"Heartbroken. This is how I feel after reading *Fighting for a Hand to Hold*. It hurts to read about children suffering. Shaheen-Hussain's book does not relieve that pain. Yet his words hold the potential to help us create broader healing, if his insights are heeded."
JOHN BORROWS, Canada Research Chair in Indigenous Law, University of Victoria Law School

"A sick child is transported by plane to a hospital 1,000 kilometres away, alone, without a parent: a state practice without pity. This practice was no mere residue of an old colonial system long gone. Instead it is a telling sign of an ongoing settler colonialism, one deeply structured to 'disappear Indians' and to declare Indigenous lives to be worth less than white ones. Samir Shaheen-Hussain's clear-eyed account reminds us that we can change but not until we recognize this ugly truth."
SHERENE H. RAZACK, distinguished professor and Penny Kanner Endowed Chair in Gender Studies, UCLA, and author of *Dying from Improvement: Inquests and Inquiries into Indigenous Deaths in Custody*

"In *Fighting for a Hand to Hold* Samir Shaheen-Hussain exposes the social, cultural, and historical structures that allow medical colonialism to hide in plain sight as it harms generations of Indigenous children and their families. It is an unflinching analysis that should be required reading in every medical school in the country."
MAUREEN LUX, professor, Brock University, and author of *Separate Beds: A History of Indian Hospitals in Canada, 1920s–1980s*

"Shaheen-Hussain argues that genuine reconciliation can't occur without reparations and restitution. Besides disclosure and acknowledgment of the harm done, this means a genuine demonstration of sorrow and regret, a promise to never do harm again, and action that ensures the harm will not be repeated. This book should be read by anyone who wants to meaningfully enter into reconciliation with Indigenous people."
MARIE WADDEN, author of *Where the Pavement Ends: Canada's Aboriginal Recovery Movement and the Urgent Need for Reconciliation*

"Its clever framing, detailed research, and frequent critical gems put *Fighting for a Hand to Hold* in the very good company of a small group of stellar books and articles about Indigenous health issues, all of them manifestos for change. It's a passionate and informed report from the medical frontlines that exposes some of the social determinants and racial subtexts that prevent us from improving and safeguarding the lives of Indigenous peoples and other minorities in Canada."
GARY GEDDES, author of *Medicine Unbundled: A Journey through the Minefields of Indigenous Health Care*

"Samir Shaheen-Hussain's *Fighting for a Hand to Hold* is a searing indictment of medical colonialism in Canada. This must-read book shatters the myth of universal and equitable healthcare as a pillar of this country's benevolent social democracy and forcefully exposes the active involvement of the medical system in upholding historic and ongoing settler-colonial power."
HARSHA WALIA, author of *Undoing Border Imperialism*

FIGHTING
FOR A
HAND
TO HOLD

McGill-Queen's Indigenous and Northern Studies
(In memory of Bruce G. Trigger)

JOHN BORROWS, SARAH CARTER, AND ARTHUR J. RAY, EDITORS

The McGill-Queen's Indigenous and Northern Studies series publishes books about Indigenous peoples in all parts of the northern world. It includes original scholarship on their histories, archaeology, laws, cultures, governance, and traditions. Works in the series also explore the history and geography of the North, where travel, the natural environment, and the relationship to land continue to shape life in particular and important ways. Its mandate is to advance understanding of the political, legal, and social relations between Indigenous and non-Indigenous peoples, of the contemporary issues that Indigenous peoples face as a result of environmental and economic change, and of social justice, including the work of reconciliation in Canada. To provide a global perspective, the series welcomes books on regions and communities from across the Arctic and Subarctic circumpolar zones.

FIGHTING FOR A HAND TO HOLD

Confronting Medical Colonialism against Indigenous Children in Canada

SAMIR SHAHEEN-HUSSAIN

Foreword by Cindy Blackstock
Afterword by Katsi'tsakwas Ellen Gabriel

McGill-Queen's University Press

Montreal & Kingston | London | Chicago

© McGill-Queen's University Press 2020

ISBN 978-0-2280-0360-1 (cloth)
ISBN 978-0-2280-0513-1 (ePDF)
ISBN 978-0-2280-0514-8 (ePUB)

Legal deposit third quarter 2020
Bibliothèque nationale du Québec

Printed in Canada on acid-free paper that is 100% ancient forest free
(100% post-consumer recycled), processed chlorine free

We acknowledge the support of the Canada Council for the Arts.

Nous remercions le Conseil des arts du Canada de son soutien.

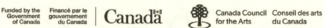

Funded by the   Financé par le
Government   gouvernement   Canada   Canada Council   Conseil des arts
of Canada   du Canada   for the Arts   du Canada

Every effort has been made to trace copyright holders and to obtain their
permission for the use of copyrighted material. The publisher would be
grateful to be notified of any errors or omissions so that corrections, if any,
can be incorporated in future reprints or editions of this book.

At the request of the author, all royalties from the sale of this book will be
directed to designated organizations in support of Indigenous children,
youth, and their communities.

Library and Archives Canada Cataloguing in Publication

Title: Fighting for a hand to hold : confronting medical colonialism against
    indigenous children in Canada / Samir Shaheen-Hussain ; foreword by
    Cindy Blackstock ; afterword by Katsi'tsakwas Ellen Gabriel.
Names: Shaheen-Hussain, Samir, 1979- author.
Description: Series statement: McGill-Queen's indigenous and northern
    studies ; 97 | Includes bibliographical references and index.
Identifiers: Canadiana (print) 20200268252 | Canadiana (ebook)
    20200268511 | ISBN 9780228003601 (cloth) | ISBN 9780228005131 (ePDF) |
    ISBN 9780228005148 (ePUB)
Subjects: LCSH: Indigenous children—Medical care—Canada. | LCSH:
    Indigenous peoples—Medical care—Canada. | LCSH: Racism in
    medicine—Canada.

Classification: LCC RA450.4.I53 S53 2020 | DDC 362.1089/97071—dc23

Je me fais une autre idée de l'amour.
Et je refuserai jusqu'à la mort d'aimer cette création où des
enfants sont torturés.
– Dr Bernard Rieux, in Albert Camus, *La Peste*

But no society can change the nature of existence.
We can't prevent suffering.
This pain and that pain, yes, but not Pain.
A society can only relieve social suffering, unnecessary suffering.
– Shevek, in Ursula K. LeGuin, *The Dispossessed*

And I understood that as long as there are dreamers left, there
will never be want for a dream.
– Frenchie, in Cherie Dimaline, *The Marrow Thieves*

Contents

Part Four The Structural Determinants of Health and Decolonizing Our Future

Figures

Foreword

How could any government think that putting sick Indigenous children on a medevac flight without a parent or caregiver's "hand to hold" was a good idea, let alone an idea worth defending?

Native American legal scholar Robert Williams (2012) links contemporary colonialism to the dehumanization of Indigenous Peoples as "savages" and the exaltation of settlers and their governments as "civilized." Williams argues that dehumanization clears the way for the unlawful taking of Indigenous lands, resources, cultures, and rights in the name of "progress" of western civilization and its attendant institutions and structures. In a landmark book, Mi'kmaw historian Daniel Paul (2006) tests the validity of the "civilized" label by analyzing the actions of Canadian governments and preceding colonial powers in relation to First Nations people, and concludes that "we were not the savages."

Paul's conclusion is supported by the Truth and Reconciliation Commission's (TRC) 2015 finding that Canada's residential schools amounted to "cultural genocide." The TRC had some powerful allies in making this proclamation, including then Supreme Court chief justice Beverley McLachlin, who delivered a speech in May 2015 affirming that Canada had attempted cultural genocide through the assimilative and often abusive residential school system, which removed Indigenous children from their families to be "properly cared for." The schools operated for more than a century, with the last one closing in Saskatchewan in 1996 (McLachlin 2015). While there were some detractors, most Canadians accepted that residential schools amounted to cultural genocide.

Yet, when the National Inquiry into Missing and Murdered Indigenous Women and Girls (MMIWG 2019a, 2019b) reaffirmed this finding four years later, many Canadians were not ready to take the next step. In June 2019, the

National Inquiry released a final report that said Canada's long history of colonial acts, including the docile response of Canadian governments and institutions to the dramatic rates of violence against and disappearance of Indigenous girls and women, was genocide – full stop.

The mainstream media pundits were largely aghast, suggesting that it was a serious over-reach to say that Canada's colonialism met the definition of genocide. The naysayers failed to present cogent arguments to counter the MMIWG report's detailed evidentiary support for the finding – instead, many said that the declaration of genocide rests on the "intent" of the wrongdoers and that Canada *did not mean* to kill and mistreat Indigenous Peoples. Interesting, but wrong. As renowned Jewish Holocaust historian and survivor Raul Hilberg (2003) notes, there was no "smoking gun" document linking Hitler to an explicit direction or intent to murder the Jews and others in the death camps, and yet reasonable people agree that Hitler was clearly responsible for genocide.

Another narrative is that genocide is obvious and will be called out as it is happening, but this too has not historically been the case. For instance, many countries chose to recast the brutal and systemic genocide in Rwanda in 1994 as merely an "act of genocide" to foreclose any obligations they may have to intervene based on international law. I believe the strength of the pushback on the MMIWG finding of genocide is sourced in Canada's colonial anointment of itself as "civilized" and Indigenous Peoples as "savage." The report confronts these myths by suggesting that Canadian governments and institutions representing the "civilized" *were, and are,* committing acts of "savagery." This is not to suggest that individual Canadians are perpetuating acts of savagery, but rather to say the construction of Canadian society enables its governments and institutions to commit acts of "savagery."

For example, in July 2019, citizens of Attawapiskat First Nation were told to open their windows if they turned on the taps in their homes because the water vapour was toxic to breathe and an independent report found that 40 per cent of First Nations deaths in northern Ontario were preventable if equitable and effective health care was available (Mamow Ahyamowen Partnership 2019). The media covered the stories, but both were eclipsed by "more important" stories like the fiftieth anniversary of the Apollo 11 mission. While there was some public outrage at the gross inequity in public services experienced by contemporary First Nations people, it was not enough to press politicians into meaningful action. Meanwhile, Prime Minister Justin Trudeau, who came into his first term in office on a reconciliation platform, told supporters at a Liberal Party fundraiser that, when it comes to reconciliation, "we have to be patient. We have to be present. We have to be unconditional in our support in a way that a parent needs to be unconditional in their love – not that there is a parent-child dynamic here" (quoted in Smart 2019). He then went on to say that it does not matter how many experts provide advice to First Nations people on how to run businesses, change has to come from First Nations. The narrative underpinning the prime minister's comment foists the responsibility for the slow pace of reconciliation onto Indigenous Peoples while immunizing "patient" and "unconditionally loving" Canadian governments from accountability.

Canadian governments voice an interest in reconciliation, but too often, this interest wanes when it involves large-scale government reform and sacrifice. This may sound harsh but with a few exceptions, it is a fair characterization. As the TRC (2015) and historian John Milloy (1999) make clear, throughout the more than one hundred years that Canada operated residential schools, people of all walks of life constantly reported the maltreatment and preventable deaths of Indigenous children. Despite this, Canada actively chose to take inadequate action to fix the problem. For example, in 1907, Dr Peter Henderson Bryce, a physician, blew the whistle on the preventable deaths of children in residential schools related to Canada's chronic underfunding of health care and the ill-treatment of the children. Bryce provided scientifically based recommendations to the Canadian government to save the children; the federal government persecuted Bryce for making his report public. The TRC (2015) estimates that 4,000–6,000 children died at the schools; Daniel Schwartz, reporting for the CBC, noted that child death rates in the schools approximated those of Canadian soldiers in the Second World War (2015). While it is proper to honour those lost in the Second World War with monuments and ceremonies, one has to ask why there is no national monument to the Indigenous children who died in residential schools in what lawyer Samuel Hume Blake characterized in 1908 as an "uncomfortable nearness with manslaughter" (Milloy 1999).

To give a more recent example, in 2016 the Canadian Human Rights Tribunal found that the federal government's inequitable provision of public services racially discriminated against more than 165,000 First Nations children and ordered the government to immediately cease its discriminatory conduct (*First Nations Child and Family Caring Society et al. v Attorney General of Canada*, 2016 CHRT 2). The Tribunal explicitly linked the federal government's conscious underfunding of child welfare prevention services to there being more First Nations children in care today than at the height of the residential school system. Canada welcomed the decision and then did little to nothing to fix the problem until it was forced into action by the Tribunal's issuance of a further ten orders over subsequent years (Blackstock 2019). The Tribunal continues to retain jurisdiction in this case and more orders are possible. This all happened on the heels of Canada's residential school apology and after the federal government had said that its most important relationship is with Indigenous Peoples.

Professionals are often viewed as safeguards to human rights abuses. Their high levels of education and training, and the ethics oaths they swear, all suggest that they hold a higher obligation to identify and address human rights violations. However, as Dr Shaheen-Hussain argues in this book, these professions are founded in colonial cultures and many were silent or actively involved in the perpetration of some of the worst colonial abuses in Canada. For example, lawyers drafted the Indian Act and its related provisions banning "Indian" ceremonies, forcibly removing "Indian" children to be "properly" cared for in residential schools, and removing Indigenous Peoples from their lands in the name of colonial progress (RCAP 1996b). Social workers served on admissions committees for residential schools and failed to turn their social justice mandate onto the obvious abuses of Indigenous Peoples (Blackstock 2013). And government and university-based medical researchers conducted nutritional experiments on First Nations people, depriving them of fundamental nutrients to see what would happen (Mosby 2013).

Federal, provincial, and territorial governments perpetuated the savage/civilized dichotomy and its attendant dehumanizing stereotypes by denying Canadians, including professionals, proper education on Canada's historical and contemporary relationship with Indigenous Peoples. By keeping the Canadian public in the dark, governments were free to violate Indigenous Peoples' rights by seizing their lands, resources, and even their children in ways that would be intolerable if applied to other Canadians. While governments in some provinces and territories are making good progress addressing the problem, the Ontario government, under Doug Ford, is rolling back the clock on reconciliation education. In a hopeful sign, teachers continue to share reconciliation knowledge and activities with their students regardless of government positions and mandated curricula.

A recent CBC poll suggests that 69 per cent of Canadians believe that Canadian governments should be doing more to support Indigenous Peoples in Canada. Still, only 9 per cent listed it as one of their top three election issues (Grenier 2019). Rinsing Canadian society from the ravages of the colonial savage/civilized dichotomy can happen if the 69 per cent who want more to be done make this a sustained and top political priority. The best hope for reconciliation has been and continues to be everyday Canadians who translate their caring into reconciliation-based action. That is why the First Nations Child and Family Caring Society has seven free ways that people of all ages and backgrounds can help achieve culturally based equity for First Nations children.

As exemplified by Dr Shaheen-Hussain's work through the #aHand2Hold campaign, individuals have the power to turn the tide in Canada's colonial relationship with Indigenous Peoples. It takes the courage to stand up to a system designed to be deaf to the suffering of First Nations, Inuit, and Métis people, but with the action of enough individuals united for this common cause, caring Canadians can make a difference in the lives of Indigenous children. Thanks to the collective efforts of the entire #aHand2Hold team, children who require medical evacuation from remote areas in northern Quebec are now able to travel with a loved one. As the saying goes, a rising tide lifts all ships. Ensuring substantive equity for First Nations, Inuit, and Métis people stands only to empower Indigenous communities while enriching Canada's national fabric at the same time. This will take confronting colonialism in governments, in professions, and in ourselves.

CINDY BLACKSTOCK

Preface and Acknowledgments

The bulk of this book was written over the summer of 2019. The copy-editing process occurred in the early months of 2020, around the time that major disruptions were happening across the country in solidarity with the Wet'-suwet'en land defence against TC Energy's Coastal GasLink pipeline, followed by the COVID-19 pandemic that exposed and worsened the faultlines of social injustices on a global scale. I received the typeset proofs just around the time that George Floyd was brutally murdered by police in the US, sparking uprisings (including against systemic racism) in many countries. At a Black Lives Matter protest, an observation by Floyd's six-year-old daughter went viral: "Daddy changed the world." It was not possible to include the many issues raised by these three major events in the book, but they underscore the urgency with which we, as a society, have to build a new world if we want humanity to survive and if we want to live lives with meaning. A new world where being empathetic, emphasizing cooperation, mutual aid, and solidarity, respecting human dignity, and living in harmony with the environment are core values. Decolonization efforts here in Canada are a necessary path toward that world.

Land acknowledgments to recognize occupied, unceded, and/or Traditional Territories of Indigenous Peoples have gained more mainstream acceptance today than even a decade ago. However, all too often, they end up being empty rituals at the beginning of an event, or a few cut-and-pasted lines in a footnote at the bottom of a page. We would like to believe that taking a few seconds to acknowledge historical colonial injustices makes us accountable and responsible for our actions today. But, in order to engage meaningfully with the politics of decolonization, we must position ourselves more explicitly and transparently. In writing this book, I have strived for intellectual rigour rooted in a commitment to decolonization and social justice.

My research and writing occurred mostly in Tio'tia:ke (Montreal), but it's important for me to acknowledge that I spent chunks of time working on the manuscript in other places (southern Quebec, southern Ontario, northeastern United States), including the Traditional Territories of several Indigenous Nations: Abenaki, Anishnaabe, Haudenosaunee, Huron-Wendat, Nanticoke Lenni-Lenape, Métis, Mississaugas of the Credit, Ramapough Lenape, Wendat. Such acknowledgments must go beyond where we live and work, however, to include Indigenous Lands where resources are exploited, and from which we benefit. For example, the electricity distributed throughout the province by Hydro-Québec powered the electronic devices, library databases, and internet access that I used to write this book. Yet, as I explain in Chapter 14, well over 80 per cent of the province's hydroelectricity is generated on the territories of the Eeyou, Innu, Inuit, and Naskapi Nations. My land acknowledgments are made in full recognition of this reality.

I would also like to highlight the courage of the caregivers and parents – including Abbygail Wellman, Alaku Qullialuk, Alexandre Stewart, Ann Kelly, Brayen Lachance, Catherine Hudon, Charlotte Munik, Enya Sérandour-Barrette, Pelle Loon, and Valerie-Lynn Gull – who spoke out during the #aHand2Hold campaign to denounce the government's non-accompaniment practice and its impacts on their children. They did so not to erase the trauma they'd experienced, but rather to put an end to forced family separation so that future generations would not suffer. To honour their spirit of solidarity, all royalties from sales of this book have been redirected to groups and initiatives that support Indigenous self-determination and are concerned with the health and wellness of Indigenous children and youth: Eagle Spirit Science Futures Camp, First Nations Child and Family Caring Society, Groundswell Community Justice Trust Fund, Minnie's Hope Social Pediatric Centre, Mohawk Language Custodian Association (Kanehsatà:ke Language and Cultural Center), and Native Women's Shelter of Montreal. Proceeds from hand sales at public events will also go to Indigenous resurgence movements and land-defence initiatives.

Fighting for a Hand to Hold relies heavily on the scholarly works of both Indigenous and non-Indigenous academics, activists, and researchers, as well as the testimonies of individuals from Indigenous Nations across the country. I hope that I have been able to make use of and build on their work in a significant way. I am also grateful to the teachers, mentors, and friends in the social justice movements I've been a part of, and to those involved in liberation struggles more broadly, for shaping my social and political lens over the years. It is impossible to name everyone, but I would like to express my heartfelt appreciation for two individuals whose words grace the pages of this book: Cindy Blackstock (foreword) and Ellen Gabriel (afterword). From the moment she learned of the injustice of the non-accompaniment practice, Cindy recognized the importance of all children having a hand to hold during emergency medevac airlifts. Her sustained and vigorous support of the campaign (including input on the hashtag early on!) was instrumental in its eventual success. This despite the great demands on her time given her tireless advocacy on behalf of Indigenous children in Canada. I met Ellen as part of a collaborative event at McGill University to counter the racist backlash on campus in the weeks following the attacks of 11 September 2001 in the United States. She generously shared her knowledge and experience mentoring many of us who founded the Indigenous Peoples Solidarity Movement (IPSM) months later, in 2002; even though IPSM no longer exists, Ellen and I have remained friends ever since. Her unwavering and fierce commitment to struggles for Indigenous sovereignty, environmental justice, and human rights spanning more than thirty years is truly an inspiration. I am both thankful for and humbled by Cindy and Ellen's indispensable contributions to this book.

Many other people made contributions I wish to recognize. A few of my colleagues in the pediatric emergency department at the Montreal Children's Hospital covered my shifts or switched with me, oftentimes at critical moments, so that I could make it to important public events, media interviews, and meet deadlines. This occurred when the #aHand2Hold campaign was active, but also during the writing of this book. Long before the idea of working on a manuscript was even conceived, several people helped me understand the situation of medevac airlifts in Quebec and/or played key roles to strengthen the #aHand2Hold campaign itself. As such, I would like to thank the following individuals: Adam Bretholz, Amir Khadir, Amy Ma, Anne-Marie Gosselin, Anne-Sophie Thommeret-Carrière, Antonio D'Angelo,

Aris Hadjinicolaou, Baruch Toledano, Camille Coltrinari, Camille Duranceau, Catherine Farrell, Catherine Rich, Christina Maratta, Cleve Higgins, Cory Verbauwhede, Debbie Friedman, Dexter Docherty, Djamila Saad, Dubravka Diksic, Elizabeth Moreau, Esli Osmanlliu, Eva Soos-Kapusy, Farhan Bhanji, Gary Pekeles, Ghislain Picard, Gillian Morantz, Gillian Seidman, Harjap Grewal, Harley Eisman, Hayley Chazan, Hélène Caron, Hussein Wissanji, Isabelle Leblanc, Jared Will, Jen Turnbull, Jessica Stewart, Joë Lance, Joe Nemeth, Julia Couture-Glassco, Julie Gauthier, Kasim Tirmizey, Kelly Martin, Kristina St-Arnaud, Laurence Alix-Séguin, Laurie Richard, Lisa Qiluqqi Koperqualuk, Margaret Butler, Marie-Hélène Cormier, Matthew Magyar, Max Silverman, Mustapha Bettache, Natan Obed, Nehal Shata, Patrick Martin-Ménard, Phil Hedrei, Radha Jetty, Raphaël Paquin, Raphael Ribeiro De Aquino Freitas, Robert Primavesi, Robert Rodrigues, Robert Sternszus, Robin Petroze, Romeo Saganash, Rosalie Cavin, Sam Wong, Scott Weinstein, Sharon Lax, Stephen Agluvak Puskas, Sue Gennerelli, Suzanne Vaillancourt, Sylvie Côté, Sylvie Côté Chew, Tamara Gafoor, Tobey Ann Audcent, Tom Sheldon, Tunu Napartuk, Véronique Hivon, Viviane Michel, Yasmine Nadifi. Many groups endorsed the campaign, but I would like to highlight the pivotal role played by the pediatric emergency department and intensive care unit at Sainte-Justine Hospital, the Canadian Pediatric Society (CPS), and Médecins québécois pour le régime public (MQRP).

In publishing this book, McGill-Queen's University Press (MQUP) had to deal with a first-time author with regular clinical duties in a busy pediatric emergency department. I am appreciative of Erin Rolfs, Jacqui Davis, Kathleen Fraser, and the entire MQUP team for understanding my social justice responsibilities and commitments to Indigenous communities; reaching consensus on certain important decisions may have been demanding, but the book is that much stronger because we aimed to achieve it. Jenn Harris put in long hours, oftentimes late into the night for days on end, to provide the book with a useful index. I would like to thank my copy editor, Kaitlin Littlechild (whom I have not yet had the honour of meeting in person), for reminding me of the importance of making deliberate decisions when rewriting colonial history by centring the realities of Indigenous Peoples. Despite the challenges stemming from my attention to detail and erratic schedule (complicated further by the COVID-19 pandemic), her work has been instrumental to make my arguments more compelling and my writing more accessible for readers. I am grateful to Mark Abley, my acquisitions editor, for having believed in this project soon after he received the proposal in April 2019. He taught me the axiom about writing, "Show, don't tell," which I've endeavoured to follow here. I welcomed his timely, insightful, and honest replies to my late-night emails, even if we didn't always agree. His editorial feedback and staunch advocacy for the book played a major role in it coming to fruition.

Much of my research was facilitated by booksellers like Another Story Bookshop, Drawn & Quarterly, Le Port de Tête, Left Wing Books, Paragraphe, and the Word, as well as municipal and university libraries. I would like to recognize the work of several staff of McGill University's library services whom I met but whose names I didn't get to know, and others whom I didn't meet but can name: Lily Szczygiel and Mary Hague-Yearl (Osler Library of the History of Medicine), and Sonia Smith (Nahum Gelber Law Library). Reference librarians at the Bibliothèque de l'Assemblée nationale du Québec also helped with fact-checking. In particular, I would like to highlight the unparalleled skills of radical librarian Andrea Miller-Nesbitt who consistently and promptly dug up crucial material that was not always easy to find, notably for the section on medical colonialism and genocide.

I could not have met my self-imposed writing timeline without the assistance of dozens of people who supported the project in different ways and to various extents by providing: advice and guidance; emotional support; fact-checking and critical feedback; leads on sources, data, and scholarly research; opportunities to speak in classrooms and at public events; permissions for use of proprietary material; sharing personal experiences and insights; technical assistance; and translation help. Explaining each person's contribution would make for a book on its own, but I nonetheless want to acknowledge the following people (including several who were vital to the success of the #aHand2Hold campaign itself): Aaron Lakoff, Abeer Majeed, Adam Clark, Adnan Ghanchi, Aisling O'Gorman, AJ Withers, Ak'ingabe Guyon, Alicia Boatswain-Kyte, Alisa Lombard, Andréa Schmidt, Angela Robertson, Anne Panasuk, Anne-Emanuelle Birn, Anne-Marie Gallant, Anne-Sara Briand, Antoine Libert, Arnold Aberman, Ashley Fortier, Aziz Choudry, Barbara Shankland, Bertrand Schepper, Bill Nelson, Brenda Epoo, Brett Burstein, Camille Gérin, Candida Hadley, Cat Tuong Nguyen,

Catherine Delisle L'Heureux, Cherie Dimaline, Chip Phi, Chris Fletcher, Courtney Kirkby, Craig Fortier, Darlene Kitty, Dave Harris, David Mandzuk, Davis Alvarado, Dolores Chew, Dramatik, Dror Warschawski, Ebba Olofsson, Edith-Farah Elassal, El Jones, Emilie Nicolas, Emsal Hasan, Éric Normandeau, Faiz Imam, Florence Tiffou, Francis Dupuis-Déri, François Van Vliet, Geneviève Bois, Ghazanfar Husain, Graham Latham, Guillaume Hébert, Hala Mreiwed, Harsha Walia, Heather Davidson, Hiba Zafran, Holly Moore, Houda Asal, Ian Mosby, Imène Kouidmi, Isabelle Picard, James Stempien, Jason Clement, Jenna Healey, Joanie Tremblay-Pouliot, Joël Pedneault, Johanne Morel, John Clarke, Jordan Topp, Jos Porter, Julien Peyrin, Karen Stote, Kate Hooton, Katia Belkhodja, Kent Saylor, Kerre King, Kira Page, Laurie Plotnick, Leanne Betasamosake Simpson, Luc Dansereau, Marc-Antoine Mahieu, Margot Latimer, Marie-Claude Goulet, Marie-Eve Lamy, Marie Serdynska, Macho Philipovich, Margaret Berry, Marie-Lyne Grenier, Martin Lukacs, Mary Foster, Mehnaz, Melissa Caza, Michael Giangreco, Michael Helquist, Michael Shevell, Minh Nguyen, Miriam Heap-Lalonde, Mostafa Henaway, Nancy Krieger, Nanky Rai, Natalie Blair, Nazmeen, Nora Butler Burke, Onye Nnorom, Orielle Solar, Paola Moquillaza Bello, Pamela Toman, Pat Cadorette, Patricia Li, Pierre-Olivier Pineau, Rachel Letofsky, Rafico Ruiz, Rami Ghazzaoui, Raphaëlle Blondin-Gravel, Raven Dumont-Maurice, Ricardo Lamour, Rita Ziadé, Robyn Maynard, Rossel Berard, Rushdia Mehreen, Saïdou (for Sidi Wacho), Saleem Razack, Samian, Samina Ali, Sara Oaklander, Sarah de Leeuw, Sarah Reaburn, Sarah Vance, Sebastien Dallaire, Sharon Hatcher, Simon Kind, Sophie Schoen, Stephen Legari, Suzy Basile, Tara Holton, Tom Swanky, Scott Park, Sze Ting Chan, Vince Teetaert, Waahli Yussef (for Nomadic Massive), Wanda Gabriel, Will Prosper, Zoua Vang.

An earlier version of the manuscript was vastly improved thanks to the supportive feedback of MQUP's anonymous peer reviewers, but also because of the critical perspectives from several people close to me, including Bhai, Helen Hudson, Karl Lévesque, and Olivier Sabella, to whom I owe much gratitude. Stef Gude was an early reader of this manuscript and her formative influence on an incomplete first draft in June 2019 has shaped this book. If it reads well now, it is due largely to her input then and her guidance and sharp skills as an editor in the months that followed. While we share friendship and politics, she let neither get in the way of making sure that indignation and passion fuelled, rather than interfered with, intellectual honesty and rigour throughout the writing process. Mandeep Dhillon, a kindred spirit, took on the task of helping me proofread the manuscript; her insightful comments and timely corrections were invaluable. Nazila Bettache was a staunch supporter of the #aHand2Hold campaign and has been behind this book-writing initiative from the beginning. She is the one who suggested approaching MQUP when other publishers hesitated. The emotional labour she has put into this book is matched only by the energy and time she has poured into helping with translations and research, providing feedback on various versions of the manuscript, sharpening my analysis, and even weighing in on the publisher's proposed title and cover. Without a doubt, she has had to bear the brunt of the demands that writing this book on such a short timeline placed on me. I am eternally grateful for her commitment to social justice and her unwavering generosity, patience, strength, and love. I would have quite simply not been able to write this book without her presence in my life.

As Mandeep reminded me recently, *nadie escribe solx* ("no one writes alone"). Despite my attempt to be thorough, I sincerely apologize to anyone whose name I have forgotten here. However, while this book would not have been possible without the assistance and contributions of many people, none of the individuals listed here is responsible for the contents of this book. Some of these people will agree with what I've written in the pages that follow, others will find I go too far, while others will say I don't go far enough. Regardless, the facts I provide, the arguments I make, the positions I take, and any resulting mistakes are solely my responsibility.

Finally, I would like to pay a special tribute to the friends and family I love and cherish, and who have shaped who I am today. The values of caring for others, working hard, living by one's principles, and striving for social justice were imparted to me by my parents and nourished in a modest but loving home through relationships with them, my siblings, and my grandmother. Other grandparents, cousins (many of whom now have children of their own), aunts, uncles, in-laws, my adored nieces, and chosen family (i.e., my caring networks and meshworks of friends) have further cultivated these values.

There are also several people who were an integral part of my life and whose deaths have left a large void, including Kavita Kulkarni, Nani Jan,

Ghanchi Uncle, Wahid Uncle, Abby Lippman. And my dear and beloved cousin Rbia, with whom I grew up and shared my childhood, who died from leukemia at the Montreal Children's Hospital when we were both still in our teens. I have only recently come to fully understand that the wounds left by her absence will never heal and that I will carry those scars forever. While researching and writing this book, and as I write these words now, I've often been overwhelmed by her memory. I recall stories about how she would spend time, when she could, with younger children who were all alone on the oncology wards, when she was hospitalized for chemotherapy treatments or medical complications. I've wondered if those kids with cancer were unaccompanied because they'd been sent from remote and rural regions of the province via emergency medevac transfer. I can't know for certain, but I suspect that at least some of them were. Rbia would have been upset to know that a rule existed that prevented children from being accompanied by a loved one for medical care and that Indigenous communities in northern Quebec were disproportionately impacted. She would have celebrated when a family-centred care policy was finally instituted (even though other health and social injustices remain). I'd like to think that those children found comfort in the warm presence of my kind and empathetic cousin until their parent or caregiver was able to join them. If this book can play a role in ensuring that Indigenous children are allowed to thrive at home with their families and in their communities, wherever they may be, then it will be a meaningful way for me to honour Rbia's memory. May her light shine on through the concluding words of these pages calling for a more just and loving world. I dedicate this book to her, and to Indigenous children who must continue – in different ways and after all these years – to fight for a hand to hold. I deeply hope that one day, soon, they will no longer have to.

SAMIR SHAHEEN-HUSSAIN
June 2020, Tio'tia:ke (Montreal)

A Note to Readers

Words carry meaning, but they also carry power. Words have the power to unearth the truth and expose injustices, but they also have the power to conceal and perpetuate them. One of the many ways that colonialism functions is to use words to strip Indigenous Peoples of their history and identity. This is why I have endeavoured to use terminology and spellings favoured by Indigenous Peoples in this book.

Indigenous Peoples in Canada and throughout the world have different cultures, languages, and histories. Indeed, more cultural similarities may exist between someone from Gibraltar and someone from Tangiers (despite being on different continents and separated by national borders) than between an Indigenous person from Nunavik and one from Coast Salish Territories (see Chrisjohn et al. 2017, 55). Yet all Indigenous Peoples share an experience of colonization. Without intending to homogenize them, "Indigenous Peoples" is used throughout this book "to refer to First Nations, Inuit and Métis peoples in Canada collectively" (Younging 2018, 64).

Certain historical expressions meet with variable acceptance or outright rejection by Indigenous Peoples. As such, I have avoided terms like Indian (often used to refer to Indigenous Peoples in the Americas, but more specifically to individuals who fall under the Indian Act in the Canadian context), Eskimo, and even Aboriginal, except when used to refer to specific individuals (e.g., Indian agents), institutions and programs (e.g., Indian hospitals, Indian Health Service), or initiatives (e.g., Royal Commission on Aboriginal Peoples), or in citations from other sources (e.g., where Eskimos is used instead of Inuit).

When referring to specific Indigenous Peoples, I use spelling (e.g., Atikamekw, Innu, Mi'kmaq, Naskapi, etc.) to best reflect transliterations of Indigenous languages in English. I generally use Eeyou to refer to the Cree of northern Quebec as this is how they self-identify (Eeyou Istchee means the People's Land), but I opt for Cree when referring to specific organizations (e.g., the Cree Regional Authority) or to other communities (e.g., in Ontario, Manitoba, etc.). I favour Kanien'kehá:ka instead of Mohawk. Inuk is the singular form of Inuit; Nunavimmiuq refers to someone from Nunavik (Inuit Land in northern Quebec), Nunavimmiuuk is for two people from Nunavik, and Nunavimmiut is for three or more individuals from Nunavik. Simailarly, Nunavummiuq, Nunavummiuuk, and Nunavummiut refer to the inhabitants of Nunavut.

Where several accepted names exist for an Indigenous Nation (e.g., Anishnawbe, Anishnabe, Anishinaabeg, Nishnaabeg), I use one single term for consistency's sake (e.g., Anishnaabe), unless I am referring to someone who has clearly identified a preferred spelling (e.g., Nishnaabeg scholar and artist Leanne Betasamosake Simpson).

I privilege using place names that centre Indigenous history (e.g., Eeyou Istchee, Nunavik, Nunavut, Unamen Shipu, etc.), even if referring to events that occurred when these lands were not recognized as such by colonial governments. I, nonetheless, decided to use Montreal instead of Tio'tia:ke because I mostly refer to the city in the context of children being transferred to the Montreal Children's Hospital.

I have adopted the principle that terms related to Indigenous institutions, identities, and collective rights (e.g., Elders, Indigenous Land, Indigenous Peoples, Indigenous Rights, Oral Histories, Traditional Territories, etc.) should be capitalized (Younging 2018, 77–81). I have also used capitalization when referring to other specific peoples (e.g., Black, South Asian). However, I did not alter citations where such practice was not employed (i.e., that instead used "indigenous land," "black," etc.). In fact, citations used in this book were generally left "as is."

All translations of French sources are my own unless otherwise noted. In circumstances where scholarly literature proved confusing or contradictory, I generally opted for terminology and dates from more recently published works and use the same terms throughout the book as much as possible for simplicity and consistency. For example, some authors refer to the federal agency responsible for Indigenous health care as "Indian Health Services" and there is disagreement as to the year it came into existence (1945 versus 1946); I have opted for Indian Health Service (IHS), including after it was renamed Indian and Northern Health Services in 1955 (Grygier 1994, 81) and also after it became the Medical Services Branch in 1962 (Bonesteel 2006, 73). For various arguments I make regarding the #aHand2Hold campaign as a case study (e.g., the cost of the Challenger plane as a percentage of the provincial health care budget), I have chosen to use the most current available data from around the time of the campaign when possible.

Finally, readers will note that I have omitted the names of Indigenous children mentioned in media reports during the #aHand2Hold campaign. Even if journalists had parental authorization to name the children, I have, nonetheless, referred to them anonymously out of respect for their privacy as the children could not consent to the use of their names and because they will still be minors at the time of publication. On the other hand, I have included the names found in published works that are not directly related to the campaign because I can only assume that these individuals willingly shared their childhood stories as adults.

It takes great courage to reveal traumatic experiences from one's early life to the public gaze with the hope of putting an end to injustice and violence. This book is meant to honour those acts of courage so that future generations of Indigenous children are no longer the victims of colonial trauma.

PART ONE

Above All, Do No Harm

Timeline

SUMMER 2017

Two young Inuit children are transferred to the Montreal Children's Hospital (MCH) from Nunavik by Évacuations aéromédicales du Québec (ÉVAQ). A decades-old non-accompaniment practice enforced on ÉVAQ's flying hospital service, which prevents caregivers and parents from coming aboard, means they each arrive alone.

19 DECEMBER 2017

A letter signed by three MCH pediatricians is sent to ÉVAQ administration and provincial government officials calling for an end to the practice.

24 JANUARY 2018

After the letter is made public, the #aHand2Hold campaign is front-page news. Health Minister Gaétan Barrette responds categorically: no imminent plans to allow caregiver accompaniment exist.

5 FEBRUARY 2018

Catherine Hudon's letter about her son Mattéo, who suffered brain death during a Challenger plane medical evacuation (medevac) to the MCH in 2008, is published. She was not allowed to accompany him. Two letters supporting the campaign (from Montreal's Sainte-Justine Hospital pediatricians and another from the Canadian Pediatric Society) are sent to elected officials.

6 FEBRUARY 2018

A petition sponsored by Joliette member of the national assembly (MNA) Véronique Hivon is launched by two concerned members of the public; thousands sign within days.

15 FEBRUARY 2018
Barrette announces an imminent end to the non-accompaniment practice, cautioning that pilots will retain the right to refuse caregiver access aboard, including for reasons of "agitation" or "intoxication."

3 MARCH 2018
Media report that Charlotte Munik, an Inuk interpreter from Kuujjuaq, had been prevented from accompanying her toddler on an ÉVAQ emergency airlift a few days prior.

21 MARCH 2018
Samir Shaheen-Hussain is invited to testify on behalf of the #aHand2Hold campaign at the Viens Commission in Montreal, characterizing the non-accompaniment practice as rooted in colonialism.

1 MAY 2018
Amir Khadir, Mercier MNA, presses Barrette at the Quebec National Assembly, where the minister invokes budgetary considerations to justify the inability to guarantee systematic caregiver accompaniment on all ÉVAQ airlifts.

4 MAY 2018
Ann Kelly's story about not being able to accompany her Inuk son on a medevac flight makes front-page news and the media reveals that a formal written "non-accompaniment policy" never existed.

10 MAY 2018
Media report that Enya Sérandour-Barrette was not allowed to board an ÉVAQ airlift transferring her toddler from Val d'Or to Sainte-Justine Hospital. The Ministry of Health is unable to provide a specific date for implementing a new family-centred care (FCC) policy.

17 MAY 2018
Samir Shaheen-Hussain's op-ed, "Separating Sick Inuit Kids and Parents Is Medical Colonialism All Over Again," is published by the *Guardian*. The #aHand2Hold campaign's reach goes global.

6 JUNE 2018
Médecins québécois pour le régime public (MQRP) calls for Quebec premier Philippe Couillard's direct intervention because children continue to be systematically sent unaccompanied on ÉVAQ flying hospital missions. Barrette tells journalists that children will benefit from caregiver accompaniment by the end of the month.

21 JUNE 2018
On National Indigenous Peoples Day, a recording of Barrette's comments that "agitated, drugged, under whatever influence" caregivers would not be allowed on medevac flights is released, prompting Indigenous activists, leaders, and politicians to call for his immediate resignation. He remains health minister until the provincial Liberals are defeated on 1 October 2018.

29 JUNE 2018
Nunavik Regional Board of Health and Social Services informs the public that the Ministry of Health and Social Services has published ÉVAQ's FCC framework supporting caregiver accompaniment: *Cadre de référence sur l'accompagnement parental.*

5 JULY 2018
Julie Ikey, from Salluit, becomes the first Inuk parent to accompany her child from Nunavik on ÉVAQ's Challenger plane.

30 AUGUST 2018
Media reports that Valerie-Lynn Gull and Pelle Loon, from the Eeyou community of Waswanipi, were prevented from accompanying their child on a Challenger medevac flight, confirming that the new FCC framework is not being applied as it should.

18 OCTOBER 2018
Gull and Loon testify at the Viens Commission in Val d'Or. Samir Shaheen-Hussain testifies on behalf of the campaign a second time, highlighting how anti-Indigenous systemic racism and medical colonialism have tainted the government's actions.

24 OCTOBER 2018

Ministry of Health and ÉVAQ representatives testify at the Viens Commission in Val d'Or, confirming that mid-September modifications to the FCC framework now allow all children to have a hand to hold during medevac flights throughout Quebec.

Introduction

To declare that social justice is the foundation of public health is to call upon and nurture that invincible human spirit that … has a compelling desire to make the world a better place, free of misery, inequity, and preventable suffering, a world in which we all can live, love, work, play, ail, and die with our dignity intact and our humanity cherished.
– Nancy Krieger and Anne-Emanuelle Birn, "A Vision of Social Justice as the Foundation of Public Health: Commemorating 150 Years of the Spirit of 1848"

In the summer of 2017, I was the treating emergency physician involved in the care of two Inuit children from Nunavik who were transferred to the Montreal Children's Hospital (MCH) by Évacuations aéromédicales du Québec (ÉVAQ), the provincially run medical evacuation airlift service. The first child was a preschooler who fell off a moving all-terrain vehicle earlier that morning and was transferred to us with a suspicion of injuries to the abdomen and head. His flight to Montreal took several hours and he was sent alone. The trauma team was quickly mobilized and a dozen of us worked together to determine the extent of his injuries. I was working as the acute care doctor in the Emergency Department (ED) that day and took on the role of trauma team leader in this case. Verbal communication with the child was limited because he spoke exclusively Inuktitut; none of us spoke the language and no interpreter was readily available. Based on our physical exam and the child's vital signs, we considered him to be clinically stable. He was quiet for most of our initial assessment, but then he suddenly began crying inconsolably. Did he develop a headache? Was he becoming disoriented? If a parent was at his bedside, would they tell us that he was slow to respond to their questions? That he was not acting like his usual self? All these questions are important because they factor into evidence-based decision-making guidelines that help us decide whether a child with a suspected brain injury requires a CT scan of the head. A significant skull fracture or a hemorrhage can be devastating; however, we don't indiscriminately send all of these children for CT scans because the radiation exposure can increase their lifetime risk of lethal malignancies. We performed another thorough clinical evaluation, but there was nothing we could find on our assessment that explained the child's sudden irritability. When an Inuktikut interpreter arrived, we finally understood why he was crying inconsolably: the child was terrified and missed his mother. She was still over a thousand kilometres away because she'd been prevented from accompanying him and would only arrive later that night on the next available commercial flight. He continued to cry for a while before our nursing and social work teams found a way to console him. The experience was heartbreaking for everyone involved.

A few weeks later, a young school-aged child was transferred from Nunavik while I was working in the ED. She had swallowed a coin that got lodged in her esophagus. Working in a tertiary care pediatric hospital, children from Montreal and neighbouring areas regularly come to us for objects that are stuck where they shouldn't be (throat, esophagus, airway, ears, nose, etc.). In some cases, removing these objects can take only a few minutes. In others, it's more of an involved process. When I arrived at her bedside to introduce myself, she was alone and remained silent. I assumed that she spoke only Inuktitut or that she had very limited knowledge of English. The transfer note from the referring centre was straightforward. However, scouring through the chart sent with her, how could I be sure that she didn't have a condition that put her at a higher risk for a swallowed object getting stuck in her esophagus? Did I know for certain that she hadn't had previous surgeries of the airway or the esophagus when she was an infant? Answers to these questions have implications for the specialists who would be removing the coin. Could I rely on the notes to be sure that she wasn't currently taking any medications or that she didn't have known allergies? Without a caregiver around, I couldn't get reliable answers to these questions from the chart sent with her. When I looked back up, she was not making a sound, but tears were quietly rolling down her cheeks. On top of the discomfort of having a coin stuck in her esophagus, I could only imagine how scared she must have been. It was, yet again, heartbreaking. The child was placed on the emergency operating room list to have the coin removed as soon as possible. I don't know if the team that removed the coin was ultimately able to explain the procedure and associated risks, and address any concerns or questions her family may have had. The parent, who wasn't allowed to accompany her, was unreachable while on the next commercial flight to Montreal.

Without knowing it or intending it – and although there will never be any justification to much of their emotional and psychological suffering – those two children became the catalysts for what would eventually become the #aHand2Hold campaign. Their experience was not exceptional. évaq had a long-standing practice of systematically separating children living in remote and rural communities from their families for urgent medical evacuation (medevac) airlifts. Caregivers were prevented from accompanying their children to tertiary care hospitals in Montreal and Quebec City; they had to wait for the next available commercial flight. Indigenous communities, particularly those in northern Quebec, were disproportionately impacted by this non-accompaniment rule.

Above All, Do No Harm

A prime directive in health care is derived from the Latin maxim *primum non nocere*, often adapted as "above all, do no harm." As a pediatrician working in a medical system that condoned this family separation, wasn't I complicit in the trauma this caused? I reimagined those two children lying alone on a crash-room stretcher in our ED and wondered whether they would remember us as caring health care providers who were genuinely trying to make them feel better. Or, would our intentions be forever overshadowed by their feelings of being alone and terrified?

I also wondered about the impacts on Indigenous caregivers and parents. I was aware of the history of forced family separation enabled by colonial policies, including through the residential school system and child welfare services. The best interests of the child had always been used to justify the forced removals, but government promises to safeguard the well-being of Indigenous children were consistently broken. How had I ignored the broader impacts of ÉVAQ's practice on these families and their communities? If my main concerns as a pediatrician are supposed to be the health and well-being of all children, why hadn't I properly considered the scope of this intergenerational trauma sooner? After all, the consequences of such violent histories reverberate for generations and influence health outcomes in the present day.

An ED colleague had heard about the child in the all-terrain vehicle accident. Days after the incident, he inquired about how the child ended up doing. When I brought up the fact that it was infuriating that a young child would be transferred hundreds of kilometres away from home without a caregiver, his email reply was succinct, but disarmingly accurate: "The root cause unfortunately is systemic racism." His observation reinforced my evolving assessment of why this situation persisted. Over the course of my residency training and now working as a pediatric emergency physician for close to a decade, I had personally cared for dozens of children who were transferred alone, and almost all were from Eeyou and Inuit communities in northern Quebec. At the MCH, hundreds of children had been impacted and the practice had become normalized for us over time. It had always been upsetting to see children sent alone, but the experiences with the two children from the summer of 2017 haunted me. For the first time, it forced me to question the normalization of the practice: inflicting emotional and psychological trauma on children should never be normal.

Politics Is Nothing but Medicine on a Grand Scale

My involvement in social justice movements since the early 2000s, including Indigenous solidarity work, has taught me that most of our lives are shaped by economic, political, and social forces. Health care is no exception, as eloquently conveyed by Rudolph Virchow's dictum: "Medicine is a social science, and politics is nothing but medicine on a grand scale" (Brown and Birn 2013, 17). Virchow was a nineteenth-century German physician, a founder of both cellular pathology and social medicine (a precursor to the field of public health). As such, he was well-placed to claim that "all diseases have two causes – one pathological and the other political" (McGibbon 2012, 19). A life-altering trip to Upper Silesia in 1848 allowed him to recognize that the typhus epidemic there disproportionately impacted impoverished peasants because of economic and political oppression (Mackenbach 2009, 181). He advocated for "radical measures rather than 'mere palliatives'" (Krieger and Birn 1998, 1604), and made the argument that social inequality must be eliminated to prevent such epidemics in the future (Mackenbach 2009, 181).

Outside of my clinical work, I've been part of grassroots collectives and coalitions involved in social justice campaigns. Early on, especially through formative experiences as a founding member of the now-defunct Indigenous Peoples Solidarity Movement in Montreal, I learned that harmful governmental practices and policies can be changed or eliminated. Some more easily than others, of course, but change is possible. When human suffering is produced by government actions (or inaction), confronting them is imperative. But it's easier to palliate injustices than to address their roots; for instance, building homeless shelters is simpler than understanding how and why the capitalist economic system produces homelessness in the first place. When I initially started exploring ÉVAQ's non-accompaniment rule in the weeks that followed the transfer of those two unaccompanied Inuit children, I didn't expect the issue to become as political as it did. In retrospect, this was a silly assumption. For some reason, I had failed to recognize this ongoing injustice as one that went beyond a simple medevac practice. Like most other injustices, it was rooted in political, economic, and social oppression. Ending the practice would require digging to the roots of the problem.

On 24 January 2018, the #aHand2Hold campaign was launched. I, along with others, had been actively involved in laying the groundwork for it, and our goal was to put an end to the practice of children being transferred alone across the province. We had one core demand: instituting a child- and family-centred policy for all medevac airlifts in Quebec. A few weeks later, then health minister Gaétan Barrette announced that caregivers would be able to accompany their children on all flying hospital medevacs in the province. However, an actual family-centred care (FCC) framework was only established on 29 June 2018. Even then, proper implementation didn't occur until months after that. The provincial government's response would highlight variations of what Mi'kmaq legal scholar Pamela Palmater calls "deny, deflect, defer" tactics that governments often use to deal with Indigenous communities (Palmater 2017, 75–6). Such an approach is marked by a lack of transparency, bad faith, and broken promises.

Inequalities in Health Care Follow the Fault Lines of Societal Injustices

The campaign exposed how the persistence of ÉVAQ's non-accompaniment rule was a contemporary example in a long-standing history of systemic anti-Indigenous racism and medical colonialism, a term used to describe the violent and genocidal role played by the health care system in the colonial domination over Indigenous Peoples in settler societies. By doing this, the campaign called into question the commonly held belief that the medical establishment is inherently benevolent. Indeed, its track record of dealing with Indigenous Peoples (as well as other marginalized and oppressed groups) paints a very different picture. After all, the medical establishment and the health care system more broadly do not operate in a vacuum; they shape and are shaped by the societal structures within which they exist. Inequalities in health care follow the fault lines of societal injustices. The campaign countered the narrative, prevalent both in Quebec and in Canada, that colonialism is a relic of the past. It challenged the notion that we live in a postcolonial era marked by a genuine commitment to reconcile with Indigenous Peoples whose ongoing dispossession and oppression continue to benefit provincial and federal governments and the non-Indigenous population who have settled and occupy these lands to this day.

In the grand scheme of things, ÉVAQ's non-accompaniment rule was arguably minor compared to other injustices impacting Indigenous communities in the province and the rest of the country. Similarly, the #aHand2Hold campaign was admittedly marginal when considering the work that needs to be done to ensure that Indigenous Peoples have meaningful access to equitable and dignified health care. However, the story of the campaign fits into a much larger narrative. Dissecting the provincial government's response to long-standing calls to end the non-accompaniment practice allows us to understand how colonialism and systemic anti-Indigenous racism operate at a societal level. It also leaves us with a fundamental question: If governments can't treat Indigenous children equitably and with dignity when it comes to health care, how will they redress the injustices imposed on Indigenous communities more broadly?

The idea for this book started germinating after then health minister Gaétan Barrette's comments perpetuating anti-Indigenous stereotypes were made public on 21 June 2018, National Indigenous Peoples Day (Hendry 2018; Gervais 2018c). Most of the media coverage and public response was critical of what he had said, but the news died down within a few days. The demand for Barrette's resignation coming from Indigenous leaders and activists was not taken up in any meaningful way by the public or by politicians. The premier of Quebec, Philippe Couillard, stood by Barrette. François Legault, head of the Coalition Avenir Québec (CAQ), an opposition party that went on to win a majority government in the October 2018 provincial elections, stayed silent about Barrette's comments. Around the same time that summer, Black and Indigenous artistic communities faced significant and sustained backlash in the public arena for having voiced their opposition to two shows – SLĀV and *Kanata* – by a prominent Québécois artist, Robert Lepage. He was criticized for how Black and Indigenous histories were treated in both of those plays. Yet, Legault, who had already been denying the very existence of systemic racism in Quebec for months (Legault 2017), stated that opposition to a show like *Kanata* was "dangerous" and expressed dismay that the show was cancelled after some of its producers backed out amid the controversy (Bellerose 2018). The contrast between the responses to these two incidents at the political level revealed a troubling double standard that had echoes in the public sphere: a health minister was able to make anti-Indigenous racist comments with impunity related to a matter of fundamental concern in pediatric care, yet an opposition leader felt compelled to dismiss Indigenous protestors' concerns in the theatre world because of a show's cancellation. The idea for this book project crystallized in January 2019, around the one-year anniversary of the #aHand2Hold campaign launch. Legault was now premier of Quebec. Since coming to power, the CAQ refused to acknowledge the existence of systemic racism in Quebec. Yet, the campaign had very publicly revealed a salient example of the harmful consequences of systemic racism, including on Indigenous children and their families.

In the weeks prior to the campaign launch, only a handful of MCH pediatrician colleagues and residents were involved. In the weeks that followed, many others got on board, including nurses, physiotherapists, research assistants, social workers, and surgical residents. At the peak of the campaign, well over twenty health care providers were involved at the MCH alone. I continued to play a coordinating role, collaborating with other individuals, institutions, and organizations supportive of the campaign's demands. On more than one occasion, Indigenous families that were impacted by the practice reached out to a campaign member, after their child was transferred alone, to share their experiences and express their frustrations, usually privately. In other cases, caregivers and parents insisted on speaking out publicly. Everyone involved with the campaign felt it was important that Indigenous voices were not only heard but that they remain central. The courage, dignity, and resilience of the families who spoke out were instrumental in providing the very real – and often deeply moving – testimony of how this practice tangibly impacted these children. Their interventions infused the campaign with urgency and humanity.

I sought to highlight these experiences and perspectives when I was invited to testify at the Public Inquiry Commission on relations between Indigenous Peoples and certain public services in Quebec. Presided over by retired superior court judge Jacques Viens, the Viens Commission was created by the Government of Quebec on 21 December 2016, over a year after Indigenous women in Val d'Or first publicly spoke out about their experiences of sexual assault and other abuses by Sureté du Québec police officers (Viens Commission 2019, 11–18). Its mandate included "making recommendations as to the concrete, effective and sustainable measures to be implemented ... by the authorities to prevent or eliminate, regardless of origin or cause, any form of violence or discriminatory practices or differential treatments in the provision of ... public services to the Aboriginals of Quebec: police services, correctional services, justice services, health and social services and youth protection services" (Viens Commission 2019, 21). The main finding of the Commission was categorical: "It seems impossible to deny that members of First Nations and Inuit are victims of systemic discrimination in their relations with the public services that are the subject of this inquiry" (Viens Commission 2019, 203). The research, interviews, exchanges, and discussions that went into preparing the presentations for my testimonies before the Commission on 21 March 2018 (in Montreal) and 18 October 2018 (in Val d'Or), cited several times throughout the final report, made this book possible. I relied heavily on the contribution and feedback provided by impacted families, as well as members and supporters of the #aHand2Hold campaign, including many examples, stories, and quotes appearing in this book.

One of the quotes I often share came from a former pediatric resident at the MCH. A few weeks after the launch of the campaign, she emailed me to convey her relief that something was finally being done to disrupt the status quo: "I can't even recall all the times in my residency that I was in a situation where this policy affected a child I was taking care of. We knew it was the rule, we knew it was awful, and yet we just kept going." Her words aptly describe our complicity in accepting the injustices inflicted on Indigenous communities. The danger with normalizing injustice is that even the most sensitive individual may become desensitized to the suffering it causes. By using the #aHand2Hold campaign as a case study to explore unsettling truths about how colonial governments deal with Indigenous children and their communities, including a focus on the medical establishment's genocidal role in colonization and colonialism, this book is meant to make a modest contribution to ensure that we no longer "just keep going."

Chapter 1

Medevac Airlifts in Quebec and the Non-Accompaniment Rule

The first task of the doctor is therefore political:
the struggle against disease must begin with a war against bad government.
– Michel Foucault, *The Birth of the Clinic: An Archeology of Medical Perception*

Health care teams are consistently working under stressful conditions to care for sick patients, many of whom are at risk of dying without appropriate medical or surgical interventions. This work is made more arduous when health care provision occurs on a plane, with limited personnel, space, and equipment. Other physiological and technical considerations that come with being on an aircraft, including altitude changes and harsh weather conditions, add to the challenge of providing this essential service; a service intended to ensure that those living in rural and remote areas of the province have equitable access to tertiary care in urban centres. This work is often underrecognized and undervalued as an essential part of our public health care system, which holds universality at its core.

From as early as the 1950s, provincial government planes were used to transfer critically ill and injured patients from remote areas of Quebec to centres in Montreal or Quebec City (ÉVAQ 2018d, 1). Until the late 1970s, local teams were typically called on to provide medical and nursing care during a medical evacuation (medevac) airlift. However, the lack of standardization (different planes, variable equipment, discrepancies in personnel training) was a significant issue (ÉVAQ 2016, 8). In 1981, the provincial government mandated ÉVAQ, staffed by physicians based at Enfant-Jésus Hospital in Quebec City, to provide medical airlift services throughout Quebec (DSMGP 2005, 3; ÉVAQ 2016, 8). Since then, ÉVAQ has added planes to its fleet to offer distinct medevac services, including an air shuttle (for more stable patients, staffed by two nurses) and a flying hospital (for more critically ill or injured patients, staffed by at least one physician and one nurse). In 2018, the ÉVAQ fleet consisted of four planes: two DASHs, which generally provide air shuttle services, and two Challengers that provide flying hospital services. Given that both aircraft personnel and health care professionals are part of the ÉVAQ program, it functions under the joint auspices of the provincial Ministry of Health and Social Services and the Ministry of Transport, while conforming to federal air transport regulations.

From the beginning, ÉVAQ has never allowed patients (regardless of age) to be accompanied by family members on its flying hospital planes. However, despite what many people believed, no official written policy ever existed. Rather, a long-standing practice had simply become the norm. A handout from as early as 1984 stated that only ÉVAQ personnel could accompany the patient for safety and efficiency considerations, as well as to ensure the aircraft's availability for any other urgent request as flying hospital planes had the capacity to transfer more than one patient at the same time (ÉVAQ 2018d, 5). Limited space, confidentiality and privacy concerns for multipatient transfers, and ethical considerations were also invoked over the years (Couillard 2005, 1). Variations on these themes remained part of the standard government response to calls for change. As of 2005, ÉVAQ has permitted parental accompaniment on its air shuttle service in certain circumstances, though more systematically so since 2012 (ÉVAQ 2018d, 6; Bernier et al. 2018, 75; Couillard 2005, 2). The air shuttle service transfers the bulk of ÉVAQ's patients, including both adults and children. However, between 2015 and 2018, close to a third of all patients being transferred required flying hospital services (ÉVAQ 2018a, 5). Based on ÉVAQ's 2012–15 data, children under nineteen accounted for 7 per cent of air shuttle evacuations, but 20 per cent of flying hospital transfers (ÉVAQ 2018c, 1). These critically ill or injured children would arguably benefit the most from having a loved one's hand to hold during a medevac airlift, but they were systematically denied.

Details about the 2018 ÉVAQ fleet and their services allow us to better understand the government's historical failure to end the non-accompaniment practice. The DASH planes can transport sick patients requiring a stretcher, but they also have between eight to twenty-two regular passenger seats depending on their configuration. Challenger planes can transport a handful of very sick patients simultaneously. Although these planes were configured with fewer seats than their DASH counterparts, they can fly at a higher altitude, are faster, and don't need to refuel as frequently (ÉVAQ 2016, 26; ÉVAQ 2018d, 3, 16). These characteristics make the Challenger planes ideal for providing ÉVAQ's flying hospital service, which includes responding to urgent medevac requests from more distant regions in Quebec.

As shown in Figure 1.1, the flying hospital (Challenger plane) covers the entire region north of Chisasibi (to the west) and Fermont (to the east). The rest of the province, including remote areas like the North Shore, the city of Gaspé, and the Magdalen Islands, benefits from "double coverage" by both flying hospital and air shuttle services most days of the week. Moreover, to ensure adequate service provision for medevac airlifts, some regional health boards (e.g., the Cree Board of Health and Social Services of James Bay) have contracts with private companies (e.g., Airmedic) that usually allow caregivers to accompany children on their planes (Millette 2018). However, most do not offer the same level of expertise and/or don't have planes that are as fast or as well-equipped as ÉVAQ's Challenger for more critical cases. Specific to Nunavik, only three communities have landing facilities to accommodate a plane with the Challenger's dimensions and size: Kuujjuaq, Kuujjuaraapik, and Puvirnituq. Evacuations from the eleven other Inuit communities are initially carried out by a regional airlift service provided by Air Inuit, which is staffed by local physician and nursing teams. These planes are smaller, not as well-equipped as the Challenger, and can't transfer children all the way to Montreal. However, caregivers are almost always allowed aboard and, despite the smaller space and the fact that children are often in critical condition, medical personnel can't recall the last time a caregiver's presence interfered in any way with caring for a sick child (Joanie Tremblay-Pouliot, pers. comm., 2019). Upon arrival at one of the three Nunavik sites where the Challenger can land, the ÉVAQ team takes over medical care for the remainder of the transfer. All these factors explained, in part, why northern Quebec, and Nunavik in particular, was disproportionately impacted by the non-accompaniment practice.

The MCH is a tertiary care centre that is part of the McGill University Health Centre. As shown in Figure 1.2, we receive children who are transferred from a catchment area that covers more than 60 per cent of Quebec, including Eeyou Istchee and Nunavik (MUHC 2019). Pediatric transfers from other dis-

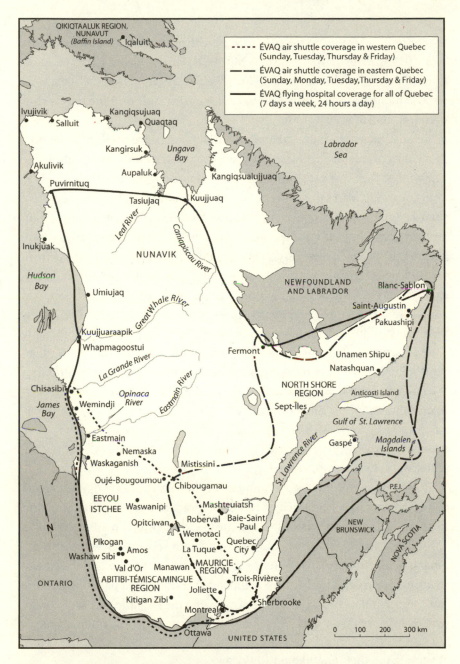

Figure 1.1 Évacuations aéromédicales du Québec (ÉVAQ) flight coverage
Cartography by Bill Nelson, based on 2002 Natural Resources Canada map adapted
in *Plan stratégique, 2016–2018* report (ÉVAQ 2016, 24).

tant or remote regions of the province are either sent to Sainte-Justine Hospital (the other pediatric centre in Montreal) or to Quebec City, based on their respective catchment areas. Thus, health care workers at the MCH were witness to the impacts of the non-accompaniment rule on Indigenous children from northern communities.

Before the launch of the #aHand2Hold campaign, precise data about how many unaccompanied children from northern Indigenous communities we cared for at the MCH was limited. No such information was made publicly available by ÉVAQ and there was no tool to systematically tabulate and extract such data at the MCH. However, by using postal code and regional information gleaned from registrations at the MCH's Emergency Department (ED), we were able to extrapolate that we cared for 219 children from Nunavik and 146 from Eeyou Istchee during the 2016 fiscal year (Shaheen-Hussain et al. 2017, 1). ÉVAQ's 2015 report stated that 116 urgent cases were transferred to the MCH in 2014–15 (ÉVAQ 2015, 23). In the early stages of the campaign, we did not know how many of these children were transferred by Challenger, nor how many were unaccompanied, but it was reasonable to assume that dozens of Indigenous children were sent unaccompanied to us per year. In 2018, months after the launch of the #aHand2Hold campaign, statistics produced by ÉVAQ confirmed our estimates: since 2012, there had been 432 such transfers from Nunavik alone (ÉVAQ n.d.). All these patients – from infants to adolescents – were unaccompanied because the practice of separating families was systematically enforced on flying hospital medevacs during that period.

At the end of the day, for everyone involved with the campaign, even one child impacted by the non-accompaniment practice was one child too many. Figuring out the numbers was only a means to an end. The numbers told a story; they lent weight to our assertion that family separation was not a marginal phenomenon given how many children were impacted, and that it was ongoing. However, numbers are cold. Numbers can tell a part of the story, but they can't paint a full picture. Recognizing the tangible effects of forced caregiver separation was the first step to understanding the full picture.

Traumatizing Unaccompanied Children

My involvement as the treating physician of the two Inuit children who were sent alone to the MCH ED by ÉVAQ's Challenger a few weeks apart in the

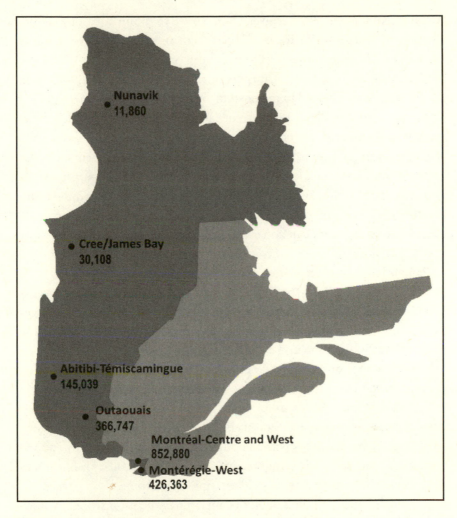

Figure 1.2 Montreal Children's Hospital (MCH) catchment area
Population data provided is for 2011. Image courtesy of Réseau Universitaire Intégré
de Santé et Services Sociaux (RUISSS)-McGill (MUHC 2019).

summer of 2017 made the impacts of being unaccompanied very clear. The
emotional and psychological trauma inflicted on those two children haunts
me to this day. These children and others like them would initially be assessed
in their home community somewhere in Nunavik. If they were from one of
the eleven communities where ÉVAQ's Challenger can't land, they would be
transferred from the nursing station there by the regional medevac team,

usually accompanied by a caregiver. Upon arrival to Kuujjuaq or Puvirnituq, they would be assessed by the health care team and transferred to the MCH via ÉVAQ's Challenger. Many had never been on a plane before, and most would not know ÉVAQ health care personnel. From the airport in Montreal, they would be transferred to the hospital by ambulance, now accompanied by a team of paramedics. Upon arriving at the MCH ED, they would be met by more unfamiliar faces, many of whom would poke and prod them while speaking a foreign language. Already vulnerable because of their age, these children would not have a family member, let alone a single person of reference, with them throughout their hours-long journey. There would be no one to explain to them what was happening; no one to meaningfully console them in a language they can understand. No one to comfort them by simply holding their hand.

Parents left behind were often overcome with worry and fear. Is my child in pain? Is she scared? Will he survive? These anxieties could only be heightened by the generations of forced separation that were imposed on Indigenous communities through colonial practices and policies, including the residential school system and child welfare services.

Given that the non-accompaniment practice had been in place for decades, it was important for me to reach out to members of the MCH's Northern and Native Child Health Program for some perspective and a sense of history. After all, they provide care for Eeyou and Inuit children through on-site consultations during fly-in visits to the different communities and by coordinating their care when these children are at the MCH. Advocacy is integral to their work. Although a change would certainly be welcome, I was warned not to have high hopes. Previous attempts, including a petition signed by hundreds of people from different Inuit communities from as long ago as the early 1990s, were simply ignored. There was little to suggest that things would be different now. To avoid certain disappointment given the government's previous responses and apparent priorities, I was well-meaningly told to not even bother trying. The pervasiveness of this feeling of demoralization was revealed after the launch of the #aHand2Hold campaign through comments made by other health care workers, impacted family members, and Indigenous leaders.

In the preliminary stages of working on this issue in the fall of 2017, I set out to show why the non-accompaniment practice was untenable. Together with a handful of nursing and physician colleagues, we explored how clinical care was compromised. These frontline health care providers identified key aspects of the medical history that could make a difference if the information was not readily available including the child's allergies, medications, previous surgeries, and medical conditions, as well as the events leading up to the injury or illness in question. Several colleagues expressed that they had, at one point or another, performed investigations because of the very real concern of missing something critical due to inadequate information. In some cases, these decisions we had to make caused harm – painful bloodwork, radiation exposure from medical imaging, etc. In rare cases, children with virtually no chance of survival were kept alive, and therefore any suffering prolonged, only to allow family members the time to arrive so that life-support could be withdrawn with a loved one at the bedside. All of this could have been avoided had a caregiver been allowed to accompany the child.

Performing investigations and procedures brings up the issue of obtaining consent to care, which must be free and informed. In the case of a child, it is a parent or guardian who must be sufficiently informed of the risks and benefits of a given investigation, procedure, or treatment, and must be given a meaningful opportunity to ask questions (CMQ 2020, 97, 158). For true emergencies, like a child requiring urgent surgery (e.g., internal bleeding following an accident) or needing acute medical resuscitation, when stakes are high and a delay in treatment could put the child's life in danger, consent is generally implied (CMQ 2020, 158). However, informing the parent about a life-saving operation or resuscitative measures being performed is crucial for pediatric practioners, but not possible when children were transferred alone. For situations where the child's life was not imminently threatened but a time-sensitive intervention was still necessary (like the child with the coin stuck in her esophagus), obtaining free and informed consent was difficult, especially if the caregiver was unreachable because they were on a commercial flight to join their child.

The role of a parent or caregiver as an advocate for the child was obvious. For children who were nonverbal (whether because of young age, development issues, or acquired complications), or who didn't share a spoken language with health care personnel, parents could act as interpreters to ensure that the child's needs, including for pain control, were properly communicated. For instance, some clinicians lamented how children's pain was inadequately treated because we weren't as attuned to their cues of discomfort as caregivers would be. Parents at the bedside were also vital to ensure the safety of the child. One physician recalled how an unaccompanied toddler fell out of his crib in the ED. A nurse shared how an unaccompanied young girl tried to run away from her room to go home because she didn't realize that she was over a thousand kilometres from where she lived. In these circumstances, and many others, harm – whether real or potential – could have been prevented if caregivers had been allowed to accompany their children. Finally, parents play an irreplaceable role in reassuring their children by explaining what's happening and being able to comfort them when they are going through scary or painful procedures.

The psychological and emotional trauma suffered by all children who were transferred alone via Challenger plane was a significant issue that colleagues brought up on multiple occasions. This trauma was compounded for children from northern Indigenous communities because of communication barriers and a history of colonial family-separation policies that spanned generations. Helped by a few pediatric residents, we searched the medical literature. It was not difficult to find studies that reiterated the importance of caregivers as quintessential to family-centred care (FCC), which is a cornerstone of pediatrics (AAP 2016, 241). As of 2001, studies in the United States and later in the United Kingdom underscored the importance of offering the option for parents to accompany their child during ambulance transportation (Woodward and Fleegler 2001; Davies et al. 2005). In the years that followed, the American Academy of Pediatrics (AAP), the American College of Emergency Physicians, the Emergency Nursing Association, the Association of Air Medical Services, and the Canadian Pediatric Society recommended, and in some cases reiterated, that parents should be offered the option of accompanying their child during medical transfers and/or being present during medical resuscitation efforts. In its most recent manual on pediatric transport, the AAP recognized that "it may, in fact, be much easier to care for the child with the parent present" during transport (AAP 2016, 241). Months later, we found original research in the *Air Medical Journal* that reported that "specific to pediatric care, parental presence as a means to facilitate FCC has been shown to alleviate patient/parent anxiety, reduce separation anxiety, and improve parental satisfaction and child cooperation with procedures" (Joyce et al. 2015, 32).

Building the #aHand2Hold Campaign

To add one last element to make our case, several of us contacted colleagues in other children's hospitals across the country to find out what their practices and policies were on this front. A colleague in the MCH ED had done his residency training on the west coast and had been wanting to address the non-accompaniment practice for a few years because he knew that things could be done differently: children transferred to BC Children's Hospital from northern (including Indigenous) communities were always accompanied by a family member. Nonetheless, my expectation was that at least some other jurisdictions would also have a non-accompaniment practice. I was anticipating that we were going to have to work with pediatric health care providers and children's advocates in other provinces to develop a country-wide coalition to force change. However, as it turned out, encouraging caregiver accompaniment for pediatric medevacs seemed to be the standard of care across Canada. Every centre we contacted seemed to have such a practice. This included BC Children's Hospital (Vancouver), Children's Hospital of Eastern Ontario (Ottawa), Children's Hospital of Winnipeg, Hospital for Sick Children (Toronto), Janeway Children's Health and Rehabilitation Centre (St John's), Stanton Territorial Hospital (Yellowknife), Stollery Children's Hospital (Edmonton), and the Royal University Hospital (Saskatoon). In the case of the latter, we learned that the Saskatchewan Air Ambulance even had a written policy explicitly encouraging family accompaniment.

In early October 2017, I was in touch with ÉVAQ administrators about this issue and was informed that it was already on their radar. They'd planned a meeting with the health care teams in Kuujjuaq and Puvirnituq later that month and this was going to be on the agenda. I was subsequently invited to submit any information that could buttress the arguments made in favour of an FCC policy prior to their next director's meeting, on 20 December 2017. I drafted a letter, cosigned by the division directors of the emergency department and the pediatric intensive care unit at the MCH. The letter was sent to ÉVAQ's administration, the Ministry of Health and Social Services, and the Ministry of Transport. It was based on all of our findings from polling colleagues at the MCH, reviewing the medical literature, and contacting health care providers in other provinces. The letter underscored the impacts of historical practices and policies that forcibly removed Indigenous children from their families, notably through residential schools, child protection services, and the health care system. We proposed an equity-based approach that recognized these historical injustices and argued that allowing yet another practice that separated Indigenous children from their parents would only breed further mistrust and contempt of the medical system (Shaheen-Hussain et al. 2017, 3–4).

I promptly received acknowledgment emails from the ministries, and a well-meaning but informal reply that ÉVAQ would do everything in its power to respond to this need. My hope had been that the incontrovertible arguments made in the letter would result in a firm commitment to quickly resolve the issue. However, I didn't receive any official response for weeks. No imminent change seemed forthcoming. Meanwhile, children throughout the province continued to be sent unaccompanied on all Challenger medevac flights. So, on 24 January 2018, the #aHand2Hold campaign was launched after a couple of media outlets obtained a copy of the letter. The overwhelming public and media response that followed was not only unexpected but unequivocally sympathetic.

Chapter 2

The #aHand2Hold Campaign: Confronting a System

I don't trust you any more, you keep saying "Go slow!"
– Nina Simone, "Mississippi Goddam"

There's a saying in the villages of the Narmada valley –
"You can wake someone who's sleeping.
But you can't wake someone who's pretending to be asleep."
– Arundhati Roy, "The Reincarnation of Rumpelstiltskin," *Power Politics*

Following the launch of the #aHand2Hold campaign on 24 January 2018, Quebec health minister Gaétan Barrette, himself a physician (he worked as a radiologist before entering politics), professed sympathy for impacted families. He initially confided to a journalist that he would be "extremely uncomfortable" if one of his children had to be transferred alone by plane for emergency medical care and told her: "I'm not saying it's possible to change, but I'll take a look at it" (Fidelman 2018a).

However, the government's tangible response invoked the same excuses as in the past: limited resources on the plane (i.e., space and personnel) and the possibility of having to pick up other patients. Physicians and health care professionals working in northern Quebec countered that there was a seat available for a caregiver on the Challenger, regardless of whether all the stretcher beds were full (Duchaine and Teisceira-Lessard 2018a). Government and hospital officials confirmed that both Challenger planes had five seats, including those reserved for medical personnel (Lowrie 2018). This suggested that there was at least one seat for a caregiver since ÉVAQ's flying hospital teams were rarely, if ever, made up of five health care professionals (most of the time, the team was made up of a nurse-physician duo). Barrette's subsequent response was confusing at best, and disingenuous at worst: "If we were to add seats we'd have to reconfigure the plane and have less capacity to transport patients" (Lowrie 2018). He was categorical with journalists: "If you are asking me today if we have plans to deconstruct or reconfigure the aircraft, at this moment that we are speaking, the answer is no" (Duchaine and Teisceira-Lessard 2018b).

When the campaign was launched, Cindy Blackstock, Gitxsan First Nation activist, professor in the School of Social Work at McGill University, and executive director of the First Nations Child and Family Caring Society, brought up a core issue, which foreshadowed a story that would follow a couple of weeks later: "What happens if something horrible happens and the child passes away during the flight? They die alone. They really need a hand to hold, someone who loves them" (Fidelman 2018a).

News reports, opinion pieces, and editorials termed the practice of separating children from their family as barbaric, cruel, discriminatory, heartless, inhumane, monstrous, offensive, paternalistic, shocking, shameful, and traumatic (Duchaine and Teisceira-Lessard 2018a; Fidelman 2018b; I. Picard 2018; Hudon 2018; A. Picard 2018; Hanes 2018; Fidelman 2018a). Such characterizations may have seemed harsh; however, the Quebec government was an outlier in Canada by persisting with such an antiquated practice. It could not plead ignorance because there were demands for change from almost three decades ago. Indeed, some historical perspective provides insight into the government's handling of this matter.

ÉVAQ and a History of Opposition

In the early 1990s, Dr Johanne Morel, a pediatrician who is now director of the Northern and Native Child Health Program at the MCH, spearheaded a petition to put an end to the non-accompaniment practice. She collected hundreds of signatures throughout several Inuit communities in Nunavik and submitted the petition to ÉVAQ and then health minister Marc-Yvan Côté (Rogers 2018). Morel never got a response from the Ministry of Health. Months later, she received a negative reply from ÉVAQ. "I was told to forget it," she recalled. "We tried to change things, but it had no impact" (Fidelman 2018b).

Another formal request to end the non-accompaniment rule occurred several years later, in 2005. The Commission des droits de la personne et des droits de la jeunesse (CDPDJ) sent a letter to then health minister Philippe Couillard, himself a physician who practised as a neurosurgeon before becoming a politician (his Liberal Party of Quebec won the 2014 provincial elections, and he remained premier throughout the time the #aHand2Hold campaign was most active in 2018). The CDPDJ decided to intervene after learning that a woman from the Magdalen Islands had been prevented from accompanying her breastfed infant on an ÉVAQ plane. *Radio-Canada* (7 July 2005) reported that the couple paid $7,700 to charter a flight so that they could accompany their baby during the transfer to Quebec City for surgery. The news story also cited an ÉVAQ report: 146 infants (i.e., less than one year of age) had been transferred without a caregiver across Quebec in 2004–05 alone, suggesting that many children (when including those beyond the first year of life) were impacted on an annual basis. As the CDPDJ's letter suggested, the practice of separating children from their caregivers contravened Article 39 of the Quebec Charter of Human Rights and Freedoms and Article 3 of the United Nations Convention on the Rights of the Child (Marois et al. 2005). In his reply, Health Minister Couillard justified the non-accompaniment practice by citing confidentiality and ethical, privacy, and safety considerations, as well as the necessity to ensure the aircraft's availability for another urgent request received during the course of the current mission (Couillard 2005, 1). He did commit to establishing a special committee, Comité sur la révision de la politique de non-accompagnement à bord de l'avion-hôpital, made up of administrators and bureaucrats from his ministry and the health care system, with a mandate to determine whether the practice should be maintained or rescinded (DSMGP 2005, 1).

There were no pediatricians or identified child advocates on the committee. Even though Indigenous children continued to be disproportionately impacted by this practice, there was no representation from Eeyou Istchee, Nunavik, or other Indigenous communities. Only two rural or remote regions were represented: Abitibi-Témiscamingue sent the coordinator of pre-hospital and emergency services and the Magdalen Islands sent the nursing director and a physician from the health centre (DSMGP 2005, 1). Perhaps this was why "these regional representatives did not report any recurrent complaints about the fact that a patient could not be accompanied aboard the flying hospital plane" (DSMGP 2005, 5). The committee cited two pediatric health care centres in California and Texas as examples where a "similar policy" was in place (DSMGP 2005, 4). The report, which was made public by the Viens Commission in March 2018, recommended maintaining the status quo (DSMGP 2005, 1).

Around 2010, Jane Beaudoin attempted to change the situation that's "been like that forever" when she became the executive director of the Inuulitsivik Health Centre, which is based in Puvirnituq and is responsible for the medical coverage of seven Inuit communities along the Hudson Bay (Fidelman 2018b). She told a journalist that she couldn't understand why minors were being transferred alone: "I would be frantic" (Fidelman 2018b). Beaudoin's request to favour caregiver accompaniment for children was also rejected by government authorities. ÉVAQ's rule for its flying hospital service remained firmly in place (Deshaies 2018).

The consequence of these refusals was imposed resignation. "We don't have a choice," Alaku Qullialuk told reporters (Duchaine and Teisceira-Lessard 2018a). Several of her children and grandchildren, including a baby of only a few weeks old, had been transferred alone from Akulivik over the years. Tunu Napartuk, who was mayor of Kuujjuaq when the #aHand2Hold campaign was launched, echoed this sentiment in an interview: "We've accepted it because that's how it's always been done" (Fidelman 2018a).

Of course, it's not true that Inuit, Eeyou, and other Indigenous and non-Indigenous communities simply accepted such a draconian practice for all these years: the actual impetus for change has always come from those directly impacted by the non-accompaniment rule. Protests could have taken the form of a caregiver simply expressing their disagreement or persistently asking to accompany their child after initially being refused. It could also take on more significant proportions, like the jarring story of an Inuk mother running after a flying hospital plane that was transferring her child who had suffered severe dog-bite injuries to the face (Duchaine and Teisceira-Lessard 2018a). Likely, hundreds, if not thousands, of individual pleas for change were systematically ignored for decades, either by frontline workers or by ÉVAQ administrators and government officials.

In her 2004 Sydney Peace Prize lecture, award-winning author and activist Arundhati Roy said: "We know of course there's really no such thing as the 'voiceless.' There are only the deliberately silenced, or the preferably unheard" (Roy 2004). Indeed, just because there's no trace of those forms of protest in official documents or through media coverage doesn't mean that they didn't happen. Every single one of those rejections was a missed opportunity to right a historical wrong.

Launching the Campaign

The #aHand2Hold campaign did not start from scratch. On the contrary, it built on long-dismissed demands for change, whether institutional or informal. This time, provincial and federal air transport regulations were invoked as additional reasons to preserve the non-accompaniment rule (Fidelman 2018a; Fidelman 2018c). The government likely counted on the media coverage to abate so that it could continue to ignore the issue. However, the opposite happened. Columnists and editorialists lambasted the non-accompaniment rule and came out strongly in favour of the campaign (Hanes 2018; A. Picard 2018; Krol 2018). In early February 2018, over a few days, public pressure exploded.

A letter in support of the #aHand2Hold campaign was drafted by Dr Laurence Alix-Séguin, a pediatric emergency medicine colleague at Sainte-Justine Hospital (the other pediatric centre in Montreal), and co-signed by the division directors of the emergency department and intensive care unit there. The letter, dated 5 February 2018, was addressed directly to Barrette and Transport Minister André Fortin and echoed many of the concerns we had brought up a few weeks prior (Fidelman 2018c). Another letter dated 5 February, written on behalf of the Canadian Pediatric Society (CPS) by Dr Radha Jetty (chair of the First Nations, Inuit, and Métis Health Committee), and co-signed by Dr Catherine Farrell (CPS president) and Dr Pascale Hamel (president of the Association des pédiatres du Québec), was also sent to both ministers. It highlighted that "separating a child from the security of their parent when they are frightened, hurt or when they may be at risk of dying not only increases the likelihood of developing post traumatic stress disorder, but it is merciless." The accompanying CPS press release referred to the forced family separation as an "antiquated" practice, and Farrell called it "cruel" (CPS 2018). Based on our December 2017 letter, anthropologist Isabelle Picard and producer Ève Tessier-Bouchard launched a petition sponsored by Véronique Hivon, member of the Quebec National Assembly for Joliette, calling for the government to devote the necessary resources to ensure children were accompanied on all medevac airlifts. Several thousand people signed on within days of its launch (Hivon 2018).

"Mon fils est mort sans moi"

Compelled by the media coverage spurred by the #aHand2Hold campaign, Catherine Hudon published a letter in *La Presse* on 5 February 2018 entitled "Mon fils est mort sans moi" ("My son died without me"). Hudon recounted how her son, Mattéo, suffered brain death while being transferred alone via Challenger a decade ago. Originally from the Montérégie region (south shore of Montreal), Hudon was working as a nurse in the northern community of Chisasibi in Eeyou Istchee (Lortie 2018). Mattéo, who had underlying medical issues, woke up that morning with a headache. The medical team at the Chisasibi Hospital felt that he had to be transferred immediately for more advanced care and that the Challenger plane would be the fastest way to do so. By the time Hudon arrived in Montreal to be at his bedside, twelve hours later, he had a dismal prognosis because of the extent of the neurological injury he'd suffered. Life support was withdrawn in the following days, and Mattéo died. In her letter and subsequent media interviews, Hudon recounted how she had been robbed of the last conscious moments of her son's life: "I was not there to tell him that I loved him. For him to hear his mother's voice in his subconscious. He was 2 years and 10 months old and he was probably terrified" (Hudon 2018). This heart-wrenching story made it impossible for the government to ignore the issue any longer.

Hudon shared how the experience tormented her, forcing her to quit nursing: "In my mourning, there's a black hole. The amnesia of that space-time that was stolen from me. I made up images of his arrival by ambulance, alone. It continues to anguish me that I wasn't by his side to comfort him. It took me years to rebuild this emptiness. To forget this injustice. To forget that I was robbed of my last moments with my child" (Hudon 2018). Sentiments of guilt for something completely beyond their control were also echoed by other parents and caregivers in the weeks following the launch of the campaign. Even though their children did not die, Alaku Qullialuk (grandmother of an infant from Akulivik), Brayen Lachance (father of a toddler from Amos), Alexandre Stewart (father of a school-aged child from Kangiqsualujjuaq), Abbygail Wellman (mother of a preschooler from St. Augustin, an isolated village on Quebec's Lower North Shore), and several others publicly described the harmful emotional and psychological impacts that the forced separation had on their families (Duchaine and Teisceira-Lessard 2018a; Duchaine and Teisceira-Lessard 2018b; Fidelman 2018d). Regardless of whether they are Indigenous or not, all of these caregivers expressed how anxious, guilty, and helpless they felt about not accompanying their children, who were themselves petrified during the transfer.

Hudon's story raised an important question: how many other children had died alone during flying hospital transfers over the years? Some of the pediatric intensive care specialists involved with the campaign knew of a few, including the case of a teenager who suffered an accidental, but fatal, gunshot wound to the head several years ago (Duchaine and Teisceira-Lessard 2018a). In how many other situations were caregivers not allowed to accompany their fatally injured or sick children? The experiences for these families contrasted sharply with a no-less-tragic situation that was handled very differently. In 2013, the *Pediatric Emergency Care* journal published an article written by Renée Semonin Holleran, an air-medevac nurse based in Ohio (United States), that highlighted the importance of ensuring parental presence throughout all aspects of medical care. Holleran's program had been involved in the transfer of a child who had suffered a severe drowning injury. The mother's "only request was to hold her hand during her transport to the pediatric care center. The child died peacefully later that day with her mother at her side" (Holleran 2013, 214).

As it turns out, Hudon herself had worked as a pediatric nurse at the MCH before moving to Chisasibi. She recalled in her letter: "I had seen Native and Inuit children sent alone, terrified, who were operated on" (Hudon 2018). She lamented how her attempts to change the practice, soon after Mattéo's death, were met with indifference. The government parroting the same old excuses now was like listening to a broken record, Hudon wrote. She wondered how the planes had never been refurbished to allow at least one caregiver to accompany their child after all these years. She suspected that part of the reason involved the personnel aboard Challenger aircraft not wanting to deal with anxious parents because many of them were not used to working with children and providing FCC like pediatric nurses and pediatricians do. Hudon stated that when prejudices against Indigenous Peoples were introduced into the mix it made the situation even more explosive. Her words reinforced what Eeyou and Inuit communities in northern Quebec had been saying for years. A Nunavik mother (who did not want to be named), whose young child had been transported alone by flying hospital a couple of years earlier, captured this sentiment well. In an interview with *Nunatsiaq News* in the days following the launch of the #aHand2Hold campaign, she said: "We've been so de-humanized, we accept it. We are stressed enough as a society, these policies just add to it. But when you strip it all down, it's racism" (Rogers 2018).

ÉVAQ administration had started consultations to explore the possibility of changing the non-accompaniment practice before the launch of the campaign. However, who knows how many years that would have taken and how many children and families would have continued to suffer in the meantime. The extent of the public indignation spurred by the #aHand2Hold campaign was impossible for the government to contain or ignore. The momentum was only going to increase with time and Hudon's letter likely accelerated this process.

Health Minister Responds: A Family-Centred Care Policy and Racist Tropes

On 15 February 2018, Barrette invited journalists to the ÉVAQ hangar in Quebec City for a press scrum, telling them: "What is obvious is that a parent should be allowed to accompany a child" (Fidelman 2018e). He candidly acknowledged that he had either been misinformed or had misunderstood, but no formal federal air transport regulation existed to justify the non-accompaniment practice after all (Lavoie 2018). "It appears that the information I got (about air regulations) was wrong," he confirmed (Fidelman 2018e). Motivated by the "human factor," he announced that a new policy allowing caregiver accompaniment would be implemented imminently; the newer of the two flying hospital planes, a Challenger refurbished in 2014, would accommodate a parent accompanying their child in a few weeks (CBC 2018a; Lavoie 2018; Fidelman 2018e; Morin 2018).

During the press scrum, Minister Barrette made two statements that caught my attention. First, one journalist reported that caregivers will be "denied for safety issues, for example, if the parent is intoxicated, has a restraining order prohibiting contact, is clinically ill or seems so agitated as to pose a risk during flight" (Fidelman 2018e). Another journalist reported that ÉVAQ pilots could refuse access to an "agitated, intoxicated or abusive parent" (Morin 2018). Second, he informed journalists that the older of the two Challengers may have to be removed from service for up to a year to make the necessary modifications, which could cost millions of dollars (Morin 2018). It is certainly true that an agitated or intoxicated person could put the personnel and patient(s) on a medevac airlift at risk, thereby jeopardizing the transfer itself. It is also possible that any necessary modifications to the plane would take time and cost money. However, subtext and context are everything. The #aHand2Hold campaign centred on the experiences of Eeyou and Inuit communities impacted by the non-accompaniment rule. As such, choosing to highlight the example of a parent who is "agitated" or "intoxicated" to make the point that certain restrictions may apply to the new policy is loaded. It evokes the colonial and racist stereotype of the "drunken Indian" (TRC 2015c, 17, 73, 76). Less stigmatizing examples could have easily been used. It is also important to note that this right of refusal is not exceptional and can be exercised by any pilot across the country (including for commercial airlines) to ensure the safety of all passengers and crew. Similarly, his assertion that it may be necessary to ground the older Challenger for up to twelve months for reconfigurations, allegedly costing millions of dollars, plays off another anti-Indigenous trope: that of Indigenous Peoples ("them") being freeloaders who are a burden on "our" (colonial government and settler society) resources and who are compromising public services (see Reading 2013, 4). These two tropes recurred in the government's response in the months that followed.

Plus ça change ...

On 3 March 2018, barely three weeks after Barrette's announcement of a new FCC policy, *La Presse* and the *Montreal Gazette* broke a story confirming our observations in the ED: nothing had changed. Charlotte Munik had been prevented from accompanying her daughter on a flying hospital medevac a few days prior. The toddler had been hospitalized with pneumonia for a week in Kuujjuaq but was transferred to the pediatric intensive care unit at the MCH because her condition had deteriorated. After an angst-ridden sleepless night waiting for the next available commercial flight, Munik broke down when she finally arrived at her daughter's bedside twenty-four hours later: "My baby had five IVs in her and was on a breathing machine" (Fidelman 2018f). The medical team had also inserted a chest tube (Duchaine and Teisceira-Lessard 2018c). Over the years, Munik had seen many mothers "crying for their children" through her work as an Inuktitut interpreter at the hospital in Kuujjuaq, but she never expected to be in the same situation (Fidelman 2018f). She denounced the "horrible" non-accompaniment practice and stated that "it has to stop." Barrette's response was pragmatic: "I feel for that mother. I am very sorry for the mother, I understand that it's unbearable. But at least she was transferred" (Fidelman 2018f).

On 21 March 2018, I was invited to testify on behalf of the #aHand2Hold campaign at the Viens Commission in Montreal. In my testimony, based on consultation with impacted families and those involved with and supportive of the campaign, I provided context and outlined the campaign, clarifying that children were still systematically unaccompanied. I labelled the non-accompaniment practice as colonial and expressed concern about the "drunken Indian" and "freeloader" tropes that had surfaced in Barrette's press scrum, pointing out that a price tag of millions of dollars to ensure that families are kept together during flying hospital medevacs (assuming this estimate was even accurate) was insignificant compared to the social cost of allowing an antiquated practice to remain in effect (Lebel 2018).

My message didn't get through. On 1 May 2018, MNA Amir Khadir pressed Barrette on this issue at the Quebec National Assembly, citing Munik's example to highlight how families continued to be separated on Challenger airlifts. The health minister invoked budgetary considerations to justify why caregiver accompaniment could not be guaranteed (CSSS 2018). During the Munik episode, Barrette confirmed to La Presse that it was only a matter of weeks before ÉVAQ staff would be trained to be able to implement an FCC policy (Duchaine and Teisceira-Lessard 2018c). Yet, on 4 May 2018, CBC and Le Devoir revealed how a four-year-old Inuk child had been transferred alone by ÉVAQ's flying hospital plane from Kuujjuaq a couple of weeks prior because of a coin stuck in his throat that needed to be removed operatively. His mother, Ann Kelly, described the contempt with which she was treated. She had been allowed to strap her son in on the plane, but then had to get off. Kelly saw that there were seats available, but a nurse told her that she couldn't come because of the decades-old rule. According to Kelly, a physician said that the flying hospital team was doing her a favour by transferring her child because his condition was not a real emergency; she was told that these flights cost thousands of dollars. Because of the limited number of commercial flights available, Kelly was only able to join her son in Montreal the following day. He was traumatized by the transfer and continued to remind Kelly weeks later that she'd abandoned him (Gervais 2018a).

The *Le Devoir* journalist who reported on Kelly's experience dug deeper into this issue to confirm what some of us had been suspecting for weeks: there was never a written policy prohibiting caregiver accompaniment! This was one of the major revelations of the campaign. However, an ÉVAQ spokesperson stated that they were now in the midst of elaborating an actual FCC policy, which would be ready in a few weeks (Gervais 2018a). The need for an FCC policy was again highlighted a few days later when the media reported that Enya Sérandour-Barrette's two-year-old child with chronic medical problems was not allowed to have a caregiver accompany her on an ÉVAQ transfer from Val d'Or to Montreal (she was followed at Sainte-Justine Hospital). Minister Barrette could not provide a date as to when an FCC policy would be implemented throughout the province (Parent-Bouchard 2018).

On 6 June 2018, the issue made headlines again because children continued to be sent unaccompanied on ÉVAQ's Challenger planes. *Le Devoir* and the *Montreal Gazette* reported that Médecins québécois pour le régime public (MQRP), whose board I was a member of at the time, was calling on Premier Philippe Couillard to intervene directly. MQRP's letter was endorsed by over twenty signatories, including unions, professional and student associations, child-advocacy organizations, and Indigenous groups (MQRP 2018). Gaétan Barrette reiterated to journalists that the implementation of an FCC policy was imminent, this time with a specific target by the end of the month (Fidelman 2018g).

A few days later, Barrette made a preelectoral visit to a Muslim community centre in his La Pinière riding on the south shore of Montreal. There, he was questioned by a member of the congregation who wanted to know why the change in ÉVAQ's practice was taking so long. As part of a lengthy reply, not knowing he was being recorded, Barrette made the following statement: "And I can tell you one thing. If you follow that in the news, I guarantee you that there will be at least one instance in the next six months that, where someone will not be made allowed, uh made, not allowed to get on the plane. Why? Because no one agitated, drugged, uh, under whatever influence would get on the plane (inaudible) at any cost, that will not happen. And that happens all the time" (CBC 2018b). Without being prompted further, he went on to drive home his point: "If you're over there, and your kid has to be transported and you're the parent … and you're agitated, you're under the influence or whatever, you will not get on the plane. As simple as that."

CBC and *Le Devoir* broke the story on 21 June 2018, National Indigenous Peoples Day (Gervais 2018c, Hendry 2018). The media furor that followed was significant, making headlines throughout the province and across the country. Indigenous activists, leaders, and politicians denounced the minister's statements, and many called for his immediate resignation.

On 29 June 2018, just over a week after Barrette's comments were made public, the Nunavik Regional Board of Health and Social Services issued a press release. The executive director, Minnie Grey, stated: "This is excellent news for the communities as well as for the well-being of Nunavik children" (NRBHSS 2018). More than four months after Barrette's initial press scrum announcing the change, ÉVAQ's FCC framework supporting caregiver accompaniment, the *Cadre de référence sur l'accompagnement parental*, was finally available on the website of the Ministry of Health and Social Services (ÉVAQ 2018b).

Several days later, on 5 July, *La Presse* and the *Montreal Gazette* reported that Julie Ikey, from Salluit, became the first Inuk parent to accompany her child from Nunavik on the Challenger plane. Ikey had been prevented from accompanying her children on two separate medevacs in the past, so both she and her preteen son were relieved that they were going to be transferred to the MCH together this time. Ikey was impressed with how the ÉVAQ team made space for her (Fidelman 2018h). Her son, who had injured himself after crashing his bike, required the care of the MCH trauma team. A pediatric nurse highlighted how having Ikey present at her child's bedside improved communication and helped establish trust to provide proper medical care, while the pediatric trauma surgical resident commented that "this is definitely a step forward" (Fidelman 2018h).

This was very encouraging. Finally, after decades, children would no longer be sent alone on medevac transfers. However, in the weeks that followed, our surveillance measures at the MCH painted a disappointing picture: around half of all children were still being transferred unaccompanied. Families and referring health care centres from northern communities were telling us that the ongoing refusals were due to the absence of a flight attendant or nurse to escort the caregiver or parent. Families were frustrated and upset. Those of us receiving these children in Montreal were perplexed because there was no mention that an escort was obligatory in the documents released by the government, including the information sheet given to parents (ÉVAQ 2018b). I wrote to ÉVAQ administrators and government officials about this issue on 9 August 2018. The three-page email reply I received the following day acknowledged that ÉVAQ had refused accompaniment requests but didn't name the absence of escorts as being the cause.

Later that summer, on 30 August 2018, *Radio-Canada* broke the story of a child from the Eeyou community of Waswanipi who had been transferred from Chibougamau to Montreal by Challenger without his parents, Pelle Loon and Valerie-Lynn Gull, because of suspected gastrointestinal bleeding. Well over six months after Barrette's initial announcement and more than two months since the announcement of the new FCC framework, Loon stated that they "were devastated and hurt" to find out that they couldn't accompany their child (Isaac 2018). Their son told Gull: "They shouldn't let sick children get on board the plane alone without their mother or father. Mom, tell them I'm only six years old. I can't do this on my own" (Niosi 2018). Panicked and heartbroken, Loon and Gull decided to make the ten-hour drive to Montreal, much of it in the middle of the night while sleep-deprived, to be with their child at Sainte-Justine Hospital. Based on ÉVAQ's figures, obtained by the journalist, close to a quarter of all accompaniment requests had been refused throughout the province (i.e., not just transfers to the MCH) since the new FCC framework had been introduced at the end of June (Niosi 2018).

So, while there had certainly been an improvement in the situation, children continued to be transferred alone. The Viens Commission returned to this issue by inviting Valerie-Lynn Gull and Pelle Loon to testify about their experience at the hearings in Val d'Or on 18 October 2018. After their testimony, I was invited to provide an update of the #aHand2Hold campaign by testifying a second time. I reported that, if our summer figures were accurate up until the beginning of September, children from northern Quebec were still being transferred alone at higher rates than the rest of the province, with around half of all children being impacted. I also highlighted that the government's response to the campaign provided an example of how medical colonialism and anti-Indigenous systemic racism tainted the government's actions. The following week, on 24 October 2018, Richard Bernier (physician and ÉVAQ medical director), Sylvie Côté (nurse and ÉVAQ coordinator), and André Lizotte (nurse and director of prehospital emergency services with the Ministry of Health) were asked to testify. Based on their figures, 40 per cent of all accompaniment requests were refused across Quebec for the period of 30 June to 1 October 2018 (ÉVAQ 2018d, 11). For the same period, this refusal rate was over 50 per cent for Nunavik transfers (ÉVAQ, 2018d, 11). They confirmed that children continued to be transferred alone over the summer because of an informal rule requiring a flight attendant or nurse escort for all caregiver accompaniments (Bernier et al. 2018, 92–3, 103). If no escort was available, the request for accompaniment was rejected.

This unwritten rule was why Gull or Loon hadn't been allowed to accompany their son (Bernier et al. 2018, 135–36). It was apparently part of a transition process to ease ÉVAQ teams into the new era of caregiver accompaniment. However, it was dropped in September because ÉVAQ personnel reported that the transfers were going "super well with the families" (92). A precipitous drop in accompaniment-request refusals followed (93). Indeed, this was reflected in our experience into the fall of 2018. To this day, children transferred to the MCH by Challenger are almost always sent with a caregiver. Even when the rare exception occurs, it seems not to be related to an oversight or an omission by ÉVAQ, but rather because of other considerations.

Histories of Broken Promises

Useful insights can be gleaned by re-visiting the timeline of the government's handling of this issue since 1990 and focusing on a few selected responses. The exercise of simply asking questions helps identify forks in the road where things could have been done differently. For instance, when Dr Johanne Morel submitted her petition with signatures from hundreds of Nunavimmiut in the early 1990s, why did she not get an appropriate and detailed response from government officials? Why was there no committee set up with the mandate to determine whether to rescind the non-accompaniment rule?

In 2005, in response to the intervention of the Commission des droits de la personne et des droits de la jeunesse (CDPDJ) in the case of the non-Indigenous infant from the Magdalen Islands (see page 29), such a committee was finally struck. The committee conducted a search to determine whether "a similar policy was used by other medevac airlift services in North America" (DSMGP 2005, 4). Why did the committee conduct what it called a "non-exhaustive" search (DSMGP 2005, 4)? Relatedly, why did the committee submit its report weeks ahead of their deadline (Couillard 2005, 2; DSMGP 2005, 6) instead of adopting a more "exhaustive approach" (Bernier et al. 2018, 58)? How is it possible that the committee identified only two pediatric health care centres in California and Texas with a non-accompaniment rule? Why did they not mention whether helicopters (that have less space and are used for shorter distances) or fixed-wing aircraft (with more space, for longer distances) were used there? More importantly, why were there no examples from other jurisdictions in Canada, where the geography and health care system are more comparable to Quebec's? Were the American examples simply cherry-picked to justify ÉVAQ's practice? How could the committee not know that other medevac services in Canada (in Yellowknife and Edmonton, for example) had been allowing caregiver accompaniment for pediatric transport for several years already? If it had, recommendations to change course on this issue could have been made over a decade ago. After all, as pediatric emergency physician and medevac expert Laurence Alix-Séguin stated, "It's not like we'd be particularly innovative or pioneers in the field" by adopting an FCC policy in Quebec (Gervais 2018a).

In March 2018, when media revealed that Charlotte Munik had been prevented from accompanying her daughter during a medevac airlift, Barrette stated that he needed to find out which plane flew Munik's child to Montreal because "one of the two Challengers is not authorized by federal regulations to bring someone aboard" (Fidelman 2018f). The implication was that if she'd been transferred on the Challenger that was authorized to have caregiver accompaniment, Munik should have been allowed aboard. However, as we learned later, all children requiring ÉVAQ's flying hospital services were still *systematically* being transferred unaccompanied. Ongoing forced family separation throughout the province had nothing to do with which Challenger was being used in March 2018. The real issue for the delay was that the process within ÉVAQ was taking longer than the minister had anticipated. In June 2018, he admitted that "changing regulations takes time" and went on to confirm that "all that remains now are the training protocols" (Fidelman 2018g). Did Barrette know that a new FCC policy had not been implemented yet when he wondered about which Challenger was used for Munik's child? On the other hand, if he genuinely believed that only one of the Challenger planes was now allowing caregiver accompaniment, how could such a significant misunderstanding between the Ministry of Health and ÉVAQ have occurred? Given that children continued to be sent alone well into the month of June, why had a realistic timeline not been clearly communicated to all impacted communities following the February press scrum? Instead, families and health care providers were left in the dark for months, leading to confusion and frustration.

In May 2018, when *Le Devoir* reported that Ann Kelly was not allowed to accompany her son on a medevac flight from Kuujjuaq, the journalist uncovered that there was never a written ÉVAQ policy prohibiting caregiver accompaniment – an instance of a falsehood that can become confused for the truth if repeated often enough. In this case, a practice became the de facto norm, which then became regarded as a policy. Government officials openly considered it as such; for example, the special committee struck in 2005, in response to the intervention by the CDPDJ, referred to the "Non-Accompaniment Policy" (*Politique de non-accompagnement*) in the very title of their six-page report (DSMGP 2005, 1). For all these years, why had impacted communities and the general public been led to believe that there was an actual written policy when there was none? Why was the practice maintained year after year from the beginning of ÉVAQ's existence in the early 1980s? Conversely, even if this was considered as a policy, why wasn't it reviewed on a regular basis? Was it ever an evidence-based practice? The state of affairs was patently Kafkaesque: a rule that was not even in a written form issued by a governmental body acquired such authority that no amount of suffering or medical pleading could change it.

Based on a working document submitted by ÉVAQ and government officials to the Viens Commission prior to their testimony, ÉVAQ formally
consulted the clinical ethics committee of the Centre hospitalier universitaire
de Québec, where ÉVAQ is based, on 10 May 2018. ÉVAQ raised several consequences of ending the non-accompaniment rule, including the concern
that parental accompaniment would compromise its teaching role because
medical trainees would "not be able to participate on missions when patients
are accompanied" by a caregiver if seating space becomes further limited
(ÉVAQ 2018c, 2). Was ÉVAQ's teaching mission so important that it trumped
instituting FCC for its pediatric transfers? More crucially, was ÉVAQ allowing
medical trainees onboard its Challenger planes all these years while stating
that there was no space for a child's parent or caregiver?

When the government released the new FCC framework on 29 June 2018,
it made a promise to all children living in rural and remote regions of the
province that, from now on, they would have a hand to hold during all
medevac airlifts. However, not all children were being accompanied because
of the informal rule instituted by ÉVAQ requiring a flight attendant or nurse
to act as an escort for the caregiver. To echo Edith Farah-Elassal, the Viens
Commission's legal counsel, now that a new FCC framework was in place,
why were families from Nunavik being disproportionately impacted by
accompaniment-request refusals (Bernier et al. 2018, 102)? Why was there
no mention of this unwritten requirement in the documents released by
the government, including the information sheet given to parents (ÉVAQ
2018b)? Why did the government simply not announce this as a transition
process from the get-go? Why did ÉVAQ administrators not mention this in
their reply to my query in early August 2018? Perhaps more importantly, if
one of the long-standing excuses to justify the non-accompaniment practice
was that there was no space on the plane, how was there now not only
enough space for a caregiver, but also for an escort to accompany them?

The decades-old practice of preventing caregivers from accompanying
their children ultimately did come to an end in 2018, but it came at a price
because many government responses and nonresponses throughout the
#aHand2Hold campaign fostered hurt and mistrust among those im-
pacted. Anyone treated this way by the government would be skeptical, sus-
picious, and distrustful of the public health care system. This is without

even considering the history of colonialism and racism that continues to shape Canada's relationship with Indigenous Peoples.

The announcement of an FCC policy made during Barrette's press scrum on 15 February 2018 was obviously welcome. However, as I observed in response, it warranted "cautious optimism" precisely because "our government lamentably has a history of broken promises to Indigenous communities," and this announcement "very well may fit into that history" (CBC 2018a). As time would tell, the government's response to ending a health care practice that separated families when they were at their most vulnerable fit into a historical pattern – including the lack of transparency, bad faith, and broken promises – all too familiar to Indigenous communities. The following chapters provide further context to this history of racism and colonialism, including the harm in perpetuating stereotypes like that of the "drunken Indian" and the "freeloader," especially by those who wield power, notably health care providers and politicians. As became obvious over the course of the #aHand2Hold campaign, these anti-Indigenous tropes were completely gratuitous, used as a straw man all along. Scapegoating and dehumanizing those most adversely impacted by unjust practices and policies is a way to divert from addressing the more significant underlying issues at play. The way the government dealt with this matter revealed and exacerbated fissures that some would like to believe no longer exist.

PART TWO

Structural Fault Lines in Health Care

Chapter 3

Social Determinants of Health: Equality, Equity, and Limitations

All animals are equal
But some animals are more equal than others
— George Orwell, *Animal Farm*

For the poor it [citizenship] consists in supporting and maintaining the rich
in their power and their idleness. At this task they must labour in the face
of the majestic equality of the laws, which forbid rich and poor alike to sleep
under the bridges, to beg in the streets, and to steal their bread.
— Anatole France, *The Red Lily*

Health care inequalities follow the fault lines of societal injustices. The reality of the non-accompaniment practice for directly affected communities was no different. As such, the #aHand2Hold campaign centred on the experiences of Eeyou and Inuit children living in northern Quebec for two reasons.

First, the impacted families seen at the MCH, where the campaign originated, were almost exclusively Eeyou and Inuit because of the catchment area that the hospital is mandated to serve (see Figure 1.2). It only stood to reason that we would blow the whistle on a practice that was impacting populations we provide care for. In no way did we ever intend to minimize or deny the harm experienced by other Indigenous (e.g., Atikamekw, Innu, etc.) and non-Indigenous communities from remote areas of Quebec. Pediatric transfers from these regions were sent either to Montreal's other children's hospital, Sainte-Justine, or to Quebec City based on their respective catchment areas. However, the detrimental impact of ÉVAQ's non-accompaniment practice on *any* child and their family was undeniable, which we proactively raised in media interviews and public outreach. Therefore, the campaign's core demand was always clear – an immediate end to the non-accompaniment practice throughout Quebec. The campaign was organized to facilitate broader involvement, including from other impacted communities, so long as support for the core demand remained central, allowing individuals (e.g., Catherine Hudon, Isabelle Picard, etc.), as well as other groups and institutions (e.g., Canadian Pediatric Society, Sainte-Justine Hospital, Médecins québécois pour le régime public, etc.) to so easily support the campaign's efforts. When individuals, leaders, and politicians from other Indigenous and non-Indigenous communities spoke out, it only strengthened the campaign further.

Second, the experiences of Indigenous families from northern Quebec were crucial because these children, and those from Nunavik in particular, seemed to disproportionately bear the brunt of ÉVAQ's non-accompaniment practice. To understand why, an overview of the social determinants of health (SDH) is necessary.

Social Determinants of Health

In 1948, the World Health Organization (WHO) defined health as a "state of complete physical, mental and social well-being and not merely the absence of disease or infirmity" in its constitution (WHO 2006, 1). This was bold at the time because the dominant medical paradigm in Europe and North America focused on the individual to understand disease using the biomedical model, "with molecular biology [as] its basic scientific discipline" (Engel 1977, 130). A minority of individuals within the medical profession sought to expand this conceptualization, but a modest paradigm shift did not meaningfully occur until an influential article was published in *Science* in 1977, entitled "The Need for a New Medical Model: A Challenge for Biomedicine" (Fava and Sonino 2017, 257). This "biopsychosocial model," widely taught in medical curricula today, recognized that the psychological and social aspects of people's lives influence illness, which is why it used a more "inclusive" and "systems-oriented" approach (Engel 1981, 107). This was an improvement from the biomedical model, but still had limitations.

The social component of the WHO's definition of health was crucial because people are part of communities and live in societies. Social well-being implies a basic level of fairness and, ideally, harmony in a society. However, throughout time, those in power have established hierarchical systems and structures that produce social, economic, and political conditions that benefit the few at the expense of the majority. As the authors of an article published in the *Global Public Health* journal insightfully explain in their historical perspective, much of the current thrust around the SDH can actually be traced back to grassroots community-based health initiatives in the 1960s and 1970s in parts of the world where "dominant medical and public health models were not meeting the most urgent needs of poor and disadvantaged populations." These local responses directly addressed social and environmental conditions, but also "political-economic structures and power relations" (Irwin and Scali 2007, 238).

In 2008, sixty years after its impactful definition of health, the WHO's Commission on Social Determinants of Health (CSDH) released its landmark report, *Closing the Gap in a Generation: Health Equity through Action on the Social Determinants of Health* (CSDH 2008). The report's premise was not necessarily novel: the reality that health is primarily informed by the social conditions in which people live has been recognized for centuries, notably by those most adversely impacted by them. The CSDH's report, however, succeeded where previous similar efforts faltered in the past. The rigorous research, multifaceted collaborations, wide scope, and global reach of this report made it impossible to ignore the importance of the SDH any longer.

The biopsychosocial medical model of clinical care, albeit an improvement from the biomedical model that preceded it, nonetheless focuses on the individual's body and behaviours to assign causality for both favourable and adverse health outcomes. For example, a central tenet of this model involves eliciting "the patient's cooperation in activities to alleviate distress and/or correct underlying derangements that may be contributing to distress or disability" (Engel 1981, 102). This individualizing approach was de-emphasized in the CSDH's report and the focus shifted to the "causes of the causes" (CSDH 2008, 42). Physicians would move away from comments like "You have diabetes because you don't exercise enough" or "Your cancer is in remission because of your positive attitude throughout chemotherapy" to recognizing that, while individual biology and behaviours play a role, people's living conditions and other broad factors generally influence disease rates and outcomes more significantly. Countless population studies have made it clear that the conditions over which individuals have little or no control dictate how healthy they are or how long they will live. The health gaps, called "death gaps" by some due to their devastating consequences (Ansell 2017, xiii), reflect significant and widening social and economic disparities both within and between countries. As the CSDH wrote in the introduction of its report, "these inequities in health, avoidable health inequalities, arise because of the circumstances in which people grow, live, work, and age, and the systems put in place to deal with illness" (CSDH 2008, n.p.).

In the conceptual framework developed for the CSDH (see Figure 3.1), these circumstances are divided into three broad categories: behavioural or biological factors (e.g., nutrition, tobacco, alcohol consumption, physical exercise, genetics); psychosocial (e.g., living and working conditions, relationships, and social support); and material conditions (e.g., housing, financial means to buy healthy food and proper clothing, work, and neighbourhood environments). These elements constitute the conditions of daily life and are part of the "intermediary determinants" of health (Solar and Irwin 2010, 6; CSDH 2008, 1, 43). The health care system itself is also considered an "intermediary determinant" because it can facilitate equitable access to care (e.g., overcoming geographic barriers) by promoting cooperation among various sectors to improve health status (Solar and Irwin 2010, 40).

The CSDH conceptual framework illustrates how the intermediary determinants then funnel down to impact on equity in health and well-being experienced at the individual level. According to the WHO, equity has to do with the "fair opportunity for everyone to attain their full health potential, regardless of demographic, social, economic or geographic strata" (WHO, n.d.). Simple variations or differences in health become social inequities in health if they are "systematic, socially produced (and therefore modifiable) and unfair" (Whitehead and Dahlgren 2006, 2).

Despite the vast potential, discussions about the SDH often end up being limited in scope, partly because the frameworks to understand them can be so varied. For example, the Canadian Council of Social Determinants of Health produced a report identifying over thirty SDH frameworks that were classified into "types" and grouped according to their "primary area of focus" (SDH Frameworks Task Group 2015, 5). The authors stated that the "report is not an exhaustive catalogue of all frameworks on the determinants of health, nor was it designed as a formal evaluation of the frameworks that

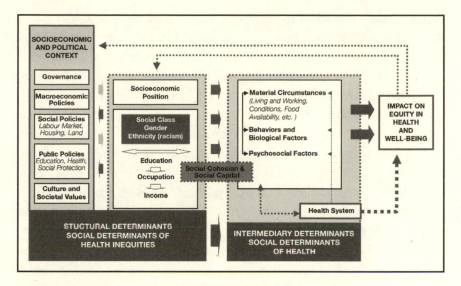

Figure 3.1 Final form of the Commission on Social Determinants of Health (CSDH) conceptual framework
Used with permission from the World Health Organization (Solar and Irwin 2010, 6).

were included" (1). However, such heterogeneity effectively demonstrates how different interpretations of, and responses to, the SDH come about. Health policy and management professor Dennis Raphael has aptly addressed how certain frameworks, which may have the potential for more substantive change, end up being de-prioritized in the Canadian context: "Various discourses that consider SDH but ignore their public policy antecedents allow governmental authorities to neglect the quality of the SDH that are experienced and their inequitable distribution" (Raphael 2011, 230). Consequently, interventions often end up focusing on mitigating the impacts of living in poverty, growing up in an overcrowded house or a dangerous neighbourhood, having precarious employment, smoking, etc. These are certainly important issues to address. However, the CSDH's emphasis on seeking out the "causes of the causes" is ignored with such an approach.

The CSDH's conceptual framework considers the conditions of daily life as *intermediary determinants*. However, the CSDH report's introduction explains that "the conditions in which people live and die are, in turn, shaped by political, social, and economic forces" (CSDH 2008, n.p.). These forces – macroeconomic, social and public policies, governance, culture, and societal values – along with socioeconomic position (informed by social class, gender, ethnicity, as well as education, occupation, and income) are referred to in the CSDH's conceptual framework as *structural determinants* or the *social determinants of health inequities* (Solar and Irwin 2010, 6). Although the intermediary determinants are often referred to interchangeably with the more generic social determinants of health, the CSDH intentionally "took a holistic view" of the concept of the "social determinants of health," and considered it to include both the conditions of daily life (or intermediary determinants) and the structural determinants (Marmot et al. 2008, 1661; CSDH 2008, 1). This holistic view is important because it avoids compartmentalizing these concepts as though they were unrelated to one another. Indeed, when we consistently prioritize addressing material conditions over the structural elements that produce them, we strip the SDH of their potential for more substantive change, which is only possible by acting on the structural aspects. As a result, the very framework intended to expand our understanding and analysis of health determinants ironically ends up limiting both.

The Priority Public Health Conditions Knowledge Network of the CSDH summarizes it well when they write that the SDH are crucial to explaining health inequities, which are directly linked to the "distribution of power, income, goods and services, globally and nationally, as well as the immediate, visible circumstances of peoples lives, such as their access to health care, schools and education; their conditions of work and leisure; their homes, communities, and rural or urban settings; and their chances of leading a flourishing life" (Blas and Kurup 2010, 5). Returning to the CSDH's conceptual framework, the structural determinants influence the intermediary determinants, which, in turn, impact on equity in the health and well-being of individuals. To be clear, "the vocabulary of 'structural determinants' and 'intermediary determinants' underscores the causal priority of the structural factors" (Solar and Irwin 2010, 6). Or, more simply, if the "causes of the causes" address the conditions that produce illness, then the structural determinants address the causes that produce those conditions in the first place.

The CSDH's report contributed to "institutionalizing" a major paradigm shift advocated for years by impacted communities, health-justice activists, socially aware practitioners, and public health experts. A new lens through which to analyze the discrepancies in health, well-being, and longevity was made widely accessible with the goal of achieving equity in health care.

Indigenous Children: Bearing the Brunt of ÉVAQ's Non-Accompaniment Rule

In the executive summary of its report, the CSDH identifies how children's life chances are dramatically impacted by where they are born: "In Japan or Sweden they can expect to live more than 80 years; in Brazil, 72 years; India, 63 years; and in one of several African countries, fewer than 50 years" (CSDH 2008, n.p.). At the same time, unexpected discrepancies occur between different regions of the world, as exemplified by the fact that "a young unskilled worker in East Baltimore [United States] has a life expectancy shorter than the average life expectancy in Bangladesh" (Navarro 2009, 428). Indeed, even when comparing only rich countries, health and social problems in the population at large – but also specifically for children – are more common in unequal societies that are marked by large income inequalities (Wilkinson and Pickett 2010, 20, 23–4). This phenomenon can be observed in some large cities, where the differences can be staggering: a twenty-minute drive from west to east on Ogden Avenue in Chicago "exposes a near twenty-year life expectancy gap" (Ansell 2017, viii). Similarly, a 2012 report by the public health department of Montreal highlighted how the average life expectancy in the west of the city could be more than ten years longer than in the east (DSP 2012, 15).

The consequences stemming from the conditions we are born into – the accident of birth – can be lethal for Indigenous Peoples. The "Inuit Statistical Profile 2018" produced by Inuit Tapiriit Kanatami, the national representational organization for the 65,000 Inuit living in Canada, reported that "the Inuit infant mortality rate was almost three times that for non-Indigenous infants and the sudden infant death syndrome (SIDS) rate was over eight times the non-Indigenous rate" (ITK 2018, 11). A study published in 2019 provided the most complete estimates to date of mortality for Indigenous youth using official government data from 1974 to 2013. In "First Peoples Lost," economists Donna Feir and Randall Akee reported that the mortality rate of status First Nations youth* between ten and nineteen years of age was at least twice as high as the Canadian average (Feir and Akee 2019, 503). For First Nations girls aged between fifteen and nineteen years living on reserve, the mortality rate was almost five times as high. In fact, for all First Nations girls living on reserve across the country, mortality rates have not improved in the last thirty years (515). In response to the study's findings, Dr Evan Adams, the chief medical officer of the First Nations Health Authority in British Columbia, commented that "Indigenous people have the worst health and are the poorest of any ethnic group in the country and that is no accident. That is a direct result of their history" (Friesen 2019a; see also Greenwood and de Leeuw 2012).

Returning to the issue of why the experiences of Eeyou and Inuit children from northern Quebec were so central in the #aHand2Hold campaign, an important study published by the government of Quebec in 2015 provides some insight. It reported that, although the absolute numbers were small (a reflection of smaller populations), the infant mortality rate in Eeyou Istchee is almost four times that of the overall Quebec population, and up to six times as high in Nunavik (RRSSSN 2015, 32). The social determinants that most adversely impacted childhood in Inuit communities include malnutrition, food insecurity, prenatal exposure to environmental contaminants, housing overcrowding, social stressors, and poverty (RRSSSN 2015, 6). Citing numerous studies across the globe irrespective of age and sex (gender wasn't mentioned), the authors identify socioeconomic status as one of the most powerful determinants of health. They explain that the impacts of poverty are felt even before a baby's birth and carry through to have implications on the child's growth and development, including school performance. As adults, they suffer from higher rates of chronic medical problems (diabetes, stroke, heart disease) and mental health issues. Mortality rates are higher at various points throughout the entire life cycle (RRSSSN 2015, 14).

Adopting the lens of the SDH made it easier to understand why children from northern Quebec, especially Nunavik, were more adversely impacted by ÉVAQ's non-accompaniment practice than children in other parts of the

---

* The authors of the study provide the following explanation: "'Status First Nations' are individuals who are governed explicitly under the Indian Act as 'Indians.' 'Indian status' is determined through genetic relation to the First Peoples classified by the federal government as 'Indians'" (Feir and Akee 2019, 491n1).

province. Simply stated, Inuit children living in Nunavik are more likely to need to be transferred by a flying hospital because of the conditions they are born into. Children from Nunavik are at a higher risk of suffering from injuries and poisonings, infectious diseases, and severe respiratory illnesses than the rest of the pediatric population in Quebec (RRSSSN 2015, 34). In fact, a large study published in 2016 reported that 5 per cent of the entire birth cohort needed to be treated at a tertiary care centre, including almost 2 per cent whose illness was so severe that they required life support. The authors highlighted that the "rates of lower respiratory tract infections in ... Nunavik are among the highest globally" (Banerji et al. 2016, E619). Local health care resources are significantly limited in terms of health care personnel, characterized by a high turnover of health care workers and professionals, as well as a marked absence of medical specialists and surgeons (Viens Commission 2019, 396–7). Diagnostic and therapeutic technologies (e.g., medical imaging, noninvasive ventilatory support, mechanical respirators) pale in comparison to what is available in some community hospitals "down south." Indeed, there is no tertiary care centre in northern Quebec. Geographic factors are also important: unlike other regions of Quebec where private medevac companies are able to airlift patients from rural to urban centres for emergency care, the regional medevac Air Inuit planes can't transport critically ill patients to Montreal because of the physical distance (Joanie Tremblay-Pouliot, pers. comm., 2019). Also, as shown in Figure 1.1, other areas of the province benefited from double coverage with the air shuttle service on most days of the week; there was no such service for Nunavik. Of course, there are no land-based alternatives. All this meant that for critical, but also urgent noncritical cases that required health care personnel for transfer, the Challenger plane was the only option to provide flying hospital services to regions in Nunavik.

While any child being transferred alone is unacceptable, families from other areas in Quebec could reduce the harm of ÉVAQ's non-accompanying rule by taking one of several commercial flights or even driving (depending on where they were coming from) to reach their child at the hospital. However, for Nunavimmiut, there was typically only one flight per day from Kuujjuaq or Puvirnituq to Montreal and the caregiver would not necessarily be able to take it: the flight could be delayed, cancelled, or at capacity already. In such circumstances, caregivers would have to wait until the following day and hope for the best. The example of the couple who chartered a flight to transfer their breastfeeding baby from the Magdalen Islands to Quebec City after they were refused to board the flying hospital in 2005 (see page 29) is an exception. It would not only be cost prohibitive for a caregiver in Nunavik to do the same, but it would be virtually impossible to do so on such short notice because of geographic and other logistical (aircraft availability, weather) considerations.

As a result, these Inuit children would sometimes be forced to remain hospitalized alone for days before a caregiver could join them. Such delays would exacerbate the effects of communication barriers with Inuit toddlers and school-aged children who usually don't learn English (or French) until they are older. Since most health care providers in the province don't speak Inuktitut, it was virtually impossible for them to effectively communicate with the children they were caring for.

Equality vs Equity

The burden of the non-accompaniment practice was disproportionately borne by Indigenous children from northern Quebec. Something needed to be done to change this. If the troubling numbers of children being transferred alone weren't enough in and of themselves, the long-standing calls for change by impacted families and communities should have been a wake-up call for the government.

Government officials and ÉVAQ administrators occasionally made it a point to highlight how it wasn't a matter of only the population in northern Quebec being discriminated against, but rather all communities across the province. For example, when Barrette made the announcement, on 15 February 2018, that he was putting an end to the non-accompaniment rule, he explained to a reporter that the newer of the two Challengers could land on all the runways in Nunavik, but that it couldn't land in the Magdalen Islands (Lavoie 2018). Even if Barrette's assertion was true, the message between the lines seemed to be that families in Nunavik were not exceptional in having to deal with suboptimal health care services. The Magdalen Islands and Nunavik are indeed similar in that neither can access their referral tertiary care hospital (in Quebec City and Montreal, respectively) solely by land. However, Barrette was wrong about the Challenger's capabilities because it can only land in three communities in Nunavik: Kuujjuaq, Kuujjuaraapik, and Puvirnituq. He was also disingenuous about the Challenger not being able to land in the Magdalen Islands (see Figure 1.1). Moreover, he failed to mention mitigating factors, like the fact that ÉVAQ provides an air shuttle service to the Magdalen Islands on most days of the week and that the DASH planes can also provide emergency medevac airlift services for these shorter distances. Nunavik doesn't benefit from these factors that could have lessened the harms of the non-accompaniment practice.

As discussed previously, Edith-Farah Elassal, the Viens Commission's legal counsel presiding over ÉVAQ's testimony, pointed out that children from Nunavik had a higher rate of caregiver refusal than the provincial average, based on ÉVAQ's statistics between 30 June and 1 October 2018. She asked why these children continued to be disproportionately impacted by the non-accompaniment practice, despite the implementation of the new FCC framework on 29 June 2018. André Lizotte, a nurse and the director of prehospital emergency services at the Ministry of Health, explained that Nunavik was impacted not because of its population, but because of logistical considerations since the flying hospital service there is provided by the Challenger plane, while the DASH (with fewer space constraints when the "caregiver escort" rule was still in effect) could potentially be used to provide flying hospital service in urgent situations for other regions. ÉVAQ did not provide statistics on how many of their flying hospital missions were done by DASH versus Challenger, but it would be safe to assume that most were by Challenger. The implication of Lizotte's reply was that Inuit communities in Nunavik were not being discriminated against but were simply collateral damage due to being geographically remote (Bernier et al. 2018, 102–5).

A last example illustrates how officials viewed communities across the province as being treated equally. During his testimony at the Viens Commission, ÉVAQ's medical director, Dr Richard Bernier, was asked by Elassal about the concerns stemming from children being sent alone and how this had safety, communication, and clinical implications. Not receiving an adequate answer, she kept pressing him including about the matter of obtaining parental consent in such circumstances. Finally, after being asked the same question for the third time, he responded that the situations she was bringing up happen in all hospitals across the province. Citing the ostensibly "frequent" example of a toddler from a French-speaking family who requires immediate lifesaving or pain-alleviating interventions, Bernier explained that it is ethically justified to intervene without consent because of the time-sensitive nature of the injury or illness. Bernier was right (i.e., consent to provide immediate life-saving interventions for critically ill or injured children is usually implied), but he still wasn't answering Elassal's question. She wanted to know his perspective on providing proper medical care to Indigenous children when caregivers were being systematically prevented from accompanying them, particularly in the context that those from northern Quebec were being disproportionately impacted (Bernier et al. 2018, 82–8).

In these three examples, Barrette, Lizotte, and Bernier didn't want to acknowledge that Inuit communities in Nunavik were disproportionately impacted. The non-accompaniment practice applied to everyone equally, and so, according to them, everyone was equally impacted by it. Even though Lizotte's reply conveys a recognition that Nunavik was an exceptional situation, he nonetheless justified this as being a logistical consideration owing simply to geography and having nothing to do with the fact that the population there is Inuit. By suggesting that everyone was being treated equally, government officials and ÉVAQ administrators glossed over the fact that their practice adversely impacted certain communities more than others. This raises the very important distinction between equality and equity.

Even if it was true that the core issue here was the geographical reality of Nunavik being in the far north of Quebec, and not that Indigenous Peoples live on that land, the fact that an identifiable demographic of children was being adversely impacted simply by virtue of geographical considerations is a problem. The Priority Public Health Conditions Knowledge Network of the CSDH asserts that "equity in health care ideally implies that everyone in need of health care receives it in a form that is beneficial to them" (Blas and Kurup 2010, 7). No one can convincingly argue that systematically preventing a parent from accompanying their child can be beneficial for either of them.

The letter sent to ÉVAQ administration and government officials, which eventually served as the basis for the launch of the #aHand2Hold campaign, proposed an equity-based approach to ending the non-accompaniment rule. Our perspective went beyond purely geographical considerations because, among other factors, we recognized that separating Eeyou and Inuit children from their parents fit into a larger history of forced removal of Indigenous children from their families, notably through residential schools, youth protection services, and disappearances within the health care system itself (Shaheen-Hussain et al. 2017). This was often justified by governments deciding what was best for the child. An equity-based approach would have meant recognizing the history of broken promises by governments and ensuring that future promises will not be broken.

Equality-based and equity-based approaches are often confused and are sometimes used interchangeably. They differ though in their conceptions of fairness, or, more specifically, how to achieve it. During presentations throughout the #aHand2Hold campaign, I used Figure 3.2a and Figure 3.2b to explain the difference between equality and equity (even though they oversimplify reality by assuming that everyone is on a level playing field). I would then show the image in Figure 3.3, labelled "reality," because it better captures the concept of SDH inequalities. The final image I used, shown in Figure 3.4 with a slide entitled "liberation," differentiates between equity-based and social justice–based approaches; equity-based approaches are to the intermediary determinants of health what social justice–based approaches are to the structural determinants of health, which aim to tackle the actual "causes of the causes." However, even this example has its limitations because it doesn't address the fact that some people can't even get into the stadium in the first place.

Essentially, an equality-based approach could make sense if we lived in a truly egalitarian society. But, in a society that produces inequalities, including one where the health care system fails those it is intended to care for, an equity-based approach must take precedence. In a document produced by the European regional office of the WHO in 2006, the authors state that the "outcome of these efforts would be a gradual reduction of all systematic differences in health between different socioeconomic groups. The ultimate vision is the elimination of such inequities, by 'levelling up' to the health of the most advantaged" (Whitehead and Dahlgren 2006, 5).

Another benefit of equity-based approaches is that their success may benefit people beyond the specific group with whom a given intervention is being planned. In Amy Sun's article, "Equality Is Not Enough: What the Classroom Has Taught Me about Justice," she uses the cartoon shown in Figure 3.5 to provide an example of an equity-based approach that results

Figure 3.2a *Top* Equality versus equity
Image download available via Craig Froehle (2016), "The Evolution of an Accidental
Meme: How One Little Graphic Became Shared and Adapted by Millions," Medium,
14 April 2016, https://medium.com/@CRA1G/the-evolution-of-an-accidental-meme-
ddc4e139e0e4.

Figure 3.2b *Bottom* Equality versus equity
Image from Maryam Abdul-Kareem (n.d.), "Here's Why We Should Care More about
Equity, Not Equality," http://muslimgirl.com/46703/heres-care-equity-equality/.

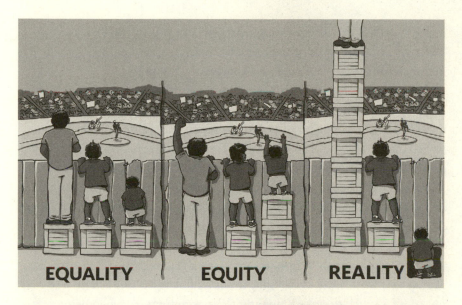

Figure 3.3 *Top* Equality, equity, and reality
Image used with permission from the Interaction Institute for Social Change,
http://interactioninstitute.org/equality-vs-equity-the-gift-that-keeps-on-giving/.

Figure 3.4 *Bottom* Equality, equity, and liberation

in more-or-less equal access to enter the school (Sun 2014). The cartoon is effective, but only hints at the more fundamental societal reorganization required for the full inclusion of people with disabilities.

In a similar vein, by centring the experiences of Eeyou and Inuit children living in northern Quebec, the #aHand2Hold campaign focused the attention on how the government's non-accompaniment practice adversely impacted these Indigenous communities. However, our goal was always for the practice to be stopped throughout the province for the benefit of all children. As such, with the campaign's eventual success, all children living in remote and rural areas requiring flying hospital services, not just Eeyou and Inuit childen, can now be accompanied by a caregiver. An equity-based approach resulted in equal access to parental accompaniment for all children in the province. Unfortunately, though, the campaign's success didn't produce a change that would also allow Indigenous adults, including Elders who may not speak English or French fluently, to be accompanied when being transferred by ÉVAQ's Challenger plane. Nor did the campaign meaningfully alter, and it certainly didn't eliminate, the persistent and pervasive inequities that disproportionately impact Indigenous children throughout Quebec. The only approach to "narrow the health gap in an equitable way is to bring up the level of health of the groups of people who are worse off to that of the groups who are better off" (Whitehead and Dahlgren 2006, 16). This is easier said than done.

Limits of the Social Determinants of Health

The conceptual framework and analytical tools stemming from the CSDH's report were crucial to understand why the non-accompaniment practice disproportionately impacted Indigenous children, those from northern Quebec in particular, and especially Inuit children from Nunavik. The "causes of the causes" that allowed such a practice to persist for so long soon became obvious: systemic racism and colonial policies rooted in capitalism. The CSDH's report was ground-breaking in many respects. However, it also had notable weaknesses. Two are particularly striking.

First, while there was a clearly articulated focus on addressing the "causes of the causes," this remained very generic. Identifying that "political, social and economic forces" shape the "conditions in which people live and die"

Figure 3.5 Equity-based approach and "levelling up"
"Clearing a Path" cartoon, originally appeared in Michael F. Giangreco (2000),
Teaching Old Logs New Tricks: Absurdities and Realities of Education (Thousand Oaks,
CA: Corwin Press). Used with permission.

(CSDH 2008, n.p.) is important, but so is actually naming these forces and attempting to understand how they operate, which the report doesn't do.

For example, particularly relevant to the non-accompaniment rule and the #aHand2Hold campaign, the CSDH's report and the conventional understanding of the SDH don't ascribe the necessary importance to colonization and colonial ideologies, practices, and policies (see Czyzewski 2011, 9;

de Leeuw et al. 2010, 286). Yet, such structural elements continue to produce significant inequalities in the conditions of daily life with devastating consequences for many people, including to children.

The second weakness of the CSDH's report, and of conventional understandings of the SDH, flows from the first. If there are systems in place that produce inequalities in health, why and how are they allowed to persist? In the executive summary, the CSDH report authoritatively states that "social injustice is killing people on a grand scale" (CSDH 2008, 26). However, social injustice does not appear out of nowhere. It has to be created and maintained. If people are being killed on a grand scale by social injustice and we are truly committed to putting an end to it, then we must go to the roots and find the "causes for the causes." We must ask why.

The answer lies in power, who wields it and how they benefit from it while harming others. It is worth quoting a critique of the CSDH report by Vicente Navarro, professor of Health and Public Policy at Johns Hopkins University, at length here:

> It is not *inequalities* that kill, but *those who benefit from the inequalities* that kill. The Commission's studious avoidance of the category of power (class power, as well as gender, race and national power) and how power is produced and reproduced in political institutions is the greatest weakness of the report. It reproduces a widely held practice in international agencies that speaks of policies without touching on politics. It does emphasize, in generic terms, the need to redistribute resources, but it is silent on the topic of whose resources, and how and through what instruments. *It is profoundly apolitical, and therein lies the weakness of the report* ... The Commission's report goes very far in describing how inequalities are killing people. But we know the names of the killers. We know about the killing, the process by which it occurs and the agents responsible. And we, as public health workers, must denounce not only the process, but the forces that do the killing. The WHO will never do that. But as public health workers we can and must do so. (Navarro 2009, 440; emphasis in original)

Navarro's critique is not solely directed at the CSDH's report because he also takes issue with the WHO (which commissioned the report) and other similar international agencies. He explains that these organizations always have to reach consensus from their member nation-states, and in order to reach a consensus, the most powerful typically wield another power: that of veto. Subjects, terminologies, and/or conclusions that more powerful groups don't agree with will simply be dropped.

The publication of the csdh's report allowed the concept of the sdh to achieve "a prominence that makes it difficult for policymakers, health researchers and professionals to ignore" (Raphael 2011, 221). It recommended that "educational institutions and relevant ministries make the social determinants of health a standard and compulsory part of training of medical and health professionals" (csdh 2008, 206). While the sdh were already taught in various health care training programs in Canada, the csdh's report anchored them permanently in the curricular landscape. Beyond classrooms and clinical-teaching settings, the sdh became adopted, albeit often selectively, in many sectors of society: governmental bodies, public health organizations, research-funding agencies, etc. Indeed, "even the business-oriented Conference Board of Canada has established an initiative focused on the social and economic determinants of health" (Raphael 2011, 221). Such widespread uptake is fascinating, but the report's two notable weaknesses likely made it more adoptable at the who and more widely accepted by institutions like the Conference Board of Canada once released. This came at a price, however: the very systems that create and maintain injustice and misery, and those who benefit from them, were not named.

Chapter 4

Recognizing Systemic Racism:
A Social Justice Approach

The opposite of poverty is not wealth; the opposite of poverty is justice.
– Bryan Stevenson, *Just Mercy: A Story of Justice and Redemption*

With so much money in the world, then why are people on the street?
I seen an old lady diggin' in the garbage bin for somethin' to eat
Some man died in the hospital, they thought he was asleep
What kind of world do we live in? When the rich don't wanna give
into the poor?
Then they wanna send us to war
To kill each other for nothin', what is it all for?
When we're fighting for ourselves to survive
'Cause you're lucky if you make it past the age of twenty-five.
– Warrior Minded featuring Dramatik, "No Justice, No Peace"

Government officials and ÉVAQ administrators perseverated until the very end that the non-accompaniment rule was applied equally to everyone in Quebec. While equity-based approaches can certainly be very useful, there are limits to their utility because they often only address the intermediary determinants of health, considered by the Commission on Social Determinants of Health (CSDH) as the conditions of daily life and the health care system (Solar and Irwin 2010, 6, 40; CSDH 2008, 1). In the correlating meme of the three children trying to watch a game in a stadium, the goal is *overcoming* barriers (see Figures 3.2a, 3.2b, and 3.3). Social justice-based approaches, meanwhile, can certainly build on equity-based approaches but are generally more holistic and radical (in the etymological sense of the word, from *radix* in Latin, meaning "root") because there is an understanding of the structural determinants of health. The goal in the correlating meme is that of *eliminating* barriers and preventing them from being put up in the first place (see Figure 3.4).

An equity framework was important in the #aHand2Hold campaign. The strict and systematic application of the non-accompaniment rule on flying hospital (i.e., Challenger) medevac transfers may have been "equal" for all children living in remote and rural areas throughout the province, but it nonetheless disproportionately impacted Indigenous children, particularly Inuit in Nunavik. Essentially, equal application of the accompaniment prohibition resulted in inequitable consequences because of the underlying inequalities in the conditions of daily life, which have direct consequences on health.

A social justice framework helped elucidate at least two structural forces at the root of those intermediary determinants of health: systemic racism and colonialism. Importantly, such a framework also played a role in recognizing the historical and political context of Indigenous children being separated from their families through government-sanctioned practices and policies (e.g., residential schools, child welfare programs, disappearances in the health care system), and how these could exacerbate the experience of being sent alone by medevac airlift.

The initial public messaging of the #aHand2Hold campaign, building from the letter sent to ÉVAQ, was framed mostly around equity. During interviews, we talked about the historical reality of colonial policies that resulted in the forced removal of Indigenous children and how the non-accompaniment rule discriminated the most against those in northern Quebec, particularly children from Nunavik. One *La Presse* headline, "Une pratique d'évacuation « barbare »," flipped the usual colonial and racist tropes, quoting Dr Joanie Tremblay-Pouliot, who was working in Puvirnituq (Nunavik) at the time. She characterized as "barbaric" the practice of separating a sick or medically unstable child from their parent and leaving them unaccompanied and alone in a Montreal emergency department, knowing full well that they often only speak Inuktitut (Duchaine and Teisceira-Lessard 2018a). More explicitly, *Nunatsiaq News* quoted an Inuk woman (who didn't want to be named), whose young child had been transferred alone in the past: "But when you strip it all down, it's racism" (Rogers 2018). Despite the significant amount of media coverage following the launch, none of the initial public messaging really addressed systemic racism or colonialism head-on. However, the government's subsequent response, sparking more public indignation, and the catalyzing role of the CPS shifted this messaging within days.

In a very firm letter, the CPS expressed its concern about the forced separation of these children causing post traumatic stress disorder and referred to the non-accompaniment practice as "merciless." The letter stated that "choosing not to revise antiquated policies reinforces the racism that has been built into our health care system" (Radha Jetty, Catherine Farrell, and Pascale Hamel, letter to the Ministers of Health and Transport, 5 February 2018). Dr Radha Jetty, the chair of the CPS's First Nations, Inuit, and Métis Health Committee persisted in an interview: "What's really distressing is that Canada does have this dark history of government-sanctioned, forced removal of Indigenous children from their families ... We have to realize that these health care systems, these policies, are racist, that they're discriminatory, and choosing not to change these antiquated policies perpetuates this racism" (CTV 2018). That a reputed, mainstream national pediatric organization whose primary mission is ensuring the health and well-being of children living in Canada came out so forcefully in support of the campaign was significant enough. The fact that it identified root systemic causes – racism and colonialism – that had allowed the non-accompaniment practice to continue unchecked all these years was unprecedented.

Understanding Racism

Some individuals tend to feel defensive and even threatened when the notion of racism is raised. When members of a dominant or privileged group hear the terms *structural*, *institutional*, or *systemic discrimination*, they often feel personally targeted. White, US-based, antiracist sociologist Robin DiAngelo explores this phenomenon explaining how "white privilege" and "whiteness as a position of status" are enabled in societies founded upon white supremacy, which she considers to be "a descriptive and useful term to capture the all-encompassing centrality and assumed superiority of people defined and perceived as white and the practices based on this assumption" (DiAngelo 2018, 23–8). In this context, she clarifies that white supremacy "does not refer to individual white people and their individual intentions or actions but to an overarching political, economic, and social system of domination" (28). Defensive reactions against the charge of racism stem from a conviction that the person is not racist, which "is rooted in the false but widespread belief that racial discrimination can only be intentional" (43). Indeed, individual racist attitudes and behaviours are often unintended because "under the surface is the massive depth of racist socialization: messages, beliefs, images, associations, internalized superiority and entitlement, perceptions and emotions" that form unconscious beliefs (42). These are what produce implicit bias. Fundamentally though, as these terms imply, structural, institutional or systemic racism refer to overarching structures and systems, not individual attitudes and behaviours. This is why it's important to first distinguish between different forms of racism so that we can be on the same page about the terms being used.

The excellent resource produced by the National Collaborating Centre for Aboriginal Health (NCCAH), entitled "Understanding Racism," elaborates on several different expressions of racism, including relational, colour blindness, epistemic, and structural (Reading 2013, 3–6). *Relational racism* (also referred to as interpersonal racism) occurs when someone experiences discriminatory behaviour in everyday human relationships, ranging from micro-aggressions (for example, making assumptions about someone's employment based on their ethnic identity) to overt sexual and physical violence, including murder.

The concept of *colour blindness* allows people to claim that they "don't see race" (hence the related term, "racelessness"). Of course, race as a biological entity doesn't exist. However, racialization – the process by which "race" has been socially constructed – does. Cedric J. Robinson, late professor of political science who developed the concept of "racial capitalism," traces "a social order of domination from which a racial theory of order emerged" in European civilization at the end of the first Christian millennium (Robinson 1983, 2, 66). This "racial ordering" continued throughout the medieval and feudal ages (67), and well into the Enlightenment period when scientific thought and the leading thinkers of the time created an "enduring racial taxonomy and the 'color-coded, white-over-black' ideology with which we are familiar" (Bouie 2018). Indeed, "colonial domination and expropriation marched hand in hand with the spread of 'liberty,' and liberalism arose alongside our modern notions of race and racism" (Bouie 2018). During the

Enlightenment, women's access to property, higher education, and professional training was curtailed locally in Europe (Perez 2019, 13), while hierarchies of domination and economic exploitation based on physical appearance and skin colour were established to justify colonialism, imperialism, and slavery abroad (Bouie 2018). The eurocentric rendering of history that persists to this day is "a political interpretation of the world based on Christianity, exploitation, economic profit, and Western Europe's blind faith in its cultural superiority" (Adams 1999, 21). Considering this historical context, "racelessness essentially ignores the social realities of racialized inequities experienced within relationships, systems and structures, thereby maintaining the status quo" (Reading 2013, 6).

Epistemic racism is tied to how the "dominance of western knowledge systems produces and promotes beliefs about racialized cultures as inferior to western culture" (Reading 2013, 3). Specifically, in the colonial context, scientific – including medical – research has exploited "vast resources and opportunities" to "observe, measure and record hypothetical racial differences" (3). Perhaps even more critically, these "disciplines of science have created and maintained racial distinctions used to segregate and oppress Aboriginal peoples" (4). As the following chapters explore, such knowledge acquisition and development have come at the expense of the health, well-being, and lives of Indigenous Peoples, including children.

Finally, *structural racism* refers to "the economic, social and political institutions and processes of society and the moral and cultural systems that underpin them," occurring when those in power produce, reproduce, or "fail to redress the structural inequities between racialized groups" (Reading 2013, 4). The Government of Ontario's 2017 antiracism strategic plan states that "systemic racism ... doesn't necessarily mean that people within an organization are racist." Rather, it "is often caused by hidden institutional biases in policies, practices and processes" or the "result of doing things the way they've always been done, without considering how they impact particular groups differently" (Government of Ontario 2017, 10).

Senator Murray Sinclair, whose traditional name is Mizana Gheezhik, chaired the TRC. He dispels the claim that an entire population is being put on trial when the subject of structural or institutional racism is being evoked: "Systemic racism is the racism that's left over after you get rid of the racists." He clarifies that "once you get rid of the racists within the justice system, for example, you will still have racism perpetrated by the justice system ... because the justice system follows certain rules, procedures, guidelines, precedents, and laws that are inherently discriminatory and racist because [they] ... come from a history of the common law, which comes from a different culture, a different way of thinking" (M. Sinclair 2017, 1–2).

An even more tangible example is provided by Kwame Ture (previously known as Stokely Carmichael) and Charles V. Hamilton in their 1967 book, *Black Power: The Politics of Liberation in America*, in which the term *institutional racism* makes one of its earliest appearances in the literature: "When white terrorists bomb a black church and kill five black children, that is an act of individual racism ... But when in that same city ... five hundred black babies die each year because of the lack of proper food, shelter and medical facilities, and thousands more are destroyed and maimed physically, emotionally and intellectually because of conditions of poverty and discrimination in the black community, that is a function of institutional racism" (4).

Many experts use institutional, structural, and systemic racism interchangeably (Allan and Smylie 2015, 5). I make a subtle but relevant distinction because, for the purposes of this book, I consider systemic racism to encapsulate both structural (or institutional) racism *and* relational (or interpersonal) racism. While somewhat semantic, this makes explicit the fluid links between structural and relational racism, and particularly the mutually reinforcing relationship that can exist when we factor in the societal power wielded by an individual like a government official, a university professor, or a physician. This interplay between individual and structural power, as well as other overarching societal forces and economic systems, is eloquently illustrated by Kwame Ture: "If a white man wants to lynch me, that's his problem. If he's got the power to lynch me, that's my problem. Racism is not a question of attitude; it's a question of power" (Clennon 2018, 2).

Systemic Racism

Most media coverage throughout the bulk of the #aHand2Hold campaign focused more on the colonial context of the practice rather than on the systemic racism that allowed it to persist. There had never been a formal discussion among those doing media interviews to intentionally avoid using systemic racism as a term. So, why wasn't it more prominent in our interviews, especially earlier on? One explanation could be that in white-dominant societies where racism is systemic, legitimate accusations of racism often must be unduly substantiated for them to be taken seriously. Even when talking about institutional, structural, or systemic racism (and not relational racism per se), people who exercise some form of power in racialized dynamics – and benefit from its maintenance – feel personally threatened because of the perceived accusation that they are individually racist. Those who call out racism may be attacked for exaggerating or for being overly sensitive. As DiAngelo explains, "white fragility functions as a form of bullying; I am going to make it so miserable for you to confront me … that you will simply back off, give up, and never raise the issue again" (DiAngelo 2018, 112). It "is much more than mere defensiveness or whining," but can rather "be conceptualized as the *sociology of dominance*" (113; emphasis in original). This chilling effect may explain, at least in part, why systemic racism's role in having allowed the non-accompaniment rule to have persisted for so long only became more prominent later on in the campaign.

Meanwhile, the government certainly didn't want to openly recognize that some racialized groups may be disproportionately impacted by the practice. An insightful example is provided by the health minister's choice, during his press scrum on 15 February 2018, to give the hypothetical scenario of a parent who is "agitated" or "intoxicated" to make the point that certain restrictions would apply in the forthcoming FCC policy (Fidelman 2018e; Morin 2018). To portray his words as racist would have been difficult because he wasn't openly talking about Eeyou, Inuit, or other Indigenous families. However, even if his intention was to "equally" address non-Indigenous caregivers from Gaspé or the Magdalen Islands, subtext and context are critically important. Given that the #aHand2Hold campaign was centred around the reality of Indigenous communities living in northern Quebec, his problematic choice of words contradicted the position that everyone was "equally" impacted by the non-accompaniment rule. For this reason, during my March 2018 Viens Commission testimony, I explicitly addressed the "drunken Indian" trope his example evoked and included several slides about the detrimental consequences of systemic racism on Indigenous Peoples' health (Shaheen-Hussain 2018a). However, two situations that occurred in the following months made it obvious that more overt forms of relational (or interpersonal) racism were at play.

The first happened later that spring when the campaign was still quite active. I was teaching a pediatric resuscitation course where I'm regularly an instructor. A participant identified me based on my public involvement in the #aHand2Hold campaign and told me that he worked as a physician with ÉVAQ. He was clearly frustrated with me. At the break, he began lecturing me about the "social conditions" of "these communities." Ostensibly to prove his point, he described a school bus in a community in Nunavik (where he had recently been with the medevac team) that reeked of pot when the doors opened to drop children off in the morning. "These kids," he explained, often live with an aunt, uncle, or grandparent, making caregiver accompaniment difficult because there is no "parent." He, himself, volunteered that these stereotypes were "cliché." His examples were irrelevant, as the campaign's central demand was about children being accompanied by their recognized caregivers, which may very well be adult siblings, aunts, uncles, or grandparents. The literature notes that "in an Inuit cultural setting, children are the centre of family life" and the "roles of being a parent or grandparent provide fundamental sources of purpose and meaning" (Karetak and Tester 2017, 7). As for the school bus anecdote, again, the problem of relevance arises. It was one anecdote and completely unrelated to the importance of a child having a hand to hold during a medevac airlift.

I didn't know whether this physician was an outlier or a person of influence within ÉVAQ's medical team, but his comment made me realize that ÉVAQ's new policy could simply end up putting into writing what they had already been doing in practice for years. As a result, the campaign expanded its demand to ensure accountability and transparency on this front, requiring any refusal to be exceptional and the justifications to be duly documented by the ÉVAQ team. Médecins québécois pour le régime public weighed in on this exact issue in full support of the #aHand2Hold campaign a few weeks later (MQRP 2018). This expanded demand was adopted, to some extent, by the government when the new FCC framework was announced at the end of June 2018.

This physician's intervention was a reminder of what I'd been hearing anecdotally from others, including people working in northern communities. Despite a genuine desire by some of ÉVAQ's administrative, medical, and pilot teams to implement a new FCC policy, others were resistant. Indeed, given that the calls for change coming from health care providers and Indigenous families in northern Quebec had been "preferably unheard" or "deliberately silenced" for so long (Roy 2004), the possibility of a climate within ÉVAQ that was resistant to revoking the non-accompaniment rule should not have been surprising.

Culture is understood to be "historically and geographically bound patterns of shared beliefs, values, and behaviors" often within identifiable social or ethnic groups (Reading 2013, 2). However, as the NCCAH notes, it is "recognized that groups in institutional boundaries have culture" as well and that this culture can be transmitted to others in various ways, including "through rules and policies" (2). Government ministries and agencies are no exception to this, which is why many supporters of the campaign had already publicly commented that institutional racism at the governmental level had played a role in allowing the non-accompaniment rule to have persisted for so long.

Jarring as the interaction with the ÉVAQ physician was, it did not prepare me for the second situation demonstrating that relational (or interpersonal) racism was at play: the health minister's comments in June 2018 explicitly perpetuating anti-Indigenous racist stereotypes. As I explained previously, Barrette responded to concerns about the non-accompaniment rule expressed by a member of the public by predicting that at least once in the ensuing six months, a parent would not be allowed to accompany their child because of being "agitated," "drugged," or "under whatever influence," and that this "happens all the time" (Hendry 2018). After CBC and Le Devoir broke the story on 21 June 2018 (National Indigenous Peoples Day), Barrette denied targeting Indigenous Peoples, saying that his comments were taken out of context and that he'd been "misunderstood" (Dalton 2018). He claimed that he was simply making a generic statement about one reason a caregiver could be prevented from accompanying their child (Dalton 2018). In the Ministry of Health's press release issued that day, Barrette states: "At no time did I make reference to an Indigenous community in the revealed excerpt" (Barrette 2018). When the full transcript of the entire exchange, which had been recorded, was uploaded on the CBC website, his very specific reference to Inuit communities in Nunavik at that point in the conversation made it clear that his comments had been directed at Nunavimmiut (CBC 2018b).

Indigenous communities – including activists, leaders, and politicians – denounced the minister's statements. Many called for his immediate resignation. Cindy Blackstock, executive director of the First Nations Child and Family Caring Society, noted that it was problematic for Barrette to state that such an occurrence "happens all the time," and expressed disappointment about his overgeneralization to all members of the community (Gervais 2018c). Tunu Napartuk, who was mayor of Kuujjuaq at the time and had worked to put an end to the non-accompaniment practice, demanded Barrette's resignation. He rejected Barrette's attempt at an apology, saying that "by not talking about the racism we experience, we effectively give permission to people to continue" (Nadeau and Gervais 2018). Charlie Watt, president of Makivik Corporation said, "He needs to go. The trust is gone" (Derfel 2018). Ellen Gabriel, Kanien'kehá:ka visual artist, environmentalist, and human rights activist, described his comments as an example of "racism and colonialism at its best" (Gervais 2018c).

The Assembly of First Nations of Quebec and Labrador issued a press release within hours of the story breaking. Chief Ghislain Picard stated that "we are not done digging up and tearing down the deep roots of discrimination and prejudice against Indigenous peoples." Addressing systemic issues, Picard firmly noted that the "utterly unacceptable statement clearly indicates that these roots are deep into the heart of Philippe Couillard's government" and wondered whether the Viens Commission "should have called Gaétan Barrette first, to assess how much discrimination in the important ministry that he manages starts from the top and how much the minister's prejudices influence the delivery of the essential health and social services to First Nations and Inuit people" (AFNQL 2018). Romeo Saganash, a member of the federal parliament for the riding of Abitibi-James Bay-Nunavik-Eeyou, wrote in a statement that "the stereotypes he expressed are rooted in colonial violence." He also made a direct connection to the non-accompaniment rule: "There is no excuse for this racist policy, and the fact that Mr Barrette felt that he could make these statements is disgusting" (Saganash 2018).

Quebec Native Women also issued a press release highlighting the systemic impacts of comments like Barrette's. President Viviane Michel asserted that provincial ministers must "be more aware of the institutionalized racism they can reproduce, and that they are responsible for dismantling." She also stated that it is "unacceptable for someone in a position of power, who is supposed to represent us, to promote such prejudice" (QNW 2018). Since women are still usually the ones to accompany children, whether they are Indigenous or not, when seeking medical care, Michel's intervention highlighted the double prejudice – racism and sexism – tacit in Barrette's comments and a reality often faced by Indigenous women in daily life.

These reactions had a significant impact on the media coverage, with Indigenous voices framing the debate about the colonial and racist attitudes imbued in Barrette's comments. Political commentators (e.g., James and Blanchet 2018) and editorialists (e.g., Chouinard 2018) recognized that it was unacceptable for Barrette to have made such comments, regardless of whether he was aware of being recorded or not. However, Patrick Lagacé, one of Quebec's most influential columnists at *La Presse*, took a very different perspective in his column titled "À la défense de Gaétan Barrette" (Lagacé 2018). Despite professing not to like Gaétan Barrette (he even explained how he had coined the term "Gaétan Trump" because of Barrette's intimidation tactics against his political opponents), Lagacé felt compelled to defend him in this case. Although he proactively acknowledged the reality of anti-Indigenous racism and the "cultural genocide" suffered by Indigenous Peoples, Lagacé wrote that he "saw neither the racism, nor the colonialism, nor the stereotypes that people were reproaching him for," and that Barrette didn't have to apologize (Lagacé 2018). Citing drug use and binge drinking statistics from Nunavik, Lagacé suggested that Barrette's comments were simply reflective of the prevalence of substance abuse problems there. Using statistical data that was either taken out of context, incompletely presented, or inadequately interpreted, Lagacé provided backing to Barrette's prediction that an intoxicated parent would be prevented from accompanying their child.

In a rebuttal cowritten with Nazila Bettache, a medical doctor and assistant professor in the Faculty of Medicine at Université de Montréal, we first provided a more complete – and necessarily complex – analysis of various demographic studies on the subject, including those cited by Lagacé (Bettache and Shaheen-Hussain, 2018). In response to his point that higher rates of binge drinking and drug use could result in parents being more likely to be refused to board the flying hospital, we cited Institut national de santé publique du Québec figures correlating higher alcohol consumption rates with higher household income. Applying Barrette's logic that was defended by Lagacé, we ironically suggested that affluent Westmount and Outremont families, more likely to consume alcohol than relatively poorer neighbour-hoods, should be advised that, in the foreseeable future, at least one parent would be prevented from accompanying their child when being transferred to the hospital by ambulance. Overgeneralizations, we argued, exposed the racist and colonial stereotypes informing Barrette's choice of words. Lagacé's point about relatively higher binge drinking rates in Nunavik and the pos-sibility of an intoxicated parent wanting to board the Challenger was simi-larly flawed. Was he suggesting that worried caregivers would rush their sick or injured child to medical attention out of concern for their well-being, only to then drink to the point of becoming so intoxicated that they wouldn't be allowed to board the Challenger plane when it arrived?

We concluded by highlighting the disastrous impacts that biased analysis and intellectual shortcuts can have on those already stigmatized by a pro-foundly unjust system when used by someone with Lagacé's public influence. Although *La Presse* provided us with generous space to respond to Lagacé's column, it is almost certain that his piece was read by more people than ours, given his fame and reach via social media. As such, not only did Lagacé's col-umn serve to amplify Barrette's comments to a larger audience, worsening their systemic effects, but he also provided them with intellectual cover.

Systemic Racism Exists in Quebec and Canada

Barrette's comments sent a shockwave throughout the media and the public in Quebec and beyond. Throughout the #aHand2Hold campaign, the intention was never to point fingers at specific individuals, but rather to understand the issue as being rooted in colonialism and racism, deeply embedded in practices and policies of a system that we've admittedly inherited and that will continue to perpetuate itself unless we choose to confront it. If these comments had been made by a random individual who wields little power, they would be part of the litany of indignities faced by Indigenous Peoples in their regular interactions with settlers. However, a health minister is not a random individual.

In *Accounting for Genocide: Canada's Bureaucratic Assault on Aboriginal People*, accountant Dean Neu and poet Richard Therrien refer to Raul Hil-berg's voluminous work on the Holocaust to conclude that "the bureaucratic machine is too complex to be the work of a few mad minds." Importantly, however, they go on to clarify that "key individuals do exercise power and control within such administrative structures" (Neu and Therrien 2003, 90).

Barrette's comments legitimized those who think similarly in the general public (i.e., relational or interpersonal racism). At a more systemic level, if a cabinet minister makes comments perpetuating racist stereotypes with impunity, how can we know that such perspectives are not embedded in health care policies, not to mention in other ministries and institutions whose mandates are ostensibly to serve the public equitably and transparently (i.e., institutional or structural racism)?

The goal for pediatric medevac transfers should certainly be systematic caregiver accompaniment in all cases. However, we always knew it would be unrealistic to expect a one hundred per cent success rate. Even ground ambulance teams, on rare occasions, bring a child unaccompanied to the hospital because of factors beyond their control. Why did Barrette choose the specific examples of "agitation" and "intoxication" as a justification for eventual refusals of caregiver accompaniment requests? Why did he perseverate on this point more explicitly with his comments about caregivers being "drugged" and "under whatever influence," and that this "happens all the time" (CBC 2018b)? If his point was to suggest that there may be some exceptions, he could have emphasized examples that are not stigmatizing, like the scenario of a caregiver with a high-risk medical condition whose health could be compromised on a flight (Fidelman 2018e). The focus in this situation would instead be on finding an appropriate substitute to escort the child because that should be the priority. Whatever his reasons, medical personnel at ÉVAQ ultimately had to publicly distance themselves from his comments.

In late-August 2018, Dr Arnaud Bocquier, a physician-clinician with ÉVAQ, was interviewed on CBC *Radio Homerun* to discuss why caregivers were still being refused in some cases. When pressed by the host about whether Barrette's infamous comments were founded, Bocquier provided the common-sense response that "if you look at the history of medical transportation throughout the world, parents being difficult is something which is marginal at best … So we are not concerned about parents being difficult at all" (Bocquier 2018). This was not surprising for most of us: we were not aware of any instance where this was an actual issue for the other medevac services that encouraged parental accompaniment, whether in Quebec (e.g., Air Inuit, Airmedic) or the rest of the country (Joanie Tremblay-Pouliot, pers. comm., 2019; Bettache and Shaheen-Hussain 2018). Indeed, in the months that followed, and throughout 2019, there was not a single media report about a parent being prevented from boarding the Challenger plane on account of being intoxicated. Barrette's "guarantee" that there would be at least one such case in the first six months proved to be wrong.

We will likely never know for certain how far the "deep roots of discrimination and prejudice" went in Barrette's Ministry of Health. However, an exploration of two critical components of the health care system in Quebec and Canada – clinical care and medical training – reveals the pervasiveness of anti-Indigenous racism and other forms of discrimination.

Clinical Care: Understanding Implicit Bias

After the chorus of demands from Indigenous activists and leaders calling for Barrette's resignation, he issued an apology. However, he didn't apologize for his comments per se, but rather for offending Indigenous communities (Barrette 2018). Instead, he proclaimed to journalists: "If there is something I am not, it is a racist" (Dalton 2018).

In reality, only a very small percentage of the North American population will self-identify as racist. After all, aside from hardline white supremacists and white nationalists, who actually wants to be known as a racist? A Canada-wide poll conducted by marketing firm Léger in February 2018 (a few months prior to Barrette's comments) is very instructive: in Quebec, only 16 per cent of respondents considered themselves "somewhat racist" or "slightly racist;" Manitobans had the highest proportion (23 per cent), while the Canadian average was 14 per cent (Roy-Brunet 2018). Another marketing firm, Ipsos, conducted a poll in Quebec a few months later with a similar sample size that took a different angle: when asked about specific groups, 63 per cent of the respondents felt that Indigenous Peoples were "strongly" or "somewhat" victims of discrimination (Ipsos-LaPresse 2018).

Comparing two distinct polls to draw reliable and valid conclusions is a perilous task. Léger asked about being racist generically, while Ipsos asked specifically about discrimination against Indigenous Peoples (among other identified groups). However, it is interesting to note that while only a relatively small minority (16 per cent) of Quebec respondents in one poll considered themselves "somewhat" or "slightly" racist, a clear majority (63 per cent) in the other recognized discrimination against Indigenous Peoples. One interpretation (among many) of this discrepancy is that respondents recognized the existence of institutional or structural racism; since a large majority do not consider themselves to be racist, the institutions and overarching structures in society must be the sources of the perceived discrimination against Indigenous Peoples. Another is that respondents simply underreported their own racism (i.e., "racism exists, but it is others who are racist, not me"). The flip side to this possible interpretation merits consideration and is informed by how I would have answered the first poll's question.

During my Viens Commission testimony in October 2018, I explained that if I was asked whether I am "somewhat racist," "slightly racist," "not very racist," or "not racist at all," my answer would be "slightly" or "somewhat" racist. This is not because I want to be racist (after all, the study's question wasn't "how racist do you want to be?"), but rather because I recognize that socialization patterns in an inegalitarian and unjust society form biases, stereotypes, and prejudices. For example, the stereotyped images that may come to mind when prompted to think of a "homemaker," "CEO," "prisoner," "nurse," "athlete," or "sex worker" are a result of implicit bias, which refers to "attitudes and stereotypes that occur unconsciously and inform our thinking, beliefs, and behaviours about social groups" (Tam 2019, 30). The troubling aspect of implicit bias is that the beliefs and ideas we hold on an unconscious level may be in very stark contrast to those we hold consciously and profess publicly. Implicit bias muddles the line between *descriptive observations* that may have some basis in reality and making *prescriptive judgments* based on our preconceived notions. However, both conscious and implicit biases operate at various levels (e.g., interpersonal, institutional, societal) to stigmatize different populations resulting in negative health outcomes (Tam 2019, 25–31, 41–6).

In the clinical context, implicit bias has adverse impacts on women, 2SLGBTIQ+, those who are racialized, low-income households and people experiencing homelessness, migrants, people with disabilities, and others marginalized by the societal systems we live in. Not only do Indigenous

Peoples, as a group, suffer from worse health outcomes than the non-Indigenous population in Canada, as outlined in Chapter 3, but they also "receive differential and less optimal care than non-indigenous groups" (Ly and Crowshoe 2015, 613; see also Allan and Smylie 2015, 27; Tam 2019, 26, 31–2). Just like the differentials in health outcomes, disparities in health care are explained by "socio-economic factors, the effects of colonisation, political and legal structures, geography, lack of culturally suitable health care services, and the impacts of racism and discrimination" (Ly and Crowshoe 2015, 613). This discrimination includes implicit bias.

A particularly brutal example is the now-infamous case of Brian Sinclair, an Anishnaabe man living in Winnipeg, Manitoba who died in the waiting room of the ED at the Health Sciences Centre, which is considered to be "the most comprehensive medical facility serving Manitoba and northwestern Ontario" (McCallum and Perry 2018, 25). Sinclair was a double amputee and used a wheelchair, suffered from cognitive impairment, and had endured homelessness in the past (Allan and Smylie 2015, 28). He was initially seen by a nurse and his family doctor at the Health Action Centre, a community clinic (McCallum and Perry 2018, 20). They deemed that his urinary catheter needed changing, so he was given a referral note by his doctor and she arranged for transport to the ED by taxi. Even though he was greeted by a triage aide upon wheeling himself into the ED at 2:53 p.m. on Friday, 19 September 2008, he was not formally registered. Health care personnel there thought that he was either simply sleeping or drunk and so he was left in the waiting room for over thirty hours despite the fact that other patients and their family members were concerned about his state and even alerted hospital staff on several occasions. He was pronounced dead at 12:51 a.m. on Sunday, 21 September, but his actual death had likely occurred hours earlier, as a result of sepsis stemming from complications of an otherwise-treatable urinary tract infection. The referral note from his doctor, to be given to a nurse at the ED, was found in his jacket pocket (20–5). In *Structures of Indifference: An Indigenous Life and Death in a Canadian City*, social historians Mary Jane Logan McCallum and Adele Perry explain how the inquest that followed Sinclair's death referred to a "perfect storm" of "weaknesses and deficiencies" tied to triage procedures, hospital systems, and personnel, but that these became "ways of diverting from issues of racism and colonialism" (McCallum and Perry 2018, 129–30, 132). Even if Sinclair had been drunk, there is no justification for him to be ignored when seeking health care. Anti-Indigenous racial bias, class-based discrimination, compounded by the prejudice faced by people with disabilities, contributed to what happened (Allan and Smylie 2015, 2). At the end of the day, Sinclair "was literally ignored to death" (McCallum and Perry 2018, 12).

There are also significant consequences to implicit bias in pediatrics. In the United States, a large study assessed triage scores (usually provided by a frontline health care worker) in a pediatric emergency department and reported that "African American, Hispanic, and American Indian [i.e., Indigenous] patients received lower acuity triage scores than Whites," which "could not be explained by available sociodemographic, clinical, or ED utilization factors" (Zook et al. 2016, 720, 725). These children were given less of a priority triage score than white children, despite ostensibly having similar clinical symptoms. A modest study published in 2012 in the *American Journal of Public Health* suggested that "pediatricians' implicit attitudes about race affect pain management" (Sabin and Greenwald 2012, 988). A more recent and larger study assessing pain management in children with appendicitis performed a cross-sectional analysis of data obtained from the National Hospital Ambulatory Medical Care Survey in the United States. The analysis did not allow assessment of outcomes for Indigenous children specifically, but it did reveal that "Black children are less likely to receive any pain medication for moderate pain and less likely to receive opioids for severe pain, suggesting a different threshold for treatment," which confirmed that "racial disparities with respect to analgesia administration exist" (Goyal et al. 2015, 996–7). Such American studies are difficult to replicate because of the limited availability of race-based demographic data, which isn't collected in the same way in Quebec and most parts of Canada. However, Indigenous community members consistently report poor interactions in the clinical setting and believe their concerns – including pain and hurt – are dismissed (Latimer et al. 2018, 1–2). Moreover, pediatric researchers have no reason to doubt that implicit bias can have detrimental impacts on clinical decisions in the ED, including for Indigenous children in Canada (Margot Latimer, co-leader of Aboriginal Children's Hurt & Healing Initiative, pers. comm., 2020).

Beyond the one-on-one clinical context, implicit bias can have broader, population-based implications. Individuals who are responsible for policy development in health care can embed – even without intending to – structural stereotypes and prejudices, which amplify the clinical impacts of those biases because policies impact more people than do individual clinical encounters by a health care provider. For example, during ÉVAQ's testimony at the Viens Commission, legal counsel Edith-Farah Elassal referred to the FCC framework document produced by ÉVAQ at the end of June 2018 to understand why there were two instances where it was written that the caregiver or parent could be refused access on board if they showed signs of intoxication due to drugs and/or alcohol based on their behaviour or speech (ÉVAQ 2018b, 7, 9). She wondered why such wording was used given that it had stigmatizing connotations. Sylvie Côté, nurse and ÉVAQ coordinator, explained that her team had referred to directives about family accompaniment in the English-language *Air Medical Journal* when elaborating the FCC framework, and that she simply translated those into French without giving the issue a second thought. Elassal followed up, reminding Côté that Barrette's comments had made headlines a week before the FCC framework was unveiled by the government, and so wondered whether "more neutral or less stigmatizing" terms could have been used to convey the same point (namely, that a parent or caregiver could be refused if they risk posing a danger to themselves or others). Côté recognized that things could have been done better, but also went on to say that she didn't have any ulterior motive when drafting that part of the document and that she wasn't targeting anyone in particular (Bernier et al. 2018, 109–16). I don't doubt that Côté was genuine in what she said. And, it is true that her team simply translated many of the elements from the screening process outlined in the 2009 article from the *Air Medical Journal*, an American authority (Funk and Farber 2009, 34–6). However, as intimated by Elassal, several considerations should be taken into account when translating such a directive, including ensuring that ÉVAQ's framework did not perpetuate stereotypes in the local (i.e., Quebec) context, particularly given that Indigenous communities had been disproportionately impacted by the non-accompaniment rule for years.

As the authors of one of the aforementioned pediatric implicit bias studies recommended, "when clinicians become aware of areas in which they hold implicit bias and situations in which biases are likely to be activated, they can be more purposeful in decision-making" to counter those biases (Sabin and Greenwald 2012, 994). Implicit bias can impact all types of decisions we make, including deciding *not* to intervene in a situation. Did implicit bias – a reflection of our unconsciously held biases, stereotypes, and prejudices – play a role in failing to prevent the inclusion of potentially stigmatizing language used in the new policy? It is very difficult to "prove" implicit bias. However, as it happens, the Saskatchewan Air Ambulance (SAA) service provides a fortuitous comparative example: their policy manual had just been updated at around the same time, namely August 2018. In their freshly worded document, there was no mention of intoxication being an issue. On the other hand, they do include "the escort's health/emotional status" as being a scenario in which "a family member or escort may not be able to accompany the patient." At the bottom of the page, it states: "The final decision to allow an escort to accompany the patient in transport shall be made collaboratively with the air medical crew and the PIC [pilot in command]" (SAA 2018, 1). David Mandzuk, a registered nurse and the manager of the SAA service, explained the rationale for his wording of the policy: "I chose words based on respect. Our medical crew must assess a number of factors related to the health and emotional status of a family member on-board. A statement that draws attention to something specific such as intoxication distracts from other reasons that someone may be excluded from the transport in the interest of safety" (David Mandzuk, pers. comm., 2019). The end result is the same (i.e., there's a clear message that a family escort could be refused to board in certain circumstances), but without any stigmatizing language and virtually no risk of perpetuating hurtful and harmful stereotypes.

In an interview with *Le Devoir* in response to Barrette's comments, I said that "racist prejudices exist at all levels of the health care sector," that "neither I nor ÉVAQ teams are an exception to this," and that prejudices "have harmful consequences on Indigenous communities" (Gervais 2018c). The goal was to drive home the point that no one who works in health care – including myself – is immune to implicit bias. Unless we are living in a truly egalitarian and just world, there is no way for anyone to completely immunize themselves from internalizing the overarching systems of power and domination that permeate society precisely because prejudices are buried in our unconscious through the specific and predictable socialization that occurs soon after we are born. In my case, even though I have vivid recollections of experiencing racism as a young Muslim child of South Asian immigrant parents, going to French-immersion elementary school, living in a mostly white mixed working- and lower-middle-class neighbourhood of a Montreal suburb, it does not mean that I don't have implicit racial bias. The only way to do anything constructive about the racial biases we hold, as I went on to say in the interview, is to "fight against these prejudices through antiracist initiatives" (Gervais 2018c). But we can't fight against systems of discrimination until we, individually and societally, acknowledge that they exist.

Medical Training: The Vicious Cycle of Exclusion

University-based processes and systems that control who gets into health care training programs, and the curriculum trainees are exposed to, play a significant role in perpetuating medical colonialism and anti-Indigenous systemic racism. This professionalization of the colonial status quo occurs in at least two ways in the field of medicine: a marked underrepresentation of Indigenous students in medical faculties and little attention paid to the impacts of colonial policies – past or present – on the health and well-being of Indigenous Peoples in Canada in medical curricula.

In the Report of the Royal Commission on Aboriginal Peoples (RCAP) released in 1996, the commissioners estimated "that only about 0.1 per cent of physicians in Canada are Aboriginal" (RCAP 1996b, 240). There has been some improvement since then, but the ratios are still not close to parity levels. In a study conducted between 2009 and 2011 of nine cohorts from four English-speaking medical schools in Ontario and Quebec, researchers asked participants to complete a survey to gain demographic information about medical students. They asked about age, gender, gender identity, sexual identity, marital status, ethnicity, rural status, parental income, and disabilities. Compared to 2006 national census data (which was the most recent available at the time of the study), Indigenous Peoples were grossly underrepresented (Young et al. 2012, 1505). This has been recently re-confirmed based on the 2016 Statistics Canada census: of the close to 94,000 physicians in Canada, less than 1 per cent identify as "Aboriginal," even though Indigenous Peoples make up close to 5 per cent of the population (Ohler 2018). Some of this can be explained by a history of institutional anti-Indigenous racism within medical faculties – and Québécois and Canadian society more generally – that impedes the social mobility of Indigenous Peoples. The medical schools study also identified other factors that are not unique to Indigenous Peoples but add further barriers even if there was no institutional racism. For example, respondents who self-identified as coming from a rural background were underrepresented compared to their population share. Participants reporting parental household incomes between $20,000 and $49,999 were underrepresented, yet a majority of participants reported parental household incomes of over $100,000 per year, which the authors noted was significantly more than the median after-tax income for a household in Canada at the time (Young et al. 2012, 1505–7). Even if medical faculties are genuinely seeking to redress their long-standing history of institutional racism, how geographically and financially accessible are they for Indigenous Peoples, particularly those from northern or remote communities across the country?

Although many of these findings weren't news to anyone, it confirmed that medical school is an elite institution where a large proportion of the general population (e.g., based not only on how people are racialized but also on family income, where they live, etc.), is not represented adequately in its student body.

The sport of vying for entry into medical school is not played on a level playing field. Among the few who can make it to the stadium, many are not allowed to enter. For the most part, this remains the case for Indigenous Peoples. Indeed, various evaluation tools used by medical schools in the admissions process are racially biased, including the Grade Point Average (GPA) and the Medical College Admission Test (MCAT), multiple mini interview, and even the recently developed Computer-based Assessment for Sampling Personal Characteristics (CASPer) (IHN 2019, 10).

The CASPer is a situational judgment test developed at McMaster University in Hamilton, Ontario. It is comprised of "a 12-section, online, predominantly video-stem-based, constructed-response test of nonacademic competencies" (Juster et al. 2019, 1198). The literature suggests that individuals "traditionally underrepresented in medicine," including Indigenous Peoples, are disadvantaged by GPAs and the MCAT (Juster et al. 2019, 1197). The CASPer has been adopted as part of the admissions process at many medical schools and other health care professional programs across North America, at least in part because it is promoted as having "the potential to widen access to medical education for a number of underrepresented demographic groups" (1197). However, anecdotal experiences suggested that

Indigenous applicants (regardless of the type of health care program) performed worse than others on the CASPer. A psychometrician confirmed this for the 2018–19 academic cycle when "Indigenous applicants slightly underperformed [on the CASPer] compared to non-Indigenous applicants in Canada, the US and Australia" (Heather Davidson, Altus Assessments, pers. comm., 2019). These differences were assessed to be less significant than those typically seen with more conventional admission tools, but it is nonetheless concerning if a flaw in a test implemented to improve access to health care professional programs still decreases the likelihood of Indigenous applicants getting into the program of their choice, including medical school, when compared with non-Indigenous applicants.

An Indigenous person making it to the point of being able to apply to medical school or other health care professions is an exception because of colonial policies and socioeconomic factors that act as obstacles and barriers. Going further upstream, the education system, dictated by colonial ministries, is also not conducive to enabling Indigenous Peoples to get that far in the first place. Assimilationist curricula that don't prioritize historical knowledge, and that don't integrate cultural and language programming into course material, compounded by chronic government underfunding, create the conditions to ensure that many Indigenous children who would like to pursue postsecondary education and training programs will not be able to. The reality is that the "educational system ... does not provide equality of opportunity, because all the nonmerit advantages that accrue to students from more-privileged backgrounds ... collectively produce ... educational outcomes" that allow for entry into coveted postsecondary programs (McNamee 2018, 105). Comparing educational-attainment data from the 2001 Canadian census, the NCCAH explained how the percentage of Indigenous Peoples fifteen years of age and older who had not completed "less than a high school education is in the order of 50%, compared to 30% for other Canadians"; specifically for Inuit, this figure was close to 60 per cent (Reading and Wien 2009, 16). Data from the 2016 Canadian census indicated that educational attainment for Indigenous Peoples had improved compared to 2006, but significant gaps persist when compared with the overall Canadian population (Statistics Canada 2017, 1–2, 7–8). In October 2018, the Quebec Ombudsman released a special report in which it found that

"54.2% of Inuit have no certificate, diploma or degree, compared to 13% elsewhere in Québec," while the high school graduation rate in Nunavik "is 25.9%, compared to 77.7% for Québec as a whole" (Corneau 2018, 13).

So, on the one hand, the elite who gain entry into medical school benefit from systems that allow them to renew themselves with each subsequent cohort. On the other, those who have traditionally been prevented from entering medical school continue to be excluded through entrenched structures. A vicious cycle is created where the elite who get into medical schools eventually rise to positions of power where they control the admissions process and curricular development. If that elite – the "white old boys' club" – fosters anti-Indigenous biases, the consequences are significant.

The Canadian Federation of Medical Students has acknowledged that medical education systems in Canada "both directly and indirectly contribute to the continued colonization of Indigenous people and their health" (Arkle et al. 2015, 1). The Indigenous Physicians Association of Canada and the Association of Faculties of Medicine of Canada made recommendations about Indigenous-focused curricula development in medical schools across the country a decade ago (IPAC-AFMC 2009, 4). Yet, "medical schools continue to offer students little opportunity to learn about broader issues of discrimination and racism, especially in the context of Aboriginal health, in which educational initiatives remain sparse or poorly integrated into core curricular activities" (Ly and Crowshoe 2017, 613).

Acknowledging the history of residential schools has started to permeate through to medical schools, in part stemming from the TRC's Calls to Action. The subject, however, is often stripped of the broader discussion about colonialism and genocide, and there is rarely a connection with how different governmental practices and policies continue to perpetuate colonial ideologies today, including those that have disastrous impacts on Indigenous children. I'm not aware of any medical faculty addressing medical colonialism as such, or of highlighting the responsibility incumbent on those of us working in health care to confront the historical and contemporary consequences of such practices.

For the 2019–20 academic year, none of Quebec's four faculties of medicine exceed twenty compulsory hours dedicated to Indigenous health and health care issues in their medical undergraduate programs. While there has been more of an effort to reach out to and involve Indigenous communities in recent years, the core curriculum on Indigenous health in undergraduate medicine programs has historically been developed and taught by non-Indigenous physicians and faculty members. If there are Indigenous instructors involved, the expectations placed on them as educators are often unreasonable (Kripalani et al. 2006, 1118). Of course, this is structural because Indigenous Peoples have been grossly underrepresented in medical schools for decades.

The overall result is an annually renewed cohort of medical students, many of whom are unaware or unwilling to learn about the role that the medical establishment, which they are now part of, plays in the colonial project, including through medical colonialism. Upon graduation, these physicians are often unable to develop meaningful relationships of trust with Indigenous Peoples in clinical settings. Ultimately, anti-Indigenous systemic racism is tolerated, enabled, and perpetuated by a medical culture that is deeply ingrained, with far-reaching consequences.

Chapter 5

Medical Culture and the Myth of Meritocracy

Mes amis, retenez ceci, il n'y a ni mauvaises herbes ni mauvais hommes.
Il n'y a que de mauvais cultivateurs.
– Victor Hugo, *Les Misérables*

The holders of power and possessors of wealth need, in all societies,
to have the assurance of the best of moral titles to their fortune.
– Michael Young, *The Rise of the Meritocracy*

I am, somehow, less interested in the convolutions of Einstein's brain than
in the near certainty that people of equal talent have lived and died in cotton
fields and sweatshops.
– Stephen Jay Gould, "Wide Hats and Narrow Minds," in *The Panda's Thumb*

Reflective of overarching societal structures, where being white and male is
the default (Perez 2019, 23), the medical establishment transmits discriminatory and oppressive norms and value systems from senior physicians and
faculty members to junior trainees. This occurs through the formal medical
curriculum where the anatomy, physiology, and pharmacology that are
taught set the "typical 70 kg (white) man" as the norm. Whatever falls outside this "norm" is deemed "atypical" or "abnormal" (196). For example, in
order to learn more about the dangers of radiation exposure on the human
body, the International Commission on Radiological Protection even developed the concept of the "Reference Man." While the 1945 atomic bombings
of Hiroshima and Nagasaki (in Japan) by the United States are widely recognized as the most notorious examples of acute and massive radiation exposure in human history (and from which much knowledge about radiation

risk has been derived), this "Reference Man" was nonetheless considered to be "20–30 years of age, weighing 70 kg, is 170 cm in height, and lives in a [temperate] climate … He is a Caucasian and is a Western European or North American in habitat and custom" (ICRP 1975, 4).

Extrapolating medical knowledge this way has significant clinical implications. For instance, there may be major variations in how medications are metabolized for those of us who aren't the "typical 70 kg (white) man." Even today, women (and transgender people) are generally underrepresented in clinical trials, creating gender-based data gaps that continue to be ignored by the medical establishment (Perez 2019, 198–9). The results stemming from this lack of knowledge can be catastrophic and lethal. As Caroline Criado Perez, author of *Invisible Women: Data Bias in a World Designed for Men*, states: "Women are dying, and the medical world is complicit" (Perez 2019, 216).

The same research gap applies to racialized people. Studies on certain diseases in the North American context have focused on "white European-Americans," even if other ethnocultural groups may be more impacted. For example, in the United States, "African American children have died from asthma at 10 times the rate of non-Hispanic white children," yet they continue to be neglected by research that could benefit them (Jacewicz 2016). Even when researchers strive to conduct more inclusive studies, these families may withhold permission because of the "lingering iatrophobia from the exploitative abuse of African American children" by the medical establishment (Washington 2006, 296). Children, in general, are penalized by the "typical 70 kg (white) man" because, as pediatricians often repeat to trainees, "children are not little adults." This is true in all respects: anatomy, physiology, and pharmacology, as well as psycho-emotively and cognitively. Nevertheless, a recent statement by children's hospitals from Australasia, Canada, Europe, and the United States states that "most drugs prescribed for children have not been tested in children and only 6% of clinical trials in one of the largest international databases involve children" (CHA et al. 2019, 2). Research forms a basis for clinical knowledge, which, in turn, is taught in medical schools. Unlike earlier periods of imposed human experimentation, including several examples I will provide in this book, patients and impacted communities "themselves have begun to demand entrance to clinical trials" (Goodman et al. 2003, 16; see also Washington 2006, 386). Until their safe inclusion happens in a meaningful way, biased research will have direct implications not only on *what* medical students and residents learn but *how* they put what they've learned into practice as clinicians.

Transmitting Medical Culture: The Hidden Curriculum

Another way that discriminatory and oppressive norms and value systems are transmitted from one generation to the next within the medical establishment is through the *hidden curriculum*. Unlike formal classroom and bedside clinical teaching that are an integral part of the formal medical curriculum, or the more informal learning that can happen between classes or seeing patients (over lunch or in the elevator, for example), the hidden curriculum is a more latent and insidious process. In "The Hidden Curriculum, Ethics Teaching, and the Structure of Medical Education," professor Frederic W. Hafferty and physician Ronald Franks explain that this "hidden curriculum" is meant precisely to replicate medical culture (rather than conveying scientific knowledge or techniques) by ensuring that medical students "will internalize ... the values, attitudes, beliefs and related behaviors deemed important within medicine" (1994, 864–5). In other words, it "refers to medical education as more than simple transmission of knowledge and skills," but also as "a socialization process" (Mahood 2011, 983). In his iconoclastic book, *Getting Doctored: Critical Reflections on Becoming a Physician* (published in 1978, but still relevant today), Dr Martin Shapiro draws on his experiences going through medical school at McGill University to explain how this "process of socialization into a set role is influenced by a number of forces": the medical curriculum, a sense of competition, rituals, a pathological compulsion to work, being politically or critically disengaged, and an assumed identity as a physician (Shapiro 1978, 27–8). Precisely because it occurs outside of dedicated learning environments, this socialization process is considered "sticky knowledge" and, therefore, often becomes more memorable than the formal curriculum itself: "Every word spoken, every action performed or omitted, every joke, every silence, and every irritation imparts values we might never have intended to impart" (Mahood 2011, 984).

As trainees advance in their training, many of them become acculturated to internalize, embody, and celebrate the norms and value systems of the medical elite. Indeed, "medical education does not take place in a cultural vacuum, within a value-neutral environment or in a place in which medical morality simply replicates lay values" (Hafferty and Franks 1994, 865). Treating certain groups of people as though they have less inherent value as human beings is regrettably often a part of this. All medical educators "have the responsibility to teach unbiased Indigenous health content" (Arkle et al. 2015, 14). Yet, "case reports may convey images that perpetuate gender, racial, ethnic, cultural or disability stereotypes" (Hafferty and Franks 1994, 865). Moreover, pejorative remarks based on stereotypes can "go unchallenged by students who feel intimidated by their preceptors, which facilitates the acceptance or perpetuation of these negative beliefs" (Ly and Crowshoe 2015, 617). Once the structures of such a cultural system are in place, it doesn't take much to ensure that it reproduces itself.

Monuments Cast Shadows: Contrasting the Legacies of William Osler and Marie Equi

Combatting the "institutional reproduction of cultural values associated with sexism, racism, and discrimination against people with disabilities ... must focus not just on individual attitudes and related behaviors but on identifying how the structure and overall milieu of the setting in question" enables and promotes them (Hafferty and Franks 1994, 867). Medical culture provides the scaffolding for the hierarchy, authoritarianism, elitism, and oppressive tendencies of the medical establishment. This cultural system was established well over a century ago, when the medical establishment as we know it was in its early stages, around the beginning of the twentieth century (Starr 1982, 4, 81–92). There is no one individual who is responsible for it, that's not how culture works. It is, nonetheless, important to recognize that influential individuals did play a role back then and that others continue to do so today.

For example, one of the most highly regarded alumni of McGill University's Faculty of Medicine is William Osler (1849–1919). He was born in Bond Head, Ontario. Osler's father was a former British naval officer who had become an Anglican clergyman. By the time Osler was born, the youngest boy of nine children, his family benefited from a "more comfortable life on the developing margin of the British Empire" because of the increasing prosperity of Anglican communities in the area (Lella 2000, xiii, 41). He initially intended on following in his father's footsteps in the ministry, but his exposure in boarding school to the rapidly advancing field of science and medicine changed that (Lella 2000, xiii). Osler spent two years studying medicine in Toronto. He graduated from McGill University in Montreal in 1872 and joined the faculty there after two years of postgraduate training in Europe (Millard 2011, 228; Lella 2000, 57). In 1884, he moved to Philadelphia to become a professor of medicine at the University of Pennsylvania (Lella 2000, xiii). In 1889, he was recruited to Johns Hopkins Hospital in Baltimore, Maryland, where he would become chief of medicine and one of the founding physicians of its medical school (Lella 2000, xiii; Millard 2011, 228). In 1905, he became Regius Professor of Medicine at the prestigious Oxford University, where he would end his prolific career (Millard 2011, 228).

Osler is often referred to as the "Father of Modern Medicine" and contributed to the professionalization of medicine in Canada, the United States, and the United Kingdom (see Lella 2000, xiv–xv). He played a formative role in training thousands of medical students and residents during his life, published hundreds of scholarly articles, and single-authored *The Principles and Practice of Medicine*, which went through sixteen editions and was translated into several languages (Millard 2011, 228). Several physical-exam findings and diseases are eponymic terms (e.g., Osler's nodes, Osler-Weber-Rendu disease/syndrome, etc.). He pioneered the practice of bedside teaching for medical trainees and was key in developing the concept of residency training at Johns Hopkins Medical School (Starr 1982, 116). His influence as a teacher has continued long after his death. For example, when I was in medical school at McGill University, the Faculty of Medicine offered each of us a book with a selection of his works intended for students. I recall being inspired by a quotation famously attributed to him: "The good physician treats the disease; the great physician treats the patient who has the disease" (Murthy and Wright 2019, 665). However, it wasn't until recently that a medical student friend informed me that Osler held racist beliefs.

In the early 1880s, when he was a professor at McGill University, Osler wrote an unpublished paper under the pseudonym Dr Egerton Y. Davis (EYD). Osler's alter ego, EYD, was a "US Army Surgeon" based in "Caughnawauga" (i.e., Kahnawà:ke), just outside of Montreal (Golden 1999, 4, 19). His essay, "Professional Notes among the Indian Tribes about Gt Slave Lake, NWT," explores "tribal marital and obstetrical customs" (19). EYD contrasts the practices of "civilized communities" with those of "squaws" and "primitive tribes" by observing various customs and traditions (20–2). For example, he insists upon "the chief" to be allowed to attend a birth as repayment for having "saved the life of his youngest and favorite squaw" (21). EYD's account objectifies the Indigenous woman giving birth and she is stripped of all agency (21–2). He also describes the "violent coitus during the early weeks of the red-man honey-moon" on one page and then refers to the "stoicism" of an Indigenous "husband" on the next (20–1). Words like "ludicrous," "disgusting," and "vile animal habit" (19, 22) are used to describe practices that EYD ascribes to Indigenous Peoples. Not surprisingly, leading authorities later found "no basis of fact for any of the tribal rites described" (27).

Another report, "Some Peculiar Observations in Obstetrics among the Caughnawaga Indians," ostensibly submitted by EYD to the Medico-Chirurgical Society of Montreal, bears resemblance to "Professional Notes." The story goes that the report was accepted, but when the evening of the presentation arrived, the text was read by Osler (who held the position of secretary) because EYD didn't show up (Golden 1999, 24). It is probable that this report never actually existed as such, but that it was the same piece as "Professional Notes." However, that didn't prevent the apocryphal story of Osler reading EYD's text from being published in reputable and widely read medical journals like the *Lancet* in 1915 and the *Canadian Medical Association Journal* in 1966 (Holmes 1915, 114–15; Bean 1966, 1034). Both of these accounts, however, were "flawed with errors and confusion relating to its subsequent publication history" (Golden 1999, 25).

The publication of "Professional Notes" remained suppressed for years. William Willoughby Francis, the first Osler librarian at McGill University and Osler's godson, considered it to be "the prime duty of me and my successors … to see that the manuscript does NOT get into print." However, the "air of mystery surrounding the suppressed paper allegedly kept 'under lock and key' in the Osler Library, together with rumors of its inappropriate content, provided it with an unwarranted reputation as well as attraction" (Golden, 1999, 26; see also Lella 2000, 12n29). The piece gained legendary status. It was only published for the first time in 1999 as part of the Osler Library's collection, *The Works of Egerton Yorrick Davis, MD: Sir William Osler's Alter Ego*.

It is well-known that Osler was a practical joker, and that using the EYD persona allowed him to "vent his more spontaneous, fanciful and creative side in almost compulsive zaniness" (Lella 2000, 82). However, even if the "Professional Notes" piece was not intended to be a serious anthropological study, the unsolicited content perpetuated harmful and dehumanizing stereotypes of Indigenous Peoples by those within the medical establishment. If it was meant as a hoax, it was nonetheless a racist prank (Lella 2000, 106). As pointed out by Jenna Healey, Hannah Professor of the History of Medicine at Queen's University in Kingston (Ontario), regardless of whether it was a hoax or not, the piece provides a window to the jokes that Osler was comfortable making with friends, but did not want publicly attributed to him. According to Healey, the essay served as an inside joke for an elite network of white male physicians who were not at all bothered by its racist and sexist content. This well-kept secret served as a basis for bonding and camaraderie for those who were in the know, but otherwise created a medical culture that was hostile to women and racialized communities, notably Indigenous Peoples, both within and outside of the medical establishment (Healey 2019; pers. comm., 2019).

Osler's racism was more explicit in other contexts. In an August 1893 letter to a medical colleague about attending the Pan-America Medical Congress, he wrote: "I hate Latin-Americans – but I do not like to desert my friends who are in it"* (Venugopal 1996, 2). When he was in his leadership role at Johns Hopkins, he "was silent on issues of racial segregation on the wards" (Millard 2011, 228). Yet, he was one of the few who had the power to end such a practice. In 1912, Osler was listed as one of the vice-presidents of the first international eugenics congress in London, which was presided over by renowned eugenicist Leonard Darwin and attracted over seven hundred delegates from around the world (McLaren 1990, 23). On 29 May 1914, a *Montreal Gazette* front-page article recounts Osler's speech at a dinner reception held at the Canada Club in London, England, in honour of the recently ap-

---

* It is worth noting that Harvey Cushing, one of Osler's most illustrious biographers, replaced "hate" with "don't care for" and removed the reference to Latin-Americans entirely when this letter was eventually published (Venugopal 1996, 2).

pointed governor general of Canada. Osler spoke about the problems facing Canada: "The question with us is what are we to do when the yellow and brown men begin to swarm over" (CAP 1914). According to him, it would be easy enough to refuse the Japanese (who were underpaid for jobs many white Canadians didn't want at the time, such as farming, fishing, and mining [Sunahara 2011]) and the Chinese (thousands of whom had worked as labourers in exploitative conditions to build the Canadian Pacific Railway [Lavallé 2008]) because Japan and China were foreign countries anyway. His concern was with "the Indians" coming from South Asia because they were "fellow citizens" (CAP 1914). Osler may have been preoccupied with news of the now-infamous *Komagata Maru* incident (Lella 2000, 105n163). On 23 May 1914, a week prior to his comments, a ship carrying 376 British subjects from India arrived at the Vancouver harbour, but the Canadian government refused to let the passengers land because they were "undesirables" (Mann 2009, 194). Two months later, the *Komagata Maru* was forced to return to India, where it was greeted by police. Several passengers were shot and killed, while "175 people were charged with political crimes, 20 were hanged, 76 were banished for life to India's convict colony, and 58 were imprisoned for shorter terms" (Mann 2009, 195). Osler's advice to the governor general and the audience of mostly Canadian businessmen about the perceived threat of Indian immigration was to respond as follows: "We are sorry, we would if we could, but you cannot come in on equal terms with Europeans." He went on: "We are bound to make our country a white man's country" (CAP 1914). The choice of words was not innocuous; they echoed what Mackenzie King, Canadian deputy minister of labour, had written when recommending immigration restrictions in a 1908 report: "Canada should remain a white man's country" (Lella 2000, 105n163). More fundamentally, Osler didn't seem bothered by the inherent injustice of a colonial power dictating who is allowed to come to a land that was stolen from Indigenous Peoples and occupied by generations of settlers, including his own family.

Osler historians recognize that there is "no artificial separation in the Osler-Davis persona; the whole being greater than the sum of the parts" (Golden 1999, 158). His admirers accept that he held prejudicial and/or racist views, but counter that they simply "reflected the Victorian and Edwardian milieu of his time" (Millard 2011, 228; see also Lella 2000, 22–3, 105–6; Venugopal 1996, 1–2; Wallis 1997, 1551). The argument that he was "a man of his age" is invoked to guard against the dilemma posed by "presentism," which is the "anachronistic judgement of historical figures according to present-day values, interests, knowledge and etiquette" (Wallis 1997, 1549, 1551). But "presentism" depends on the vantage point we choose to take. Who determines which "values, interests, knowledge and etiquette" are circumscribed to a given period of history? Were colonizers and slave-owners in North America simply "men of their age?" If that's the case, what about those, including the colonized and enslaved, who fought to end their oppression? Were they not also people "of their age?" Asking these questions reveals how those who wield power shape the present and recast the narratives of the past. Suggesting that influential and powerful figures of the past were simply "individuals of their age" or a "product of their time" is "a way of framing historical racism that can minimize agency and the real complexity and diversity that already exists in any society ... as well as different degrees of willingness to participate in various kinds of violence" (Chapman and Withers 2019, 307). As it turns out, the "presentism" argument is moot in the case of Osler because he had contemporaries who proved that his racist views, and those held by so many others in the medical establishment, were not immutable.

One such contemporary was Dr Marie Equi (1872–1952). Equi was born in New Bedford, Massachusetts, a city considered "one of the most diverse populations in America" at the time (Helquist 2015, 16). She was the fifth child in a family of eleven children, but several of her siblings died before she was ten years old (17–18). Her Irish mother and Italian father were both first-generation working-class immigrants who raised her to "abhor absolutism, monarchy and oppression" (Krieger 1983, 56). Equi did not have an easy childhood. One account reports that she began working in the textile mills, while still attending school, when she was only eight years old (56). It was not uncommon for some children to work for part of the day and then attend school for the remainder (Helquist 2015, 21). Despite being devoted to her studies in high school, Equi had to drop out after her first year to help support her family by working in the textile mills where, along with hundreds of teenage girls and women, she became part of an exploited labour force that worked in the city's factories under hazardous conditions (20–1). Equi's early teenage tuberculosis – along with her desire to help others, have professional autonomy, and follow in the footsteps of other women physicians – may have pushed her to enter medical school (Krieger 1983, 56).

Equi moved with her classmate companion, Bessie Holcomb, to San Francisco in 1897 (Helquist 2015, 39, 47–8). Her trajectory was exceptional: her "determination and audacity transcended the limits of her working-class roots and carried her to the steps of a medical college" (Helquist 2015, 43). In 1899, Equi entered medical school in San Francisco, but then transferred to the University of Oregon in 1901 (Helquist 2015, 44, 49; Krieger 1983, 56–7). She was part of demographic groups that were under-represented in medicine at the time: 6 per cent of all physicians in the US were female and only 17 per cent of all women physicians were US-born children of at least one immigrant parent (Helquist 2015, 41, 52; Michael Helquist, pers. comm., 2020). The hostility from male medical students and faculty took a toll on Equi, but she persevered; when she graduated in 1903, she became "one of the first sixty women physicians in Oregon" (52; see also 13, 47–50). About half of all physicians undertook advanced training; however, going to Europe (like Osler had) or even the East Coast of the US was not possible for Equi, at least partly due to prohibitive costs. She was, nonetheless, able to secure a six-month internship in California along with her new companion, Mary Ellen Parker. Equi worked under the supervision of respected San Francisco-based surgeon and national leader in homeopathic medicine, Dr Florence Nightingale Ward (52; see also 49–50). She returned periodically to San Francisco to advance her skills over the years, assisting reputable surgeons in bladder, kidney, and gynecological procedures (53).

In November 1903, Equi returned to Oregon and registered with the Umatilla County authorities, joining the practices of eleven – all male – physicians in Pendleton, Oregon. The Cayuse, Umatilla, and Walla Walla Nations were at the nearby Umatilla Indian Reservation, where the "population had been decimated by diseases of the white men." Equi wasn't one of the contract physicians serving the reservation, but historians suggest that she may have occasionally provided health care services to Indigenous Peoples living in the area. A journalist wrote of Equi's "unstinted courage and dedication on the range," riding "on horseback in the countryside providing medical care to Indians and cowboys." Such accounts of "Equi's doctoring in the remote stretches of Umatilla County burnished her reputation" (Helquist 2015, 54).

By 1905, she had established a general medicine practice in Portland "with an emphasis on obstetrics and gynecology as well as maternal and childhood health." Her time in San Francisco "had helped her develop a reputation as a skilled diagnostician," while "her background in New Bedford gave her a natural rapport with Portland's working-class and immigrant populations" (Helquist 2015, 56). Not forgetting her roots, Equi became "a physician for working-class women and children" (Krieger 1983, 56–7). Indeed, her "ease with working-class patients and among laborers who worked the farms, factories, and forests made her distinctive among other doctors in the Pacific Northwest," while her "willingness to help women with birth control and abortion when both were illegal set her further apart from many of her colleagues" (Helquist 2015, 13). Her ability to collaborate with people on a variety of issues was impressive, including emergency medical relief when she integrated into US Army operations as part of a delegation of physicians and nurses from Portland to assist the victims of the devastating 1906 earthquake in San Francisco (Helquist 2015, 67–9; Krieger 1983, 57). She was recognized for these efforts by President Theodore Roosevelt and was the first woman to be honoured with the rank of "doctor" in the US Army (Krieger 1983, 57; Helquist 2015, 15).

Equi had already become quite active in the women's suffrage movement, but, in 1913, a patient prompted her to get involved with the women's strike at the Oregon Packing Company fruit cannery (Krieger 1983, 57–8). The main issue was low wages, but also punishing working hours (sometimes exceeding fifteen hours per day) and unsanitary conditions, and the strikers were "primarily immigrants, the kind of people for whom Equi was both physician and advocate" (Krieger 1983, 58–9). Equi's radicalization was triggered by witnessing the violent arrest of a speaker, Agnes O'Connor, a thirty-year-old pregnant Indigenous woman (Helquist 2015, 118). Equi was enraged and "rallied the crowd to follow the police to the station – with O'Connor under arrest – and demand the release of all the strikers." She even "punched two officers in the face during a struggle at the jail" and castigated the sheriff and his deputies. Although other detainees were not released that day, O'Connor was (118).

Equi lived openly as a lesbian, and, after becoming radicalized as a result of police brutality and state repression, she "embraced anarchism as the means to obtain economic and social justice" (Helquist 2015, 12). She was a suffragist who also "campaigned against US imperialism in Latin America and the Caribbean" (Krieger 1983, 61) and continued to support antiracist campaigns well into her sixties (Helquist 2015, 229). None of these causes were popular in Equi's time, but she couldn't bear injustice. She stood by her convictions, even if it meant being surveilled and imprisoned: US Department of Justice agents filed over eight hundred pages of reports on her day-to-day movements leading up to her arrest, trial, and indictment in 1918, for "saying that workers should not participate in a war where they would be killing fellow workers at the bidding of their masters" during an antiwar speech (Krieger 1983, 66; Helquist 2015, 14). Her political development, successes, and failures should be "sources of both inspiration and critical lessons for all who, like Equi, would act to rid the world of exploitation and oppression" (Krieger 1983, 56).

Equi and Osler overlapped in the medical world over a span of almost two decades, including several years when both were in the United States. Yet, the contrast in their respective legacies is striking. Equi had a reputation as an excellent diagnostician who embodied a holistic and radical approach to health care that sought to address root causes of illness; she generated significant media coverage locally, regionally, and nationally during her life, with over three hundred articles over forty years since her arrival in Oregon in 1892 (Helquist 2015, 14). Nonmedical institutions in Oregon, like the National Park Service and the Secretary of State, have only very recently recognized her contributions (Helquist 2019) and an integrative clinic "to enrich the health of the Trans, Queer, Gender Diverse and Intersex communities through trauma-informed care, culturally affirming medical services and social justice advocacy" in Portland was named after her in 2019 (Equi Institute n.d.). Yet, she's been relegated to anonymity within – and by – the medical establishment. She's been forgotten "mainly because she was the sort of person traditional historians would rather ignore: a powerful woman, a lesbian, and a revolutionary and militant fighter for the working class" (Krieger 1983, 56).

On the other hand, Osler's legacy has been extensively cultivated. In Montreal alone, a street, an amphitheatre at the Montreal General Hospital, and the McGill Faculty of Medicine's library bear his name. He is considered by many as a "patron saint of medicine, of 'humanistic' physicians, and of the history of medicine" (Lella 2000, xv). Others note that his "learning and urbanity made him the profession's favorite doctor" (Starr 1982, 116). There are Osler societies in North America, Europe, and as far as Japan (Lella 2000, xv). An open-access medical education website to promote clinical excellence was named CLOSLER as a tribute "to guide us all 'closer to Osler'" (Murthy and Wright 2019, 667). The year 2020 marks the 50th annual meeting of the American Osler Society. Biographers have cited Horace's poetry to convey the significance of Osler's legacy to medicine: "I have erected a monument more lasting than bronze" (Golden 1999, 158). Indeed, Osler has attained mythological status within medical culture. However, there are many drawbacks to creating mythologies around individuals. Monuments cast shadows. Perhaps the most damaging consequence of erecting monuments for individuals, including for men like Osler, is that they invisibilize the work of others who, as part of larger collectives and movements, could serve as inspiring examples for future generations of health care providers committed to social justice. It is difficult to imagine that Osler's colleagues and the future generations of physicians he trained would be immune to the racist views he endorsed and promoted, even if he didn't say anything directly to them in the classroom or at the bedside. This is how the hidden curriculum works.

Of course, Osler is just one of many influential physicians who contributed to developing the framework that shapes the cultural norms and value systems of a physician elite made up of a white old boys' club within the medical establishment. In various ways, this scaffolding has been buttressed over the years by those in positions of power and influence. Once in place, this medical culture allows the system to reproduce itself unless there are active attempts at interrupting or disrupting the status quo. Remaining neutral allows it to continue. When a few outliers try to interrupt or disrupt the system, even in very modest ways, it often comes at great personal and professional cost.

The Case of Medical Admissions Reform: When Privilege Strikes Back

In 2013, Dr Saleem Razack, a pediatric intensive care physician and assistant dean in the Office of Admissions, Equity, and Diversity at McGill's Faculty of Medicine at the time, came under fire from members of the Montreal anglophone community for instituting reforms to conform to national accreditation standards (Seidman 2014; Reiter and Aalamian 2013, 3). Among several of the measures that were implemented, applicants were no longer required to complete the Medical College Admission Test (MCAT) as of 2010 because it discriminated against francophones and others for whom English may not be the first language. The MCAT also added very little beyond information obtained from GPAS (Reiter and Aalamian 2013, 3), and the cost was prohibitive for those who couldn't afford to pay hundreds of dollars for preparatory courses and exam fees (*Montreal Gazette* 2014). Razack's team also implemented pipeline initiatives to reach out to francophone students, particularly from rural areas (including Indigenous communities), and lower socioeconomic groups, to increase the pool of applicants. The intent was to recognize that a "diverse population needs a diverse medical profession to serve its needs" (Seidman 2013). In his view, "when the percentage of students from high-income families is about eight times more than the general population, you have to look at whether there are qualified applicants not making it through the process" (Seidman 2013).

Much of the backlash he faced seemed to stem from frustrations that francophone students and those from lower socioeconomic backgrounds would be taking spots that some McGill alumni felt their children were entitled to. One McGill alumnus and assistant professor in the Faculty of Medicine, whose daughter was rejected twice, stated that the new policies "stink." In her *Montreal Gazette* opinion piece, she affirmed: "Smart kids come from smart parents, and smart parents make more money" (Finestone 2013). An external review of the admissions process commissioned in the months that followed noted that some critics of the reforms were concerned "that selection based upon meritocracy would be sacrificed in the name of 'social justice'" (Reiter and Aalamian 2013, 5). Yet, not only did the changes implemented during Razack's tenure help to make incoming classes less elite and more representative of the population at large, but incoming medical students' median GPAS rose – from 3.80 to 3.84 – since the MCAT requirement was lifted (Montreal Gazette 2014). The report concluded that the faculty and administrative staff had "provided a vision and pathway which is eminently reasonable and defensible" (Reiter and Aalamian 2013, 13). However, as one journalist noted, the university's "financial vulnerability" was mentioned repeatedly in the report, hinting at the possibility that "frustration and unhappiness the new direction … sparked among some of McGill's traditional stakeholders … may have translated into a decline in donations" (Seidman 2014). An anonymous observer, from another faculty at McGill, aptly termed this saga "When Privilege Strikes Back." Indeed, institutional discomfort with the concept of equity in admissions persists to this day (Razack et al. 2019, 5).

Undoubtedly, medical school is demanding on multiple levels – physically, emotionally, mentally, intellectually, and spiritually. However, this does not mean that only the most talented and hard-working individuals get in. Rather, medical school, even more than university programs in general, selects those who have, for the most part, benefited from various forms of privilege, often from birth. Perhaps the admission process reforms struck such a sensitive cord precisely because they challenged a core, staunchly defended mythology of western liberal democracies: meritocracy.

Myth of Meritocracy

The cultural myth of meritocracy suggests that "medicine is a profession for 'the best and the brightest'" (Razack et al. 2019, 2). The premise is that the privileges people benefit from – political power, social status, income, and wealth – accrue based on individual merit. It presupposes an egalitarian society where everyone starts on a level playing field, and in which one's lot in life is then determined primarily by talent and work ethic. Those who enjoy relative affluence do so because they make the most of their opportunities, while those who are forced to live in misery have only themselves to blame for their failures. Various permutations of the "American Dream" are predicated on this notion that individuals can achieve success based only on their merit. The myth of meritocracy "provides cover to institutional white male bias" (Perez 2019, 93). In capitalist societies, it allows the rich to justify their affluence by positing that they "earned it"; the system is maintained, in part, because people who are relatively poorer are immersed in this common hegemonic culture, holding on to the hope that one day, they too will "make it" if they work hard enough (see McNamee 2018, 204).

The vast SDH literature exposes the folly of such a pervasive school of thought. We have no control over the economic, social, and political conditions into which we are born (i.e., accident of birth), nor over how the hand that we are dealt can have a powerful impact in dictating the circumstances and opportunities present throughout our lives. This is limited not only to mortality indicators but to the full spectrum of health and social wellness (see Wilkinson and Pickett 2010, 18–26). Without diminishing the role of individual agency or the power to change social and economic conditions as part of collective struggles, the SDH recognize that structural realities play more of a role in determining our lot in life than do our talents and work ethic. These structural determinants can limit the prospects for upward social mobility throughout the entire lifespan of individuals.

For example, as Richard Wilkinson and Kate Pickett explain in *The Spirit Level: Why Equality Is Better for Everyone*, income inequality – itself a product of multiple structural factors – is inversely proportional to upward social mobility because, while "those at the top can maintain their wealth and status, those at the bottom find it difficult to climb up the income ladder" (Wilkinson and Pickett 2010, 160–1). Since the 1980s, the rich have gotten markedly richer, while the poor have remained poor (and have therefore gotten relatively poorer). This gap has widened between the richest and poorest countries (CSDH 2008, 37), but also within the population of Quebec (Bernier and Posca 2020, 3), Canada (Dirks 2018), the United States (McNamee 2018, 62, 204; Moriarty 2012, 18) and many countries around the world (Wilkinson and Pickett 2010, 244–5). These growing disparities have alarmed international agencies like the Organisation for Economic Co-operation and Development and the WHO (Bernier and Posca 2020, 2). Even financial institutions like the World Bank and the International Monetary Fund, whose policies exacerbated such disparities in the first place (see Gershman and Irwin 2000, 32–3; Schoepf et al. 2000, 99), have expressed concern not only because of compromised economic expansion, but also because of the social consequences (Bernier and Posca 2020, 2). Larger income discrepancies and greater inequalities ensure that "equal opportunity is a significantly more distant prospect" (Wilkinson and Pickett 2010, 169).

Of course, some people do benefit from upward social mobility. But, even then, obstacles, barriers, and glass ceilings exist along the way. For example, women now make up the majority of Canadian medical students (Young et al. 2012, 1503), yet "they remain under-represented at higher levels of professorial rank, in leadership positions and in surgical specialties" (Razack et al. 2019, 3). In McGill University's Department of Pediatrics, one of the largest in Canada, "women represent 60% of the faculty, yet remain underrepresented in high-level roles" (Plotnick et al. 2018, 49). So, even though women have been able to gain admission to medical schools and faculties in greater numbers than fifty years ago, systemic factors still discriminate against them.

Studies challenge the notion of medical meritocracy by showing that "if merit in medicine was essentially obtainable to all who accept that they have to work hard and well, women would outrank men" (Razack et al. 2019, 3).

Nonetheless, a few people may be able to genuinely claim a "rags to riches" story in business, sports, medicine, and the arts, among other fields. However, they are are exceptions to the rule of limited upward social mobility (Moriarty et al. 2012, 7). These stories also often ignore the role of other non-merit factors beyond our control, like circumstances, opportunities, and luck (McNamee 2018, 24–5,149). Meanwhile, annual lists like the Forbes 400 of the wealthiest Americans downplay structural factors "that enable wealth, such as tax policies, other government policies that favor the wealthy, and the importance of being born to the right family, gender and race" (Moriarty et al. 2012, 6). Indeed, in a 2012 report produced by United for a Fair Economy, almost two thirds of those on the Forbes 400 list came from an upper-class background, 90 per cent were men, and 96 per cent were white, while well over half of their combined income came from capital gains (Moriarty et al. 2012, 9, 13–15). The authors argue that the Forbes list is "carefully constructed to reinforce the 'rags to riches' narrative" that glamorizes "the myth of the 'self-made man'" (Moriarty et al. 2012, 6). Such stories, whether embellished or not, are held up as examples precisely because they serve the useful purpose of further anchoring the mythology in our collective consciousness. Yet, such examples are, by design, impossible to replicate on a mass level. The myth of meritocracy is necessary to maintain the façade that individuals have earned their societal privileges – whether it's wealth, income, social status, or political power – based solely on merit. It doesn't question whether having such privileges *at all* is even justified.

In their seminal work, *The Meritocracy Myth*, which was originally published in 2004, sociology professors Robert K. Miller Jr and Stephen McNamee explain how "discrimination is not just a nonmerit factor; it is the antithesis of merit" (McNamee 2018, 203). Yet, from a population (versus individual) point of view, not only can disadvantageous conditions into which we are born and grow up restrict our capacity to realize our full potential, but the reverse is also true. The most obvious example is that of inheritance (i.e., the initial starting point in life based on parental position), which "includes a set of cumulative nonmerit advantages for all except the poorest of the poor" (McNamee 2018, 62). Certainly, for the wealthy these "birthright privileges" include the transfer of estates from one generation to the next, but also the conversion of wealth "into social and cultural capital, providing distinct nonmerit advantages ... to the children of the rich and powerful" (McNamee 2018, 85; see also Moriarty et al. 2012, 6). With respect to individual achievement and what is commonly perceived as success, "the effects of inheritance come first, *followed by* the effects of individual merit – not the other way around" (McNamee 2018, 43; emphasis in original). This is why inherited wealth in particular is "a poor indicator of genuine merit" (Wilkinson and Pickett 2010, 237). Ultimately, when it comes to inheritance versus meritocracy, it's a zero-sum game: "the more there is of one, the less there is of the other" (McNamee 2018, 222).

The irony about the very term meritocracy is that Michael Young, the late British politician and sociologist who is credited with having popularized its usage decades ago, actually intended it as a warning to society, not as a prescription to be followed. In his 1958 satirical novel, *The Rise of the Meritocracy*, Young wrote about a future dystopian society, which bears some resemblance to our own, where the education system determines those who will possess political power (and, therefore, wealth) by a simple formula: "I + E = Mt," or "intelligence and effort together make up merit" (Young 1994, 84). The goal of society was to establish "not an aristocracy of birth, not a plutocracy of wealth, but a true meritocracy of talent" (11). However, the narrator points out how society "had to recognize that nearly all parents are going to try to gain unfair advantages for their offspring" (20). For example, wealthier parents with less talented or less motivated children "bought places at private schools which would never have been awarded on merit" (88). As the meritocracy becomes more entrenched, inequalities become more structural. Over time, inheritance and merit become intertwined (166). Nepotism becomes effectively normalized. There's a push to guarantee a privileged education for the children of the elite who, "in their eyes, [are] not just children but rulers born to a high destiny" (167, 171). The mechanisms that are meant to allow some upward social mobility become limited before being questioned altogether: "some intelligent parents were stimulated to go further and ask whether equality of opportunity is not a wholly outdated idea" (171).

In "Down with Meritocracy," an opinion piece published in 2001 (the year preceding his death), Young explained that the central argument of his book was inspired by a historical analysis of what had been happening in British society since the 1870s, "when schooling was made compulsory and competitive entry to the civil service became the rule." In the piece, he drew parallels between his novel and contemporary society, oftentimes blurring the lines between the two, by explaining how the "business meritocracy is in vogue" and how the "new class has the means at hand, and largely under its control, by which it reproduces itself." The result, then, is worsening inequality over time. Young was "sadly disappointed" by his book because the word he coined went into such wide general circulation without the ironic meaning he intended, and he implored political leaders to stop using the term in a favourable light (Young 2001).

The belief that we live in a meritocracy runs counter to what the vast SDH literature tells us. The ideology of meritocracy at best glosses over and at worst categorically ignores the very existence of pre-existing societal inequalities. The SDH not only recognize the existence and impacts of inequalities on people's lives but also identify that the only viable remedy is to target their causes. While broader social, political, and economic ideologies, forces, and systems frame people's daily conditions of life and produce misery and suffering for large segments of the world's population, the ideology of meritocracy is especially pernicious because it allows for societal injustices to remain stubbornly entrenched through cultural mechanisms. More fundamentally, meritocracy in capitalist societies holds, at its core, that "success" has to do with the accumulation of wealth and power. But, as goes the saying popularized by comedian Lily Tomlin in the 1970s, "The trouble with the rat race is that even if you win you're still a rat" (*People* 1977).

The capitalist economic system values profits more than people, smothers sentiments of solidarity, promotes competition, and celebrates crass individualism, all of which allow the ruling class to benefit from tried-and-tested divide-and-rule tactics. In Young's novel, a resistance movement led by feminists seeks to reframe the concept of "equality of opportunity." In their manifesto, they write that equality of opportunity "should not mean equal opportunity to rise up in the social scale, but equal opportunity for all people, irrespective of their 'intelligence,' to develop the virtues and talents with which they are endowed, all their capacities for appreciating the beauty and depth of human experience, all their potential for living to the full" (Young 1994, 160). Indeed, what would our lives be like if being empathetic,

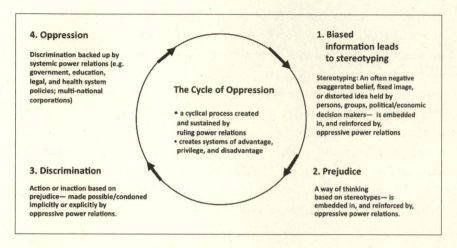

Figure 5.1 Ruling power relations and the cycle of oppression
Used with permission from Fernwood Publishing (McGibbon 2012, 27).

emphasizing cooperation, mutual aid, and solidarity, respecting human dignity, and living in harmony with the environment became core values?

Instead, meritocracy imposes a cultural societal norm that is rarely questioned, enabling a cascade of cognitive framings that promote harm and injustice. This cultural hegemony, which is especially entrenched in the medical establishment, allows those in positions of power and privilege to hold biased and stereotyped perspectives about others who are disadvantaged primarily by the accident of birth (based on their gender, the colour of their skin, etc.). Stereotypes are "social distortions" that "can form a mental framework among members of the dominant racialized group ... about how to 'deal with' the racialized other" (Reading 2013, 3). Canada's chief public health officer's report, *Addressing Stigma: Towards a More Inclusive Health System*, states that "stigma begins with the labeling of differences and negative stereotyping of people, creating a separation between 'us' and 'them,'" which results in those who are stigmatized being "devalued and subjected to discrimination" (Tam 2019, 22). "The Cycle of Oppression" framework in Figure 5.1 shows this interplay between biases, stereotypes, and prejudices – all embedded in power relations in an unjust society – that can ultimately result in discrimination and oppression at the systemic level (McGibbon 2012, 27–31; see also Salée 2005, 64).

It should come as no surprise that the Commission on Social Determinants of Health (CSDH) report discussed in Chapter 3 considers "biases, norms, and values within society" as one of several structural drivers of the circumstances of daily life (CSDH 2008, 42). The medical establishment's biases, norms, and values have been dictated for decades by an elite, white old boys' club that has historically excluded "the other" from its ranks. While that may have been changing in some ways in the last few years, the hidden curriculum has promoted the dehumanization of "the other" for decades based on relationships rooted in domination, which is not easily undone. This dehumanization is necessary before committing atrocities, including against Indigenous children through medical colonialism.

PART THREE

Medical Colonialism and Indigenous Children

Chapter 6

A Little Matter of Genocide: Canada and the United Nations Convention

All my life, I've had to listen to rhetoric about the United States being a model of freedom and democracy, the most uniquely enlightened and humanitarian country in history … It's a lie. The whole thing's a lie, and it always has been. Leaving aside the obvious points which could be raised to disprove it by Blacks and Chicanos and Asian immigrants right here in North America … there's *a little matter of genocide* that's got to be taken into account right here at home.
– Russell Means, American Indian Movement, in Ward Churchill, *A Little Matter of Genocide: Holocaust and Denial in the Americas, 1492 to the Present*

Canada's a liar. It's hypocritical and two-faced. Look in Canada's back yard, its crimes, inequities and injustices are there to see. Of course, all this is hidden. That is one of the main occupations of Canada's capitalist governments to keep the grisly offenses, and ugly injustices hidden from view especially from the international scene.
– Howard Adams, *Tortured People: The Politics of Colonization*

As I've explained previously, despite the massive media coverage that followed the launch of the #aHand2Hold campaign on 24 January 2018, the public messaging that initially came through focused more on equity rather than explicitly addressing systemic racism or colonialism. Meanwhile, the government's dismissive response did not succeed in shutting down debate on this issue. Instead, critics of the practice became emboldened.

The Canadian Pediatric Society (CPS) and its First Nations, Inuit, and Métis Health Committee not only called out the racism that is "built into our health care system" in their letter to government officials, but they also wrote about the "need to work together to dismantle these colonial systems"

(Radha Jetty, Catherine Farrell, and Pascale Hamel, letter to the Ministers of Health and Transport, 5 February 2018). Importantly, they provided context by recognizing the intergenerational trauma resulting from the forced removal of Indigenous children that occurred through residential schools for over a century, and from the mass evacuations of Inuit in present-day Nunavik from the late 1940s to the 1960s due to the tuberculosis epidemic.

In an interview later that spring, Dr Johanne Morel suggested that the colonialism of the non-accompaniment practice had parallels with the residential school era: "We go get the child and we tell the parents that we don't need them. 'We are the ones who are going to tell you what your child needs'" (Gervais 2018a). Morel is well-placed to make such an analogy: as a pediatrician, she has spent decades working with Indigenous communities in northern Quebec and had just recently taken over the directorship of the Northern and Native Child Health Program at the MCH. Her efforts to put an end to the non-accompaniment rule back in the early 1990s were ignored by ÉVAQ and the Ministry of Health at the time.

A few weeks following Morel's interview, Médecins québécois pour le régime public (MQRP), where my term as a board member was coming to an end, took on a prominent role in supporting the #aHand2Hold campaign. Since children continued to be transferred alone despite Health Minister Barrette's months-old promise that things would change within weeks, MQRP sent a letter directly to then premier of Quebec, Philippe Couillard. MQRP, whose primary mandate is safeguarding and strengthening the public health care system in Quebec, had not openly taken positions in opposition to colonial medical practices and policies in the past. This made its stance even more remarkable. It reminded the premier that "for decades, young Indigenous children were torn away from their families, often by plane, and placed in residential schools or foster homes," and that "given this colonial reality, it is all the more unacceptable to separate parents and children." The letter went on to state that for health care providers working in these communities, "transferring these children without caregivers is simply unjustifiable. In 2018, Québec can and must do better" (MQRP 2018).

All these interventions progressively created space for the campaign to become more explicit about some of the root causes – systemic racism and medical colonialism – that allowed the non-accompaniment rule to persist for so long. The social justice approach adopted by the #aHand2Hold cam-

paign and its supporters sought to place ÉVAQ's non-accompaniment practice – and its consequences – in the larger social, political, and historical
context. The residential school system, child welfare system, and tuberculosis
mass evacuations were all examples that had had significant impacts on Indigenous communities throughout Canada, including – and in certain cases,
especially – northern Quebec. In both of my testimonies on behalf of the
#aHand2Hold campaign at the Viens Commission, I mentioned these ex-
amples, but also referred to other "colonial and genocidal policies" that have
resulted in intergenerational and multigenerational trauma: forced displacement and relocation of entire communities, including into settlements (see
QIA 2014, 17, 22–6; RCAP 1996a, 395–7, 409–10); the *qimmit* (sled-dog) kill-
ings in Inuit communities (see QIA 2014, 39); missing and murdered Indigenous women and girls (see MMIWG 2019c). More broadly, I highlighted the
chronic underfunding of health care, education, housing, and social programs impacting Indigenous communities throughout the province, much
like in the rest of the country (Shaheen-Hussain 2018a and 2018c; see also
Blackstock 2011).

I made the argument that ÉVAQ's ongoing non-accompaniment practice
was rooted in colonialism and that by choosing not to remedy it despite calls
to do so for years, ÉVAQ and the government were perpetuating and institutionalizing a form of discrimination against Eeyou and Inuit children
transferred to the MCH. As the National Collaborating Centre for Aboriginal
Health (NCCAH) explains, "structural racism is perpetrated when policy
makers and power brokers [re]produce or *fail to redress* structural inequities
between racialized groups. In this way, the ideological concept of race is given
material power in the social order, as it becomes linked to political and economic structures and systems" (Reading 2013, 4; emphasis added, brackets
in original). We'll likely never know whether ÉVAQ's original intention was
to discriminate against children from Eeyou Istchee and Nunavik; since there
was never an actual written policy in the first place, it becomes difficult to
find official documents we can trace back to decide one way or the other.
However, whether it was ÉVAQ's intention to discriminate or not, my point
was that a failure to redress the practice years ago resulted in institutionalized
discrimination becoming the de facto reality on the ground.

Putting an end to the non-accompaniment practice was a political issue.
The #aHand2Hold campaign maintained its pressure for months, insisting

at public events and in media interviews that this was a problem rooted in colonialism for which the government was ultimately responsible and, therefore, had the power to resolve. However, what was the reality on the ground? Weren't health care providers the ones who were ensuring that the non-accompaniment rule was strictly applied and enforced? Weren't we the ones who had normalized these children arriving alone at our hospital's EDs? Something Catherine Hudon, whose son Mattéo suffered brain death while unaccompanied on a Challenger medevac in 2008, said during a *Radio-Canada* interview stuck with me: "We are punishing parents and children. We are causing trauma" (Radio-Canada 2018). How can health care personnel *cause* trauma, when we are supposed to alleviate it? How do we deal with the cognitive dissonance that this creates? Is there an aspect of the dominant medical culture that allows this to happen? Systemic racism, as discussed in previous chapters, certainly plays a significant role. When it comes to Indigenous Peoples, however, there's another component as well: medical colonialism.

In May 2018, I was invited to submit an opinion piece about the #aHand2Hold campaign to the *Guardian*, which has a global readership. I contextualized the non-accompaniment practice by highlighting "the medical establishment's role in the displacement and genocide of indigenous peoples over the last century." Interestingly, the title assigned by the *Guardian*'s editors helped bring the issue into better focus for me: "Separating Sick Inuit Kids and Parents Is Medical Colonialism All Over Again" (Shaheen-Hussain 2018b). During my second testimony at the Viens Commission in October 2018, I proposed the term *medical colonialism* as a framework to describe the violent role played by the health care system in settler societies to support a system of colonial domination over Indigenous Peoples (Shaheen-Hussain 2018c).

Medical Colonialism: Beyond Complicity

The colonial apparatus is very effective at making it seem as though settler-society violence and suffering inflicted on Indigenous communities by and through the health care system are discrete aberrations in Canada's national narrative rather than a core theme. However, history doesn't bear this out. In "Disease, Medicine and Empire," historian David Arnold wrote how "medicine became a demonstration of the superior political, technical and military power of the West, and hence a celebration of imperialism itself" toward the end of the nineteenth century. Importantly, medicine "registered the imperial determination to reorder the environment and to refashion indigenous societies and economies in light of its own precepts and priorities" (Arnold 1988, 17). Similarly, Canadian medical anthropologist John O'Neil wrote that "so-called biomedicine developed historically during a period of colonial expansion of European power into all parts of the world, and the system of medicine that we now rely on not only assisted that expansion, but was assisted in its development and domination by the colonial process of subjugation and resource exploitation" (O'Neil 1993, 39).

Clearly, the medical establishment has been an integral part of the colonial project since its inception. However, it has not simply been a passive tool that has aided in colonial conquest. On the contrary, more than being only complicit in such violence, it has played a significant and active role in shaping nation-states and colonial agendas. As the editors of *Useful Bodies: Humans in the Service of Medical Science in the Twentieth Century* point out, the conflation of "disease and race was invented by medical science," which "thus provided the modern state with a new language that scripted its relationship to society" in the first half of the twentieth century (Goodman et al. 2003, 5). They also explain that physicians' race-based thinking and nationalist interests made it impossible for them to empathize with those "they perceived as uncivilized, undisciplined, unhealthy, dysfunctional, irrational, unproductive, primitive, degenerate, and impulsive," identifying instead "with the state they served and were shaping" (11). As author and poet Gary Geddes explains in *Medicine Unbundled: A Journey through the Minefields of Indigenous Health Care*, Canadian physicians played a role in the expropriation of Indigenous land through early iterations of the Indian Act by apprehending Indigenous Peoples for quarantine or incarceration: "Declaring individuals contagious was a good means of control, keeping them out of trouble or out of circulation while the task of clearing the land was underway" (Geddes 2017, 13). In *Colonizing Bodies: Aboriginal Health and Healing in British Columbia, 1900–50*, historian Mary-Ellen Kelm explains that "medicine, its perspectives, and its practitioners, have been instrumental in shaping colonial relations, both within the dominant society through formulations of colonial power, and between the colonizers and their subjects" (Kelm 1998, 100).

Searches for "medical colonialism" in social science and medical literature yield varied results. Drawing on work in the field, however, Kelm has suggested that medical colonialism refers to how "colonial governments appropriated medical power by encouraging the production of knowledge about indigenous bodies that justified racial hierarchies" and that the "same medicine reified those hierarchies by providing segregated and inequitable services on the basis of race" (Kelm 2004, 335; Brown et al. 2011, 104n2; Brown et al. 2012, 48). This useful formulation explains how health care providers can be complicit in the injustices committed against Indigenous Peoples without consciously intending to hurt anyone. However, reflecting similar trends in other parts of the world, the medical establishment in Canada has not simply followed the lead of colonial governments but has proactively carried out their agenda. For the purposes of this book, medical colonialism refers to a culture or ideology, rooted in systemic anti-Indigenous racism, that uses medical practices and policies to establish, maintain, and/or advance a *genocidal* colonial project.

Waging Genocide: Targeting Indigenous Children

As the NCCAH observed in 2014, "some critics find the term genocide too controversial; however, it is not being used here to provoke but rather to center racialized colonialism within a framework that shows the extent of damage it has had on Indigenous populations" (Loppie et al. 2014, 6–8). To this end, it is worth going back to the term's origins. A recent commentary, "Canada's treatment of Indigenous peoples fits the definition of 'genocide,'" written by Canadian criminal-defence lawyer Michael Spratt provides some insights. The opinion piece is a response to the backlash faced by the commissioners of the National Inquiry into Missing and Murdered Indigenous Women and Girls (MMIWG) for their conclusion, made public in June 2019, that the genocide of Indigenous Peoples has occurred in Canada (MMIWG 2019d). Spratt explains how the term *genocide* was coined in the 1940s by a lawyer, Raphaël Lemkin, who defined it as the destruction of a nation through the "disintegration of the political and social institutions, of culture, language, national feelings, religion and the economic existence of national groups, and the destruction of the personal security, liberty, health, dignity and even the lives of the individuals belonging to such groups" (Spratt 2019).

This definition first appeared in Lemkin's seminal 1944 publication, *Axis Rule in Occupied Europe*, even though he had been developing the concept of genocide, including how it applied to different groups of people, for well over a decade (Stote 2015, 129; see also Churchill 1998, 67–75). In fact, Lemkin "was aware of the effects of colonialism on Indigenous peoples of North America", and considered colonial "acts perpetrated by the English and the French in the Americas as equal instances of genocide" (Stote 2015, 130, 154). At least in part due to Lemkin's efforts, the United Nations started developing a formal definition of genocide to be recognized at the international level. Three experts, including Lemkin, were commissioned to work on developing an initial framework, entitled "Draft Convention on the Crime of Genocide" (Starblanket 2018, 46). In this draft, genocide was declared "a crime directed against racial, national, linguistic, religious, or political groups" and it "detailed at considerable length what were referred to as the biological, physical and cultural dimensions of genocide" (Stote 2015, 131; Starblanket 2018, 46–7). Cultural genocide included the forced transfer of children to another group, prohibiting the use of the national language, and the systematic destruction of historical or religious monuments (Starblanket 2018, 46–7; Stote 2015, 131). Lemkin strongly favoured the inclusion of the cultural dimensions in the definition of genocide because his "view was that the diversity of cultures was as important as the physical integrity of a nation" (Starblanket 2018, 47). Moreover, it was recognized that "cultural genocide often preceded physical or biological genocide" (Stote 2015, 132). However, nation-states like Canada, the United Kingdom, and the United States successfully opposed its inclusion (133). They were concerned that "including cultural genocide within a convention prohibiting genocide would outlaw implicitly and explicitly stated assimilatory practices and policies imposed on Indigenous and minority populations" (133).

The United Nations General Assembly adopted the Convention on the Prevention and Punishment of the Crime of Genocide (Genocide Convention) in 1948; it came into effect in 1951. Article 2 defines genocide as "any of the following acts committed with intent to destroy, in whole or in part, a national, ethnical, racial or religious group," including: killing members of the group; deliberately inflicting on the group conditions of life calculated to bring about its physical destruction in whole or in part; causing serious bodily or mental harm to members of the group; imposing measures intended to prevent births within the group; and forcibly transferring children of the group to another group (UN 1951). The Genocide Convention's definition includes *any* of the five acts listed in Article 2. As I will demonstrate in the chapters that follow to develop the concept of medical colonialism, the violence inflicted by the medical establishment on Indigenous children in Canada applies to *all* five acts.

The decision to focus on children is not meant to minimize or ignore the suffering inflicted on adults and Elders by the medical establishment's colonial ventures into Indigenous communities. Using the Genocide Conventions' five acts as a framework is also not intended to lend undue credence to the Genocide Convention itself, which is far from being flawless; Canada's role in excluding cultural genocide is but one example of how flawed it is. Rather, I am using the Genocide Convention as an instrument that is familiar to many and has currency around the world to make a moral argument highlighting the hypocrisy of countries like Canada that contravene the spirit, if not the letter, of international conventions that they are signatories to. In Canada's case, these include agreements like the United Nations Declaration on the Rights of Indigenous Peoples (Articles 7.2, 14.2, 14.3, 21.2, and 22) and the Convention of the Rights of the Child (Articles 17d, 29d and 30), both of which have specific provisions to protect Indigenous children (UN 2007; UN 1990). As such, for the purposes of what follows, I consider Indigenous children as a distinct group to show how the medical establishment, enabled by and/or in collaboration with provincial and federal governments, has actively participated in committing genocide against Indigenous Peoples more broadly in Canada.

To be clear, I am not setting out to make a legal argument since I am not confining myself to the strict framing of the Genocide Convention. For example, I consider that cultural genocide should have been included as part of the Genocide Convention as Lemkin originally intended. Also, my purpose is not to prove genocidal *intent* as required by the Genocide Convention's definition, but rather to firmly establish the genocidal *effects* of the acts listed in its definition. Importantly, however, when taken together as a whole, the genocidal effects leave little doubt as to the intent. I adopt the basic moral premise discussed by world-renowned linguist and "libertarian socialist" intellectual Noam Chomsky: "Honest people will have to face the fact that they are morally responsible for the predictable human consequences of their acts" (Chomsky 1987, x, 27).

The chapters that follow provide multiple accounts of medical colonialism waged against Indigenous children, the proactive role that the medical establishment – with physicians often leading the charge – has played in the genocidal colonial project, and the impunity that allows such injustices to persist in various forms to this day. This important context became a critical focus for the #aHand2Hold campaign, providing a broader framework to understand the violence of a practice that systematically separated Indigenous caregivers from their children during emergency medical care.

Chapter 7

From the Smallpox War of Extermination to Tuberculosis Deaths in Residential Schools

Canadian colonialism is an infectious disease.
– Anonymous participant, *Red Women Rising: Indigenous Women Survivors in Vancouver's Downtown Eastside*

At first glance, some may find it difficult to think of examples where the medical establishment has been actively involved in killing Indigenous Peoples, as outlined in the first act of the Genocide Convention (UN 1951). However, as legal scholar and political philosopher Tom Swanky states in his meticulously detailed *The True Story of Canada's "War" of Extermination on the Pacific* (2012) and *The Smallpox War in Nuxalk Territory* (2016), in the years immediately preceding Canada's formal existence as a nation-state, settler physicians on the west coast (including the colony of Vancouver Island) actively participated in a war of extermination, a term we would simply refer to as genocide today (Swanky 2012, 237). Over the span of several weeks in 1862, smallpox epidemics were intentionally fomented in many Indigenous communities on Vancouver Island and the mainland interior, especially coveted Nuxalk and Tsilhqot'in territories (Swanky 2016, 182, 202–5). In what will be a recurrent theme in the sections that follow, such actions were orchestrated and/or carried out by colonial regimes and capitalist commercial interests whose primary objectives have driven Canadian policy ever since: "to get rid of Indigenous Peoples through whatever means necessary, with a view to securing permanent access to Indigenous lands and resources for the settler population" (Palmater 2014, 30). In other words, colonization and colonialism. In this case, while mineral mining (gold, silver, copper, lead, mercury) certainly played a role, "the desire to profit from colonization and resettlement preceded the gold rush era" (Swanky 2012, 30, 35–6). Indeed, the "colonists pictured a new homeland dominated by Anglo-Saxon, Judeo-

Christian capitalists" (26). The intentional spread of smallpox – via official expulsion policies, through the forced mixing between infected and healthy people at gunpoint, and by speculators and settlers bringing smallpox into Indigenous communities – was openly or tacitly backed by the governor of the Colony of British Columbia James Douglas and Attorney General George Cary (Swanky 2016, 121–4, 182–91, 206). These actions resulted in the deaths of half or more of the entire Indigenous population on the west coast, "perhaps 100,000 souls in a few-terror stricken months" (Swanky 2012, 1). In 1865, the British Crown annexed the territory to British Columbia, which joined the Canadian Confederation a few years later (Swanky 2016, vii).

Smallpox and the War of Extermination

Key physicians played their part, including several who had vested corporate interests (Swanky 2012, 239). Perhaps the most notorious example is that of Dr John Helmcken, who was a partner of the Hudson's Bay Company, an influential speaker of the Legislative Assembly, and a large investor at Bute Inlet. He also happened to be Governor Douglas's son-in-law (79, 239). According to Swanky, part of Helmcken's role seems to have been to create the expectation that there would be "a natural large loss of life" caused by smallpox outbreaks among Indigenous Peoples in 1862 "as a cover for genocide" (239). That is, if smallpox was occurring "naturally," then it could obviously not be considered intentional. However, even if the smallpox epidemic that began devastating Indigenous communities in the late spring and early summer of 1862 had truly been a "natural disaster," and had not been planned and orchestrated by colonial powers, physicians, nonetheless, had a responsibility to mitigate its impacts. In fact, the "Vaccination Act of 1855 imposed a legal duty on doctors to vaccinate children" and it "was impossible for any doctor or senior official in the Colonies to have been unaware of it" (242). So, if "[Governor James] Douglas truly intended to treat natives as British subjects, he would have required doctors to vaccinate native children," which was the standard of care "in English law and medicine" at the time (242). This didn't happen. Several high-placed physicians left Indigenous Peoples, including children, vulnerable to a disease they knew to be lethal.

In July 1862, although Indigenous Peoples "were dying everywhere by the thousands ... Helmcken could say that 'the Colony was in a very healthy condition' apparently because the Douglas Regime was making itself believe that natives were sub-human and their plight could be overlooked" (Swanky 2012, 246). Helmcken's main worry was that a smallpox epidemic "might decrease the Colony's attraction to settlers" (246). This posed a problem for individuals like him who stood to profit from the land-grab initiated by Douglas as any and "every barrier to a pleasant settlement experience would decrease the value of property held in anticipation of more settlers flooding in to inflate the price" (32). At the "smallpox hospital" for Indigenous Peoples that had been set up, observers noted that it was "only a place where the victims may die in a heap without being obnoxious to anyone and not where they may obtain relief and attention as its name implies" (247). However, with "proper medical care ... the native recovery rate may have been substantially higher" (247). The fact that colonial powers withheld "medical care from an identifiable ethnic group is evidence of a public policy for creating the conditions of life calculated to see them die, i.e. of genocide" (Swanky 2016, 121). But, trying to save the lives of Indigenous Peoples infected with smallpox was never the goal.

As Swanky's research demonstrates, the "war of extermination" was not simply a case of Indigenous Peoples dying in massive numbers because they had no previous exposure to smallpox. This dominant colonial narrative implies that deaths resulting from settler contact are inevitable but unintended. However, deaths through colonization are both predictable and intentional. In this case, colonizers exploited an immunological reality (i.e., Indigenous vulnerability to smallpox) to orchestrate the annihilation of entire Indigenous Nations (Swanky 2016, 119–24).

Crimes, including genocidal ones, occur by acts of omission or acts of commission. In the case of this "war of extermination," many preventable deaths resulted from both. Indigenous children were not spared. During the smallpox epidemic through until 1863, the European hospital, under Helmcken's leadership, actively refused Indigenous patients (Swanky 2012, 245). Colonial and capitalist commercial interests, with the active involvement of physicians, ended up using "medical knowledge about the rhythm of infection to further increase the kill rate," which "proves genocidal intentions" (268). As Swanky astutely observes, "those exceptionally well qualified to stop a disease are also exceptionally well qualified to deploy it" (240). The result is one of the earliest examples of biological warfare on these lands. Ultimately, "this was mostly 'a made in Canada' genocide" (250).

Residential Schools: Killing the Indian in the Child

The smallpox "war of extermination" may have been unprecedented in terms of the scale of the devastation but it is not an isolated or exceptional case. Mounting evidence exists of the Canadian medical establishment's active participation in the orchestrated or preventable deaths of Indigenous Peoples. The residential school system experience reveals not only the medical profession's failure to safeguard the health and well-being of Indigenous children but also its role in precipitating and hastening their deaths. This was not the work of a few rogue individuals, but rather a consequence of the practices and policies that were implemented by administrators and bureaucrats, including physicians, and carried out by health care personnel (as well as the clergy, nuns, and principals running the schools, and the teachers staffing them).

The residential school system in Canada is the most notorious example of Indigenous children being forcibly removed from their families as a result of colonial government policy. Genuinely meeting the children's educational needs was never the actual goal of these government-funded, church-run schools. Rather, the purpose of the forced removals was to cut family ties while stigmatizing Indigenous identity and culture by indoctrinating "children into a new culture – the culture of the legally dominant Euro-Christian Canadian society, led by Canada's first prime minister, Sir John A. Macdonald" (TRC 2015a, v). Indeed, as early as 1883, the assimilationist thrust behind the residential school system was openly stated in the House of Commons by Prime Minister Macdonald, who was also the first superintendent general of the Department of Indian Affairs when it was created in 1880 (Moore 1946, 140). Referring to Indigenous parents and community members as "savages," Macdonald justified "that Indian children should be withdrawn as much as possible from the parental influence, and the only way to do that would be to put them in central training industrial schools where they will acquire the habits and modes of thought of white men" (TRC 2015a, 2).

A key figure in the establishment of residential schools, Duncan Campbell Scott "was known as a writer who was exceptionally sympathetic to Natives and their culture" (Neu and Therrien 2003, 89). However, he masked his political conservatism "behind romantic verse that extolled the freedoms of the savages while lamenting their inability to become civilized – though it was through the auspices of his own office, ironically, that serious attempts to force them into civilization were being made" (89). Instrumental in establishing the elaborate system that sought to "kill the Indian in the child," an expression that seems to have been incorrectly – but aptly – attributed to him (Abley 2013, 36–7), Scott spent his entire career as a civil servant in the Department of Indian Affairs, initially being given a position as a copying clerk by Macdonald, who was a friend of the family. Both before and after 1913, when he was nominated to the highest position for a bureaucrat, deputy superintendent or superintendent general (a powerful role he held until 1932), Scott was key in shaping residential school policies (Lux 2001, 130; Milloy 1999, 3; Neu and Therrien 2003, 91). During later parliamentary hearings, he asserted his assimilationist views by infamously stating that "our object is to continue until there is not a single Indian in Canada that has not been absorbed into the body politic, and there is no Indian question, and no Indian Department" (TRC 2015a, 54).

In 1894, an amendment to the Indian Act authorized the Canadian government to "secure the compulsory attendance of children at school" (TRC 2015c, 13). Subsequently, "the Regulations Relating to the Education of Indian Children granted Indian agents and justices of the peace the power to authorize the apprehension and placement of Aboriginal children in industrial or boarding schools," if they deemed that parents or guardians were "unfit or unwilling to provide for the child's education" (TRC 2015c, 13). Indian agents were able to ascribe "police powers" to "truant officers" and the Department of Justice even developed a warrant that would help standardize the removal of Indigenous children (TRC 2015c, 13). This was all before the beginning of the twentieth century.

The residential school system was framed as a way for Canada to fulfill its treaty obligations to provide education for Indigenous children; instead, it was "a cost-effective abrogation of that responsibility, since the 'teachers' were no such thing, the 'schools' were prisons, and the 'curriculum' nonexistent" (Chrisjohn et al. 2017, 101). Residential schools "aimed to Christianize Aboriginal children, to inculcate within them clear roles for men and women within a nuclear family and to instruct them to become a subservient class of workers within the Canadian political economy" (Stote 2015, 34; see also RCAP 1996a, 309–10, 326). Living conditions (food, clothing, housing, health care, etc.) were abysmal. Children suffered from cultural, emotional, psychological, physical, sexual, and spiritual abuse, including extreme environmental exposure and forced labour, as well as "starvation, deliberate infection of diseases, beating, torture, rape, solitary confinement, assaults" (MMIWG 2019d, 24–5; see also Chrisjohn and Young 2006, 49–51; Starblanket 2018, 113–27). Some resisted by running away (Cherrington 2007, 17) or by setting fire to their school (Shield 2018; TRC 2015b, 322–4). However, thousands of children died as a direct result of the horrific conditions they were forced to live in. Young children, like Duncan Sticks from Williams Lake Residential School (Starblanket 2018, 120) and Chanie Wenjack from Cecilia Jeffrey Indian Residential School (Downie and Lemire 2016), died trying to escape, while others committed suicide (Starblanket 2018, 120; TRC 2015b, 217–20).

Survivors of the system have filed thousands of court cases against the federal government and the churches that ran most of the residential schools (Anglican, Catholic, Presbyterian, and United). These lawsuits culminated in the largest class-action lawsuit in Canadian history, which was settled by the Indian Residential School Settlement Agreement that came into effect in 2007 (TRC 2015a, v, 130).

In June 2008, addressing over 80,000 living Survivors of residential schools, the prime minister of Canada, Stephen Harper, issued an official apology on behalf of the Canadian government for having "so profoundly" failed Indigenous Peoples. He acknowledged that "some sought, as it was infamously said, 'to kill the Indian in the child,'" but barely mentioned the criminal acts that occurred in the schools, referring vaguely to "physical and sexual abuse and neglect of helpless children" (Harper 2008). There was no recognition that genocidal practices and policies enabled the harm caused by the residential school system in the first place. Many criticized or outright rejected the apology because it minimized the suffering of Survivors and made no promise to prevent ongoing harm or reverse the damage that's been done (Starblanket 2018, 26–7; Chrisjohn et al. 2008, 205; see also Coulthard 2014, 124–6; Palmater 2014, 28; Simpson 2016, 438–9).

Residential schools were in place for well over a hundred years; the last one closed in the 1990s (TRC 2015a, 70, 360). In many cases, multiple generations of the same family went through the system. By the federal government's own admission, at least 150,000 Indigenous children were separated from their families by the residential school system (Harper 2008). The Settlement

Agreement issued compensations to Survivors from 139 residential schools and residences (TRC 2015a, 3). A dozen of these were located in the province of Quebec, including several in Eeyou Istchee and Nunavik: Amos, Fort George,* Inukjuak, Kangirsualujjuaq/Fort George, Kangirsuk, Kuujjuaraapik/ Whapmagoostui, La Tuque, Mistissini, Mashteuiatsh (Pointe Bleue), Sept-Îles (TRC 2015a, 359).

A cornerstone of the Settlement Agreement was the establishment of the Truth and Reconciliation Commission of Canada (TRC). The horrors of the residential school system were documented in its reports, published in 2015; it is here that the TRC qualified the establishment and operation of residential schools as "cultural genocide" (TRC 2015a, 1).

The TRC's final report accounts for the known deaths of over 3,000 Indigenous children (TRC 2015a, 92). The residential school death rate was anywhere between two and almost five times higher than the death rate of the general Canadian school-aged population (based on five-year averages for the period spanning 1921 to 1965). Tuberculosis (TB) accounted for a significant proportion of the reported deaths (close to 50 per cent); when combined with the next most common causes (influenza, pneumonia, "general lung disease"), the share of deaths caused by communicable infectious diseases shot up to over 70 per cent (TRC 2015a, 91–3). As the TRC highlights, the "tuberculosis health crisis in the schools was part of a broader Aboriginal health crisis that was set in motion by colonial policies that separated Aboriginal people from their land, thereby disrupting their economies and their food supplies" (TRC 2015a, 94).

Tuberculosis in Residential Schools: "A National Crime"

In 1907, Dr Peter Henderson Bryce, Chief Medical Officer of the Department of Indian Affairs, published his "Report on the Indian Schools of Manitoba and the North-West Territories." A questionnaire he had sent to the principals of thirty-five residential schools was completed and returned by fifteen of them. The results were shocking: "Of a total of 1,537 pupils reported upon

---

* The Eeyou of Fort George Island were forced to relocate to the mainland as a result of the James Bay hydroelectric project imposed by the Quebec government in the 1970s. The Cree Nation of Chisasibi was established in the early 1980s (Cree Nation of Chisasibi 2020).

nearly 25 per cent are dead, of one school with an absolutely accurate statement, 69 per cent of ex-pupils are dead, and that everywhere the almost invariable cause of death given is tuberculosis" (Bryce 1907, 18). That same year, a lawyer responsible for advising the government was blunt about the extent of the crime and of who bore ultimate responsibility: "In doing nothing to obviate the preventable causes of death, brings the Department within unpleasant nearness to the charge of manslaughter" (Milloy 1999, 77). Ward Churchill, a former professor of American Indian Studies at the University of Colorado and author of *Kill the Indian, Save the Man: The Genocidal Impact of American Indian Residential Schools*, provided perspective to these statistics from residential schools in Canada by comparing them to the death rates at Nazi concentration camps like Dachau (36 per cent), Buchenwald (19 per cent), and Mauthausen (58 per cent), where malnutrition and disease were also major factors (Churchill 2004, 34). Bryce's numbers were self-reported by church-run boarding schools (Milloy 1999, 91). It is, therefore, reasonable to assume that these were underestimates; the TRC has confirmed that an unknown number of children's deaths were never reported (TRC 2015a, 90).

In 1904, Bryce had been appointed to the position of medical inspector to the Department of the Interior and of Indian Affairs after having spent years working in public health as the secretary for the Provincial Board of Health of Ontario (Bryce 1922, 3). Perhaps this prior experience allowed him to better identify how a confluence of known risk factors (overcrowded classrooms and dormitories, poor sanitation and ventilation systems) exacerbated an already volatile health crisis for these children bearing the brunt of the tuberculosis epidemic.

In Bryce's report, he wrote that "we have created a situation so dangerous to health" that he was "often surprised that the results were not even worse than they have been shown statistically to be" (Bryce 1907, 19). The health crisis detailed in the report made headlines across the country and articles ran in several media, including the *Montreal Star, Ottawa Citizen,* and *Saturday Night* (Milloy 1999, 91). Bryce had also issued seven recommendations, which were not initially made public by the government. In 1922, when he was no longer a civil servant, he detailed them openly in *The Story of a National Crime – Being an Appeal for Justice to the Indians of Canada* (Bryce 1922, 15). These recommendations included the federal government taking over the management of the schools from the churches and each school effectively becoming a sanatorium through the promotion of "fresh air methods in the care and treatment of cases of tuberculosis" by its medical staff (Bryce 1922, 4; TRC 2015a, 96). As Bryce recounted, these recommendations were consistently ignored and even proactively suppressed by Scott who, for example, intervened to prevent discussion of Bryce's findings at the National Tuberculosis Association meeting in 1910 (Bryce 1922, 5–8). Bryce went on to call Scott a "reactionary" whose "dominating influence … prevents even the simplest effective efforts to deal with the health problem of the Indians along modern scientific lines" (13).

Soon after Scott's appointment as deputy superintendent in 1913, he withdrew Bryce's mandate to perform regular inspections of residential schools (Bryce 1922, 7). A few years before, Scott had referred to Bryce's work in a letter to the British Columbia Indian Agent General and acknowledged that, at one point within the entire system, "fifty per cent of the children who passed through these schools did not live to benefit from the education which they had received therein" (RCAP 1996a, 331). Yet, influenced by Scott, the government did not heed Bryce's 1907 recommendations. Instead of changing its policy, it began negotiating contracts between the Department of Indian Affairs and the churches who were running the residential schools. These negotiations culminated in 1911 and required, among other conditions, that no children be admitted to a residential school "until, where practicable, a physician has reported that the child is in good health" (TRC 2015a, 97).

Based on his research for the Royal Commission on Aboriginal Peoples, John Milloy's landmark study, *A National Crime: The Canadian Government and the Residential School System, 1879 to 1986*, explains how regulations issued in 1894 already stipulated "that children had to have a medical certificate signed by a doctor before admission" to residential schools (Milloy 1999, 89). This potential safeguard failed then as it did after the implementation of the new contracts. For example, in 1911, a Dr O. Edwards filled out and signed the form of a child named Louise Plaited Hair, documenting enlarged right neck glands in response to a question about whether the child exhibited signs of tubercular disease. Despite this observation, he did not interrupt the child's admission process to St Mary's Boarding School on the Blood Reserve. Instead, the Department of Indian Affairs accepted his form without question. Years later, in 1925, Scott recognized that the actions of medical officers in such cases were not an aberration; hundreds of Indigenous children suspected of having tuberculosis had been admitted to residential schools despite the very regulations that were intended to prevent this from happening. Importantly, he realized that it was "our own officers who are picking up orphans, delinquents and others, that are causing the difficulty, as occasionally no application forms are forwarded" (Milloy 1999, 89). As the TRC details, "because the government was slow to put in place policies that would have prohibited the admission of children with tuberculosis, and ineffective in enforcing such policies once they were developed, healthy children became infected," highlighting how "pre-admission medical examinations appear to have been perfunctory, ineffective, or non-existent" at some schools as late as the 1950s (TRC 2015a, 97).

Bryce's 1907 report was particularly scathing of medical professionals, noting that the lamentable "actual situation" had "not been fully realized … by the medical officers except in a few instances," and that "even physicians were at times inclined to question or minimize the dangers of infection from scrofulous or consumptive pupils" (Bryce 1907, 17). The *Ottawa Citizen* headline following his report's release proclaimed: "Schools Aid White Plague" (Milloy 1999, 91). Doctors and other medical personnel played their part by not intervening to prevent children with tuberculosis from being admitted to these schools, many of which were known for their high death rates, and by exposing previously healthy children to conditions that virtually guaranteed that they would contract the illness. Instead of defending the best interests of the children and potentially subverting the system by refusing admission to all Indigenous children since residential schools were known to be high-risk zones at the time, physicians not only inflicted suffering but also sentenced hundreds, if not thousands, of children to their deaths.

Of course, the right thing to do at the time would have been to push for the shutdown of the entire residential school system. This would have prevented tens of thousands of children from experiencing the misery and violence that they suffered, beyond the effects of tuberculosis. Unfortunately, even Bryce wasn't calling for this. He did not consider Indigenous Peoples to be equals. Indeed, in the introductory paragraph of his 1907 report, he states how "restrained through diplomacy, force and the interests of trade by the great fur-trading companies, the widely distributed and wandering bands of Indians would still have been savages, had it not been for the heroic devotion of those missionaries who, attaching themselves to some band, moved with it in its wanderings, or travelled from post to post where the Indians were assembled while bartering their furs" (Bryce 1907, 7).

When Bryce's seven recommendations from 1907 were finally made public in 1922, it became obvious that he was not against the idea of residential schools. His third recommendation implied that he didn't challenge the "educational" mission of the residential school and even suggested that Indigenous families should eventually be forced to pay tuition: "As the Indians grow in wealth and intelligence they should pay at least part of the cost [of the schools] from their own funds." His fourth recommendation confirms that he was not opposed to assimilation policies: "That the school studies be those of the curricula of the several Provinces in which the schools are situated, since it was assumed that as the bands would soon become enfranchised and become citizens of the Province they would enter into the common life and duties of a Canadian community" (Bryce 1922, 4). As Roland Chrisjohn and Sherri Young point out in *The Circle Game: Shadows and Substance in the Indian Residential School Experience in Canada*, Bryce "didn't have any problem with the 'civilizing' mandate of the Indian Department" (2006, 144–5n79). That mandate resulted in great suffering for Indigenous Peoples.

Bryce's understanding of tuberculosis was rooted in racial prejudice and eugenics. For example, he believed that some of the Indigenous Peoples who suffered the least from tuberculosis were those who had undergone an "advance in general intelligence of how to live, through the valuable admixture of White blood with its inherited qualities" (Lux 1998, 285–6). In *Our Own Master Race: Eugenics in Canada*, historian Angus McLaren includes Bryce among a handful of influential doctors "preoccupied by hereditary defect" who would "play an increasingly powerful role in public health reform and government service" (McLaren 1990, 30). He led the Canadian Purity Education Association for several years and proposed that one way of stopping degeneration was by proactively "preventing the unfit to marry and reproduce their kind" (McLaren 1990, 54, 71). Meanwhile, "Bryce and his colleagues were suggesting ... that immigrants were posing a double threat" to Canada (55). As such, he was one of the physicians who "took a leading role in employing eugenic arguments in the immigration debate" (50), particularly through the power he exercised as chief medical officer of the Department of Immigration for almost twenty years beginning in 1904 (52). Bryce's fundamental beliefs about immigrants were revealed in his writings: "the old Anglo-Saxon heart must be the centre; … it must animate and control the many other racial influences which come amongst us, by assisting each into its proper economic place, by educating their uninformed minds … so … that unconsciously and automatically he will have to march in time and full accord with the mighty forces which are, we hope, forging us into a great, free, liberty loving and duty performing people" (McConnachie 1987, 100). In 1919, the federal government issued a grant of $10,000 to the Canadian National Committee of Mental Hygiene and Bryce's renamed Department of Immigration and Colonization to launch a study biased by the premise that "immigrants contributed disproportionately to the institutional population and burdened Canada with social problems;" Bryce pledged his "hearty co-operation" (McConnachie 1987, 92).

Bryce's whistle-blower report was crucial in exposing some of the horrors of residential schools and he paid a heavy professional price for this. However, as historian John Milloy explains, referring to "The Story of a National Crime" report, "much of Bryce's 1922 narrative is the self-interested tale of his failed ambitions in the Department and of his unsuccessful attempt to secure appointment as the first deputy minister of the Department of Health" (Milloy 1999, 95). It is true that "the core of his charges was undeniable" (95), but Bryce's prejudices didn't allow him to recognize the foundational national crime that gave rise to all the others: Canadian colonialism. As some critics point out, perhaps he "was not the hero we might wish him to be" (Chapman and Withers 2019, 293).

Frontline physicians did not subvert the residential school system by refusing admission to all Indigenous children. Bryce, one of Indigenous children's most well-regarded physician-advocates, recommended only reforms that he felt would improve their health, instead of demanding the end of the schools – and their colonial agenda – altogether. Meanwhile, at the top levels of government, physicians continued to provide cover for such acts while shaping Indigenous health policy. In some cases, like that of Dr Harold Wigmore McGill, an elected official who served as the director of the Department of Indian Affairs, doctor-politicians would erect barriers "to keep

Indians in abject subjugation and away from the locus of power" (Shewell 2004, 157). For example, in 1937 (during the Great Depression), McGill, described as "a bigoted, authoritarian man" (157), sent instructions to restrict health care services for Indigenous Peoples. Funding for the surveillance and treatment of chronic tuberculosis was eliminated; hospital care was "restricted to those who absolutely needed it, and then for the shortest possible duration" (Lux 2001, 219; Lux 1998, 290). Medication spending was cut in half (TRC 2015a, 98; Lux 2001, 220). Even if these cuts didn't target residential schools specifically, children who had been impacted by their criminal practices and policies for decades, including through the contraction of tuberculosis, certainly suffered from the consequences.

The following year, in 1938, another physician, Dr Percy Elmer Moore, would join the Indian Affairs Branch of the Department of Mines and Resources as assistant superintendent of medical services. He would later go on to become the acting director and then director of the newly created Indian Health Service (IHS) in the Department of Health and Welfare in the mid-1940s (Grygier 1994, 65, 190; Nixon 1989, 166; Lux 2016, 39). A biographical profile appearing in a 1989 journal article states that "over a 35-year career as a public servant, Dr Percy Elmer Moore affected the course of native health care policy in the Canadian North more than any other single individual" (Nixon 1989, 166). What follows will corroborate this assessment of Moore's contributions, but not in the favourable light depicted by the profile author.

Chapter 8

Experimental Laboratories: Malnutrition, Starvation, and the BCG Vaccine

Both the federal government and private corporations have devised large-scale research abuses ... This medical ill-usage has not strictly paralleled scientific knowledge: Rather, it has mirrored the larger American cultural beliefs as well as politics and economic trends.
– Harriett A. Washington, *Medical Apartheid: The Dark History of Medical Experimentation on Black Americans from Colonial Times to the Present*

Science has emerged as one of the most dangerous tools of colonial domination, as disciplines of science have created and maintained racial distinctions used to segregate and oppress Aboriginal peoples.
– National Collaborating Centre for Aboriginal Health, "Understanding Racism"

The lack of transparent and accountable oversight of the residential schools and the impunity with which authorities could act in Indigenous communities meant that children were vulnerable to the abuses of doctors and scientists. The knowledge that was gained through such experiments throughout most of the first half of the twentieth century benefited the Canadian government, medical researchers, and the settler population first and foremost. Such research serves as a salient example of epistemic racism. Fundamentally, many of these experiments were only possible because of the pervasive malnutrition and starvation imposed on Indigenous Peoples by colonial governments, thereby "deliberately inflicting on the group conditions of life calculated to bring about its physical destruction in whole or in part" (UN 1951, n.p.). I now turn my attention to this next act of the Genocide Convention.

Nutritional Experiments: "Thank you for all the pricks you gave us"

In 2013, historian Ian Mosby published a seminal article detailing inhumane nutritional studies conducted on Indigenous children on reserves and in residential schools in the 1940s and 1950s. He provides a "narrative record of a largely unexamined episode of exploitation and neglect by the Canadian government" (Mosby 2013, 145). The article situated these nutritional studies "within the context of broader federal policies governing the lives of Aboriginal peoples, a shifting Canadian consensus concerning the science of nutrition, and changing attitudes towards the ethics of biomedical experimentation on human beings" (145).

The first experiment discussed by Mosby was related to a medical survey organized by the Medical Division of the Indian Affairs Branch in 1942, with support from the Hudson's Bay Company, the Milbank Memorial Fund of New York City, and the Medical Branch of the Royal Canadian Air Force. The initial survey involved travelling to Cree communities in northern Manitoba (specifically God's Lake, Cross Lake, Norway House, and The Pas) to assess the nutritional status of the population. This was at a time when many Indigenous communities had been forced off their lands and away from their traditional diets of wild game and plants, and were now required to obtain "store food," made up "largely of white flour, lard and sugar" (Moore et al. 1946, 228). Over 400 Cree were examined, including children, and records were kept on 215 individuals, most of whom were from Norway House (228). The results were published in the *Canadian Medical Association Journal*, which was considered to be the official mouthpiece of the physicians' national organization (McCallum 2005, 118n3). The authors concluded that the "dietary intake failed to meet the recommended daily allowances for most nutrients," with marked deficiencies in vitamin A, vitamin B2 (riboflavin), and vitamin C (ascorbic acid) based on clinical examinations. They also recognized that the "infant mortality rate, the crude mortality rate and the death rate from tuberculosis are many times higher than in the white population," and that it is "probable that the Indians' great susceptibility to many diseases, paramount amongst which is tuberculosis, may be attributable among other causes to their high degree of malnutrition arising from lack of proper foods" (Moore et al 1946, 233). Just before this statement, however, they remarked that "it is not unlikely that many characteristics, such as shiftlessness,

indolence, improvidence and inertia, so long regarded as inherent or hereditary traits in the Indian race, may, at the root, be really the manifestations
of malnutrition" (233).

What wasn't published was a related two-year experiment that began that
same year on test subjects in Norway House. Thiamine (vitamin B1), riboflavin (vitamin B2), or ascorbic acid (vitamin C) supplements, or a com-
bination of the three, were given to 125 Cree individuals. Another 175 acted
as the control group (i.e., they received no supplements). The local nurse
regularly visited those enrolled to ensure they were taking their supplements
and to remove "unreliable" individuals from the study. Detailed medical
examinations were conducted on both groups, with colour photos taken of
the eyes, gums, and tongues. The goal was to determine whether physical
manifestations of different diseases could be treated with vitamin supplementation only (Mosby 2013, 151). It is not known why the results of this
experiment were never published, but they were likely inconclusive, owing
in part to increasing numbers of individuals dropping out of the study (165).
There is some documentation to suggest that the results had "not yet been
clear enough to publish" (166n66).

Several physicians, with varying degrees of influence and power, were
actively involved in this research. For example, Dr Percy Moore was acting
superintendent of the Medical Service of the Indian Affairs Branch, which
would be replaced by Indian Health Service (IHS) in the Department of
National Health and Welfare a few years later (Moore et al. 1946, 223). Dr
Frederick Tisdall, a wing commander in the Royal Canadian Air Force
(Mosby 2013, 146), was "a famed nutritionist, a former president of the
Canadian Paediatric Society and one of three paediatricians at The Hospital
for Sick Children (Toronto, Ontario) who developed Pablum infant cereal
in the 1930s" (Macdonald et al. 2014, 64).

The second experiment described by Mosby focused on Indigenous children in residential schools, where families had been warning of conditions
that led to punishing hunger and malnutrition for decades (Milloy 1999,
109–23). Major funding cuts to an already-restricted budget during the Great
Depression of the 1930s worsened the situation for many (TRC 2015a, 87). It
wasn't until 1944 that dietitians working for the Canadian Red Cross Society
and the Nutrition Services Division of the Department of Pensions and
National Health conducted investigations of various residential schools to

assess the situation. They quickly realized what children and their families had been saying for years, that the food "typically failed to meet the government's own stated basic nutritional requirements" (Mosby 2013, 159). Perhaps more critically, even "when kitchens were well equipped, there were rarely sufficient funds to purchase the kinds of daily menus outlined" in Canada's Food Rules (159). In 1947, Dr Lionel Bradley Pett, head of the Nutrition Services Division, concluded that "no school was doing a good feeding job" (TRC 2015a, 88). That same year, he "began planning an ambitious research project using Aboriginal students as experimental subjects" (Mosby 2013, 160).

Dr Lionel Bradley Pett was a medical doctor with a PhD in biochemistry (Mosby 2013, 152). As Mosby points out, "the seemingly intractable situation in Canada's residential schools provided Pett with an unprecedented scientific and professional opportunity" because without the "necessary changes to the per capita funding formula for the schools, there was little likelihood that the students' nutritional status would improve in any meaningful way" (160). Residential schools became social and scientific "laboratories" with the children serving as "experimental materials" (171). In 1948, with the full support of the Department of Indian Affairs and Dr Percy Moore at Indian Health Service (in the Department of National Health and Welfare), Pett sought to assess the impacts of malnutrition firsthand and initiated a series of experiments based on the diets of almost one thousand Indigenous students at six residential schools across the country (161). Many different health care providers (including dentists, doctors, nurses, and nutrition professionals) were recruited to conduct the various aspects of the experiments, which included "medical and dental examinations, blood tests, intelligence and aptitude tests, as well as collection of menu and dietary records from each of the schools" (161). Relying on the information that was already known from previously conducted nutritional surveys, each school was assigned a different dietary intervention.

The children at the Alberni school in British Columbia were known to have multiple vitamin deficiencies but had the highest incidence of riboflavin (vitamin B2) deficiency of all the experimental schools. Milk and dairy products are rich sources of riboflavin. As such, Pett chose to triple the children's daily milk consumption from its 8-ounce ration (less than half of the quantity recommended by the Food Rules at the time) to 24 ounces. However, the suboptimal intake of 8 ounces per day was initially maintained for two years to ensure a baseline for the assessment of any changes that followed the tripling the daily milk intake. The children at the Shubenacadie school in Nova Scotia were considerably more likely to have anemia and gingivitis in the winter months. So, Pett and his team designed a randomized study to assess the impacts of ascorbic acid (vitamin C) supplementation on blood hemoglobin and the gums of these children. The control group received a daily placebo, while the intervention group received a 100-milligram tablet of ascorbic acid. The children at the Blood school in southern Alberta were suspected to have thiamine (vitamin B1) deficiency. Accordingly, after another two-year baseline period, the children's diet was supplemented with "Canada Approved Vitamin B Flour," which used an alternative milling technique to preserve more of the wheat's nutritional value than other white flours; government nutrition experts had introduced this product in the early years of the Second World War. At St Mary's school in Ontario, Newfoundland Flour Mix was introduced into the children's diet because of the thiamine, riboflavin, niacin, and bonemeal that were added to it, despite the fact that Canada's laws against food adulteration prohibited it from being legally sold outside of Newfoundland (which was not a part of Canada until 1949). The children at the Cecilia Jeffrey Residential School, also in Ontario, were given the option of eating whole wheat bread, combined with educational training for staff and children; the purpose was to "study the effects of educational procedures on choice of foods and nutrition status in a residential school." Finally, even though it was known that malnourishment was rampant at St Paul's Residential School in southern Alberta due to insufficient intake of several vitamins (A, B, C) and minerals (iron, iodine), there was no intervention to the diets of the children there because the school served as a control to compare with the five others in the experiment (Mosby 2013, 161–2).

Pett's research team also proactively intervened to avoid necessary health interventions that would disrupt the conditions of the laboratory they were trying to create. News that dentists from the IHS would implement treatments that could help prevent gum disease and tooth decay during their visits to residential schools alarmed Pett because those involved in the nutritional experiments would also be included in such interventions (Mosby 2013, 161–3; TRC 2015b, 280). A flurry of notices sent to local and regional authorities promptly followed as early as 1948. Pett intervened directly in some cases, but many of the letters were from Dr H.K. Brown, a dentist and chief of the Dental Health Division of the Department of National Health and Welfare (TRC 2015b, 280–1). In 1950, Brown wrote a letter to the assistant director of IHS confirming that the "condition of the teeth and gums is used as one of the indices of nutritional status" in the experiments. He went on to assert that "Dr. Pett and I wish to avoid the possibility of any specialized type of dental program using sodium fluoride or dental prophylaxis being instituted in any of the schools under study as these procedures would affect the clinical picture" (Napier 2000, 3). He concluded his letter by requesting the specific exclusion of preventative interventions while allowing only end-of-the-line treatments like fillings and extractions because they wouldn't impact on the research experiments (Napier 2000, 3; TRC 2015b, 280). In an interview from 2000, when Pett was ninety years old, he continued to justify his team's actions by saying that "it was not a deliberate attempt to leave children to develop caries except for a limited time or place or purpose, and only then to study the effects of Vitamin C or fluoride" (Napier 2000, 1, 3).

A collection of letters sent by children at the Alberni Residential School to the Nutrition Services Division in 1952 provide some perspective on their perceptions of the experiments. In reading through them, Mosby was troubled that the letters were "likely spurred by a set of specific instructions from the teacher" because a "common … theme … was that many children wanted to reassure the doctors that their tests had not hurt" (Mosby 2013, 169). An excerpt from the letter of one student is particularly jarring: "Thank you for all the pricks you gave us. I hope we are all going to be healthy all through the year, and not to take so many teeth out. We will all try not to get sick" (169). The last line illustrates how these children were expected to be individually responsible for their own health despite being placed in conditions that created starvation and malnourishment, which, in turn, made them susceptible to illness. The children's very specific concern raised about dental extraction (itself a consequence of the grossly inadequate dental hygiene fostered at these schools, often due to bureaucratic wrangling [TRC 2015b, xiv]) is not surprising based on testimonies of residential school Survivors who reported extractions performed by unqualified personnel without any anesthesia: "He used the pliers, and pulled my tooth, just put Kleenex in there or something, and there's no pain pill, you have to suffer"

(TRC 2015d, 178). Marian MacFarlane, a white staff member at the Alberni Residential School around that time, described how it was an accepted institutional practice for residential school dentists to hoard government-supplied local anesthetics for their own private practice (in Port Alberni), and then "just work on the Indians without painkillers" (Cherrington 2007, 17). Clinical interactions with dentists, nurses, and physicians, including the physical examinations that were a regular part of the experiments, "could be confusing, painful, and potentially traumatic;" most photos taken of the experiments showed laughing children and smiling researchers, but some, nonetheless, captured "looks of fear and confusion ... particularly those [photos] showing blood extraction and dental work" (Mosby 2013, 168). Some study results were presented at conferences and workshops, while others were published in journals (170). Aside from the results from the Alberni Residential School that confirmed that milk servings should be increased to the levels that were already recommended by the Canada Food Rules at the time, the health impacts of the nutrition experiments on the children were limited at best and harmful at worst (TRC 2015b, 287–8). For example, in 1952, although he didn't name the experimental schools, Pett presented a paper at the American Institute of Nutrition in which he revealed that the Newfoundland Flour Mix actually seemed to cause anemia in the children it was supposed to treat, presumably at St Mary's school (Mosby 2013, 164).

Similar to the studies conducted in northern Manitoba Cree communities by Moore, Tisdall, and others, the solution to the medical problems being studied in the residential school experiments (anemia, gingivitis, etc.) was known at the time – ending malnutrition and starvation. Instead, the upstream causes of these medical problems, namely the pervasive conditions promoting starvation and malnutrition in the first place, were allowed to persist. As the Hospital for Sick Children noted in a 2019 apology, "while Dr. Tisdall's body of work benefited many children; the same was not true for Indigenous children" (SickKids 2019). Not only did they not benefit, but captive children in residential schools became suitable guinea pigs for doctors and nutritionists who conducted experiments by maintaining them in conditions of deprivation – a situation that would certainly contravene the UN Convention against Torture and Other Cruel, Inhuman or Degrading Treatment or Punishment today (UN CAT 1987).

Consent, Ethics, and the Self-Interest of Professionals

Such experiments would not pass current ethical standards, but policies and rules governing medical research ethics were basically nonexistent in the 1940s. Subjects were not legally protected by the need to give their informed consent to participate in a research study. In the residential school experiments, Indigenous children and parents were not given the chance to provide informed consent; there also seems to be little to suggest that the details of the prior food-supplement experiment conducted in Norway House were explained to the Cree population enrolled there (Mosby 2013, 165).

However, the absence of a legal framework for medical ethics shouldn't have precluded these physician researchers from adopting a more just approach. After all, a long-standing prime directive for doctors is *primum non nocere* (often adapted as "above all, do no harm"). Yet, as a Canadian Pediatric Society editorial states, "the basics of alleviating malnutrition (adequate food) were well-known even before these experiments began" (Macdonald et al. 2014, 64). This prior knowledge, which rendered the very *raison d'être* of the experiments superfluous, set it apart from other ignoble examples of human experimentation on marginalized populations where advances in treatment only became known in parallel to the research studies themselves. The classic example is the infamous Study of Syphilis in the Untreated Negro Male ("Tuskegee Syphilis Study") launched by the US Public Health Service and Tuskegee University in 1932: despite being told that "they were being treated, not studied," standard of care at the time (i.e., arsenic compounds) was withheld from Black men (Washington 2006, 157, 162), and the study's objective of observing the natural history of the illness "continued long after penicillin became available to treat syphilis" (Macdonald et al. 2014, 64). In *Medicine Betrayed: The Participation of Doctors in Human Rights Abuses*, the British Medical Association recognized that "all citizens have a moral duty to oppose illegal brutality," but the authors underscored that "more is expected of the medical practitioner" (BMA 1992, 195). Ultimately, a simple litmus test for the physician researchers conducting the nutrition experiments would have been to ask themselves whether they would have allowed their children to be enrolled in such studies, and whose interests the research was truly serving. Not only did they fail in their responsibility to safeguard and promote the health and well-being of Indigenous children who were, through colonial legislation like the Indian Act, wards of the Canadian state, but they actively threatened their health by allowing suffering to persist, often making them suffer more and even putting their lives in danger.

These two experiments discussed by Mosby were conducted at a time when the field of nutritional studies was burgeoning. All the prominent physician researchers had financial and professional self-interest in the domain. Moore had long advocated for incorporating nutritionally fortified foods in the diets of Indigenous Peoples, including the development of a special "carrot" biscuit, "blood sausage," and "meat spread," some of which were rejected by the Department of Agriculture because of the addition of bonemeal (Mosby 2013, 155–6, 163). Pett was already a "well-respected scientific researcher and was the co-author of a pioneering national survey of low-income families in Edmonton" before his appointment as director of the Nutrition Services Division in 1941 (160). Tisdall had co-developed Pablum, a processed cereal for infants, which was included on a list of "foods of high nutritive value" (as per the Indian Affairs Branch in 1945) that individuals from northern Indigenous communities could purchase with their family allowances (156). The emergence of the Research Institute at the Hospital for Sick Children, where Tisdall worked as a pediatrician, was partly funded by royalties derived from Pablum (Daneman 2017).

Given their expertise in the field and the privileged access to the health status of the children involved in these experiments, all three knew – or should have known – that malnutrition and starvation were the direct results of willfully maintained conditions brought about by the underfunding and/or misappropriation of funds by colonial authorities, including for food supplies and nutrition services, in Indigenous communities and residential schools. Nutritional supplements would have modest results, at best. As Mosby points out, "none of these experiments and studies conducted between 1942 and 1952 had much in the way of long-term positive effects on the lives of those being studied" (Mosby 2013, 170). Referring specifically to the nutrition experiments in residential schools, Mosby states that, whether they "met the ethical standards of the time or not, it is clear that they did little to address the underlying causes of malnutrition in residential schools" (168).

Addressing the underlying causes would have meant demanding a major overhaul of the current systems in place, including an immediate end to the residential school system. Instead, as physician bureaucrats and policy makers in the mid-1950s, Moore and Pett continued pushing for technological solutions through nutritional engineering. When it came to policies that could have an impact on the health of Indigenous Peoples, they, for example, "jointly opposed introduction of a cash relief system, instead lobbying for continuation of an 'in-kind' system of relief and family allowances as well as for the introduction of a nutritionally improved 'bannock mix' to be distributed as part of these federally administered social welfare programmes" (Mosby 2013, 170–1).

Even if Moore, Pett, and Tisdall genuinely believed they were doing good for Indigenous Peoples, their approach was infused with the racist colonial biases, stereotypes, and prejudices that have long been inscribed into the culture of the medical establishment and which they continued to perpetuate. Given the influence and power they wielded, these views would have significant consequences on future generations of medical trainees and the clinical care that Indigenous Peoples received across the country.

For instance, Tisdall and Moore were involved with another medical survey in 1947 that spanned two years. Led by Dr R.P. Vivian and Dr Charles McMillan from the Department of Health and Social Medicine at McGill University, the James Bay Survey included the Cree communities of Attawapiskat in Ontario and Waskaganish (previously known as Rupert's House) in Quebec (Vivian et al. 1948, 506). It sought to replicate what had been done in the 1942 survey of Cree communities in northern Manitoba. In speaking about the James Bay Survey and in a context when colonization had already violently disrupted traditional subsistence mechanisms in Indigenous communities that were previously autonomous and self-sufficient, Tisdall commented to a parliamentary committee that "we do not know as much as we should as to what motivates the Indian. We have to find out what incentive we can place in front of him. The Indian is very different from us. We have to find out how the Indian can be encouraged, how his work can be diversified, his efforts diversified, so he can make himself self-supporting, so he can obtain the food he needs" (Mosby 2013, 154). If Tisdall would make such paternalistic statements in parliamentary hearings, to what extent did such beliefs influence how he treated Indigenous children and their families as part of his clinical work at the Hospital for Sick Children? Given his prominence in academia and through his teaching appointment at the University of Toronto that conferred supervision responsibilities of medical trainees, what was Tisdall's role in transmitting the cultural value systems of the medical establishment to future generations of pediatricians through the hidden curriculum?

Moore also publicly expressed his prejudiced views about Indigenous Peoples. In an article appearing in the Canadian Public Health Journal in 1941, Moore offered advice to readers about how to deal with Indigenous Peoples: "The Indian in an institution has the psychology of a child. He is fearful and timid. Try to gain his friendship and his confidence. Do not alarm him by speaking within his hearing of procedures that he does not understand" (Moore 1941, 16–17). In 1946, he wrote that the federal government accepted responsibility for health services to Indigenous Peoples, in part, "for self-protection, and to prevent spread of disease to the white population" (140). In *Enough to Keep Them Alive*, social work professor Hugh Shewell relies on testimony before the Special Joint Parliamentary Committee on the Indian Act in 1946 to explain why Moore felt "that Indian Affairs administrators had failed so far" in their objective of assimilation. The reason for their failure was "because they had been insufficiently guided and informed, and as a result they did not fully understand the difficulties facing Indians in their adjustment to civilization" (Shewell 2004, 155). As the new "professional voice of the bureaucracy," Moore called for "a base of scientific knowledge on which to build successful programs for Indian integration" (155–6).

The impacts of initiatives led by Pett and Moore went beyond medical trainees and had more significant impacts on a broader population because their respective positions allowed them to exert their influence at the policy level. Indeed, Moore wielded significant power and influence in his role as director of IHS that spanned three decades (Nixon 1989, 166). In 1946, IHS oversaw sixteen hospitals with a combined capacity of 1,200 beds, employed twenty-seven full-time medical officers (including seven in the Northwest Territories and the eastern Arctic) and seven hundred part-time doctors to provide health care to well over 130,000 Indigenous Peoples across the country, including over 7,000 Inuit (Moore 1946, 140–1). It would only increase in the years that followed; by 1960, there were "twenty-two institutions with more than 2,200 beds for the treatment of Aboriginal people" (Lux 2016, 3).

The concluding words in Mosby's research paper are fitting here: "These experiments therefore must be remembered and recognized for what they truly were: one among many examples of a larger institutionalized and, ultimately, dehumanizing colonialist racial ideology that has governed Canada's policies towards and treatment of Aboriginal peoples throughout the twentieth century" (Mosby 2013, 172).

The Buried History of Residential Schools

The now-infamous nutrition experiments highlight how the professional interests of physician-researchers trumped the physical and emotional well-being of Indigenous communities, including children, oftentimes in situations where their lives were under constant threat. In the residential school experiments, very basic human precepts of body autonomy and consent were ignored (although contemporary understandings of free and informed consent could never be obtained in light of the horrible conditions these children were in and the fact that they had been forcibly removed from their parents in the first place). The doctors used Indigenous children's bodies to acquire medical knowledge through colonial science (see Mosby 2013, 148n9). This allowed them to advance their careers, while the knowledge gained was mainly used to benefit the dominant (i.e., white settler) population.

This quest for medical knowledge at any cost put children in residential schools at high risk because, as wards of the state, they were held captive and at the mercy of Canadian health care personnel, researchers, and scientists. Soon after Mosby's article was published, Justice Murray Sinclair, who was heading the TRC at the time, stated in an interview with the CBC that some "medicines were tested in aboriginal communities and residential schools before they were utilized publicly," yet they were "withheld from children in residential schools" once it was known that they worked in the general population (CBC 2013). So, while Indigenous bodies were used to develop medical knowledge, they did not necessarily benefit from it. A few days later, news broke of a 1954 report detailing how a local doctor and nurse had experimented with over a dozen different medications to treat ear problems at the Cecilia Jeffrey Residential School (Porter 2013). In 2015, the *Winnipeg Free Press* revealed the story of a bizarre extrasensory perception (ESP) experiment in the 1940s using playing cards that involved dozens of children at the Brandon Indian Residential School in Manitoba and was conducted by a former Duke University staff member at the parapsychology lab (Paul 2015; TRC 2015b, 227). As suggested by Assembly of First Nations Regional Chief Bill Erasmus, "what's already been exposed represents only a fraction of the full, true and tragic history of the residential schools. There are no doubt more revelations buried in the archives" (CBC 2013).

BCG Vaccine Trials: Poverty Was the Greatest Threat to Indigenous Babies

While residential schools ended up functioning as social and scientific "laboratories" with Indigenous children serving as "experimental materials" (Mosby 2013, 171), those who were not in the residential school system were also used as human subjects by physicians who had the institutional backing of different levels of government and/or universities. For example, in *Medicine That Walks: Disease, Medicine and Canadian Plains Native People, 1880–1940*, medical historian Maureen Lux describes a pivotal tuberculosis vaccine trial involving Indigenous babies in the Qu'Appelle region of Saskatchewan, part of Traditional Lands of the Assiniboine, Cree, Saulteaux, and several other Indigenous Nations (Lux 1998, 278; for more about Treaty 4, see 292n4). The study, conducted in the 1930s and 1940s, was led by Dr George Ferguson and Dr Austin Simes, who was a local physician and medical officer on the File Hills reserve and would later become superintendent of the Fort Qu'Appelle Indian Hospital (Lux 2001, 208). Ferguson, whose loyalty to the church superseded that to medicine, was superintendent (1917–48) of the Fort Qu'Appelle sanatorium, which only accepted Indigenous patients when they were deemed to pose a higher risk to white people whose need for hospital care had started to decline (Lux 2001, 203; Jones 2019, 309). Ferguson considered white people to be biologically superior. In a preliminary Bacille Calmette-Guerin (BCG) vaccine trial report, he attributed Indigenous Peoples' increased susceptibility to tuberculosis to the same cause as their "primitiveness": lack of "white blood" (Jones 2019, 309–10).

The purpose of the study, supported by the Department of Indian Affairs and the National Research Council, was to confirm the effectiveness of the BCG vaccine to confer immunity to tuberculosis. The vaccine relied on a bovine strain of the tubercle bacillus that was rendered less virulent (Lux 2001, 202). Until then, 400,000 children had been vaccinated with BCG, mostly in

France and Germany, without serious complications. However, the vaccine remained controversial because the scientific validity of the European trials was disputed, and the vaccine's safety was put into question due to the concern that it would regain its virulence over time. This latter concern was likely heightened for some following a disastrous experience in Germany where 71 of 249 infants died after having received oral doses of BCG at the Lubeck municipal hospital in the early months of 1930, presumably as a result of contamination (210). At the time, there was consensus that isolating infected individuals, lengthy sanatorium treatment, and improved living conditions were part of the standard of care for tuberculosis. The potential use of the BCG vaccine offered the option of a less expensive alternative for the future (210). Meanwhile, the threat of tuberculosis spreading to the white settler population was constantly looming for those in power, including Ferguson who led the BCG study (Jones 2019, 309). So, from 1933 to 1945, 306 infants in Qu'Appelle were vaccinated while another 303 were not (they were considered controls). Dr Simes skirted the difficulties that would come with obtaining consent by vaccinating the babies born at the File Hills Colony cottage hospital, while the infants who were used as controls were born at home on the reserve under the care of Indigenous midwives (Lux 2001, 208, 210–11).

Some may argue that current understandings of informed consent for research purposes can't be applied to the period when this study took place. However, this is contradicted by Ferguson's clinical practice for non-Indigenous children. For example, he considered it "necessary to obtain parental consent" before even doing screening tests for tuberculosis on non-Indigenous children as far back as 1921 (Lux 2001, 208). On the other hand, as late as 1966, there is documentation that Dr G.D. Barnett and the Saskatchewan Anti-Tuberculosis League vaccinated Indigenous children with BCG without informing the parents because Barnett "felt it was good for them" (Lux 2001, 208; Lux 2016, 111).

The results of the trial suggested that the vaccine was safe and effective. Vaccinated infants seemed to be less likely to contract tuberculosis and were less likely to die when they did. However, the study revealed a deeper concern: high mortality rates from all causes (i.e., regardless of whether the infants had received the vaccine or not). In Canada, the first BCG trials were actually undertaken in 1926 by Dr J.A. Beaudoin, who was based at Université de Montréal; trial subjects were taken from "lower middle class and poorer sections of the community" (Lux 1998, 289). The non-tuberculosis death rates of the children in the Qu'Appelle study (primarily caused by gastro-enteritis and pneumonia) were at least twice those of their counterparts in the Montreal study (Lux 2001, 211). As Lux highlights, "the most obvious finding of the BCG vaccine trial was that poverty, not tuberculosis, was the greatest threat to Native infants" (211).

In a striking parallel to the nutritional survey studies and experiments by Moore and his colleagues, Ferguson and Simes conducted a BCG vaccine trial involving Indigenous children that lasted over ten years with the aim of reducing tuberculosis deaths, when the actual solution to reducing deaths from all causes would have been advocating to end the imposed conditions of poverty these children were forced to live in (Lux 1998, 278). Even when the tuberculosis epidemic impacting these Indigenous communities was better controlled, it did not result because of any "improvements in their economic condition but [rather because] of antibiotic drugs [used] after the Second World War" (Daschuk 2019, 177–8). As Lux concludes in her original research paper on the subject: "As for the ghastly background of disease and death that the BCG trial inadvertently highlighted, there was no vaccine. The BCG trial was a success, but unfortunately the patients died" (Lux 1998, 291).

Chapter 9

Cruel Treatment: Indian Hospitals, Sanatoria, and Skin Grafting

Of all the forms of inequality, injustice in health is the most shocking and the most inhumane.
– Martin Luther King Jr, in Harriett A. Washington, *Medical Apartheid: The Dark History of Medical Experimentation on Black Americans from Colonial Times to the Present*

The five acts outlined in the Genocide Convention may overlap. That is, many examples categorized in the other acts also fall within the act of "causing serious bodily or mental harm to members of the group" (UN 1951) discussed in this chapter. As such, even though the examples in the pages that follow focus more specifically on bodily and mental harm suffered by Indigenous children, the themes from the last two chapters – experimentation, imposed poverty, malnutrition, and starvation resulting in illness and death – continue here.

Indian Hospitals: A Segregated System to Break the Child and to Break Up the Family

Aboriginal Peoples Television Network journalist Holly Moore's award-winning investigative report, "The Cure Was Worse," explores the "Indian hospitals" that spread across Canada for most of the twentieth century. The only thing "Indian" about these hospitals was the patients; they were anchored in the dominant biomedical model, staffed by white physicians, and run by the colonial government (Lux 2017). As medical historian Maureen Lux explains in *Separate Beds: A History of Indian Hospitals in Canada, 1920s–1980s*, "racially segregated institutions reassured [white Canadian] citizens that their access to modern hospitals need not be shared with Aboriginal patients" (Lux 2016, 4). At its peak in the early 1960s, this part of the segregated Canadian health care system had a total capacity of over two thousand beds in more than twenty Indian hospital institutions throughout the country (3).

Marilyn Buffalo, whose grandmother was first a patient and then worked as a ward aide and caregiver at one of these hospitals, makes a direct link between the residential school system and the Indian hospitals: "One system fed into the other, but I learned very early in life that it's just one system, one policy. And that was to break the child, to break up the family" (Moore 2017). Joan Morris, whose mother was hospitalized for almost two decades, states that "the Indian Hospitals didn't operate on their own. They always worked with the residential schools. To me, the hospitals were a hundred percent worse" (Moore 2017).

One of the many parallels and direct links with the residential schools was the pervasiveness of tuberculosis (TB), a major reason for the number of Indigenous Peoples institutionalized in these Indian hospitals and also in some non-segregated (or mixed) hospitals. Residential school children diagnosed with TB could be transferred to an Indian hospital. However, residential schools were not the only point of entry. As will be discussed further in Chapter 11, many Indigenous Peoples across the country were forcibly removed from their communities to be hospitalized, oftentimes hundreds, if not thousands, of kilometres away. Some were prevented from leaving once hospitalized. An Indigenous nurse who worked at one of the hospitals compared it to being "like a jail. The patients couldn't leave" (Meijer Drees 2013, 175). The prison analogy is apt. In 1951, Dr Percy E. Moore, who played a major role in the development and administration of this segregated hospital system as director of Indian Health Service (IHS), recommended that amendments be made to Section 72 of the Indian Act to include "compulsory hospitalization and treatment of infectious diseases among Indians" (Lux 2016, 116). The 1953 Indian Health Regulations subsequently made it possible to fine, detain, and/or incarcerate Indigenous Peoples deemed a danger to the health of the (white) public (116–17). Police forces were called upon to enforce such policies (Lux 2016, 116–17; Meijer Drees 2013, 174). Many Indigenous Peoples would spend years in these institutions, including much of their childhood.

Indeed, hospitalization for TB treatment felt like an eternity. One Inuk woman from Nunavik has shared how the protracted and strict bed rest enforced as part of her treatment (despite, in her case, not feeling sick) contributed to losing track of time: "I really don't remember if I was gone for two or three years" (Olofsson et al. 2008, 135). Thamasie Simarapik, also from Nunavik, recounts how all the Inuit – children and adults – who underwent treatment at the time were marked by the bed rest routine "that would continue even once antibiotic drugs became standard treatment" (136).

A Cruel Existence: Aggressive Treatments, Experimentation, and Abuse

Dr William Barclay, one of the doctors who practised at the Charles Camsell Indian Hospital in Edmonton, explained that "rigorously enforced" bed rest was a "cornerstone of therapy." Forced immobilization by applying plaster casts, strict bed rest, and iatrogenic pneumothoraces (surgically collapsing the lung by injecting air into the chest) were all part of their "therapeutic armamentarium" (Grygier 1994, 109). Surgical procedures, including thoracoplasty (removal of portions of the ribs), described as "a painful and deforming procedure," were performed under only local anesthesia (109).

Despite the advent of antituberculosis medications in the 1940s and even more effective antibiotics in the 1950s, thoracic surgery was simply "made more daring and heroic" and "did not easily give way to the new chemotherapy regime, particularly for Aboriginal patients" (Lux 2016, 65). Dr A.L. Paine, the medical superintendent at the Manitoba Sanatorium, "undertook what he called 'salvage surgery,' or lung resections to reduce the perceived risk of relapse once Aboriginal patients returned home" (Lux 2016, 66). In 1958, Paine explained the double-standard: "More white patients with residual minimal lesions are being treated conservatively, though resection is still favoured to prevent relapse in those of Indian blood" (66).

In 1959, British specialist Dr P.E. Baldry visited several Canadian sanatoria. He was disturbed by the number of surgeries performed there and was surprised that lung resections were still being used for even small foci of infection, despite effective oral antibiotics being widely available (Lux 2016, 66). Surgical interventions seemed to be favoured for all Canadian patients with tuberculosis, compared to the United States and England, but "Aboriginal patients underwent chest surgery to a greater extent than other Canadians," and were subjected to "more aggressive treatment" (66–7). Baldry also noted that physicians working in Canadian sanatoria had "little faith in their patients and … separate[d] them from their homes for rather long periods" (66). His visit occurred at a time when Indigenous Peoples made up increasing proportions of the patients hospitalized for tuberculosis treatment. For example, Inuit patients made up over 50 per cent of hospitalizations at the Mountain Sanatorium in Hamilton, Ontario, in 1956; the following year, "there were only Aboriginal patients in the institution" (66). Whether knowingly or not, Baldry was likely alluding to the IHS* policy not to treat Indigenous tuberculosis patients "on an out-patient basis in view of the fact that we cannot supervise their activities very closely while they are at home and in the majority of cases their medication would not be taken regularly" because they did "not have the educational background for home therapy of active tuberculosis" (Lux 2016, 67). So, not only did Indigenous Peoples not benefit from effective antituberculosis medications and the shift to out-patient treatment that it afforded primarily to non-Indigenous (i.e., overwhelmingly white) patients (Grygier 1994, 12; Lux 2016, 67, 118), but overly aggressive surgical interventions continued unabated. Perhaps this explains (at least in part) why, as late as 1965, the Saskatchewan Anti-TB League reported that "the average length of treatment for non-Aboriginal patients decreased from the previous year, from 10.11 months to 8.63 months" while the average for Indigenous patients increased from 14.41 months to 17.93 months (Lux 2016, 67).

All Indigenous patients could be subjected to these treatments, but there were particularities to the children's experiences. Medical and surgical procedures, done without the child's parents, must have been terrifying. Doreen Callihoo, an Indigenous woman from Villeneuve, Alberta, was a young child when she was admitted for TB treatment at the Charles Camsell Indian Hospital, where she ended up spending the bulk of her childhood. As a child, she she received streptomycin injections and pneumothorax treatments twice a week. In adolescence, "she had two separate thoracoplasties … performed under local anesthetic," and a few years later, one of her lungs was surgically

---

* Indian Health Service (IHS) was renamed Indian and Northern Health Services in 1954 (Bonesteel 2006, 73) or 1955 (Grygier 1994, 81)

removed because of a chronic lung infection (Lux 2016 3, 13). Barclay recounted how the "most heartbreaking chore" practising at the hospital was streptomycin rounds for children with suspected tuberculosis meningitis. The medication was given by intramuscular injection, and also "through a spinal tap to the children who dread the whole procedure." This was often done in vain, as the medical teams "saved very few of those early cases" before other medications were developed (Grygier 1994, 110). Barclay stated that they used "these treatments more on blind faith and trust than on any scientific evidence that they were effective." For Indigenous Peoples who were "hospitalized far away from home and friends, it was a cruel existence" (109).

The harshness of aggressive medical and surgical treatments for tuberculosis (and other illnesses), and the fact that loved ones would far too often not return home, raised the suspicion among many Indigenous Peoples that they were being used as "guinea pigs" in hospitals across the country (Lux 2001, 180; Lux 2016, 110–13). Some were "positive that there was experimentation" going on (Meijer Drees 2013, 182; see also Lux 2016, 102; Selway 2016, 170). Joanasie Salomonie, an Inuk evacuated aboard the *C.D. Howe* ship in 1954, was hospitalized at the Parc Savard Indian Hospital in Quebec City for two years. He was sure that the doctors were conducting "a medicine experiment using different things on us" and "practising on us" (Grygier 1994, 115; see also Lux 2016, 112). Kathleen Steinhauer, from the Saddle Lake reserve in northeastern Alberta, worked as a nurse at the Charles Camsell Indian Hospital for a couple of years after graduating in 1954, and then returned there toward the end of her career in the 1970s. In a 2004 interview, Steinhauer recalled that both patients and staff felt that new tuberculosis treatments "were pioneered on patients in the Indian Hospital system." Even when patients were being informed about the treatment, she believed that "they often did not fully understand what was being asked of them" (Meijer Drees 2013, 168–75).

A 1976 hospital policy review submission suggests that the IHS actually boasted about being "one of the first hospitals to experiment with the use of streptomycin and to achieve a breakthrough in tuberculosis treatment" in the late 1940s (Lux 2016, 112). In 1956, it undertook a trial using different forms of the common antituberculosis drug para-aminosalicylic acid (PAS) on Indigenous patients. Extensive blood work was taken from dozens of Inuit patients for this and other studies, including tests conducted for the

Defence Research Board, as well as American researchers (112). Such research, conducted without proper consent, was clearly done with the full knowledge of IHS director Moore, for whom hospital staff using the hospital laboratory to perform such studies could be considered a legitimate expense of public funds (113).

More recently, the CBC broke the story of Florence Genaille. In 1953, the Ojibway girl from Rolling River First Nation was being treated for tuberculosis at the Brandon Sanatorium in Manitoba, where "doctors bound her to a gurney, pumped her body with electric currents and then took notes as her fingers curled, her arms shook and her neck strained backwards." Genaille was at a loss to explain why the medical team would have performed such tests but recalled that her "fingers were beginning to twist sideways, it was so incredibly painful" (Carreiro 2017).

Such treatment would not be surprising given that the abuse of Indigenous children occurred, to some extent, in most health care institutions across the country at the time. Some hospitals and sanatoria may have been better or worse than others, but all shared in the foundational violence inflicted on Indigenous children: the removal from their families and the transfer to the colonial-run medical system without a parent or guardian.

At the Charles Camsell Indian Hospital, Barclay recalled how "children resented being immobilized and did their best to prevent us from applying a cast from which they couldn't subsequently wiggle free" (Grygier 1994, 110). Staying in bed for indefinite periods would not be easy for most people, but it was especially "difficult for many of the Inuit who were used to an active life outdoors to be confined to bed – particularly the children" (Olofsson et al. 2008, 136). This was exacerbated by the fact that many of them "did not feel particularly sick, hated being in bed all the time, and did not understand that it was essential" (Grygier 1994, 110). Children "were often physically restrained to teach the discipline of bed rest" (Lux 2016, 105). Some would be placed in plaster casts. In fact, hospital staff would joke about "a condition they called 'cantstayinbeditis,' for which the treatment was 'castitis': immobilization by applying plaster casts on both legs with a bar connecting the casts" (Lux 2016, 105; see also Grygier 1994, 110). Children who managed to free themselves of the leg casts were fitted with body casts that extended all the way up to their chest (Lux 2016, 105). Titus Allooloo, an Inuk who had been evacuated to Quebec City and then transferred to the Mountain Sanatorium in Hamilton when he was six years old, was physically restrained with a har-ness and received a strapping if he was caught without it (Grygier 1994, 110). Markoosie Patsauq, an Inuk from Nunavik, was hospitalized at the Clear-water Lake Indian Hospital in The Pas (Manitoba). During his time there, children would be punished for not staying flat in bed during rest periods, including the strapping of the hands with a ruler for sitting up, a straight-jacket for a day if caught with "even just one foot, not both" on the floor, and spanking and a straightjacket for four days for having played with another child (Olofsson et al. 2008, 136).

William Tagoona was five years old when he was hospitalized in the same institution, where he stayed for eighteen months in the mid-1950s. In a 1998 interview conducted when he was living in Kuujjuaq, Nunavik, he shared an experience that scarred him for life. After throwing up macaroni, food he'd never tasted before, onto his plate, he recalled that the "nurse got really angry and mixed up the macaroni and vomit and force fed it to me." Tagoona re-membered how most of the children were constantly afraid because nurses would beat them with thick, leather belts for stepping out of line, like looking away from the nurse's face when being read bedtime stories or turning away from the nurse at the time of the goodnight kiss (McKinley 1998; see also Lux 2016, 102). Other Nunavimmiut who were hospitalized for tuberculosis treatment at different southern institutions as children also remembered that some "nurses would patrol the wards with a ruler or a yardstick to hit any misbehaving children" (Olofsson et al. 2008, 137).

Over the last few years, reports of sexual assault have also come to public attention. Ann Hardy was a child living in Fort Smith, Northwest Territories, when she was diagnosed with tuberculosis and transferred to the Charles Camsell Indian Hospital, more than 700 kilometres away. Hardy asserts that she and other children were sexually abused and assaulted by the staff there, and she is now the representative plaintiff in a $1.1 billion class-action lawsuit filed on behalf of "Indian hospital" patients against the federal government. The statement of claim asserts that "systemic failures created a toxic envi-ronment in which physical and sexual abuse was rampant" (Pelley 2018). A lawyer described the treatment at the twenty-nine segregated hospitals across Canada that are listed in the claim as "horrific" (Pelley 2018). Such legal actions seeking redress are important but rarely succeed in forcing governments to deal justly with Indigenous Peoples by putting an end to colonial practices and policies. However, such class actions do push for some accountability, even if it is much too late. Joan Morris, whose mother was hospitalized at the Nanaimo Indian Hospital for seventeen years, focuses on the medical establishment in saying, "We can't let these people, the medical profession, get away with what's been done to our people" (Moore 2017).

The treatments, experiments, and abuses suffered by Indigenous Peoples, including children, in the segregated Indian hospital system have contributed to a deep-seated sense of mistrust of health care providers and the medical establishment. According to Lux, such patient narratives from Indigenous patients also point "to a wider suspicion of the intentions of the colonizing state's myriad policies and its institutions [that are] intended to eliminate their languages and cultures" (Lux 2016, 113).

Skin Grafting in Igloolik: The Scars Don't Go Away

Another example of physicians conducting experiments on Indigenous Peoples with government and academic institutional support made headlines in June 2019, when the Canadian Press reported that several Inuit had filed a multimillion-dollar lawsuit against the federal government for biological and medical experiments performed on them between 1967 and 1973 (CP 2019b).

These experiments are not well known, even though they occurred as part of an extensive collaboration through the International Biological Program. Discussions were initiated almost a decade prior, in 1959, with over 150 participants from scientific academies worldwide who were involved in planning meetings; subcommittees were struck in 1965 for seven program areas. One of them was "Human Adaptability" (NAS n.d.).

As Nancy Wachowich details, at least part of the Human Adaptability Project took place in Igloolik and Sanirajak (Hall Beach), at the northern end of Foxe Basin in the Qikiqtaaluk region of Nunavut, where North American researchers and scientists arrived in large numbers to perform extensive tests on the Inuit population, which was estimated to be over 750 in 1969 (Wachowich 1999, 288n4). Personal histories were obtained, including through psychosocial interviews, and IQ testing was performed on many. Medical examinations were done, with many undergoing dental evaluations. Pictures were taken and various body parts were measured. Blood, hair, and urine samples were obtained. Several hundred Nunavummiut underwent radiological imaging studies of various areas of the body, including the chest and skull. Selected subjects underwent exercise testing, cold tolerance experiments, and skin grafting (Wachowich 1999, 175, 288n4).

The five Nunavummiut who are suing the Canadian government underwent skin grafting, among other abuses. It is unclear how old they were at the time, but it is likely that at least some of them were minors given that the lawsuit is seeking aggravated damages for "young age" and "vulnerability" (Uttak et al. 2019, point 25). Rhoda Kaukjak Katsak is not part of the lawsuit, but she was in her early teens when she underwent skin graft experiments in Igloolik (Wachowich 1999, 174). In the 1990s, Katsak shared her recollection of what happened when the researchers arrived. She underwent various exercise tests, a physical exam including blood pressure, and had blood samples taken. While Katsak couldn't remember all the testing she underwent, she was never able to forget the skin grafting. She recalls that after making the "whole skin area numb … they took this very long, thin cylinder, like a stick, sharp on one end, and they kind of drilled it into my arm to cut the skin … They did that twice." She was with Jake and Oopah, two of her older siblings. Jake was two years older than she was and, therefore, also a minor at the time (162). They underwent the same procedure that she did and she received one skin graft from each of them (i.e., each sibling received grafts from the other two). She mentioned that it didn't hurt at the time because of the anesthetic, but that it did hurt later (174–5).

Eminent physician and researcher Dr John B. Dossetor details the skin graft experiments in his 2005 memoir. He explains that the goals of his research team were, first, to study the human leukocyte antigen (HLA) system in the Inuit and, second, to apply this knowledge to test theories about the impacts on skin grafts at a time when the field of organ transplants – including transplant rejection – was still being actively studied (Dossetor 2005, 118–19, 121). The HLA system plays a major role in regulating the immune system and, therefore, in the success or failure of organ and tissue transplants. The researchers needed to find individuals who shared specific HLA factors. They felt that this would be more likely among siblings in "relatively in-bred populations" who were geographically isolated, and so the Inuit were selected because of their "relatively contained gene pool" (Dossetor 2005, 115, 117–18).

Dossetor's initial trip, in July 1971, was to Inuvik and Tuktoyaktuk (Inuit Lands in the northwest region of the current Northwest Territories, near the Beaufort Sea) to obtain ordinary tissue typing of Inuit families. Dossetor and his research team of twenty anthropologists, physicians, and physiologists then went to Igloolik in January 1972 to draw blood samples from the population to determine HLA typing, and in June 1972, the research team performed skin grafts on selected individuals (Dossetor 2005, 118–19). Although Dossetor's book doesn't mention how many people were part of the skin grafting experiments, the lawyer who filed the lawsuit on behalf of the five Inuit is aware of at least thirty people (CP 2019b).

The skin grafting procedures were conducted by Edmonton-based plastic surgeon Dr Mac Alton. Dossetor explains that the two of them exchanged skin grafts and used grafts of their own skin onto themselves (or auto grafts) as controls. Their purpose in doing this was to show the Nunavummiut what a persistent "take" and a rejected graft looked like while demonstrating that they were not harmed by the procedure (Dossetor 2005, 121).

Dossetor (2005, 119) explains that the "expeditions were greatly facilitated by Dr Otto Schaeffer, who had practised medicine in the North for ten years or so, could speak several dialects, and was known and trusted by the Inuit." The research team relied on Shaeffer to obtain consent, which "was mainly 'community consent,' although we also asked for individual consent." Dossetor recalls that Shaeffer obtained "community consent after meeting with the community elders in various ceremonies and explaining why we wanted their help" (Dossetor 2005, 119). HIV had not been identified yet, but Dossetor admits in retrospect that they did not discuss the possibility of hepatitis B and hepatitis C transmission, even though the risks for these infectious illnesses were known at the time. Dossetor acknowledges that his research would have been "disastrous" if these viral infections were more "prevalent in the North at that time" (121).

Dossetor (2005, 121) considered the experiments "successful" insofar as they showed "that skin grafts lasted longer in the Inuit than in Caucasians and that the system could be used to predict long-term survivors from the short." However, upon learning of Katsak's account years after the experiments took place (the *Globe and Mail* published an excerpt of her account from Wachowich's book in February 2000), he was "disturbed to read that one's research was so poorly understood, and that the subjects could not recall receiving adequate information or giving informed consent" (121).

He seemed surprised that the skin graft experiments were "not willingly undertaken by cheerful confident subjects, as we thought" (Dossetor 2005, 121–4). As a pediatrician, I can confirm that, after years of working with children and over a decade in pediatric emergency medicine where I've seen thousands of children over the years, I have yet to meet a child who would cheerfully subject themselves to getting poked for blood tests.

Limited Understandings of Consent

In his book, Dossetor (2005, 123) recognizes that "community consent" was not enough and that his team "should have found a way of explaining it in detail to each graft recipient, and making sure they not only understood what it was about, but also gave individual consent." The conclusion he draws is that "relying on the elders was not enough" (Dossetor 2015, 123). However, this didn't compel him to "reach out or apologize to those he experimented on" (Oudshoorn 2019). He seems to resent and even blame the Elders, by implying that they broke "their promise to explain to the community what they had agreed to," despite Dossetor and his team meeting with them "in their own community meetings, in their own language" (Dossetor 2005, 124). He expresses dismay that Katsak (whom, it is worth noting, he refers to by her first name only, Rhoda) didn't mention the fact that he and Alton had exchanged skin grafts and that the grafting on all subjects was done by "one of Canada's leading plastic surgeons." According to Dossetor, there was "only minimal risk involved and that diminishes, but by no means abolishes, the need for fully informed consent" (124).

Of course, precisely because so little was known about tissue transplantation at the time, that Dossetor and Alton exchanged skin grafts, and the fact that the grafts were performed by an ostensibly expert plastic surgeon are quite irrelevant when it comes to free and informed consent. Neither consideration would have had any bearing on limiting the potential spread of hepatitis B or hepatitis C if either (or any other blood-borne infection) was endemic in the community. The fundamental tenet of free and informed consent is the prospective study subject deciding for themselves whether they want to participate or not, with the option of ceasing their participation at any time; whether researchers are willing to do part of the experiment on themselves or a surgical procedure is carried out by an expert surgeon is inconsequential.

More importantly, a bioethicist with an international reputation justifying, in 2005, that the minimal risk involved in an experiment diminishes the need for fully informed consent is disturbing. It makes one wonder whether other liberties were taken with research ethics when these experiments were conducted in 1971 and 1972. This occurred at a time when a framework for ethical requirements for human participation in research didn't yet exist in Canada; the Medical Research Council of Canada put together its first such framework in 1978 (Oudshoorn 2019). However, research ethics principles for human experimentation were outlined in the Nuremberg Code, over twenty years prior, and prominent scientists have written from as early as the mid-1800s that "the principle of medical and surgical morality consists in never performing on man an experiment which might be harmful to him to any extent, even though the result might be highly advantageous to science, i.e., to the health of others" (Goodman et al. 2003, 8).

Katsak's recollection of the experiments is particularly illuminating on the issue of consent. Her understanding was that the researchers were trying to figure out if a burn victim "could get a graft from [a] sibling's skin" (Wachowich 1999, 177). Her mother was likely present, but as Katsak reflects: "I don't think it was a matter of her consenting. I don't think she thought of it that way" (175).

In speaking about her mother, Katsak mentions that it "would never have even occurred to her that she could say no to the Qallunaat"* (Wachowich 1999, 177). Katsak goes on to explain how researchers often came to study the Inuit in Igloolik when she was growing up, commenting how it "was like they couldn't get enough!" (176). They would basically do what they wanted and didn't explain what they were doing very well. She found it odd that community members complained to each other, but that they would nonetheless participate. She described this tendency as stemming from politeness, for lack of a better word. But she also provides a significant insight: "I guess what it comes down to is that the Qallunaat have always been the

---

* The term *qallunaat* "is subject to debate, but it is used variously to refer to 'Southerners,' 'white people,' or even 'English speakers'" (Aodla Freeman 2015, xiii).

people with the authority. I learned that in school. Even my parents always treated them that way. It was normal for Qallunaat to ask us to come over and do things for them, even things like giving them our skin ... We just did whatever they told us to do. They were the ones who ran the town" (176).

In the section of his book about the skin graft experiments, Dossetor doesn't explore the impacts of colonialism and racism, nor of how institutionalized relationships of domination impact on medical research. Indeed, as the editors of *Useful Bodies* point out, "the overwhelming concentration on the issue of informed consent, with its focus on the relationship between doctors and patients, has ... obscured the important question of the relationship among medical researchers, doctors, and the state as well as between state and society" (Goodman et al. 2003, 5; see also Simpson 2014, 15). The focus on a limited understanding of consent has "diverted attention away from the issue of experiments per se," allowing "humans to be used in the name of science ... provided that they are willing scientific objects" despite the fact that "individual or collective decision to participate in an experiment might be founded on misinformation, misplaced trust in the profession, or pecuniary circumstances" (13). Importantly, "human experimentation, even when informed consent has been obtained, may still violate the patient's autonomy" (4). These are precisely the themes Katsak was referring to; her vantage point meant that she had perspectives on medical ethics that differed markedly from those of an "expert" like Dossetor.

Katsak is certainly not alone in her views. When this story made headlines in May 2019, Lazarie Uttak, who underwent the skin graft experiments with her sister, said: "I feel like we were being used" (Oudshoorn 2019). Paul Quassa, former Nunavut premier, said he never gave his consent to be experimented on for skin graft testing and was skeptical about the details that were allegedly shared with community members in Inuktitut. Importantly, he categorically dismissed the idea that "community consent" could be unilaterally granted by Elders for invasive medical procedures. Quassa echoed Katsak's sentiment of Inuit being very trusting back then and simply doing what they were told (Oudshoorn 2019). The lawsuit filed against the Canadian government (both Uttak and Quassa are named as plaintiffs) addresses this point by providing historical background to the experiments conducted in Igloolik. It explains how the government of Canada asserted its authority over the region of Nunavut and the Inuit who lived there by "controlling all aspects of their life." It did so by establishing the presence – whether occasional or permanent – of police forces, courts, and judges, Department of Indian Affairs representatives, and various regulatory enforcement personnel (e.g., Fisheries and Wildlife Officers), as well as social workers and health care professionals. In so doing, the Nunavummiut were forced "to perceive Canada, which was largely represented by Qablunaq (non Inuit), and anyone associated with Canada as powerful, superior and influential" (Uttak et al. 2019, points 5 and 6). Those conducting the experiments "did not appear to be Inuk or Nunavummiut, but rather were Qablunaq, and apparently representing Canada" which compelled the individuals filing the claim to "believe that they had no choice but to submit to the Experiments" (point 12).

The biological and medical experiments for which compensation is being sought included skin grafting but also involved exposing the subjects to extreme cold conditions, assaulting subjects with sharp objects to assess pain responses, and inserting "objects into body cavities" (Uttak et al. 2019, point 13). As reported by the *Canadian Press*, the statement of claim "alleges the plaintiffs suffered irreparable psychological harm, along with other severe impairments and disabilities, including mistrust of people in positions of power, humiliation and betrayal, and avoidance of medical practitioners" (CP 2019b). The lawsuit names the University of Alberta, the University of Manitoba, McGill University, and the International Biological Program because of various researchers' affiliations (Uttak et al. 2019, point 16). However, it asserts that Canada had an obligation "not to allow the Nunavummiut to be subjected to experimental procedures without their informed and meaningful consent" (point 8). Whether the Canadian government was actively involved or not, it had a "proactive duty to prevent the Experiments" (point 11) or "terminate" them (point 21). According to the Nunavummiut filing the claim, Canada "breached fiduciary duties and obligations" by, among other things, allowing Inuit "to be subject to Experiments which were demeaning and disregarded their inherent value as human beings and having the right to be treated with dignity" (point 19).

Quassa, who characterized the details revealed in Dossetor's memoir as "sickening," made it a point to mention that "We are not monkeys, we are not animals, we are another human being that deserves respect." He lamented the researchers' approach because the Nunavummiut "never got any information from them about why this was happening and the reason why they did it. I never found out" (Oudshoorn 2019). As is often the case with such research rooted in epistemic racism, there was "no medical or cosmetic reason or benefit" to the Inuit who were experimented on (Uttak et al. 2019, point 14). In Kutsak's account, she certainly didn't talk about any benefit, but she does confirm that she's had the scars ever since: "They don't go away" (Wachowich 1999, 177).

Chapter 10

Gendered Violence: Forced Sterilization and Coercive Contraception

La mémoire se transmet par le sang. Mémoire écorchée, démembrée, violée.
Mémoire effacée de la conscience du peuple. Un grand vide se creuse d'une
génération à l'autre. Lorsque le récit n'est pas raconté il y a privation.
– Natasha Kanapé Fontaine, *Nanimissuat – Île-tonnere*

Physicians and other health care providers in Canada used Indigenous children for their professional interests (and career advancement) under the veneer of scientific knowledge in processes that were firmly rooted in epistemic racism. This was done with little concern for the health, well-being, or dignity of those being experimented on. The medical establishment also carried out pharmacological and surgical interventions on Indigenous women and girls that had little to do with advancing scientific knowledge – and certainly had nothing to do with providing dignified health care. Rather, they served to advance the mission for Canada to remain a "white man's country." These interventions were rooted in the eugenics movement that had gained force in the country in the first half of the twentieth century, which saw the deployment of willfully imposed measures intended to prevent the birth of Indigenous children in various settings.

Eugenic Practices in Canada

In her landmark book, *An Act of Genocide: Colonialism and the Sterilization of Aboriginal Women*, women and gender studies professor Karen Stote addresses head-on the fourth act of the Genocide Convention: imposing measures intended to prevent births within the group (UN 1951). Stote states unequivocally that the "sterilization of Aboriginal women did take place in

Canada and was often coupled with other policies or practices relating to the control of births, including coercive abortions and the indiscriminate prescription of contraceptives, and always within the larger historical and material context of colonialism and assimilation" (Stote 2015, 92). She explains how compulsory sterilization for specific segments of the population (e.g., people living in poverty, individuals deemed to be less intelligent based on IQ testing, etc.) was legislated through the Sexual Sterilization Act in Alberta (1928–72) and British Columbia (1933–73) and was propelled by eugenic ideologies. Although the records of sterilizations performed under this Act in British Columbia are thought to be lost or destroyed, it is estimated that at least a few hundred sterilizations were performed. In Alberta, records indicate that over 2,800 sterilization procedures were performed under its Act (Stote 2015, 46–50). Other Canadian jurisdictions (e.g., Ontario, Northwest Territories) did not succeed in implementing such legislation despite the attempts of eugenic movements to do so, but hundreds to thousands of Indigenous women were nonetheless coercively sterilized up until the 1970s outside of Alberta and British Columbia (53–9, 79). In these situations, the federal government wasn't able to enact legislation openly facilitating the sterilization of Indigenous Peoples. However, as Stote points out, "through its refusal to condemn the practice, by enacting policies and legislation affecting other aspects of Indigenous life that made sterilizations more likely and through its financial support, it allowed sterilizations to be carried out more effectively" (58). Part of the financial support she refers to is government payment for sterilization procedures billed by physicians (57–8).

Leilani O'Malley was one of the women who courageously fought to hold governments accountable for the violence they inflicted. Her highly publicized lawsuit (filed under her married name, Leilani Muir) against the Alberta government blew the lid on eugenics practices that had continued in Canada until the 1970s. She was awarded over $700,000 in 1996 in litigation that paved the way for other Survivors to fight for compensation as well (Ha 2016).

Lawsuits and settlements in the 1990s made this chapter of Canadian history known to the general public. However, what is less commonly known is that children were often impacted. For example, O'Malley, who was not Indigenous, had been admitted to Alberta's Provincial Training School (PTS) for Mental Defectives in Red Deer by her abusive family just prior to turning eleven years old in the 1950s. When she was only fourteen years old, the medical team there told her that she had to have her appendix removed. Years later, unable to conceive a child, she found out that "an appendectomy was indeed performed on her, but her fallopian tubes were also removed" (Ha 2016).

Targeting the Young: "I was just a child"

O'Malley was not the only person who was a minor at the time of forced sterilization. Using archival records, sociology professor Jana Grekul and her colleagues explain, in "Sterilizing the 'Feeble-Minded': Eugenics in Alberta, Canada, 1929–1972," that "women, teenagers and young adults, and Aboriginals were particularly targeted by the Alberta Eugenics Board" that was created by the Sexual Sterilization Act (Grekul et al. 2004, 358).

A handful of "feeder" institutions presented individuals to the Eugenics Board for sterilization: Alberta Hospital in Ponoka, Alberta Hospital in Edmonton, Deerhome in Red Deer, and PTS (Grekul et al. 2004, 366, 369, 381n12). Based on estimates, teenagers (defined as being between the ages of fifteen and nineteen) represented less than a tenth of the provincial population at the time but made up well over a quarter of the cases presented to the Eugenics Board for sterilization (Grekul et al. 2004, 374). Because consent was often unnecessary for minors, and because it was known that obtaining consent often delayed sterilization procedures, teenagers consequently accounted for 40 per cent of all Albertans who were sterilized (374). Based on "race and ethnicity," Indigenous Peoples were "the most prominent victims of the Board's attention" because they were "noticeably over-represented" of all individuals presented to the Eugenics Board for sterilization. They were also more likely to be diagnosed as "mentally defective" and consequently deemed to be not competent to provide consent and, therefore, couldn't refuse the procedure. As such, almost 75 per cent of all Indigenous Peoples who were presented to the Board were eventually sterilized, which was a gross overrepresentation when compared to the 60 per cent of all patients who were presented to the Board and underwent the same fate (375). Finally, a gender-based analysis confirmed that there was a two-stage bias when it came to women: they were more likely to be presented to the Eugenics Board and were more likely to be sterilized once presented (373). Based on these conclusions, it follows that Indigenous teenaged girls and young women were disproportionately targeted by the sterilization legislation that was in place in Alberta for over four decades.

In terms of absolute numbers, the Eugenics Board considered a total of 4,875 cases and "passed" (i.e., recommended sterilization for) 99 per cent of those. Even the remaining 1 per cent weren't refused but, rather, were deferred. Essentially, the Eugenics Board simply "never said 'no'" (Grekul et al. 2004, 367). As mentioned earlier, approximately 60 per cent of those who were "passed" were sterilized. The remaining 40 per cent were never sterilized only because of consent requirements that may have delayed the operation indefinitely; an example would be an instance where consent was withheld by the person or the next of kin (367).

Physicians and other health care professionals were making all of these decisions. The provincial government relied heavily on a few very powerful physicians who were able to exert their influence on the province's mental health institutions for a long period of time. Dr W.W. Cross was the minister of health from 1935 until 1956, while Dr Malcolm Bow served as deputy minister of health from 1932 until 1952. Dr R. MacLean led the Mental Hygiene / Guidance Clinics beginning in the 1930s and was the medical superintendent at Alberta Hospital in Ponoka, where he acted as the director of the Mental Health Division from 1948 until 1965 (Grekul et al. 2004, 379). The Sexual Sterilization Act stipulated that the Eugenics Board would have a total of four members. Notably, two members were to be physicians. For over forty years, there were only two chairs (one of whom was a physician, Dr R.K. Thompson), which meant that no more than nineteen other individuals served as members for the three remaining positions, with most being professionals, including medical doctors, psychiatrists, and social workers (366). The minimal turnover of members, with a legislated preponderance of physicians (predominantly white men), ensured that an elite and cohesive group wielded almost total control over the fate of those brought before the provincial Eugenics Board for decades.

At the institutional level, physicians were usually responsible for "presenting" individuals from the different "feeder" establishments in front of the Eugenics Board to undergo sterilization (Grekul et al. 2004, 366). For example, Dr Leonard Jan Le Vann, the medical superintendent of PTS, was a particularly zealous and unscrupulous proponent of eugenic sterilization. He identified himself as a psychiatrist but had reportedly never been fully ac-credited (Ha 2016). The overwhelming majority of individuals who were presented to the Eugenics Board from the PTS (where Leilani O'Malley had been admitted) were diagnosed as "mentally defective" under his leadership. This meant that neither the individual being presented for sterilization nor a relative had to provide consent for the sterilization procedure, which vir-tually eliminated any chance that the procedure could be delayed (Grekul et al. 2004, 370). It is worth noting that Le Vann published research articles after using institutionalized children "as guinea pigs for experiments with pow-erful antipsychotic drugs … without obtaining consent from parents or guardians" (Wahlsten 2003, 329). It should, therefore, come as no surprise that the minutes from a Eugenics Board meeting in February 1951 noted that Le Vann went so far as to propose that even young children should be pre-sented for sterilization. The Eugenics Board, which we'll recall never said no, stayed true to form and ruled that PTS could present these children for ster-ilization, but only when they reached adolescence (Grekul et al. 2004, 370). In 1955, records indicate that the Eugenics Board discussed a new admission form developed by PTS that asked parents to provide consent for sterilization upon admission, even if their child didn't fall under the jurisdiction of the Sexual Sterilization Act (370). Given that Le Vann remained in his position for the better part of a quarter of a century, hundreds of children were im-pacted by his practices, disproportionately so in the case of Indigenous girls and young women.

Archived material allows for a more in-depth exploration of the situation in Alberta, but Indigenous children underwent sterilization procedures in other parts of Canada as well. For example, in British Columbia, steriliza-tions were performed on minors institutionalized at Woodlands, a facility whose mandate was to house disabled children, those abandoned at birth, and wards of the state, including Indigenous children (Stote 2015, 53, 103). Emboldened by the sterilization legislation that was successfully passed in Alberta and in many American states, campaigns in favour of sterilization began to gain ground in Ontario in the late 1920s (McConnachie 1987, 214). The full extent to which Indigenous Peoples were impacted by sterilization is unknown. However, we can surmise that Indigenous children, girls in par-ticular, were targeted much like they were in Alberta. In Ontario, as early as 1928, when being classified as "mentally unfit" was often a prerequisite to sterilization, researchers suggested that "Indian children suffered from a greater level of retardation than whites and that IQ seemed to rise with the admixture of white blood" (Stote 2015, 55). The Simcoe County Council passed a resolution "calling for all children in provincial institutions for the mentally handicapped to be sterilized, then discharged" (McConnachie 1987, 214). A subcommittee of the 1936 annual Convention of Ontario Mayors endorsed a resolution calling for "the compulsory predischarge sterilization of all feeble-minded in institutions" (McConnachie 1987, 214–15; see also Stote 2015, 54). As historian Kathleen McConnachie explained in her 1987 doctoral dissertation, even though the Convention ultimately rejected the resolution, "the degree to which it entered public debate, indicated its growing acceptance as the economic burdens of the Depression grew worse" (McConnachie 1987, 215). Meanwhile, across the country, Indigenous children may have been sterilized while they were institutionalized in residential schools (Stote 2015, 78). The TRC has confirmed that cases of coerced and forced sterilization were brought to its attention, generally in situations where child welfare caseworkers or social workers were involved (Kirkup 2018c).

Modern-Day Forced Sterilization and Coercive Contraception

Even though there was no longer any Canadian jurisdiction that had sterilization legislation by the early 1970s, this didn't mean that sterilizations weren't occurring. In April 1973, a CBC public affairs program reported that "Inuit women were sterilized without their consent in the North and while at the Charles Camsell Hospital, and it discussed the linguistic barriers and climate of paternalism that led women to be sterilized 'for their own good.'" Perhaps for the first time, it "also featured charges that some Inuit children were separated from their families, sometimes never to be seen again after being sent to southern hospitals for medical treatment" (Stote 2015, 71). A few years later, Catholic missionary Robert Lechat charged that Inuit women (and men) in current-day Nunavut were being pressured to undergo sterilization procedures. In Igloolik (where the skin graft experiments occurred around the same time), over a quarter of the women of child-bearing age had been sterilized (Lechat 1976, 5). Inuit women publicly declared that "if we had known exactly what the operation we were made to undergo meant, we would never have accepted it," prompting Lechat to term such cases "an extorted consent" (6). Although the Canadian government repeatedly denied any official directive, Lechat demanded to know the "reasoning behind the Canadian government's intensification of its sterilization policy among the Inuit" (5). Information about these procedures was revealed in a formal parliamentary inquiry stemming from Lechat's demands and a similar request from the National Indian Brotherhood (Stote 2015, 80). It became clear that even if openly eugenicist ideology no longer framed the public debate as it did in the interwar period, coerced and forced sterilizations had continued through to the late 1960s and early 1970s. From 1971 to 1974, "at least 580 sterilizations were performed at Indian Health Services hospitals" spread across the country, including the Charles Camsell Indian Hospital and Inuvik General Hospital; Indigenous women made up 95 per cent of those sterilized (Stote 2015, 80). Although there was suspicion that numbers were being underreported by health and government authorities, the information obtained, nonetheless, suggested that almost 350 Indigenous (mostly Inuit) women had been sterilized in "Northern Zones" between 1970 and 1975 (83–7). The initial CBC story suggested that "there was a calculated attempt to reduce the birth rate of Indian peoples in northern Canada" (Stote 2015, 71). Lechat suspected that the federal government's motivation was its interest in keeping a low Inuit birth rate given the risk a larger population would pose to its finances and its access to the natural resources on those lands (Lechat 1976, 7). Of course, the government maintained throughout that there was no formal sterilization policy. However, as Stote asks, when "do we begin to consider consistent and longstanding practices not as isolated instances of abuse but as policy, whether explicitly and openly stated or not?" (Stote 2015, 91).

When eugenically motivated invasive surgical procedures done *en masse* without proper consent had started falling out of favour, recently developed pharmacological options became more viable to produce the same effect of preventing Indigenous births. As early as 1964, oral contraceptives (Enovid and Ortho-Novum) were distributed in large numbers by both nurses and physicians at various clinics, dispensaries, nursing stations, and hospitals that were mandated to provide care to Indigenous communities. Soon thereafter, the distribution of oral contraceptive pills would be carried out by physicians only (Stote 2015, 63). However, the use of contraceptives for birth control purposes was illegal in Canada until 1969 (65, 67).

Attempts to get the federal government to intervene to end such practices were unsuccessful. For example, Kahn-Tineta Horn, from the Kanien'kehá:ka community of Kahnawà:ke (near Montreal), was informed that one of the physicians mandated to serve her community had been told "to issue birth control pills, contraceptives and other means of birth control to Indians that he takes care of, but not to the Roman Catholic French Canadians who are in his practice." She conveyed this in a letter sent to the director of the Indian Affairs Branch of Indian and Northern Affairs in January 1966, asking whether the doctors providing care to her community are treating them "the same or differently from their other [non-Indigenous] patients" (Stote 2015, 64). Dr Harry A. Proctor, who had served as long-time assistant to Dr Percy E. Moore and had succeeded him in the role of director of IHS* (Lux 2016, 245n25), responded by pleading ignorance about any such practice and denied any governmental responsibility (Stote 2015, 64–5).

However, just a few months prior, in August 1965, Proctor had solicited the input of his zone superintendents from across Canada to determine "whether the size of the required prototype [Indian] home could be reduced if birth control techniques were actively advocated among the Indian population" (Stote 2015, 60). According to Stote (2015), the responses made it "clear that prior to the legalization of birth control for contraceptive purposes, it was considered viable to promote their use in Indigenous communities and these were prescribed with the express intent of limiting the number of births within the group" (60). For instance, the zone superintendent from the Atlantic Zone initially cautioned about the routine use of oral contraceptives because they had not yet proven safe for birth control purposes. However, he went on to write how children could be targeted: "Obviously, with the high illegitimacy rate amongst our Indians, to exert sufficient control over the sizes of families, it would be necessary to feed the pills to a very large percentage of the single females, even those in the 14 and 15 year old category" (60–1).

Despite knowing that coercive prescribing was occurring, which had possibly even been encouraged through communication initiatives like Proctor's,

---

* In 1962, the IHS, which had become Indian and Northern Health Services in the mid-1950s (Grygier 1994, 81), merged with other federal programs to become the Medical Services Branch. It was renamed the First Nations and Inuit Health Branch in 2000 (Bonesteel 2006, 73).

the federal government denied that prescribing birth control to Indigenous communities was an official policy (Stote 2015, 66–7). Yet, a memorandum written by John Munro, minister of National Health and Welfare, months before the legalization of birth control in Canada openly recognized that "our policy for our lay dispensers now is that they will try to prescribe and persuade, but that they don't encourage any public education or information campaigns" (68). Munro's memo to his deputy minister, Dr J.N. Crawford, begins by referring to the "genocide question," intimating that a formal policy openly targeting Indigenous communities would be risky. The issue was obviously on their radar. His solution was to unduly influence Indigenous women, once contraceptives for birth control became legal, through public education campaigns that were ostensibly directed at the general Canadian population. As Stote clarifies, once legalized, "the sale and advertisement of contraceptives would increase the effectiveness of efforts to reduce the size of the Indian population while allowing government to avoid criticisms that federal policy was genocidal in its application" (68).

In September 1970, the year following the legalization of contraception for birth control in Canada, the federal government announced a formal program framed around "the right of Canadians to exercise free individual choice in the practice of family planning" (Stote 2015, 68). Women's control over contraceptive methods was an important demand for some feminist movements at the time. However, it is worth noting that the mainstream feminist movement of the early twentieth century had "created a space for itself as a colonial agent by reinforcing sexist and racist notions of womanhood" through its participation in capitalism and "in the colonization of Aboriginal peoples and their lands in ways that also made the sterilization of Aboriginal women more likely to occur" (27). As such, "family planning" for Indigenous communities was a de-historicized and de-politicized euphemism for governmental birth control initiatives that targeted Indigenous women. In October 1971, Dr J.H. Wiebe, director of the Medical Services Branch, sent a letter to regional directors advising them that birth control initiatives would be expanded in Indigenous communities where "abnormally high birth rates" were deemed to be an issue (69). Some of the goals of these initiatives included reducing the incidence of "unwanted children," "child neglect and abuse," and "child abandonment or desertion" (69–70).

In correspondence with Dr Maurice Leclair, the deputy minister of National Health and Welfare, Wiebe had written that he was "acutely aware" of the charges of genocide levied by Indigenous Peoples. This awareness may have been informed by Harold Cardinal, of the Sucker Creek Cree First Nation, who famously described Canada's 1969 White Paper as a "thinly disguised programme of extermination through assimilation," which offered "nothing better than cultural genocide" (Cardinal 1999, 1). Contraceptive devices and drugs were, therefore, framed as being relegated to the individual doctor-patient relationship (Stote 2015, 69). As Stote points out, the new government program not only "now made it more difficult to intervene in coercive practices in Aboriginal communities," but it "also allowed the federal government to avoid responsibility for these [practices] by hiding behind the rhetoric of individual choice and non-interference due to doctor-patient privilege" (69).

This is instructive because it recognizes how genocidal practices can be carried out without official governmental policies. When such practices have been in place for decades, the ambient culture within the medical establishment can continue to perpetuate them without government endorsement, whether official or implicit. Wiebe's 1971 letter to regional directors sheds light on this culture. He acknowledged that the matter of "family planning" had been "included in the curricula of departmentally directed courses of instruction, such as those for the indoctrination of health workers" even prior to the legalization of contraception for birth control purposes, but that the Medical Services Branch had had to remain "aloof from active advocacy of family planning in the practice of public health on Indian reserves" at the time due to "provisions of the criminal code and other legislation" (Stote 2015, 69).

In other words, at a time when the government was not able to launch public education and information campaigns about contraceptives for birth control purposes in the general population because such use was illegal, its own Indigenous health care department was promoting the indoctrination of physicians and other health care providers on this matter through curricula that it had developed. For generations of physicians dealing with Indigenous Peoples, it is reasonable to speculate that even long after such courses of instruction had ceased, the hidden curriculum would continue to ensure the transmission of ideologies that sought to justify the coerced and forced sterilization in Indigenous communities, particularly of girls and women. Indeed, far from being a relic of a bygone era, echoes of this practice continue to be heard to the present day.

In 2015, news broke of several courageous Indigenous women who spoke out about having been coerced or forced to undergo tubal ligation surgery immediately after childbirth in Saskatoon since the 1970s. Other women have subsequently come forward, including some who had been forcibly sterilized as minors. Storyteller, social activist, and author Morningstar Mercredi, originally from Fort Chipewyan (in Alberta), was inspired by these women to go public about her own experience. In the 1970s, Mercredi slipped on ice in Saskatoon while pregnant and had some bleeding. She went to the hospital and was told that she required surgery. When she woke up, the doctors had performed an abortion and she was informed that her chances of becoming pregnant were now less than that of most women. "How in God's name could that be when I was just a child?" Mercredi questioned in an interview. She was fourteen years old at the time. Mercredi would later learn that she had undergone surgery to remove an ovary and a fallopian tube. She has stated how only now, when she is well into her adulthood, does she feel strong enough to fight for her childhood self who had to go through such a traumatizing experience all alone (Kirkup 2018b). She is certainly not the only teenager who has had to deal with being coercively or forcibly sterilized in recent decades.

In 2017, an external review conducted by two Métis women – Yvonne Boyer (a lawyer with a background in nursing) and Dr Judith Bartlett (a physician and researcher) – highlighted the experiences of seven women who underwent such procedures in public health care institutions in Saskatchewan. Overarching themes outlined in the report included that women felt profiled, coerced, and powerless (Boyer and Bartlett 2017, 17–21). Intimating cultural factors within the medical establishment, Dr Alika Lafontaine, former president of the Indigenous Physicians Association of Canada, aptly observed around this time that "these forced tubal ligations would have never happened if these individuals had been treated like people instead of caricatures" (Kirkup 2017). The release of the report by Boyer and Bartlett, which also addressed the presence of anti-Indigenous systemic racism, prompted the Saskatoon Health Region (since amalgamated into the Saskatchewan Health Authority) to issue an apology (Hamilton and Quenneville, 2017).

That same year, a class-action lawsuit was filed by two Indigenous women against physicians, health authorities, the government of Saskatchewan, and the government of Canada for coerced and forced sterilizations in 2001 and 2008 (Kassam 2017). In an interview from 2018, Boyer commented that if "it's happened in Saskatoon, it has happened in Regina, it's happened in Winnipeg, it's happened where there's a high population of Indigenous women" (Moran 2018). Indeed, in a May 2019 letter to the UN Special Rapporteur on Violence against Women, Alisa Lombard, a lawyer leading the lawsuit, confirmed that her firm had been contacted by dozens of Indigenous women across Canada, bringing the total for claims of unwanted sterilization procedures to over a hundred, including one woman who reported being forcibly sterilized as recently as December 2018 (Lombard 2019, 2).

In late 2018, along with Amnesty International Canada, the Maurice Law firm raised the issue with the UN Committee Against Torture, highlighting how the "modern-day forced sterilization of Indigenous women" was occurring in "publicly funded and administered hospitals in Canada" (Kirkup 2018a). The Committee recognized that "forced or coerced sterilization of Indigenous women *and girls* dating back to the 1970s and including recent cases" is a form of torture (UN CAT 2018, 12; emphasis added). In January 2019, the Inter-American Commission on Human Rights (IACHR) issued a press release confirming that it had "received, in a consistent and systematic manner, reports from indigenous women, girls and adolescents who claim to have been subjected to sterilizations without their full, free and informed consent in Canada." In the release, the president of the IACHR and Rapporteur on the Rights of Women stated in no uncertain terms that deciding if or when "to have children is a fundamental right that was taken away from them without their consent, as a result of misogynistic and racist stereotypes. This form of gender-based violence must immediately stop and the State must take all of the necessary measures for doing so." Importantly, the IACHR also called for "adequate reparations" (IACHR 2019).

Government Responses and Legislated Violence Against Indigenous Women

Niki Ashton, member of parliament for the federal electoral district of Churchill-Keewatinook Aski (Manitoba), raised the issue of forced sterilizations of Indigenous women in the House of Commons (Kirkup 2018c). She affirmed that "this is what genocide looks like," and reminded the government that the United National Committee Against Torture "also demanded an explanation for the lack of reparations and sanctions" (Ashton 2018). In his response, Prime Minister Justin Trudeau didn't address the issue that such practice is genocidal, but did recognize that Indigenous Peoples "can face systemic barriers in accessing services, including discrimination and racism" and committed to working "with partners to ensure [that] all indigenous peoples have access to culturally safe health services, no matter where they live in Canada" (Trudeau 2018).

The federal government subsequently invited all provinces and territories to form a working group that would examine the issue of Indigenous women being sterilized against their will across the country. In February 2019, the Coalition Avenir Québec government dismissed the invitation to the working group. It claimed that health is a provincial issue and that it was already having talks with various Indigenous communities in Quebec about the matter (CP 2019a). However, this narrative was disputed in an open letter drafted by Suzy Basile of the Atikamekw Nation and professor at the School of Indigenous Studies at Université du Québec en Abitibi-Témiscamingue; the letter was signed by several Indigenous activists and leaders, including Ellen Gabriel (past president of Quebec Native Women), Viviane Michel (current president of Quebec Native Women), and Marjolaine Siouï (executive director of the First Nations of Quebec and Labrador Health and Social Services Commission). The letter clarified that Indigenous health still falls under federal jurisdiction and exposed that the provincial government had "not yet initiated any formal dialogue on the subject." They denounced the provincial government's refusal to participate in the working group as perpetuating a "colonial attitude" that further entrenches "the silence and denial it has shown on all too many First Nations and Inuit issues in Quebec." At the time that they wrote the letter, they could not "determine with certainty whether or not there have been forced sterilizations of First Nations and Inuit women in Quebec," but they went on to clarify that the information available to them suggested that such practices had very likely occurred at different times in Quebec history (Basile et al. 2019). Media articles in 2019 seem to confirm this (Hoye 2019). It's only a matter of time before the public learns about such instances of coerced and forced sterilizations in Quebec targeting Indigenous women and girls, the circumstances in which they occurred, and how pervasive they were. Similar to the rest of Canada, the question is not whether such practices have occurred, but to what extent they continue.

Beverly Jacobs, a Kanien'kehá:ka lawyer and professor from Six Nations, argues that the reality of violence against Indigenous women must be placed "in the larger context of Canada's colonial relationship to Indigenous peoples" (Jacobs 2017, 49). She explains that foundational violence occurred when Canada's colonial government "violated peace and friendship treaties, which were based on nation-to-nation relationships, by unilaterally establishing its government through legislation in which it had control over 'Indians and lands reserved for Indians' (section 91(24) of *British North America Act*, 1867)." This legislation then gave the government "authority to establish the most racist and sexist piece of legislation called the *Indian Act*" (Jacobs 2017, 49–50). The patriarchal Indian Act had far-reaching consequences on Indigenous women's identity, belonging, and roles in the family and traditional governance structures (50).

This context of hostility and violence against Indigenous women is important as it has allowed the persistence of a medical culture that treats Indigenous women and their bodies with contempt (MMIWG 2019c, 102–3; Vang et al. 2018, 1867–8). This explains, at least in part, why the issue of coerced and forced sterilization targeting Indigenous women and girls has continued years after formal eugenic legislation was ended.

Chapter 11

Breaking Up Families: Child Welfare Services, Mass Evacuations, and Medical Disappearances

It began as a rumor, that they had found a way to siphon the dreams right
out of our bones, a rumor whispered every time one of us went missing,
a rumor denounced every time their doctors sent us to hospitals and
treatment centers never to return.

– Miigwans, in Cherie Dimaline, *The Marrow Thieves*

The first four of the five acts in Article 2 of the UN Genocide Convention
have to do with members of all ages from the group in question, even though
my focus has been on Indigenous children. The fifth act deals directly and
exclusively with children: "Forcibly transferring children of the group to
another group" (UN 1951).

As stated earlier, the residential school system is the most notorious legislated example of the forced transfer of Indigenous children from their communities to establishments run by colonial forces – missionary churches and
the federal government. While the TRC deemed the residential school system
as having committed a "cultural genocide" (TRC 2015a, 1), Indigenous and
non-Indigenous academics, activists, community leaders, journalists, lawyers, and physicians (among many others) have argued that it qualifies as
genocide proper based on the UN Convention. Most recently, the National
Inquiry into Missing and Murdered Indigenous Women and Girls (MMIWG)
included the residential school system among a slew of colonial practices
and policies that allowed it to conclude that genocide against Indigenous
Peoples has taken place in Canada (MMIWG 2019d, 24–5).

As I've sought to highlight thus far, by promoting the entry of Indigenous
children into residential schools where tuberculosis (TB) was both endemic
and had reached epidemic proportions, by inflicting abusive treatments and

conducting experiments, and by having ordered or performed sterilization procedures, frontline physicians played a significant role in carrying out this genocide. Meanwhile, physicians in positions of administrative, bureaucratic, and political power were the architects that allowed medical colonialism to thrive, notably, but not exclusively, within the walls of residential schools and Indian hospitals. However, physicians are not the only health care providers who have played an active role in such crimes.

Child Welfare Services: The Paving Contractor for the Road to Hell

The forced removal of Indigenous children from their families and communities through the residential school system was often couched as being motivated by the child's own well-being. As of the 1940s, "residential schools increasingly served as orphanages and child-welfare facilities" (TRC 2015a, 138). In 1953, when there were around 11,000 Indigenous children in residential schools across the country, well over 4,000 of them may have been there because they "were thought to be suffering from 'neglect' at home" (TRC 2015c, 11). In 1960, "the federal government estimated that 50% of the children in residential schools were there for child-welfare reasons" (TRC 2015, 138). Social workers became active participants by placing Indigenous children in residential schools throughout the 1960s (Blackstock 2009, 30). Among other factors around this time, due to Indigenous communities' resistance to the residential school system through the work of the American Indian Movement and Red Power activism (Chapman and Withers 2019, 333), and the long-overdue provincial enforcement of federal fire regulations at the schools (TRC 2015b, 325–31), enrollments declined and a number of buildings closed. This trend continued until the abolition of the system entirely in the 1990s (TRC 2015a, 64). However, residential schools shutting down coincided markedly with the development of a new dynamic: Indigenous children were targeted for mass removal and apprehension by child welfare agencies in order to be placed in foster care. The era of forced separation of Indigenous children from their families did not end. Instead, "child welfare services carried on where the residential schools left off" (TRC 2015c, 11). This time, social workers were leading the charge.

Although commonly referred to as the "Sixties Scoop," the practice extended beyond the 1960s and well into the 1980s (TRC 2015a, 138). In some instances, the number of children removed from reserves was so significant that buses were necessary to transport them (Blackstock 2009, 30). By the 1970s, a third of Indigenous children in Canada had been "separated from their families by adoption or fostering" (R. Sinclair 2017, 9). Between 1960 and 1985, well over 10,000 Indigenous children were removed from their families and communities to be placed in non-Indigenous homes spread across Canada, the United States, and around the world (10). Not unlike the experience of residential schools, adopted children or those "placed with white foster parents were sometimes abused" and "suffered from identity confusion, low self-esteem, addictions, lower levels of educational achievement, and unemployment" (TRC 2015c, 15). Because no steps were taken to preserve their culture and identity, these Indigenous children "sometimes experienced disparagement and almost always suffered from dislocation and denial of their Aboriginal identity" (TRC 2015c, 15; TRC 2015a, 138).

In Manitoba, amid charges by Indigenous communities of "cultural genocide" and the "selling of babies" in the early 1980s, the province banned the adoption placement of Indigenous children outside of provincial boundaries and appointed a committee to address the situation in 1982 (Kimelman 1985, 1–2). Edwin C. Kimelman, associate chief judge of the Manitoba Provincial Court, was appointed to lead the Review Committee on Indian and Métis Adoptions and Placements. In his final report, "No Quiet Place" (released in 1985), Kimelman defined cultural genocide as having occurred if even "one native child has been placed out of province where there was no need for it" (328). Based on his review of the files made available to him, he noted that the "placement of children out of province has not been the exception," but rather "constituted a regular ongoing practise which took advantage of a readily available pool of adoptive parents" (329). He highlighted the potential financial motivations underlying such a practice: "With the closing of the residential schools, rather than providing the resources on Reserves to build economic security and providing the services to support responsible parenting, society found it easier and cheaper to remove the children from their homes and apparently fill the market demand for children in Eastern Canada and the United States" through out-of-province adoption (330). Kimelman was unequivocal that "cultural genocide has been taking place in a systematic, routine manner" (328). His conclusion was scathing: "The appalling reality is that everyone involved believed they were doing their best and stood firm in their belief that the system was working well ... The road to hell was paved with good intentions, and the child welfare system was the paving contractor" (276). As a result of Kimelman's report, Manitoba changed some of its child welfare services practices and policies impacting Indigenous communities; other provinces and territories followed suit (Blackstock 2009, 30; R. Sinclair 2017, 10).

The Millennium Scoop: Violent Gestures of Care

Over three decades later, however, little has changed. Some have labelled this ongoing reality the "Millennium Scoop" (CBC Radio 2018). As the TRC highlighted in its 2015 report, "more Aboriginal children are removed from their families today than attended residential schools in any one year" (TRC 2015c, 11). Based on data from the National Household Survey in 2011, Statistics Canada (2013, 5) revealed that while Indigenous children aged fourteen years and under made up 7 per cent of children in Canada, they accounted for almost half (48.1 per cent) of the children in foster care across the country. A spattering of studies from around the same time suggest that Indigenous children from the western provinces (Alberta and British Columbia) made up more than half of the children in care, despite accounting for less than a tenth of the total population of children (Sinha et al. 2011, 5). In central Canada (Manitoba and Saskatchewan), the figures were even more staggering with Indigenous children making up over 80 per cent of the children in care, even though they made up less than a quarter of all children in each of those provinces (Sinha et al. 2011, 5). In Quebec, Indigenous children made up 10 per cent of the children in care despite constituting only 2 per cent of the total population of children (Sinha et al. 2011, 5). The Viens Commission's final report states that "compared to non-Indigenous children, the percentage of First Nations children placed in alternate care (regular foster care, kinship foster care, extended family, rehabilitation centres or group homes) is nearly eight times higher," while "Indigenous children are ... five and a half times more likely to be placed in foster care than non-Indigenous children" (Viens Commission 2019, 121–2). These figures may be an underestimate because, unlike in other provinces, not all youth protection centres in Quebec keep track of the number of Indigenous children in foster care (Curtis 2019). Regardless, the "over-representation of Indigenous children in Québec's youth protection service is a recognized fact" (Viens Commission 2019, 121).

Reports of abuses, too, continue. In December 2018, cbc *News* revealed that Inuit youth were not allowed to speak Inuktitut among themselves in two Montreal group homes. The same news story reported that the Viens Commission heard testimony from an Atikamekw couple whose daughter, who was staying at a youth rehabilitation centre in Trois-Rivières in 2007, had been punished for speaking her language by being put in isolation; she told her parents that other Atikamekw youth had received similar punishment, even for speaking their language at lunchtime (MacLellan 2018).

In November 2019, a scathing report on how youth protection services in Montreal dealt with Indigenous children and families was released. The action research project had found that Indigenous families faced systemic discrimination and that Indigenous Peoples are grossly underrepresented among the staff of youth protection services, though there is no budget to educate non-Indigenous staff about "the historical and ongoing effects of colonialism on Indigenous communities" (Fast et al. 2019, 8–10). An expert commenting on the report was blunt: "Indigenous kids are being warehoused in the system until they age out of it" (Curtis 2019).

In a 2017 special issue of the "First Peoples Child & Family Review" on Indigenous children in foster care, Sixties Scoop Survivor and social work professor Raven Sinclair explains how racial bias, systemic racism, and colonial ideologies in child welfare and legal systems have allowed such a situation to persist. Sinclair also points to the role of financial incentives as being an explanation for these practices to continue in various jurisdictions across the country: "From speaking with many people working in Indigenous child welfare agencies across the country, I have learned that Provincial Ministries benefit through per capita transfer payments for Indigenous children in care and also receive the per capita child tax benefits for any child who is in the care of the system." Echoing the implied criticism about economic factors underpinning the practice in Manitoba from Kimelman's 1985 report, Sinclair goes on to state that "if the Indigenous child welfare system has become an economy and is operating to the benefit of foster parents and mainstream social work infrastructures, the will to disassemble that system will be limited and, indeed, actively resisted" by those who gain from it (R. Sinclair 2017, 14).

In Cindy Blackstock's 2009 article, "The Occasional Evil of Angels: Learning from the Experiences of Aboriginal Peoples and Social Work," she explored why and how social workers – individually and as a profession – have not only allowed this decades-long travesty to continue but have played a major role in its execution. She identified that "professional oversight bodies did not effectively monitor the quality of child welfare services mainstream social workers began providing on reserves," which, accompanied "by a systemic ignorance of the impacts of colonization often resulted in mass removals" (Blackstock 2009, 30). She listed the default arguments that are often invoked to exceptionalize and/or justify such complicit or overtly harmful behaviour (e.g., people were just doing their job, they acted based on the norms of the time, etc.), and then debunked them one by one (32). Blackstock concluded that "social work misplaced its moral compass and in doing so perpetrated preventable harms to Aboriginal children" (35).

Building on the considerations raised by Blackstock and others specifically about residential schools and the Sixties Scoop in their recent book, *A Violent History of Benevolence: Interlocking Oppression in the Moral Economies of Social Working*, professor Chris Chapman and anti-poverty organizer A.J. Withers provide a critical and insightful observation about the role played by health care workers in a system that is anything but apolitical: "Care, whether professional or otherwise, might very well be genuine, heart-felt, and sometimes even appreciated, but this characterization doesn't disentangle it from the political dream in which it's rooted. If that political dream is one in which others' lifeworlds are to be extinguished for the good of all, then the violences of genocide and eugenics live on in even the gentlest and most necessary gestures of care" (Chapman and Withers 2019, 310).

"Shipped like cargo": Mass Medical Evacuations

Over the span of more than a century, genocidal practices and policies institutionalized the forced transfer of Indigenous children to residential schools and, right up until the present day, through the child welfare system. Health care professionals, including physicians and social workers, played important roles in these initiatives, but it can be argued that the practices and policies themselves were not necessarily dependent on health care providers to succeed because governments ensured their execution.

There is, however, a harrowing example in Canadian history of physicians, at the helm of federal health care services, piloting the forced removal of Indigenous children. The large-scale evacuations of Indigenous Peoples suspected of having tuberculosis throughout Canada, but particularly the Nunavimmiut and Nunavummiut, resulted in their mass institutionalization in medical establishments in southern Canada under the direct care of non-Indigenous physicians in a colonial medical system. These doctors, predominantly white men, decided who would be hospitalized, for how long, and under what conditions. Indigenous Peoples of all ages were evacuated from their communities, sometimes hundreds and even thousands of kilometres away, but children were particularly impacted by these forced removals.

One such child was Titus Allooloo. He was barely school-aged in the 1960s when he was evacuated from Mittimatalik (Pond Inlet), Nunavut, to Quebec City, and then to Hamilton because he was suspected to have TB. At the Mountain Sanatorium there, he suffered physical abuse, including being restrained in a harness and getting strapped if he took it off (Grygier 1994, 110). After a few months at the sanatorium, he was found to be clear of TB after all. He spent time with a foster family awaiting transport home before being bused to Toronto and then sent by plane to Iqaluit. Once there, he repeatedly ran away from his assigned family in nearby Apex: "I was on my own, basically." He remained there for almost half a year until "Indian and Northern Affairs found me and said I'm going home." He did ultimately return to Mittimatalik (Grygier 1994, 121–2).

Beginning in the late-1940s, the federal government finally decided to address tuberculosis-related illnesses and deaths that had reached catastrophic levels in Inuit communities scattered throughout the Arctic and Subarctic regions of the Canadian landmass. After ignoring multiple and repeated warnings about alarming conditions for years, if not decades, the federal government was forced to respond amid pressures both within and outside of its bureaucracies, but also for self-interested reasons (see Grygier 1994, 56–65; Lux 2016, 25–46; Olofsson et al. 2008, 129; Selway 2016, 24–30; Tester et al. 2001, 122–4; Tester 2017, 31–3; Vanast 1991, 55–73).

The role of physicians in what would become known as the mass medical evacuations of Inuit was significant, which I explore further in Chapter 13. Dr Percy E. Moore was director of Indian Health Service (IHS) in the Department of Mines and Resources until these medical responsibilities were transferred to the Department of Health and Welfare in the mid-1940s (Nixon 1988, 76). There, Moore quickly went about instituting the policy of evacuating "serious but treatable" and long-term patients to medical facilities (i.e., hospitals and sanatoria) in southern Canada (Nixon 1988, 77, 82n29; Grygier 1994, 74). The Eastern Arctic Medical Patrol (EAMP) would locate cases of TB, while "redundant military hospitals were purchased for the treatment of Inuit evacuees" (Nixon 1988, 76). Meanwhile, "the controversial BCG vaccine, although selectively employed in southern Canada, was aggressively applied to all Inuit" whose TB skin tests were negative (Nixon 1988, 76–7).

The EAMP first sailed to northern areas aboard the CGS *Arctic* in 1922, with only one medical officer aboard (Hicks 1969, 537). Historically, the medical mission was only a component of the Eastern Arctic Patrol which was "initially a part of the resupply of Hudson Bay Company posts and a physician usually travelled with the ship" (Martin 1981, 80–1). The Eastern Arctic Patrol "made its annual voyage through the long, late Arctic summer days, ploughing through ice, storm, and fog, calling at tiny isolated settlements, supplying goods and personnel, carrying scientific expeditions, checking on administration and health, administering justice, dispensing medicine, and transporting Inuit to and from hospital and between settlements" (Grygier 1994, 86). Over time, the medical component took on more prominence than other aspects of the Eastern Arctic Patrol (Grygier 1994, 100).

In 1933, the Hudson's Bay Company provided the RMS *Nascopie* for the EAMP (Hicks 1969, 538). The first evacuations of Inuit from northern communities occurred on this vessel in 1946, but a shipwreck the following year temporarily put the novel intensive medical survey approach out of commission (Selway 2016, 104; Grygier 1994, 89). The federal government replaced it with the *C.D. Howe*, a coastguard ship. Built in Quebec and specifically designed as a medical and cargo vessel for the Arctic by a Montreal-based enterprise, it was capable of carrying 1,000 tons of cargo and eighty-eight passengers. Operated by the Department of Transport, the ship was equipped with health care facilities that included "an operating room, a sick bay with beds for six patients, a dispensary, a complete dental office, an x-ray room, and a darkroom" (Grygier 1994, 89). Clinical services were provided by a team of two dentists, an eye specialist, a handful of general practitioners, a radiologist, and several nurses (Martin 1981, 81). There was even a helicopter and landing pad.

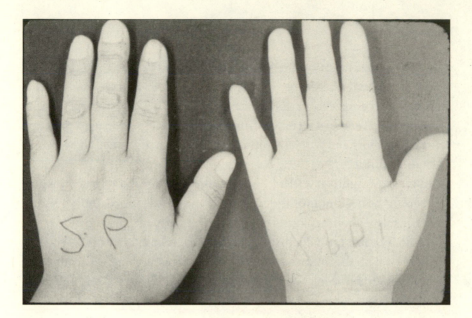

Figure 11.1 Markings on the hands of an Inuk, 1958.
Image from Johanna Rabinowitz fonds (original in colour). Used with permission from Health Sciences Archives, McMaster University.

The *C.D. Howe* allowed the EAMP evacuations of Inuit to occur on a mass scale, beginning with its inaugural voyage in 1950 (Hicks 1969, 538). The ship was decommissioned in 1968 "when other means of servicing the eastern arctic Inuit were found to be more efficient and practical" (Martin 1981, 81). What occurred in the intervening years "is likely the largest relocation of people within Canada for medical reasons" (Tester 2017, 32).

After 1945, the EAMP personnel was enlarged. Assessments conducted in the ports where the *C.D. Howe* stopped were run like a "production-line system" (Grygier 1994, 88). All Inuit community members were summoned. After registering, individuals would be assigned a serial number that was written on a hand or arm based on the order in which they were seen on the ship, which Inuit referred to as *matavik*, or "where you strip" in Inuktitut (Lux 2016, 99). They would then have their chest X-ray taken, a physician and dentist would perform a physical examination, and a nurse would immunize them. As shown in Figure 11.1, letters were written on the other hand as the individual went through the process: X, P, D, and I, representing X-ray, physician, dentist, and immunization (Olofsson et al. 2008, 131). Inuit "were 'shuffled through' mostly by signs" (Grygier 1994, 96). At the end of this process, an arrow drawn underneath the letters written on their hand served as a pass to get off the ship and return to the mainland. However, if the individual was deemed to be infected, "TB" was written instead, marking them for evacuation to a medical facility in southern Canada (Olofsson et al. 2008, 131). This cold, methodical process dictated by the ship's time constraints and with an emphasis on efficiency applied to everyone, including children.

At the community level, there was no consultation about the entire process. From the beginning of the expanded EAMP evaluations, Inuit were not even consulted about exploring options of TB treatment closer to home (Selway 2016, 19). Robert Williamson, a former federal welfare worker who had spent years with the Inuit as an anthropological researcher, recalled that the "way in which the people were picked up and herded into the ship and taken away" was "coercive and insensitive" (Grygier 1994, 97).

On an individual level, informed consent was nonexistent for a multitude of reasons. Interpretation services were imperfect at best, and even if communication was possible, prospective patients "had little chance of talking or arguing with the officials even if they felt so inclined" (Grygier 1994, 96). Records suggest that a standard consent form, titled "Agreement to Accept Medical and Surgical Treatment," was used on the *C.D. Howe* as of 1957 and possibly even before that (Selway 2016, 120). However, there are no indications that it was translated to Inuktitut. The relevant section reads as follows: "I authorize to be performed on my person whatever examination, treatment, or operation is indicated in the opinion of the medical authorities and I undertake to co-operate fully in all measures to maintain treatment and discipline" (120). This was the antithesis of what we now regard as free and informed medical consent. Signing was basically foregoing all control of health care decisions over one's body – or, if signing as a child's guardian, giving up such parental rights – for an indefinite period, and over all medical and surgical interventions. There is no mention of the necessity of the treatments or the risks involved. Most non-Indigenous people would never have been forced to sign such a far-reaching document for medical care. Some Inuit were resigned to being evacuated "because they recognised that they were ill and felt that the hospitals in the South were their only hope" (Olofsson et al. 2008, 134). However, it is important to realize that others complied "in part because they did not feel it was within their power to refuse" and that, tellingly, "many felt intimidated by non-Inuit Canadians, the police, the minister, and others working in the North" (Olofsson et al. 2008, 134). The federal government also coercively tied material support for Inuit families and their communities with participation in the medical assessments, by "streamlining the Welfare Section's operations with regard to the follow-up of patients, [and] the administration of relief in the settlements" (Grygier 1994, 99). Medical historian Maureen Lux explains that government officials "flat out would not pay people their treaty annuity until they had their chest x-ray" (Moore 2017). Consent requires that it be given freely; without a major effort to level out the playing field, can this ever have been possible in a colonial context when such a significant power discrepancy existed between the government and its medical establishment on the one hand, and Inuit communities on the other?

As outlined in the Qikiqtani Truth Commission (QTC) report, medical professionals who were part of the EAMP on the *C.D. Howe* "screened Inuit for tuberculosis and other infectious diseases or ailments, and those found to be infected or sick were removed without notice for indefinite stays in southern hospitals" (QIA 2014, 46). A government official confirmed that it "was not unusual for an Inuit person to be evacuated immediately on board this vessel" (Martin 1981, 81). In fact, not only was it not unusual, but Inuit identified for evacuation were confined to the ship, certainly in the earlier years of these expanded medical patrols: "the evacuees were not allowed to go ashore to collect belongings, to say goodbye, or to make arrangements for their families or goods" (Grygier 1994, 96). If a mother was judged sick but her children were not infected, they were given to another Inuk woman going off the ship and returning to the community; this included unweaned babies who were still dependent on their mothers for breastfeeding (96). Inuit children of all ages suspected of having tuberculosis "would be taken from their parents and sent with the boat" without a caregiver (Olofsson et al. 2008, 131). This is an early example of how the medical system felt justified in carrying out such a practice of transferring children for health care services without family accompaniment. Whether a child or their caregiving family member(s) had been evacuated to the South, the result was the same: "Children were without parents for an extended period of time" (Tester 2017, 33).

The QTC report stated that "those sent south for treatment often endured weeks on board the ship before they spent many months or years in treatment, far away from their families" (QIA 2014, 46). The average duration of institutionalization for TB in southern medical establishments (hospitals or sanatoria) at the time was around two-and-a-half years (Grygier 1994, xxii; Nixon 1988, 67). In some cases, children were hospitalized for as long as "six or seven years without any contact with their parents" (Grygier 1994, 95). Maggie Hatuk, a Nunavimmiuq from Kangirsuk, was evacuated in 1945 in the very early days of the anti-TB southern hospitalization program and before the construction of the *C.D. Howe* (evacuations also occurred aboard other ships and, as early as the 1950s, by plane [Grygier 1994, 102, 105]). She eventually arrived at the Weston Sanatorium in Toronto and underwent treatment and extensive surgeries for two years for presumed tuberculosis of the spine (Selway 2016, 178). It is no wonder that to "the Inuit, it was often as though a child had been kidnapped and lost for ever," while "their inability to do anything about it except ask the 'kidnappers' for news (which, if it came at all, came slowly, rarely and sparsely) must have made the anguish even worse" (Grygier 1994, 128).

Being ordered to be evacuated by medical professionals was understandably a frightening experience because many "had seen other members of the community, friends and relatives leave for a hospital in the South, never to return" (Olofsson et al. 2008, 131). This helps explain why some individuals would "hide out on the land once they had heard that the hospital boat was arriving" (131). As testimonies at the QTC confirmed, however, those "who refused to be screened or were known to be sick were sometimes tracked down ... by the ship's helicopter" and brought to the ship to be examined (QIA, 2014, 46; see also Olofsson et al. 2008, 131).

The lack of news about loved ones while hospitalized was also a key factor contributing to the fear of being forcibly evacuated. Anglican missionary Brian Burrows, who had spent five years in Puvirnituq (Nunavik) in the 1960s, was critical of authorities for not having provided meaningful and regular updates to families in the North about their loved ones hospitalized in the South, including informing parents where their children were. He concluded that this was because the government "refused to believe that they [Inuit] were people" (Grygier 1994, 123). Because the communication between southern medical establishments and northern communities was so deficient, "and because so many of the patients taken out in the early days were far advanced in the disease and required many years of treatment (or indeed died of it in the South), the Inuit regarded going out on the boat virtually as a death sentence" (97).

Being on the *C.D. Howe* was, in fact, a death sentence for one twelve-year-old Inuk boy. A 1954 article in the *Vancouver Sun* reported that the child was returning on the *C.D. Howe* and slipped off the Churchill docks. He drowned while the ship's crew looked on. When asked why he hadn't intervened, one witness – a six-foot-tall man who admitted he could swim – responded that "no man could last in that water." However, as the *Sun* journalist went on to note, "the water in the Churchill River, where the tragedy occurred, was so warm that children were swimming" in it. The "needless death was made even more tragic" because the Inuk boy was "happily returning to his people" after having survived tuberculosis treatment at a southern hospital (Burke 1954, 3). In *A Long Way from Home: The Tuberculosis Epidemic among the Inuit*, Pat Sandiford Grygier (1994, 94) suggests that the "lethargy and inexperience of the crew and the poor state of readiness of the equipment may well have been at least partly responsible" for this boy's death. The journalist who was accompanying the ship was less forgiving of the crew (Burke 1954, 3). Safety concerns about the ship and its crew had been raised over the years; critical reports were filed internally, and media articles were published in the mainstream press (Burke 1954, 3; see also Grygier 1994, 91–2). It is unclear to what extent concerns about Inuit safety and well-being were addressed. For example, there were no instructions for boat drills, fires, or other emergencies on the ship in Inuktitut, despite the fact that "most Inuit were on a ship for the first time and would not be likely to know what to do in an emergency" (Grygier 1994, 92).

Depending on the ship's route and where they lived, some evacuees spent two to three months at sea (Grygier, 1994, 87, 98). Titus Allooloo, forcibly evacuated for tuberculosis treatment as a young child, couldn't eat or do anything because he was suffering from motion sickness, "throwing up all the time" for the first two weeks on the *C.D. Howe* (108, 121). Once aboard the vessel, Inuit "were unable to communicate with the crew or most of the government party and were now totally dependent on the authorities" to return home (97). Some Inuit referred to the ship's crew as "the big fools" (Burke 1954, 3). Thinking back to his experience as a passenger on the *C.D. Howe* among the Inuit in 1953–54, anthropological researcher Williamson recounted that "in the stormy seas they were sick, they were terrified, they were demoralized. They were frightened of what was happening to them, of what was likely to happen to them" (Grygier 1994, 86). Indeed, Inuit evacuees "were sick, unused to sea travel, confined for most of the time to the least comfortable and most crowded part of the ship, with little to do but worry" (97).

It is true that the crew and first-class passengers were in separate quarters, while the Inuit were put in the bow of the ship (Grygier 1994, 89). However, their experience went beyond simply being confined to the "least comfortable" and "most crowded" part of the ship. Jonah Apak, a Nunavummiuq from Kanngiqtugaapik (Clyde River), was also a child when he was evacuated. During his testimony at the QTC, he shared how the EAMP had "segregated the Inuit to the area where it was the bumpiest. We were treated like lower-class people" (QIA 2014, 46). Despite its sophistication, the ship nonetheless reflected the segregation that was the norm for Indigenous Peoples in the health care system at the time.

In the early years of the southern hospitalization program, "Inuit requiring hospitalization treatment, whether for TB or for some other cause, were sent, in the words of one doctor, to wherever there happened to be a bed vacant," except for British Columbia, New Brunswick, and Prince Edward Island, where there were no Inuit evacuees (Grygier 1994, 75). Hospitalization was loosely regionalized. Inuit from the western Arctic (including the Northwest Territories and what is now known as the Kitikmeot region of Nunavut) would usually be admitted to the Charles Camsell Indian Hospital in Edmonton. Those from the central Arctic (including the Kivalliq region of Nunavut) would be sent to medical facilities in Manitoba and Saskatchewan. Evacuees from the eastern Arctic (including the Qikiqtaaluk region of Nunavut, and Nunavik) were initially scattered throughout hospitals in the Maritimes, Quebec, and Ontario (Grygier 1994, 72). Inuit evacuees were admitted to Indian hospitals (some of which are shown in Figure 11.2) but were hospitalized at nonsegregated federal or provincial health care institutions as well. Between the 1940s and 1960s, Inuit evacuees were sent to eighty or so hospitals – whether segregated or not – across the country (Grygier 1994, 81).

Once *C.D. Howe* evacuees arrived at port in Quebec City, some would be transported, typically by train, to hospitals and sanatoria in other parts of

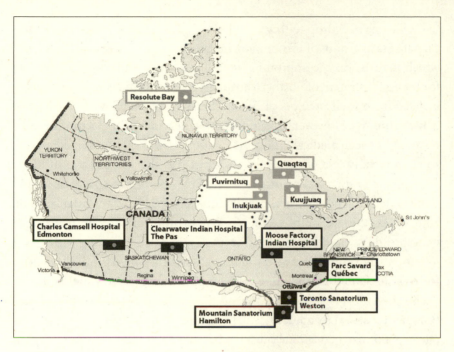

Figure 11.2 "Indian hospitals" and sanatoria used for tuberculosis treatment in Canada
Original map by Scott Park, used with permission (Olofsson et al. 2008, 130).

the province (there were a handful of institutions, mostly concentrated in or around Montreal) or to other provinces (see Grygier 1994, 77). If they stayed in Quebec City, they would be hospitalized at the Parc Savard Indian Hospital, which had previously been a quarantine hospital for immigrants (Lux 2016, 115). In June 1953, the largest number of Inuit evacuees were admitted to the Charles Camsell Indian Hospital (130 patients) and the Parc Savard Hospital (102 patients); the institution with the third-largest population of Inuit admissions was the Mountain Sanatorium in Hamilton, Ontario, where there were eight evacuees (Grygier 1994, 77). Around this time, the advent of isoniazid (or isonicotinic acid hydrazide, INH), a more effective antituberculosis medication, played a role in shifting the hospitalization of evacuees coming from the eastern Arctic and northern Quebec directly to the Mountain Sanatorium (where the staff had developed experience using isoniazid), instead of Parc Savard Hospital. This shift also occurred by transferring patients who were already admitted in another institution (Selway 2016, 34–6, 40, 43).

Serving as backdrop to this was the IHS's decision "to concentrate Inuit TB patients in groups of fifty or more in three or four sanatoria in the South," which, in turn, was a "compromise" to respond to mounting pressures calling for the establishment of northern hospitals because Inuit were being forcibly isolated from their own people in southern hospitals (Grygier 1994, 80–1; Selway 2016, 35). However, Lux importantly identifies other factors for these transfers between medical facilities (Lux 2016, 118–21). She cites "medical reasons" (for example, a surgical procedure not available at a given institution) and "bureaucratic convenience" (i.e., making use of bed space) as factors that would influence transfers of individuals in specific circumstances (Lux 2016, 119). At the level of the health care system more broadly, the increasingly widespread use of effective antituberculosis medications along with a shift to out-patient (rather than in-hospital) treatment afforded primarily to non-Indigenous (and overwhelmingly white) patients heralded what the Canadian Tuberculosis Association dubbed the "miracle of the emptying beds" (Grygier 1994, 12; Lux 2016, 67, 118). Institutions whose beds were at full capacity maximized on federal subsidies based on a per capita funding system that followed Indigenous Peoples to the institutions where they were hospitalized (Selway 2016, 19). As such, Indigenous patients "found themselves moved about (and it is fair to assume they were never consulted) for reasons that had less to do with medical treatment" and more to do with keeping beds filled and safeguarding the financial bottom line of health care institutions (Lux 2016, 68, 120). To put it simply, these health care institutions were benefiting financially from the suffering of Indigenous (i.e., not only Inuit) patients evacuated from their communities across the country.

Very early on in the southern hospitalization program, Dr Percy E. Moore himself wrote that it was the policy of his IHS to prioritize "patients whose condition is such that they are likely to improve with specialist treatment," while leaving those "with no hope of recovery" in their northern communities (Grygier 1994, 73–4). As such, it would stand to reason that children were a significant proportion of the Inuit who were evacuated through this program since they are generally healthier than adults. In 1952, out of ninety Inuit admitted at Parc Savard Indian Hospital, over a third were children (Lux 2016, 114). Some health care institutions, like the Mountain Sanatorium, opened an additional pavilion with a school and a sixty-bed unit for children in 1951; by October 1955, 150 of the institution's 686 patients were children (Selway 2016, 36, 143). Many of these children had already been evacuated once, moved thousands of kilometres to a hospital in the South, and were then at the mercy of the IHS when it came to being transferred again. Predictably, "children were especially vulnerable" (Lux 2016, 119).

Harry Kegiuna was a child when he was evacuated from the North by ship and plane, to eventually be hospitalized at the Charles Camsell Indian Hospital in Edmonton. No one knew his full name there, so he was called "Harry Hospital." After spending seven years at the hospital, he was woken up one night and transferred across the country to Ottawa by train without any explanation (Lux 2016, 119). In October 1953, forty-two of forty-eight transfers from Moose Factory Indian Hospital expected at the Mountain Sanatorium were children, presumably all Inuit (Selway 2016, 35). In January 1955, thirty Inuit children were to be received from Quebec (35). Mini Aodla Freeman, born in 1936 on Cape Hope Island (Nunavut) in James Bay, had been sent to the Moose Factory Indian Hospital and then to the Mountain Sanatorium for a "spot" on her lung when she was a teenager. In her memoir, she wrote critically about not only the fact that Indigenous Peoples were transferred from one institution to another, but also about the dehumanizing nature of the experience: "No preparation, no warning, no choice, and no reason given why they had to go so far away to be cured … we were shipped like cargo and meant to be like cargo" (Aodla Freeman 2015, 189–90).

The evacuations and transfers, along with government bureaucracies that failed to keep track of Inuit admitted to southern hospitals, had severe consequences. Some evacuees disappeared in the system. In certain cases, even the IHS didn't know "where all the hospitalized Inuit were" (Grygier 1994, 75). Government officials and bureaucrats "had, in fact, lost control over the movements of 'their' population" (75). Children were understandably at risk of being "misplaced" for a variety of factors (Lux 2016, 119–20). For instance, most younger Inuit were forced to pick up English or French (depending on where they were evacuated to), but this wouldn't occur immediately upon hospitalization because they'd be learning a completely foreign language. A former naval officer who was chief of the Arctic Division of Northern Affairs and officer-in-charge of the Eastern Arctic Patrol in 1954 acknowledged that "there were a lot of children who were lost because nobody bothered to send their [identifying] discs with them" (Alia 1994, 44; see also Selway 2016, 77, and Grygier 1994, 91). In a letter to a high-level government official in 1954, Anglican missionary Donald Marsh affirmed that Moore himself had publicly stated that he was aware of fifteen unidentified children who could not go home because no one knew where home was for them (Selway 2016, 97). Even when children remained properly identified and were being sent back up north, they were "sometimes off-loaded in the wrong location and had to be accommodated there for a year until the ship returned to take them to where they belonged" (Tester 2017, 33). Titus Allooloo's experience as a young child, described earlier, is evocative in this regard. Babies were not safe either. According to one account from the 1960s, a nurse was asking Nunavimmiut in Inukjuak if the baby she was escorting back home belonged to anyone there. Fortuitously, Rita Burrows, whose spouse was a missionary in Puvirnituq, about 240 kilometres farther north, recognized the baby as belonging to a family from there. The baby reportedly reached its mother eventually (Grygier 1994, 122–3). In other cases, no escort ensured the safe return of a child. For example, Grygier writes about a five-year-old boy who was returned to his home in the North in stages while wearing southern clothing. Staff at a nearby nursing station learned "that a mining exploration charter plane was going near his home and persuaded the party to take the boy along and deliver him on their way." The plane took him but dropped him off on the ice of a frozen lake near the family's hunting camp. They did not wait for someone from the camp to get the boy, nor did they confirm that it was the right camp in the first place. The family rushed out to get the boy, "who was terribly confused, frightened – and cold" because of how inappropriately he'd been dressed for the weather. Echoing Aodla Freeman's scathing critique of the evacuations and hospital transfers, Grygier explains that "in this outfit he had been dumped, like so much cargo, on a sheet of ice" (124).

These stories are of children who were not lost forever in the abyss of the system that IHS had developed. Their stories can be told because they survived their ordeal. How many children didn't make it back to tell their stories? The reality is that "many patients died at hospital and were never returned home, their families left to worry and wonder where they might be" (Lux 2016, 121). The sanatoria deaths were more significant in the earlier years of the forced evacuation program (Grygier 1994, 128). IHS director Dr

Percy E. Moore "cited the ratio of deaths to discharges … as … 13 per cent in hospitals in the South" (74). This mortality rate was better than in northern institutions, but it nonetheless suggested that for every nine people discharged from these hospitals in the South, at least one evacuee had not survived. Communication to advise families of deaths was woefully inadequate, because "the hospital notified the IHS, and the IHS notified Northern Affairs, which in turn notified its contact in the patient's community (usually the Royal Canadian Mounted Police (RCMP) or missionary), who told the relatives" (128). Predictably, "many messages never got through" and even in those that did, there "were no details about the cause of death, no information about the burial, no letter of explanation or condolence – just a radio call or cable or, later, a telephone call through an official" (128). In some cases, it was simply a phone call to a missionary: "Would you tell so-and-so that their baby has died?" (123)

Patients were buried in unmarked graves in a local cemetery, on a reserve, or in the closest municipality, but "the relatives were not told where" (Grygier 1994, 128). If "the family wanted to transport and bury their loved one at home, it would be at their own expense" (Lux 2016, 121). Such a policy "was particularly harsh for northern communities, who could rarely afford the costly flights to return their [deceased] family members" (122). In 1964, Dr Thomas Orford, the IHS regional superintendent for Saskatchewan, stated that the "disposal of the body of an Indian after death is a matter which concerns Indian Affairs Branch. Indian Health Services is concerned only with the living" (Lux 2016, 122). The Indian Affairs Branch, for its part, refused to cover transportation "if this will exceed the cost of burial at the place" where the patient died (122). So, while health care institutions cashed in on federal funding tied to Indigenous bodies occupying hospital beds, no money was allocated to ensure that the individuals who had died in those beds received a dignified burial at home.

Some Indigenous children disappeared into the medical system, dying before they could return to their families; others, some of whom didn't have TB but had been evacuated to southern hospitals with their parents, experienced a permanent rupture from their families and communities after they were placed in the foster care system. Many children were orphaned after being left behind in their communities following their parents' evacuation. While some of these children ended up staying with relatives (either in their community or in another one), others were placed in foster homes, including in "southern" (i.e., white) families (Grygier 1994, 101–2). When several family members were evacuated together, children with tuberculosis were usually "separated from their parents and sent to the children's ward" (Olofsson et al. 2008, 137). The first planeload of Inuit patients who were transferred directly from Iqaluit to Hamilton in 1953 for TB treatment were of all ages, including very young healthy children and babies who were evacuated with their mothers (Grygier 1994, 105–6). Aodla Freeman, who later became an official government interpreter, met this group at the airport. She recalls that "women were crying, really, because they were being separated from the children and the babies they had at their breast" (Grygier 1994, 106).

Indeed, some babies "came with their sick mothers as infants at the breast," while others were "born in hospital when pregnant women were brought out" (Grygier 1994, 125). Because the medical teams did not want to keep the babies in the sanatoria, and a rule prevented any infant less than six months of age from being sent north, these children were placed with foster families (Grygier 1994, 125; Tester 2017, 33). Some doctors would use their contacts with the government bureaucracy "to place the children in care on a local Indian reserve," usually on "a ward of an Indian Affairs hospital, where they received only minimal care and little stimulation" (Grygier 1994, 126). Some of these children may have been fostered or informally adopted by non-Indigenous health care staff, which occurred more commonly if the mother died in hospital. Whether due to maternal death, inadequate records and communication, or the precipitous separation of the infant from its mother, identifying the families of many infants from northern communities was often difficult, which is why "quite a few children were 'lost' to the Inuit community this way and remained down south" (Grygier 1994, 126). One physician at the Dynevor Indian Hospital in Selkirk, Manitoba, "hoped to keep one of his 'cute' Inuit patients" through adoption, but this did not happen because the child expressed that he wanted to return home to his family (Lux 2016, 119–20).

In 1956, the government "began to organize foster-home placement for Inuit children who were orphans or were disabled and required special care which families could not provide" (Grygier 1994, 126). Social worker Betty Marwood, integral to the EAMPs in the late 1950s and early 1960s, played an important role in getting the Children's Aid Society of Hamilton and the

Protestant Children's Homes in Montreal to arrange foster care for these children (127).

Predictably, the forced transfer of Inuit children to southern medical institutions and placement in foster care (even if temporary) had major impacts on language and culture. Sarah Saimaiyuk, a Nunavummiuq from Pangnirtung transferred to Moose Factory by plane and then Hamilton by train in the 1950s, has explained how language barriers, being on a plane for the first time, and a profound fear of white people prevented her from asking for something as basic as water for herself and her younger siblings during the flight (Saimaiyuk 1990, 21). Upon arrival at the hospital, proficient interpreters were rarely present to orient those who only spoke Inuktitut or to provide medical explanations for their conditions and transfer (Olofsson et al. 2008, 135). In some cases, Inuit children would get yelled at in French or English, which they didn't initially understand (137). Testimonies provided to the QTC revealed that Inuit children were "forbidden to speak Inuktitut" in the schools that they attended while being treated (QIA 2014, 46). Even in situations when children were not actively prevented or punished for speaking Inuktitut, the younger ones often lost their language during their prolonged hospitalizations.

Former evacuee Aodla Freeman visited Inuit patients at the St Boniface Hospital in Manitoba as an interpreter in 1957. There, she met a child who could no longer speak Inuktitut at all. She lamented that "this was as sad as any illness. How will he communicate with his parents when he goes home?" (Lux 2016, 119). Life for those children who were eventually able to return home from Quebec hospitals was particularly challenging because they had "learned French in the hospital school, lost what Inuit language and skills they had, and then returned to an Inuktitut-speaking family and an English-language school system" (Grygier 1994, 125). A woman from Kuujjuaq who had been hospitalized at Roberval, in Quebec, shared how difficult it was "trying to talk to your Mom when you don't understand them and they don't know what you're saying. It was hard" (125). Furthermore, many of the hospitalized children had lost their traditional skills (like hunting and sewing); if they had been very young when evacuated, they might never have acquired these skills in the first place (Olofsson et al. 2008, 141). Individual and collective autonomy, culture, identity, Traditional Knowledge – and, ultimately, survival – were all at play. As such, children who returned after long hospitalizations had to work to reclaim these skills because "language, sewing and hunting were important to master not only for survival but also as outward proof of Inuit identity" (141).

The medical system, with physicians calling the shots, knowingly and forcibly transferred Inuit children to southern health care institutions where many would subsequently be placed in foster care. Children's ties to their family, community, and culture were abruptly severed, oftentimes permanently.

Medical Abductions and Disappearances: Assimilation, Oppression, and Death

Further explored in Chapter 13, many connections and parallels can be drawn between the mass tuberculosis evacuations of Nunavimmiut and Nunavummiut from the late 1940s to the 1960s and the disproportionate burden of ÉVAQ's non-accompaniment practice borne by northern and remote Indigenous communities in Quebec from the 1980s until the fall of 2018. However, another important historical aspect serves as a narrative bridge between these two discrete periods.

In the last few years, disparate Indigenous communities in Quebec have been speaking out about their children having been disappeared by the medical system. From the 1950s until at least the 1970s (before ÉVAQ was established by the provincial government), Indigenous children were transferred – almost always by plane and alone – to hospitals in both rural and urban centres for emergency medical care, and never returned home.

In November 2015, investigative reporter Anne Panasuk of Radio-Canada's *Enquête* revealed that eight individuals (revised to nine in a subsequent report) had disappeared from the Innu community of Pakuashipi in 1972. They had been transferred to the hospital in Blanc-Sablon, 200 kilometres away and never returned (Panasuk 2015). This accounted for a tenth of the entire population of Pakuashipi, located in Quebec's Lower North Shore, which had a total of around eighty people at the time. To put this in context in terms of relative demographic weight for a city like Montreal, this would be equivalent to the disappearance of the entire population of its most populous borough, Côte-des-Neiges-Nôtre-Dame-de-Grâce, which makes up 9.8 per cent of the population of Montreal (Ville de Montréal 2018, 5). There is a nuance to this comparison, of course; in the case of

1972 Pakuashipi, the disappeared were all children, including babies. They had been evacuated by plane, alone, because their parents had been prevented from accompanying them. They never saw their children again, alive or dead. The families didn't know what happened; they received no death certificate or medical file. Some believed that the children had been adopted in secrecy, while others believed that they'd been medically mistreated or even killed. Four decades after the medical disappearances, with help from the *Enquête* investigative team, the families finally got access to some of their children's medical records and received the heartbreaking news that all of the children had died. The cause of death was bronchiolitis or bronchopneumonia (respiratory illnesses) for all except for one of them; the medical chart for Monique indicated that although she had been admitted for this reason, she died from an upper airway obstruction, presumably as a result of choking. Agnès Poker, her mother, wondered why the medical team would have given her something to eat that she could have choked on as "she was only three months old and only took the bottle" (Panasuk 2015). As Charles Mark, a member of the Pakuashipi community, stated in an interview (through an interpreter), "when you're not a witness and you don't have proof, it's normal to have doubts" about what happened to those children (Panasuk 2015).

Following Panasuk's initial exclusive for *Enquête*, she was contacted by Indigenous families from other communities with similar disturbing stories. In November 2017, *Enquête* ran a second feature with a focus on the Atikamekw communities of Manawan, Opitciwan, and Wemotaci. Panasuk affirmed that not a single Atikamekw family from Quebec's Upper Mauricie region was spared from the disappearance of a child in the late 1960s and throughout the 1970s (Panasuk 2017). Several families shared their stories.

Diane Petiguay had been transferred from Wemotaci to the hospital in La Tuque for pneumonia at around six months of age but was placed with a white foster family without her parents' knowledge. She found her birth family as an adolescent but was only able to communicate with them in French. The family later learned that a priest had given Diane's mother a form to sign around the time of the hospitalization that she'd understood to be an authorization for Diane to receive medical care. It turns out that the form was a waiver to confirm parental abandonment. The form was in French; Diane's mother spoke only Atikamekw (Panasuk 2017).

Marcel Awashish, from Opitciwan, broke his arm while playing near his bed and was transferred to the hospital in Amos, but then was disappeared by the health care system. Years later, his family found him in Montreal, where he had been put on an adoption list. He was reunited with his family, but his sister Suzanne explained that while he was happy to be home, it was difficult to communicate with him because he now only spoke English (Panasuk 2017).

Lauréanna was sent from Manawan to a hospital in Joliette – alone, by plane – when she was only two months old. After reportedly improving, she died suddenly one month later. The family was informed about her death in this case and made the 200-kilometre trip intending to bring her back to bury her in their community. However, she was quickly buried in Joliette. The family maintains that the body they were shown was not of their baby, but of a much older infant. They remained skeptical of the medical authorities' claim that she was buried at the cemetery in a common grave for unclaimed bodies. A former social worker later confirmed that Lauréanna had not been buried in the cemetery, but rather in an adjacent field. The family is convinced that infants were switched at the hospital and that their child is still alive (Panasuk 2017; Nadeau 2017).

In a subsequent follow-up report aired by *Enquête* in February 2019, Panasuk reported that thirty-four children were missing from that era between all three Atikamekw communities. Had they died? Were they placed in foster care or adopted? The parents had to fight against a heavy medical bureaucracy to try to get any information; in a Kafkaesque twist, hospitals informed them that since their children would now be adults, only they can ask for their medical files. The families ended up filing "missing person" reports for their children, forcing the provincial police, the Sureté du Québec, to create a special unit to investigate the matter (Panasuk 2019). In early 2020, the Assembly of First Nations of Quebec and Labrador, along with opposition parties and the Quebec Ombudsman, criticized the provincial government's response as being inadequate and undignified (Sioui 2020).

In 2017, *La Presse* investigative journalists Gabrielle Duchaine and Olivier Jean ran an exclusive investigative story about two Algonquin siblings from Pikogan, in the Abitibi-Témiscamingue region, who disappeared into the medical system barely a year apart. In 1958, Tony Ruperthouse, one-and-a-half years old at the time, was flown out to the hospital in Amos for respiratory difficulty. The following day, his mother was told that he had died. In the part of the chart that they were able to obtain, the journalists made note of three words scribbled by the physician –"transfer, Quebec, lungs" – with the diagnosis of "bronchopneumonia" and a question mark appearing beside "TB." There is no paper trail of Tony's presumed hospitalization in Quebec City. Over a year later, on 29 December 1959, he was admitted at Sainte-Anne Hospital in Baie-Saint-Paul, where he died at seven years of age in 1965. He was buried in a common grave reserved for patients without family. The family was not informed of any of this at the time. In the summer of 1959, Emily Ruperthouse, who was around five years old, was hospitalized in Amos after being stung by a bee while playing outside. She was then airlifted to another hospital that the family had understood was in Montreal. By December 1959, she also ended up at the Sainte-Anne Hospital, but there's no indication that the hospital made any connection between the siblings who overlapped in their institution for several years. In the early 1990s, Françoise, one of Emily's siblings, found her with the help of the Quebec Native Friendship Centre after an uncle had heard that she may be alive. At Sainte-Anne Hospital, her name was now Germaine and the medical staff had always been under the impression that she didn't have any family. She was in her thirties and could not walk or speak. The family never found out what happened to her for all those years. They managed to place her in a long-term care facility closer to them, in Amos. She died in 2010 and was buried in a cemetery in Pikogan (Duchaine and Jean 2017; Shingler 2018).

These stories, and many more like them, were shared with the National Inquiry into Missing and Murdered Indigenous Women and Girls (MMIWG) when it held hearings in the province of Quebec. In its Quebec-specific report, the MMIWG Inquiry stated that "some witnesses are convinced that the babies were kidnapped to be used in medical experiments or sold to non-Indigenous families" (MMIWG 2019c, 107). As highlighted in the testimonies heard by the commissioners of the MMIWG Inquiry, "the parents were not informed of the state of their children's health ... they were not consulted about the care provided to their children, and ... they were denied the power to consent or to withhold consent regarding their children's transfer to specialized centres or long-term care facilities" (MMIWG 2019c, 109). The medical establishment, physicians in particular, bear a significant responsibility for this, especially because when "their children died, the parents were not told the truth about the circumstances of the deaths or where their children were buried (109).

The MMIWG's Quebec-specific report highlighted that "health-care and religious authorities acted paternalistically, appropriating those [parental] rights and exercising them arbitrarily to the detriment of Indigenous parents, and made decisions they had no right to make" (MMIWG 2019c, 109). This is borne out by the interviews and news coverage on the matter. For Panasuk's investigative report about the disappeared Atikamekw children, she interviewed Marie-Pierre Bousquet, an anthropologist and the program director of Indigenous studies at the Université de Montréal. Bousquet stated that she never found a specific governmental directive to account for the placement of Indigenous children who had been hospitalized, but "this sort of case was common enough" in many Indigenous communities in Quebec (Panasuk 2017). In another interview, Anne-Diane Béliveau, a social worker hired to develop services in Manawan in 1973, highlighted how certain physicians working with Atikamekw communities at that time took it upon themselves to signal a child for placement in foster care for unjustified reasons (Panasuk 2017). Lucia Ferretti, a scholar who has studied the history of Sainte-Anne Hospital where the Ruperthouse siblings Tony and Emily spent most of their lives, explained to *La Presse* journalists that several children with a presumed "intellectual deficiency" from Indigenous communities around Sept-Îles and Chicoutimi were admitted there between 1945 and 1955. According to her, nurses working in dispensaries and nursing stations identified babies who appeared to be "intellectually handicapped." The decision to place them was made by one of three figures who had the power to do so in Quebec at the time – priests, public health inspectors, and doctors (Duchaine and Jean, 2017). In the interview with Panasuk, however, Marie-Pierre Bousquet argued that the problem was much more pervasive: "It wasn't necessarily the doctors or the social workers or the missionaries or the representatives for Indian Affairs who took those sorts of decisions. It was a general mentality" (Panasuk 2017). In March 2018, after hearing the testimonies of many Indigenous children having been disappeared by the medical system, MMIWG commissioner Michele Audette told the CBC that "after looking at all the documents that we will subpoena, we'll see if there might be a link with the Sixties Scoop" (Shingler 2018).

According to the report from the National Inquiry into MMIWG, the testimonies "support the conclusion that there were other attempts at assimilation and oppression, in particular through various forms of abduction and disappearances of children" and that the disappearances of Indigenous children in Quebec "are a reminder that the actions of governments and churches at that time were aimed primarily at assimilating Indigenous peoples into Canadian society" (MMIWG 2019c, 107–8). These disappearances occurred prior to ÉVAQ being established as *the* governmental medevac airlift service for the entire province in the early 1980s. However, they demonstrate that many Indigenous communities have a long history of traumatic experiences with emergency medical transfers; to some, ÉVAQ's non-accompaniment rule may have been perceived as a continuation of the same practices that resulted in their children never coming home.

The broader context of what happened to the Innu of Pakuashipi illustrates governmental assimilationist motives well. In 1961, the Innu of Pakuashipi had been deported by the federal government on order of the powerful Catholic priest Alexis Joveneau, who, according to a slew of devastating MMIWG testimonies, is alleged to have sexually abused and assaulted Innu children for decades (Page 2017). Jouveneau felt that all the Innu of the region should be in one place, in Unamen Shipu (also known as La Romaine). Many Innu defied what they considered then – and anthropologists recognize now – to be nothing less than deportation by undertaking the month-long, 175-kilometre journey to return to their lands near the Saint-Augustin River in 1963 (Panasuk 2015; Savard 1975, 59). This enraged Joveneau (Panasuk 2015; Page 2017). The community was "ostracized by the civil and religious authorities because of its refusal to remain at Unamen Shipu" (MMIWG 2019c, 108). As a result, government support was cut, which impacted health, nutrition, and other living conditions there (Savard 1975, 60–1). In the early 1970s, the federal government decided to impose the construction of houses (community members were living in canvas tents at the time) with the promise of stemming the high infant mortality rate. However, all the babies born the year following the construction of the houses in 1971 reportedly died (Savard 1975, 60). Anthropologist Rémi Savard, who spent months with the Innu of Pakuashipi, identified the social and political context that led to these newborn deaths: "The infant mortality is related to the social disorganization aggravated by the construction of the houses. This, let's not forget, is part of a more encompassing process of dispossession" (60). In the concluding paragraph, Savard addresses the structural determinants, the "causes of the causes," that certainly also played a role in the conditions leading to the disappearance of Innu children transferred by plane for severe respiratory illnesses months later: "The move from tents to houses at [Pakuashipi] is therefore one episode in a larger process. The forms it takes are sometimes more brutal, sometimes more subtle. Its name is genocide" (Savard 1975, 62; translation from MMIWG 2019c, 108).

Chapter 12

Oral Histories and the Narrative of Genocide

The colonial and genocidal structures maintained for centuries in Canada, as well as in Quebec, provide an environment where racism and indifference towards Indigenous people continues.
– National Inquiry into Missing and Murdered Indigenous Women and Girls

The United Nations' Convention on the Prevention and Punishment of the Crime of Genocide (Genocide Convention) states that "genocide is a crime under international law" (UN 1951). Since the Genocide Convention does not include cultural genocide in its definition, it does not give rise to legal obligations with respect to that form of genocide. This explains, at least in part, why provincial and federal governments are occasionally willing to recognize the finding of cultural genocide when it comes to the state violence inflicted on Indigenous children in Canada. Examples include Justice Edwin Kimelman's report for the Review Committee on Indian and Métis Adoptions and Placements in Manitoba (1985) and Justice Murray Sinclair's final report for the TRC (2015). Yet, when the National Inquiry into Missing and Murdered Indigenous Women and Girls (MMIWG) concluded that the genocide of Indigenous Peoples has occurred in Canada (MMIWG 2019d), it was met with significant backlash. The acceptance of cultural genocide by governments, but also by the public, likely stems from the interpretation that it is somehow considered less grave than the definition set forth in the UN Genocide Convention. However, a fundamental flaw with such an interpretation is that it ignores a critical reality: when survival is taught through culture (language, history, ceremony, etc.) and a direct connection to the land, as is the case for many Indigenous communities, cultural genocide is genocide proper.

As discussed in Chapter 6, colonial nation-states, including Canada, went to great lengths to exclude cultural dimensions from the definition used in the Genocide Convention because they knew that including cultural genocide within such a convention would prohibit assimilationist practices and policies imposed on Indigenous Peoples (Stote 2015, 133). The Canadian government's "assimilative policy" was officially enacted through the Act for Gradual Enfranchisement of Indians in 1869 and the first iteration of the Indian Act in 1876, but its origins can be traced to the "pre-Confederation period of Imperial control of Indian affairs" (Milloy 1999, 9). Over a few years, colonial governments abolished Indigenous governance systems and imposed their own patriarchal worldview, thereby undermining Indigenous women's prominent roles in their communities, including as decision makers (Jacobs 2017, 50). Through reserves and band councils, Canadian colonial legislation controlled all aspects of public and private life in Indigenous communities, including who could identify as "Indian" (Milloy 1999, 20–2). The federal government's thrust was "to divest itself of its legal and financial obligations to Aboriginal people and gain control over their land and resources" (TRC 2015a, 3). Assimilation effectively sought to eliminate Indigenous Peoples *as people* because if "every Aboriginal person had been 'absorbed into the body politic,' there would be no reserves, no Treaties, and no Aboriginal rights" (TRC 2015a, 3). In "Genocide, Indian Policy, and Legislated Elimination of Indians in Canada," Mi'kmaq legal scholar Pamela Palmater writes that "the primary objective of early Indian policy was to ensure the eventual disappearance of Indians – a goal which has not changed in hundreds of years" (Palmater 2014, 27). This is why she refers to *elimination* rather than *assimilation* when speaking of Canadian colonial policy vis-à-vis Indigenous Peoples (Palmater 2014, 32). This is also why some activists and scholars have clarified that what Canada has termed "assimilation" should actually be called "genocide" (Chrisjohn et al. 2017, 101). In *Suffer the Little Children: Genocide, Indigenous Nations and the Canadian State*, Ahtahkakoop Cree legal scholar Tamara Starblanket further explains how "doctrines of racial superiority to address the 'Indian problem' were codified into the Canadian state's destructive colonial legal framework" to take over Indigenous lands and resources to terminate "the national identity of the Original Nations" (Starblanket 2018, 93). The direct destruction of Indigenous bodies and communities since the beginning of colonization has occurred in parallel and in addition to these attempts to eliminate Indigenous identities and nationhoods.

The "traditional" paradigms of genocide (the Holocaust, the Armenian Genocide, the Rwandan Genocide) took place over relatively shorter periods, which has "allowed the Canadian consciousness to dismiss Canada's colonial policies as racist and misconceived, rather than acknowledge them as explicitly genocidal and, even, ongoing" (MMIWG 2019d, 11). As the MMIWG commissioners point out, however, "the insidious and gradual nature of the obliteration of Indigenous peoples ... differentiate *colonial genocide* from our traditional understanding of what constitutes a genocide" (MMIWG 2019d, 11; emphasis added). This explains their position that a nation-state's "specific intent to destroy a protected group can only be proved by the existence of a genocidal policy *or manifest pattern of conduct*" and that "this is particularly inescapable in the context of colonial genocide where ... the internationally wrongful act is slower, more insidious, structural, systemic, and often spans multiple administrations and political leadership" that use "varied tactics against distinct Indigenous communities" (MMIWG 2019d, 9, 20; emphasis added).

The examples provided thus far in this book are not meant to be a comprehensive or exhaustive study of medical complicity and/or active participation in colonialism and genocide. However, they must be viewed together as operating within a larger colonial system, structured by the Indian Act and other similar legislation, with the primary goal of eliminating Indigenous Peoples – legally and/or physically – and claiming their lands, rather than as isolated events or aberrations. Medical colonialism has played an integral role in the genocide of Indigenous Peoples in Canada, including by targeting children. In Chapter 6 (i.e., the introduction to the "medical colonialism" part of this book), I explain that my purpose is not to prove genocidal *intent* as required by the Genocide Convention's definition, but rather to firmly establish the genocidal *effects* of the acts listed in its definition. Proving individual, institutional, or national intent to commit genocide is a perilous exercise (see Hilberg 2003, 1062), especially when such intention is directly embedded in the colonial agenda and policies of the Canadian state in the first place. Indeed, "Canada has displayed a continuous policy, with shifting expressed motives but an ultimately steady intention, to destroy Indigenous peoples physically, biologically, and as social units, thereby fulfilling the required specific intent element" (MMIWG 2019d, 24). The intervening chapters, drawing on multiple examples for each of the five acts of the Genocide Convention, demonstrate that the genocidal *effects* of Canadian medical colonialism waged against Indigenous children, when taken together as a whole, leave little doubt as to its *intent*.

Oral Histories versus the Gatekeepers of Colonial Knowledge

The intergenerational and multigenerational trauma stemming from these acts, practices, and policies go beyond the pure realm of health care, given their impacts on Indigenous languages, culture, and relationships to the land (among others). The atrocities described could only have occurred, and continue to occur, because of systemic anti-Indigenous racism and medical colonialism that are rooted in a capitalist economic system, all working together to inflict their damage. And while racism and colonialism are manifested in practices and policies in various spheres of society (e.g., economic, social, and political), there's also a cultural component within the medical establishment that enables such atrocities. The hidden curriculum results in medical trainees internalizing, embodying, and perpetuating the norms and value systems of the medical elite. Treating certain groups of people as though they have less inherent value as human beings is a part of this, historically and today. Anti-Indigenous racism has been – and to many extents continues to be – a part of this culture. Underpinning this medical culture is a sense of relative and absolute impunity, particularly when it comes to the violence inflicted on Indigenous bodies, which persists to this day.

For example, the Indian Health Service (IHS) policy of not covering the cost of returning Indigenous bodies to their communities for burial after death in public hospitals from the 1940s through until at least the 1960s "provided IHS with access to bodies for autopsy without having to secure the family's consent" (Lux 2016, 122). Would we be right to assume that such a practice is part of a bygone era? In 2018, the Viens Commission heard testimony by an Atikamekw woman (whose identity is protected through a publication ban) that would suggest otherwise. Her seventeen-year-old child had died following a protracted hospitalization due to a seizure disorder caused by a rare encephalitis (HC-77 2018, 68, 73). The adolescent's body underwent an autopsy against the mother's wishes (65). The mother found out by happenstance from one of the staff members of the funeral home – and not directly from the medical treating team – that an autopsy had been performed despite her explicit refusal when she'd been approached about it initially (75–9). After burying her child, the mother later learned that the medical team had removed the adolescent's brain to run various tests (81–4). She insisted that they stop all testing and eventually retrieved the brain, but had to wait for the spring thaw to complete the burial process because the ground was frozen at the time. She shared how devastating it was for her to feel like she had to bury her daughter twice due to "the bad decision of doctors" who believed that "they could do whatever they wanted because it's an Indigenous person" (86). This happened in Quebec City in 2014, not in some obscure era of the past. The sense of impunity that serves as a bedrock for this medical culture allows such acts to continue to happen.

Like this testimony, virtually all the horrors detailed herein were initially recounted as a form of Oral History, though many went on to be meticulously and incontrovertibly documented, forcing various levels of government and/or other colonial institutions to acknowledge their own actions and issue apologies for what they had done (e.g. residential schools, nutritional experiments, Sixties Scoop, sterilization of Indigenous women, mass medical evacuations of Inuit, etc.). While the form of communication is different, oral traditions are as legitimate a method of acquiring knowledge as written ones (Younging 2018, 113). Just because something is written doesn't make it true. Similarly, just because something is spoken doesn't make it less reliable. This was essentially the finding of a landmark decision issued by the Supreme Court of Canada in 1997: "The laws of evidence must be adapted in order that this type of evidence [Oral Histories] can be accommodated and placed on an equal footing with the types of historical evidence that courts are familiar with, which largely consists of historical documents" (*Delgamuukw v. British Columbia* 1997, 1067–9).

In the preface of a revised version of his landmark book, *Prison of Grass*, which tells "Canadian" history from an Indigenous perspective, late Métis activist and scholar Howard Adams asserts: "It is known that indigenous people are constrained by the colonizer from recording and writing their own history" (Adams 1989, 6). In a situation where the colonial power is not only the main repository but also the primary gatekeeper of knowledge that is considered official, Oral Histories are often the only way for truths that inconvenience colonial powers to get out. For instance, women and gender studies professor Karen Stote explains that "after spending countless hours sifting through government documents reporting the actions and words of bureaucrats, lawyers, and members of parliament, I cannot help but be struck by the tendency for rhetoric, ignorance and sometimes outright racism on the part of many of those who make decisions on our behalf" (Stote 2015, 5). In some cases, documentary records are simply destroyed. For example, "in 1957, Indian and Northern Health Services was instructed to destroy 'correspondence [including reports by dentists, doctors, and nurses] re routine arrangements re medical and dental treatments of Indians and Eskimos, such as transportation, escort services, admission to hospital, advice on treatment, requests for treatment, etc.' after a period of two years" (TRC 2015a, 90).

Perhaps more shocking, legal scholar and political philosopher Tom Swanky uncovered evidence suggesting that colonial officials in the Dominion of British Columbia deliberately destroyed public records in the months before the fomented smallpox epidemic in the summer of 1862 that is discussed in Chapter 7 (Swanky 2012, 212–13). This "puzzling gap" in the official records "occurs precisely in the period during 1861 where we would expect to see evidence of executive planning for a policy implemented in March 1862" to intentionally spread smallpox among Indigenous communities (212). Yet, as Swanky expounds: "Canadian historians, basing their collective judgment in the lack of a formal confession by the Governor [James Douglas] and in a long practice (seemingly located in the deep-rooted colonial minded origins of Canadian intellectual history) of denying native and eyewitness evidence to the contrary, still claim that smallpox arrived in the Pacific colonies innocently and killed through an invisible hand" (214). Swanky, whose research was compelled by Indigenous Elders sharing Oral Histories about the displacement of their Peoples' sovereignty with him (pers. comm., 2020), exposes the false dichotomy between oral versus written traditions of recording history: "Requiring of an official oral record the same precision, detail or elements as one can expect from a documentary record is already bad faith," especially when "the perpetrators and their subsequent apologists will have had custody of the bureaucratic record with a motive, opportunity and practice in manipulating it" (Swanky 2016, viii).

The reality is that while many acts of medical colonialism are now well-documented, other examples provide glimpses into what are likely more far-reaching phenomena. For instance, testifying or going public about painful experiences and memories is demanding on multiple levels, so perhaps it shouldn't come as a surprise that there are "only" dozens of reported cases of Indigenous children in Quebec disappeared by the health care system following a medevac airlift over the last few decades. Over the relatively short course of the #aHand2Hold campaign, families reached out to several health care providers expressing the desire to share their stories publicly, but then later decided against doing so. There can be all kinds of reasons for this, and the families certainly didn't owe anyone any explanations for changing their minds. But I often wondered whether there was a concern about facing backlash from the health care system. The communities that many of these individuals come from are relatively small (i.e., populations of hundreds to a few thousand), and so there is a higher likelihood of people knowing each other, whether Indigenous or not. If an Eeyou or Inuk parent denounces an aspect of the health care system because they are frustrated with the care their child received, what would happen the next time they would go to the community's only nursing station or hospital, where care is often provided by non-Indigenous health care providers? During Janice and Jobie Kasudluak's testimony at the Viens Commission in November 2018, they expressed how some Nunavimmiut living in Inukjuak already felt that white people (e.g., teachers), are evacuated quicker by medevac airlifts than Inuit (Kasudluak and Kasudluak 2018, 39). If a parent or a caregiver were to denounce ÉVAQ's non-accompaniment rule, what would happen if ever their critically ill child needed to be urgently transferred by Challenger? Would their care be compromised? Throughout the campaign, there were "only" dozens of public testimonies by families impacted by the non-accompaniment practice, even though we know that there were hundreds of children who were transferred unaccompanied each year for decades (with a significant proportion being Indigenous) and that they were almost all traumatic experiences for the family. Yet, there are not thousands of such stories on the public record. Returning to the example of children disappeared by the health care system following a medevac airlift (i.e., before ÉVAQ's existence), just because the public knows that these stories have occurred in certain remote Indigenous communities (e.g., Manawan, Opitciwan, Wemotaci, Pakuashipi, Pikogan) doesn't mean that they haven't occurred in others. In fact, it is probable that they have. The governments responsible for these atrocities will not readily admit to them, which is why so little is known to the public about the Canadian health care system's past, including its ongoing role in medical colonialism, rooted in anti-Indigenous racism.

The previously discussed atrocities were carried out mostly or exclusively by physicians and other health care providers with public funds, administered by elected officials through public (including governmental) entities and employees. Basic precepts of accountability call for the Canadian population to know about the horrors its dollars are funding because, ultimately, the responsibility for those horrors is a shared one. In order to put an end to the violence inflicted against Indigenous communities by the medical establishment and the health care system, the ideologies that underpin medical colonialism must be actively confronted. Such action will reveal both historical and ongoing examples that will only further consolidate the narrative of genocide that the Canadian government has refused to acknowledge for so long.

PART FOUR

The Structural Determinants of Health and Decolonizing Our Future

Chapter 13

Capitalism and the Cost of Caring

Starvation is the life of the oppressed … It is the disease that makes up our life and wipes out our existence. This is the capitalist system and our legacy of suppression and death … Like a road map to the grave, the signs are clear: sunken dark eyes, shallow complexion, swollen lips, bleeding gums, emancipated limbs and a swollen belly. It is the curse of dying slowly, day by day, hour by hour. This is not the life of some unknown person in some unknown third-world country. This is the life of the Aboriginal in Canada.
– Howard Adams, *Tortured People: The Politics of Colonization*

Throughout history, whenever the mentality of a people has been corrupted by selfish greed, unimaginable horrors have occurred for humankind … Greed created in the ruling class of the empire-building countries of Europe an insatiable need to dominate, gather power, and accumulate wealth. The invasion of the Americas was driven by greed. This is the only credible conclusion that can be made.
– Daniel N. Paul, *We Were Not the Savages*

When describing the trajectory of the #aHand2Hold campaign in Chapter 2, I briefly touched on an important exchange between MNA Amir Khadir and Health Minister Gaétan Barrette about the continued unaccompanied transfer of Indigenous children from northern communities using ÉVAQ's Challenger plane (CSSS 2018). Khadir cited the case of Charlotte Munik, an Inuk interpreter from Kuujjuaq who was prevented from accompanying her sick toddler to Montreal weeks after Barrette's February 2018 announcement of a family-centred care (FCC) policy. Khadir wondered: "If this was a child from Westmount, is this what we would do?" (CSSS 2018).

In referencing one of Montreal's whiter, wealthier neighbourhoods, Khadir pointed out how social class, along with systemic anti-Indigenous racism, factored into the government's inadequate response by stating what many already knew to be true: in a society where affluence confers power, much of it is wielded by white people; those who are rich and white can forcefully defend their interests from any perceived threats. The corollary, of course, is that impoverishment is disempowering; historically exploited and oppressed communities are structurally disadvantaged and limited in their abilities to fight back against the injustices imposed on them. This explains, at least in part, the sense of imposed resignation about the non-accompaniment rule that filtered through the media interviews with Alaku Qullialuk from Akulivik, former Kuujjuaq mayor Tunu Napartuk, and an anonymous Nunavimmiuq early on in the campaign (Duchaine and Teisceira-Lessard 2018a; Fidelman 2018a; Rogers 2018). Many of my MCH ED colleagues pointed out that the practice would never have been allowed to persist were it not for the fact that northern Indigenous communities were disproportionately impacted. Week after week, month after month throughout the campaign, I would hear this same refrain. But Barrette didn't seem to hear it.

Budgetary Constraints: Bailouts for Corporations and Pay Hikes for Doctors

Claiming that governments must deal with a "sum of discrete situations," of which children being transferred unaccompanied for medical care was only one consideration among many others, Barrette's response was very telling: ultimately, a bill must be paid by Quebec citizens, who "already pay too much in taxes" and are "very happy to have the health care system that we have" (CSSS 2018). Stating that "at some point, difficult choices have to be made," Barrette invoked the government's "budgetary capacities" to justify why caregiver accompaniment could not be guaranteed, contending that the reconfiguration of the older Challenger to accommodate a caregiver would be too costly, and would risk compromising ÉVAQ's service because only one flying hospital, the newer Challenger, would remain active during that time. Instead, his government was choosing to ensure accompaniment on the newer Challenger, while caregivers and parents would still occasionally be refused on the old one when it was being used (i.e., during maintenance of the newer one). Once the older Challenger became obsolete in a few years, the government would purchase a new aircraft to ensure parental accompaniment on both ÉVAQ flying hospital planes. Barrette qualified this decision as the most "rational" one to make (CSSS 2018).

This wasn't the first time that Barrette brought up financial considerations, invoking the anti-Indigenous "freeloader" trope. During his initial announcement of the FCC policy, he told journalists that the older Challenger would have to be withdrawn from service for up to a year for reconfiguration work, allegedly costing "millions" of dollars (Morin 2018). He hadn't provided detailed cost estimates or explained whose expertise he was relying on. In his response to Khadir, Barrette derisively dismissed the option of buying a new, adapted Challenger as being too expensive (CSSS 2018).

Yet, purchasing the most recent Challenger plane in 2014 cost the Quebec government $19.6 million, which included $13 million for specialized medical equipment and $6.4 million for the used Challenger itself (Derfel 2014). Even adjusted for inflation in Quebec, this made up less than 0.06 per cent of the province's $38.5 billion health care budget in 2018 (Government of Quebec 2018, 2; MSSS 2019, 3). Invoking financial considerations when the lives of children are at stake is callous. Ann Kelly, the mother of a four-year-old Inuk child who had been transferred alone in April 2018 (more than two months after Barrette's 15 February announcement) addressed this point directly, asking "when a child dies in a plane far from their parents, how much does that cost?" (Gervais 2018a). Can a price tag be placed on the lives of Indigenous children? Catherine Hudon wrote in her heart-wrenching February 2018 letter that parental accompaniment "would have cost the health care system much less to this day than the psychological collateral damages" stemming from the rule that prevented her from being with her son when he suffered brain death on a medevac airlift from Chisasibi (Hudon 2018).

The health minister refused to reconfigure the old Challenger or purchase a new one citing financial constraints, but his government had used $1.3 billion in public funds in 2015 as "corporate welfare" to bail out Bombardier – the for-profit, privately owned, and privately run corporation that manufactures Challenger planes (Milke 2015). Surely, given this generous gift to become a minority shareholder to save the C-Series aircraft project, the government could have negotiated a deal for a new flying hospital plane from

Bombardier in 2018. Airbus became the majority shareholder of the C-Series in 2017, plummeting the value of the Quebec government's gift to less than half its original contribution; its shares in the venture trickled from 49.5 per cent down to 19 per cent (Arsenault 2017). In February 2020, Bombardier sold its remaining shares in the Airbus A220 (formerly the C-Series); Airbus's share in the project increased to 75 per cent and Quebec's share increased to 25 per cent, but still half of its original value (Van Praet 2020, B1). In the 2014–15 fiscal year, the federal government and a handful of provinces collectively provided close to $29 billion in business subsidies; in Quebec, the rate was $500 per capita, second highest in the country after Alberta (CBC Radio 2019). The Quebec government's original investment would have been better spent if it had been infused into public health care and social services. Instead, quite the opposite occurred.

In February 2018, the provincial government's agreement with the Fédération des médecins spécialistes du Québec (FMSQ), the province's powerful medical specialists' association, came under fire. It called for exorbitant increases in the remuneration of medical specialists, something the FMSQ had begun pushing for under Barrette's reign for years (he stepped down as president of the FMSQ in 2014 to run as a provincial Liberal candidate). As health minister, he acknowledged that physicians' incomes couldn't keep increasing; between 2008 and 2017, family physicians' remuneration had increased by over 40 per cent and that of specialists by almost 60 per cent, with the result that physicians are heavily over-represented among the richest 1% of the province (Bernier and Posca 2020, 5). For a confluence of reasons, Barrette was removed from the 2018 negotiations with the FMSQ and was replaced by Pierre Arcand, his colleague from the Treasury Department. All of this was happening in the context of punishing government cuts of billions of dollars to public spending, imposed over several years through sweeping austerity measures (Beaulne 2018). Several hundred million dollars were slashed from health and social services across the province (Nguyen 2016, 6). So, while different forms of protests by nurses, patient-care attendants, orderlies, social workers, and other health care personnel for better working conditions and dignified incomes were being ignored by the provincial government, medical specialists – the elite of the elite – were rewarded with unprecedented income increases. Family doctors had also benefited from a surge in their remuneration not long before the specialists did. The pay hikes were a slap in the face for almost everyone else who worked in or needed the services of the health care system in Quebec. The public backlash was significant. A petition opposing the hikes, launched by Médecins québécois pour le régime public (MQRP), was signed by hundreds of physicians (as well as medical trainees) and made international headlines (Levinson-King 2018). Barely a few weeks later, in March 2018, the provincial government announced a 2017–18 budget surplus of over $850 million and projected a surplus of over $900 million for the 2018–19 budget (Bloomberg 2018; CP 2018). The only way to understand the government's rhetoric of "budgetary capacities" is that the health and well-being of Indigenous children was simply not a priority.

An FCC framework was ultimately implemented in 2018 without compromising the ÉVAQ fleet and without breaking the budget. Testifying at the Viens Commission in October of that year, André Lizotte, the Ministry of Health director of prehospital emergency services, revealed that the newer Challenger had already been configured to accommodate a caregiver all along, not requiring any major modifications. Meanwhile, the older Challenger was refurbished, without costing millions of dollars, to allow caregiver accompaniment (Bernier et al. 2018, 76, 106).

To this day, it's unclear to me whether there was ever any basis to Barrette's threat that implementing the FCC policy would either necessitate withdrawing the old Challenger from service for a year or result in millions of dollars in reconfiguration costs (or both). However, his unsubstantiated financial arguments – despite corporate bailouts, exorbitant increases in physician's incomes, and significant budget surpluses – relies on the anti-Indigenous trope of Indigenous Peoples ("them") being freeloaders who drain "our" (colonial government and settler society) resources and compromise services. This exercise obscures a foundational injustice promoted by capitalism: the wealth of colonial-settler societies is actually predicated on the theft of Indigenous Lands and the dispossession of Indigenous Peoples. The leitmotif of both provincial and federal governmental colonial policies is patent: disregard its legal and financial obligations to Indigenous Peoples while taking over their land and resources (TRC 2015a, 3). Such historical and contemporary economic motives reveal the contours of important structural determinants of health – the causes of the causes – that shape reality for Indigenous Peoples in Quebec and the rest of Canada.

Taking a closer look at the federal government's policy of mass evacuations of Inuit from Nunavik and Nunavut for tuberculosis (TB) treatment in the late 1940s until the 1960s provides but one example of the economic imperatives dictating Canada's colonial policies: exploitation (e.g., for resources) on the one hand, and neglect (e.g., of services) on the other. Important connections and parallels can be made with the provincial government's inadequate response to long-standing calls by Indigenous communities in Quebec to end ÉVAQ's non-accompaniment practice.

The Few Get Rich Because Many Are Made Poor

A complex mix of factors contributed to the high rates of tuberculosis infections and deaths in Inuit communities long before the federal government implemented its plans to intervene in the late 1940s. Any meaningful search for "the causes of the causes" would expose European invaders as being the most significant. For centuries, Inuit had been spared the ravages of the decimating diseases that were prevalent in Europe. While land colonization through settlement did not occur in the North to the same extent as it did in the southern parts of Canada, invasion and colonization nonetheless did occur: "The strangers had taken over Inuit land for their own purposes and considered it all theirs: crown land – Canadian government property" (Grygier 1994, 41). These strangers felt more than entitled to invite themselves over to profit from Inuit Land and to exploit its people. Who were they? Fur traders from the Hudson's Bay Company set up a temporary post in Umiujaq (in Nunavik) as early as 1749, and the company's first permanent post in Nunavik was established in Ivujivik in 1909 (30). Whalers (usually American) had been coming to Inuit lands since the 1800s (29). In the early 1900s, the federal government granted mineral exploration permits to commercial enterprises (Vanast 1991, 61). Roman Catholic (Oblates of Mary Immaculate) and Anglican missionaries sought to convert Inuit in various communities to Christianity in both the western and eastern Arctic (and the Subarctic) as of the 1800s (Grygier 1994, 33–4). The Northwest Mounted Police (NWMP), which later became the RCMP, was established in 1873 to "seize resource-rich Métis land ... and to control Métis resistance as well as potential native allies farther west who also revolted against the forceable take-over of their land by the Canadian government" (Pedicelli 1998, 16). The goal was for the NWMP to "civilize the wild, barbaric heathen Indians," and its "mission was violently and enthusiastically carried out by its racist officers" (Pedicelli 1998, 16). In the North, the NWMP was used "to police this area and assert Canadian sovereignty over it" (Grygier 1994, 41). Officers "not only had to enforce southern laws; they were, in effect, colonial administrators in much the same way that British colonial service officers were in India and Africa" (46).

These invaders and colonizers introduced a variety of ills as they invaded, occupied, and exploited Inuit Land. Tuberculosis was certainly one of them: "The introduction of many communicable diseases, some of which were previously unknown, in many cases, almost totally eliminated the native peoples" of the North (Martin 1981, 80). These stark health disparities are commonly attributed to Indigenous Peoples' "inherent susceptibility" to various diseases. However, as medical historian David Jones argues in *Rationalizing Epidemics*, "the disparities in health status ... actually reflect the disparities in wealth and power that have endured since colonization" (Jones 2004, 19). This is why it is important to recognize that "disease is a social and political category imposed on people within an enormously repressive social and economic capitalist system, one that forces disease and death on the world's people" (Navarro 2009, 440). Indeed, the ills introduced through colonization were not restricted to a narrow understanding of health and disease. Rather, they included imposed participation in a completely foreign and inherently dehumanizing economic system, from which it eventually became impossible to escape: "Inuit were to go from a predominantly hunter/gatherer society to a materialistic one and the relations that are part of a capitalist culture and economic system" (Karetak and Tester 2017, 8–9; see also Chrisjohn et al. 2017, 103–4).

Broadly speaking, Indigenous Peoples were used to producing what they needed, "with a low consumption level and sharing-based exchange," which was in stark contrast to the "industrial (capitalist) philosophy [that] dictates that one produce for profit and [that] exchanges are market-based (with a high consumption level)." A family-based division of labour with overlapping gender roles was pitted against a class-based model characterized by a high degree of occupational specialization. Finally, in Indigenous societies, "property relations were egalitarian and collective," while in colonial systems "they were (and are) stratified and private" (Wesley-Esquimaux and Smolewski 2004, 33). Across the country, the federal government was determined to "subdue Indians and to teach them lessons in liberal economic theory and individual survival in the marketplace" (Shewell 2004, ix). However, the process of colonization and the imposition of a foreign economic system threatened their very survival *as a people*. Conservative estimates suggest that the population of Indigenous Peoples in what is now known as Canada went from 500,000 prior to "initial sustained contact with Europeans" to 102,000 in 1871. As noted by the commissioners of the Royal Commission on Aboriginal Peoples, "It would take more than 100 years – until the early 1980s – before the size of the Aboriginal population again reached the 500,000 mark" (RCAP 1996a, 21). Since Indigenous Peoples were not capitalists themselves, "the imposition of a capitalist economy was, by definition, oppressive (as it was for Europeans themselves when capitalism first came into being)" (Chrisjohn et al. 2017, 102). Economic oppression, as explained by sociologist Erik Olin Wright, occurs when "material benefits of one group are acquired at the expense of another" (Wright 2003, 376; see also Raphael 2012, 46). In other words, in a capitalist economic system that values profits over people, the few get rich because many are made poor.* This holds true for the Inuit experience.

Canadian colonial policies, as well as the activities of fur traders, whalers, and miners (among others), transformed the land and waters, causing the depletion of the wildlife (through changes in migration patterns and/or overhunting) that had sustained Inuit for thousands of years (Grygier 1994, 55; Vanast 1991, 72). Government officials have recognized for some time that before the arrival of the Europeans "there was little garbage, very little gastroenteritis and no sign of tapeworms or tuberculosis" and "health was also excellent" (Martin 1981, 82). However, with the imposition of a "more permanent settlement life," social patterns changed "rather dramatically with catastrophic results on health" (82). The Inuit had previously adapted to life in the tundra by learning how and when to move around on the land. Within

---

* Climate justice activist Greta Thunberg popularized a variation of this concept in her speech at COP24, the UN Climate Change Conference that was held in Poland in December 2018: "It is the sufferings of the many which pay for the luxuries of the few."

a relatively short period of time, they had to adopt a more sedentary existence to survive. In 1969, 90 per cent of Inuit in the eastern Arctic were living in settlements (Hicks 1969, 538). Major transformations in their diet occurred within only a few generations; cramped dwellings, malnutrition, and starvation made Inuit particularly susceptible to tuberculosis (Grygier 1994, 28, 55).

Tuberculosis: A Problem to Be Solved by Physicians

This context is necessary to understand how tuberculosis became endemic and reached epidemic proportions in Inuit communities during the early decades of the twentieth century, especially in Nunavik. Due to irregular reporting and underestimates early on, compared to more systematically collected information from the late 1940s onwards when expansive screening programs were instituted, reliable aggregate statistics regarding the first half of that century are not easily obtained. Nonetheless, various players, including physicians and missionaries, painted a picture of the undeniably devastating impact of TB in Inuit communities.

In 1939, in response to a query from Encyclopedia Britannica about "the health of the Eskimos, with particular reference to tuberculosis," Dr George Jasper Wherrett, executive secretary of the Canadian Tuberculosis Association (CTA), suggested that the health care services for tuberculosis inspections and medical treatment in Inuit communities were "as satisfactory as can be effected" (Grygier 1994, 64). He changed his tune when he visited these communities for the first time a few years later. The results of his subsequent research study on the health conditions and medical hospital services in the Northwest Territories were published in 1945 (Grygier 1994, 60; Nixon 1988, 74). Wherrett focused on the Mackenzie River District, home to an estimated 7 per cent of the Northwest Territories' Inuit population; he identified a high rate of pneumonia-related deaths and an alarming infant mortality rate. The tuberculosis-related death rate in this area, "314.6 per 100,000 of population as opposed to the Canadian average of 52 per l00,000," was "staggering" (Grygier 1994, 64). However, he suspected that his figures were a gross underestimate of the reality.

In "Writing for Our Lives: The Language of Homesickness, Self-Esteem and the Inuit TB 'Epidemic,'" the authors report that "the death rate per

100,000 [people] for tuberculosis of the respiratory system for Canada (excluding what was known at the time as the Northwest Territories) dropped from 45.4 in 1938, to 9.9 in 1953," while the "death rate for TB of the respiratory system was reported as 153.6 per 100,000 in 1938, and had risen to 298.1 by 1953" for Inuit, after peaking at "478.3 per 100,000 in 1947" (Tester et al. 2001, 123). The source for these statistics is not clearly indicated in the journal article, and it is also not specified whether these figures capture the reality for Nunavimmiut; however, as I'll explain later in this chapter, the Northwest Territories, via the federal government, did have some jurisdiction over communities in Nunavik back then, so they may very well have been included in those statistics (assuming the figures themselves are reliable). Regardless, conditions for several communities living along Ungava Bay (in Nunavik) were particularly harsh during this period owing to economic and political factors (Grygier 1994, 154; Vanast 1991, 72). As such, it is unlikely that they suffered any less from the devastating impacts of tuberculosis than Inuit living in other areas; on the contrary, they were probably hit even harder. Whatever the actual numbers may have been, no one now denies that the situation was dire for Nunavimmiut.

Physicians played a significant role in the mass tuberculosis evacuations of Inuit. The origins of physicians' involvement can be traced back to at least 1937 when a consultative process was initiated between the federal government and the CTA. At a conference held by the CTA in June 1937, the "view which developed ... was that tuberculosis was essentially a medical, as opposed to broader social-economic, phenomena and therefore was to be solved, if at all, by medical practitioners" (Nixon 1988, 75). Tuberculosis specialists today would certainly disagree with the CTA's conclusions now that the social determinants of health (SDH), broadly speaking, are well-recognized as having major impacts on tuberculosis epidemiology. However, this knowledge was available back then as well because, several decades earlier, public health physicians like Dr P.H. Bryce had issued reports that were widely covered by the media and made it clear that broader conditions impacted tuberculosis infection and mortality rates in residential schools (Bryce 1907, 17–19). The conclusions reached by the CTA were not surprising though because, "as would become the norm, 'representatives' were drawn exclusively from the medical profession, including those from within the relevant federal and provincial ministries, the CTA, sanatoria, and private physicians with experience in the tuberculosis field" (Nixon 1988, 75).

Wrestling Control: Colonial Health Care in the North

The Advisory Committee for the Control and Prevention of Tuberculosis Among Indians came into existence by order-in-council on 30 January 1945. It had the authority "to inquire into the present methods of tuberculosis prevention, detection, treatment and aftercare" and to make recommendations to the federal government about "the best possible use of monies" to both eradicate and prevent the spread of tuberculosis "among Indians" (Nixon 1988, 75). The Advisory Committee referred to "Indians," but it had "a great influence on the tuberculosis program that was eventually set up for the Inuit" (Grygier 1994, 63). The Advisory Committee was made up of twelve members. Ten of them, including the head, would be nominated by the Department of Health and Welfare, making clear that it was "designed to be the voice of the medical profession" (Nixon 1988, 75). Dr Percy E. Moore, a key figure in the nutritional surveys in Cree communities and nutritional experiments in several residential schools across Canada (Chapter 8), and in the expansion of the segregated Indian hospital system (Chapter 9), was, in his capacity as director of the Indian Health Service (IHS), one of the original members of the Advisory Committee (76). Later that year, when the medical responsibilities of the Indian Affairs Branch of Mines and Resources were transferred to the Department of Health and Welfare, Moore would be transferred there as well (76). As detailed in previous chapters, he would go on to play a major role in shaping Indigenous health policy for years to come (Nixon 1989, 166).

One of Moore's immediate priorities was to "wrestle control of health care" from the Christian missions who had, up until then, taken on this role (with federal government funding) in many northern regions (Nixon 1988, 76; Lux 2016, 43–4). In the shorter term, along with the backing of the "authoritative and powerful" CTA, the Department of Health and Welfare instituted its "own aggressive case finding, immunization, and southern Canada based treatment program" (Nixon 1988, 76). It is around this time that Moore and the Department of Health and Welfare instituted the policy of evacuating "serious but treatable" and long-term patients to medical facilities in southern Canada (Nixon 1988, 77, 82n29; Grygier 1994, 74). Over the longer term, Moore undermined church-run hospitals by establishing "a system of primary health care facilities, including nursing stations and lay dispensaries in the north" (Nixon 1988, 77).

Establishing secular medical infrastructure in northern communities was not inherently problematic, especially when the alternative was church-run hospitals where proselytizing and conversion were at the core of their missions. The issue was that Moore was slow to respond and didn't go far enough to ensure that these communities had the necessary resources to provide for adequate local health care services, both in terms of personnel and infrastructure. In fact, since at least the early 1930s, some physicians and clergy had been calling for properly staffed hospitals to be built in northern communities in direct response to the devastating toll of tuberculosis (Grygier 1994, 56–7). When Moore was director of the IHS, such calls not only continued but increased. In 1944, Dr Falconer, the medical officer of the Eastern Arctic Patrol, "suggested that a TB sanatorium be set up at Kuujjuaq to serve the northern Quebec Inuit" (62). Dr George Hooper, also a physician with the 1944 Eastern Arctic Patrol, was similarly convinced of the need for a hospital that would serve the Inuit living around Ungava Bay (Vanast 1991, 66–7). Dr R. Miller, medical assistant to the Department of Pensions and National Health, suggested "again that three TB centres be set up in the North for open cases of tuberculosis" (Grygier 1994, 62). He even went so far as to deem the forced evacuations to southern institutions as being "not good practice" and proposed that "the avoidance of removal of northern natives to southern institutions should be a stated principle as far as possible" (62). Similar calls would come from physicians involved with the medical component of the Eastern Arctic Patrol the following year as well (Selway 2016, 129). But these physicians didn't wield enough power to change practice or policy.

All such recommendations and requests for expanding health care services in the north continued to be rejected by the federal government. Moore cited a multiplicity of reasons for his opposition including a lack of health care professionals willing to work in northern communities, an anticipated decrease in tuberculosis cases rendering extra beds superfluous, and the al-

ready-existing capacity of northern facilities to remove the source of infection from within communities through isolation measures (Grygier 1994,
73). He clearly favoured the policy of mass evacuations and used two main
arguments to justify it: limited budgetary capacities and higher survival rates
for those treated in southern institutions (74).

Comparing survival rates was flawed. According to Moore's calculations,
the ratio of deaths to discharges was 29 per cent in northern institutions versus 13 per cent in southern hospitals (Grygier 1994, 74). His argument of
higher survival rates in southern hospitals provided a disingenuous justification against building new hospitals and health care infrastructure locally
in northern communities because he created the very rules that allowed for
such a discrepancy: it was IHS policy to forcibly evacuate relatively healthy
individuals who were more likely to survive tuberculosis treatments while
leaving those considered "not treatable" or "terminal" to die in northern
church-run hospitals and nursing stations (Nixon 1988, 77, 82n29; Grygier
1994, 73–4). It is no surprise, then, that both survival rates would be so
skewed, significantly exaggerating any actual difference that may have existed
between the two. The conditions were rigged to produce favourable data that
would align with Moore's plans of not expanding health care services in
northern communities (Nixon 1988, 82n29). He deemed forging ahead with
mass evacuations as being the only option. In terms of the budgetary considerations, Moore's calculations suggested that per diem costs for admission
to a mission hospital in the North were double that of a government-run
hospital in the South. As such, given the prolonged nature of tuberculosis
hospitalizations, evacuating Inuit to the South was cheaper, according to
Moore, even when factoring in the cost of transporting evacuees (Grygier
1994, 74). This argument is misleading since, again, the cost differential was
by design due to relative underfunding of health care for Indigenous Peoples;
many Nunavimmiut were sent to Indian hospitals for tuberculosis treatment
where "the cost of care continued to be half that of surrounding community
hospitals' rates" (Lux 2017).

Setting aside any methodological flaws and disingenuous calculations,
the more fundamental question is whether such cold numbers and economic
considerations can ever justify a policy that promoted the forced evacuation
of Inuit, including children, to southern institutions hundreds or thousands

of kilometres away from their families and communities for months to years at a time. Although the policy may have saved some lives, we'll never know what would have happened if the governments of the day had instead focused on developing infrastructure to treat tuberculosis locally in northern communities, especially after the widely available use of more effective antibiotics in the early 1950s, when hospitalization rates for non-Indigenous people in southern institutions for tuberculosis was decreasing precipitously (Lux 2016, 66–7, 118). Indeed, the imposed mass evacuations were likely not necessary. Importantly, the "argument that dealing with TB in the North was too expensive is questionable if one considers the social impacts that TB evacuations had upon family relations, intergenerational communication and the relationship of these considerations to many social problems currently experienced by Inuit families" (Tester et al. 2001, 137). This is a clear example of medical colonialism manifesting through policies that act as "causes of the causes." Upstream of this structural determinant of health, of course, are the twin forces of capitalism and colonization: if Inuit Land had not been invaded, occupied and exploited resulting in the forced impoverishment of Inuit communities in the first place, tuberculosis would likely never have been such a devastating force in the North.

Quebec vs Canada Jurisdictional Disputes: Taking the Land, Not Caring about the People

Moore and his predecessors had not been keen on significantly expanding health care services in northern communities in Quebec until the late 1940s. What is less clear is whether the actual reasons were the two discussed earlier (budgetary capacities and survival rates) or whether other factors were at play. For example, one significant but overlooked element is a major jurisdictional battle between Quebec and Canada around the same time, which had tremendous ramifications for health care and social services for Nunavimmiut. In a succinct historical review of Nunavik, Inuk writer and broadcaster Zebedee Nungak explains that Inuit territory went from "Rupert's Land" in 1670 to become part of the Northwest Territories that entered the Canadian Confederation in 1870. In 1912, ancestral Inuit Land was transferred to Quebec through "an Act respecting the extension of the Province of Quebec by the annexation of Ungava" (Nungak 2017, 23). Nungak qualifies the Act as "the work of pure colonialism," and states categorically that the "impact of this law would forever change the lives of Nunavik Inuit" because it "was a blueprint for governments forcing subservience on Inuit subjects" (Nungak 2017, 23–4). One of the central conflicts between the provincial and federal governments had to do with which jurisdiction was responsible for Inuit welfare. To paraphrase Nungak, Quebec wanted the land, but not the people on it, claiming that the responsibility for the Inuit rested with the federal government (Nungak 2017, 27).

This issue would ultimately be addressed at the Supreme Court of Canada in the 1930s, when Isaac Mikpighak, a fourteen-year-old Inuk from Kuujjuaraapik was caught in the cross fire. Mikpighak's story is detailed by neurologist and medical historian Walter Vanast in an insightful historical account about medical care in Nunavik, entitled "Hastening the Day of Extinction: Canada, Québec, and the Medical Care of Ungava's Inuit, 1867–1967." In 1930, Dr B.H. Hamilton, a government physician, cared for Mikpighak who had suffered an open fracture of his arm. Hamilton brought Mikpighak to his residence in Moose Factory, Ontario, because medical infrastructure in Kuujjuaraapik was absent at the time (Vanast 1991, 56). Not long after arriving in Moose Factory, Hamilton's house burned down and Mikpighak's clothing was destroyed in the fire. Hamilton bought new clothes for the adolescent, but then died suddenly soon thereafter. Mikpighak now had to live with an RCMP officer, who sent invoices for the cost of his clothing, room, and board to the federal government. Instead of making interim payments, Ottawa forwarded the bill to Quebec (Vanast 1991, 61–2).

Such billing procedures paralleled what was happening on a much larger scale between Canada and Quebec. The Hudson's Bay Company (HBC) would advance "survival credits" to Nunavimmiut who were drastically impacted by the Great Depression and a significant drop in fur prices. In order to recuperate these amounts that it had advanced, HBC would then bill the federal government, but Canada refused to pay and instead passed the buck to Quebec (Grygier 1994, 154). In 1929, the two entities had reached a fragile compromise about cost sharing for various already scant services provided to the Inuit in Nunavik: "Ottawa would provide relief for Quebec Eskimos; Quebec would then reimburse the federal government for the expenses incurred" (Diubaldo 1981, 35). However, by mid-1932, this compromise broke down, as the impacts of the Great Depression and cost cutting set in (Vanast

1991, 61; Diubaldo 1981, 35). Meanwhile, Quebec refused to pay for Mikpig-hak's basic care. If Canada was to foot the bill, Quebec's position that the federal government was responsible for Inuit health care and social welfare would be legitimized. So, the two governments continued passing the buck, making it one of the earliest recorded cases of what Jordan's Principle would seek to end almost seventy-five years later.

Named in honour of Jordan River Anderson, Jordan's Principle states that jurisdictional disputes cannot compromise public services for First Nations' children when and where they need them. Jordan was a child from the Norway House Cree Nation in Manitoba who was born in 1999 with a rare genetic defect requiring significant medical support. He could have been dis-charged from the hospital when he was two years old, but the federal and provincial governments argued over who should pay for his care in the com-munity because of Jordan's First Nations status. He died in the hospital at five years of age never having spent a day in his family's home. The House of Commons adopted Jordan's Principle in 2007, but the failure to implement it forced the First Nations Child and Family Caring Society and the Assembly of First Nations to bring the issue to the Canadian Human Rights Tribunal, which has ordered that it be a legal obligation throughout Canada in multi-ple rulings since 2016 (Viens Commission 2019, 174). Jordan's Principle has since been extended to include Inuit. Both the TRC and the National Inquiry into MMIWG recommended that it be fully implemented in all jurisdictions across the country (TRC 2015a, 142–3; MMIWG 2019a, 66–7; MMIWG 2019b, 195). The Viens Commission's final report also recommended the full imple-mentation of Jordan's Principle for all Indigenous (including Inuit) children, and to extend its application to Indigenous adults as well (Viens Commis-sion 2019, 396).

As of 1933, the two levels of government worked on developing their re-spective legal arguments on this jurisdictional issue for the Supreme Court of Canada (SCC). As the federal government's team researched the matter, one of its legal counsels was certain that the SCC would favour the province's position. The Canadian government went ahead anyway. The case was fi-nally heard in 1937 and a decision was rendered in 1939 (Diubaldo 1981, 36). The SCC decided in Quebec's favour: Inuit of Nunavik were "Indians" within the meaning of Section 91(24) of the British North America Act and the fed-eral government was, therefore, responsible for their welfare (SCC 1939, 104).

However, once the Second World War ended, Ottawa hoped to have the ruling overturned by the Judicial Committee of Privy Council, based in London, the highest Commonwealth court and the highest Canadian court of appeal at the time (Vanast 1991, 63; Diubaldo 1981, 39–40). In the interim, "overzealous federal bureaucrats actually *reduced* food and ammunition 'relief' supplies to needy Inuit by almost 90% from levels they had reached in the late 1920s" (Vanast 1991, 63; emphasis in original).

Major D.L. McKeand, a federal government official in charge of the Eastern Arctic Patrol at the time, made the argument that even if Inuit were "Indians," this did not absolve Quebec from its health care-provision responsibilities, pointing out the irony of Quebec's position while it continued collecting hefty taxes on furs traded by Inuit hunters from Nunavik. Although McKeand's treatment of Inuit over his years in power was deplorable, he did have a point in exposing Quebec's hypocrisy: the province was content to exploit Inuit labour and land, but refused to provide the necessary relief, health care, and social services. Despite the Supreme Court's decision, the federal government continued to justify its refusal to provide necessary health care services in northern Quebec as being a jurisdictional matter. Before 1939, it stated that Quebec was responsible for Inuit on "its" (i.e., colonial) territory; after 1939, it stated that Quebec was responsible because health care was a provincial matter (Vanast 1991, 64–7). The federal government did everything in its power to maintain its position of "deliberate and cultivated neglect" of the Inuit in Nunavik (Diubaldo 1981, 39). However, due to the devastating conditions that the Inuit of Nunavik were living in, the federal government was finally forced to take on more of an active role in northern Quebec by administering health care as it had begun doing in other Inuit communities years prior (Vanast 1991, 61). It could no longer shirk its responsibilities because of supposed jurisdictional issues.

This change occurred in response to pressures within its bureaucracies, but also from public shaming. The American military, which had built a base in Kuujjuaq (Fort Chimo) during the Second World War, often ended up providing medical care to Inuit because local authorities would not. When the local press in Quebec City got a hold of Dr George Gowie's scathing report following the return of the *M.V. McLean* Arctic patrol ship in 1946, the press coverage was damning of the Canadian government (Vanast 1991, 64–8). After witnessing the atrocious conditions in some Nunavik communities along Hudson's Strait, Gowie didn't mince his words. According to him, no people had been more "neglected and misused and exploited" than the Inuit (67). Gowie scornfully wondered whether the "ultimate destruction" of the Inuit was the goal of the Canadian government's northern policy, because "if so, let us continue as heretofore and do all in our power to hasten that day of extinction," which he anticipated could occur as quickly as in a few years if conditions didn't change (67). Such damaging press coverage publicly exposed Canada's hypocrisy on the international stage as well. On the one hand, it was calling for international aid at the UN in support of "underdeveloped nations;" on the other, it had precipitated the "ultimate destruction" of an entire people (Vanast 1991, 67–8).

As is often the case when governments are shamed or forced to act, they reframe obligations and responsibilities as being carried out for "humanitarian reasons" (Moore 1946, 140). Although they are significantly underplayed in historical narratives, national and corporate capitalist interests likely trumped any true "humanitarian" concerns in expanding health care services in Nunavik, much as they had in parts of the eastern and western Canadian Arctic in the preceding years (Vanast 1991, 61). Increased health care services in the North were directly linked to capitalist commercial interests from the South, particularly with the ever-looming "threat to the health of transient whites" (73). For example, the early Cold War years signalled the return of an American presence in the Canadian North to build radar stations for an early warning system in the event of a Russian attack. Concerned about the need that construction companies would have for Inuit labour, Moore himself identified tuberculosis as being a "barrier to the acceptability of the Eskimo for employment in non-native settlements" (73). In "Disease, Medicine and Empire," historian David Arnold provides an astute explanation that applies in this case: "Capitalism's internal contradiction between the pursuit of labour efficiency (and thus of workers' health) and the pursuit of profit impelled European colonial regimes and the commercial and industrial enterprises that worked under them towards greater involvement in indigenous health care" (Arnold 1988, 15). So, after resisting calls to build nursing stations and hospitals in Nunavik for years, medical services were promptly expanded in just over a decade.

In the late 1940s, nursing stations were established in Inukjuak and Kuujjuaq. In the early 1960s, nursing stations opened in Puvirnituq, Salluit, and

Kuujjuaraapik (Grygier 1994, 81–2). Nunavik's first hospital would be built in Kuujjuaq in 1967 (Grygier 1994, 155). Moore had promised "substantial numbers" of Inuit on the hospital staff of southern medical institutions in the 1950s when Inuit were being mass evacuated (80). However, most health care professionals at nursing stations and hospitals in Nunavik are not Inuit to this day. Nonetheless, some basic infrastructure was put into place – albeit decades late and without the meaningful involvement of Inuit – to provide limited medical services to the population locally.

In the concluding indictments of her study about the federal government's handling of the tuberculosis epidemic among Inuit, Pat Sandiford Grygier wrote: "When the will and money were there, the difficulties could certainly be overcome" (1994, 177). The reality is that colonial governments have little interest in ending injustices they've created and maintained because they profit from them so significantly. Finding just solutions, instead of resorting to policies like mass evacuations for tuberculosis treatment or practices like ÉVAQ's non-accompaniment rule for emergency medevac airlifts, have always been less about the money and more about the lack of political will. However, the more ambitious goal of breaking away from colonialism demands more than money and political will; it requires a complete reformulation of Indigenous-settler relations. And in order to get there, we have to know how we got here.

Chapter 14

History Matters: Colonialism, Land, and Indigenous Self-Determination

It ain't the clash of civilizations, it's the backlash of colonization
Break your mental incarceration
Like Waahli said, I guess the feeling is mutual:
You cannot be neutral.
– Nomadic Massive, "Duty"

Ils veulent tomber la pluie, sans la foudre ou le tonnerre.
Ils veulent changer les choses, sans la rage et la colère.
Ils veulent des roses sans épines, des raisins sans pépins.
Ils veulent des livres scolaires sans le massacre des Indiens.
– Sidi Wacho, "Ils nous emmerdent (Nos cagan)"

The dominant medical paradigm in North America is centred around the biomedical model of clinical care. As I briefly touched on in Chapter 3, this model places undue emphasis on the individual's body and behaviours for both favourable and adverse health outcomes. Even shifting to the limited biopsychosocial model of clinical care has been slow. The Commission on Social Determinants of Health (CSDH) report certainly tried to shift focus to the "causes of the causes" (CSDH 2008, 42). But the biomedical model, and its emphasis on the individual, remains entrenched. Broad economic, political, and social forces are rarely considered in disease processes or how a given illness is experienced.

For example, undertaking a more comprehensive historical exploration of a health issue, like the structural determinants (capitalism, colonialism, anti-Indigenous systemic racism) leading to the mass evacuations of Inuit discussed in Chapter 11, may seem irrelevant to our current reality for many health care providers. Some may argue that that era is too far gone to have any significance or applicability in the current context, even believing that Indigenous Peoples should just "move on" and "get over it." However, taking this position is a grave mistake. Not only are some of the structural determinants the same (as highlighted in Chapter 13), but their impacts are felt for generations. Indeed, jarred by the accounts of the tuberculosis mass evacuations as told to him by Inuit Elders, international AIDS advocate Stephen Lewis has charged that "what the Canadian governments have done cumulatively to Indigenous persons across this country is a crime against humanity." He explains that the "excruciating violations, the racism around TB in the 50s and 60s has so traumatized people *to this day* that it's part of the stigma" tied to being tested or even talking about tuberculosis (Moore 2017; emphasis added). In 2019, Prime Minister Justin Trudeau issued an apology to Inuit for Canada's "colonial" approach of mass medical evacuations. He made a "promise, on behalf of all Canadians, to build a brighter future" together with Inuit, and recognized that the current incidence rate for Inuit "is more than 300 times that of Canada's non-Indigenous population" (Trudeau 2019). Indeed, the Inuit experience "of TB in the Canadian North, like that of residential schools across the country, is one of ongoing trauma" (Hick 2019, 90). The devastating and long-lasting impacts on Inuit communities reverberate to this day. A summary sheet prepared for the Viens Commission at the time of the release of its final report suggests that mistrust of the health care system on the part of Nunavimmiut, informed in part by the mass evacuations to Indian hospitals and sanatoria, contributes to the high rates of tuberculosis that persist in Nunavik (Couturier and Lévesque [2019?], 3). The reporting rate of new tuberculosis cases has once again become the highest in Canada, and the prevalence was the ninth highest in the world in 2015. The authors confirm that the dominant strain is the one introduced by Europeans at the beginning of the twentieth century. Even today, up to 10 per cent of the Inuit population continue to be treated in centres away from their communities (Couturier and Lévesque [2019?], 1–2).

History Matters

Similarly, the impacts of ÉVAQ's now-defunct non-accompaniment rule on Indigenous communities are inextricably linked to patriarchal colonial policies, systemic anti-Indigenous racism, and an exploitative capitalist economic system, among other factors that shape peoples' material reality. As previously discussed, the forced removal of children from their families and communities, including through medical and social service systems (e.g., residential schools, tuberculosis evacuations, foster care placement, disappearances after medevac airlifts, etc.), was a decades-long reality for many Indigenous communities living in northern and remote areas of Quebec. We can wish that these horrors didn't happen but wishing things doesn't make them true. And, so long as they happened, we have to act and respond consequently.

We must also strive to learn about and understand that history. The biomedical and the more recent biopsychosocial models do concern themselves with the individual's history – a physician may ask: When did your symptoms start? Is this the first time such episodes have occurred? Have you had any surgeries in the past? When did your stressors at work become overwhelming? However, by ignoring histories that go beyond the individual, the model effectively erases those broader histories "to create the normative dominance of one experience over another" (Hick 2019, 91).

Yet, history is the trace left by time. Like time, history, too, is continuous. It doesn't take a break, nor does it reset itself. Understanding history can allow us to respond better to challenges in the present so that we can safeguard a meaningful future. For health care providers, pretending like people don't have or are not part of collective histories is doing them a disservice by ignoring a part of who they are.

Although it was not explicitly considered as such in the WHO's CSDH model, I support the notion that history – along with macroeconomic, social and public policies, governance, culture and societal values, and socioeconomic position (Solar and Irwin 2010, 6) – should be considered a structural determinant of health (Brown et al. 2011, 113). As a 'Namgis Elder has explained, "History matters. Throughout history our people have been challenged by outside forces, government, religious institutions and residential schools that almost took our identity away" (Brown et al. 2012, 51). Only through a historical lens can we start to grasp the origins of practices and policies impacting people's health and well-being, in turn allowing us to understand how and why the other structural determinants of health function as they do.

One of the weaknesses of the CSDH report was its failure to specifically name the structural determinants of health, or the "causes of the causes," which could allow us to identify the individuals and systems perpetuating the "social injustices" that are "killing people on a grand scale" (CSDH 2008, n.p). After all, "it is not inequalities that kill, but those who benefit from the inequalities that kill" (Navarro 2009, 440). As raised in the discussion of SDH in Chapter 3, to meaningfully do this we must get to the roots by asking "Why?" The answer invariably points to power, who wields it, and how they benefit while harming others. As such, we must focus our attention on what goes on in corporate boardrooms and behind closed government office doors, where decisions with disastrous consequences for much of the world's population are made. The identities of the individual culprits making these decisions are not always publicly known and the overarching systems they profit from seem invisible to many of us. Yet, these systems are pervasive and destructive. Professor in nursing and public health researcher Elizabeth A. McGibbon (2012, 27–31) explains that structural power is at the heart of oppression: "Ideas about domination, power and discrimination are interconnected, and there are many different and synergistic kinds of oppressions ... [that] include sexism, racism, heterosexism, ableism, ageism and classism, to name a few." She recognizes that this is a noncomprehensive list, but nonetheless takes on the important task of naming the different kinds of oppressive systems by exploring how they play out in real life. Because many of these overarching forces and systems are normalized in many of our day-to-day lives, naming and exploring them is an important first step to confront and ultimately put an end to them.

Colonization Is Ongoing

These deep-rooted systems all too often go unnamed despite the harm they cause to populations worldwide. For example, although there are dozens of references to Indigenous Peoples in the CSDH report, there are only two references to "colonization" and none to "colonialism." Even the references to colonization don't explicitly label it as a structural determinant. Yet, the Symposium on Indigenous Health, held in Australia in April 2007, after being initiated and endorsed by the CSDH itself, stated that while the realities of Indigenous Peoples are different between and within countries, there was a clear consensus that "the effect of colonization" was a "critical" social determinant of health, and that it "is not simply an historical process. It is ongoing" (Mowbray 2007, 30). In its 2013 report, the First Nations of Quebec and Labrador Health and Social Services Commission wrote that anti-Indigenous racism and discrimination are structural because of their roots in colonial history (Bacon 2013, 8). It went on to compare the 1876 Indian Act that remains in effect in Canada to this day to the now-defunct apartheid system in South Africa (9). In their 2015 report, *First Peoples, Second Class Treatment*, the Wellesley Institute authors assert that colonization "is recognized as a foundational determinant of Indigenous health globally" and emphasize that "racism and colonization are inextricably intertwined" (Allan and Smylie 2015, 6). In its 2019 report, *Just Societies: Health Equity and Dignified Lives*, the Pan American Health Organization called to "recognize and reverse the health equity impact of ongoing colonialism and structural racism," which it considers as structural drivers (PAHO 2019, 67). The National Collaborating Centre for Aboriginal Health (NCCAH) has written that "through colonization, colonialism, systemic racism and discrimination, Aboriginal peoples have been denied access to the resources and conditions necessary to maximize SES [socioeconomic status]" (Reading and Wien 2009, 13). This is important and reflects the earlier point made about the few getting rich because others are made poor in an economic system that values profits over people. A relatively recent historical example illustrates this point.

Stolen Eeyou Istchee and Inuit Land: "Offering Us What Is Ours"

In *Wrestling with Colonialism on Steroids: Quebec Inuit Fight for Their Homeland*, Zebedee Nungak explains that, in 1964, the governing provincial Liberals sent the first political delegation in Quebec's history to Nunavik, and "a brash, switched-on Minister of Natural Resources named René Lévesque opened up Le Grand Nord" (2017, 15–16, 38). This occurred fifty years after Inuit Land became part of Quebec through a 1912 colonial decree and twenty-five years after the Supreme Court of Canada ruled that the welfare of Nunavimmiut was a federal, not provincial, responsibility (SCC 1939, 104). As Nungak remarks, "Some strains of colonialism take their own sweet time to get around to examining their acquisitions" (Nungak 2017, 38).

A few years later, in 1971, the government of Quebec boastfully announced its James Bay hydroelectric project, dubbing it the "Project of the Century" (Nungak 2017, 39). The first phase of the ambitious megaproject involved diverting four rivers (Great Whale, Eastmain, Opinaca, and Caniapiscau) to create a series of seven reservoirs stretching almost 800 kilometres inland along the La Grande River (Richardson 1991, 20–1). Elizabeth Shashaweskum from the Eeyou community of Wemindji recalls, "When people heard that Sakami Lake would be flooded, they knew right away that the fish in this lake would be destroyed" (van Rosen 2010). James Shashaweskum, also from Wemindji, accompanied Elders to sites where rivers would be diverted and lands flooded, conveying how integral the land, waters, and wildlife are to the Eeyou: "It seemed, by the way the elders were reacting, that someone we loved had died" (van Rosen 2010).

The James Bay hydroelectric project was motivated by several factors, coming on the heels of Quebec's Quiet Revolution in the 1960s. It was an era marked by major political and social upheavals, rooted in the francophone majority's working-class consciousness, seeking to break free from anglophone economic domination (Vallières 1971, 42–9). Referring to himself as "a proletarian" and "a colonized man," journalist and revolutionary Pierre Vallières wrote that since the establishment of New France in the seventeenth century, "the workers of Quebec" have been "the servants of the imperialists constitut[ing] a reservoir of cheap labor whom the capitalists are completely free to" exploit, oppress, and criminalize (Vallières 1971, 13, 21–2). However, this historical subordination by the anglophone ruling class, which had undeniably nefarious consequences on all but the elite of the francophone majority in Quebec, should not obscure the fact that colonizers can be colonized, only to become colonizers once again. Philosopher Alain Deneault nuances this history by suggesting that "Québécois are not a colonized people, but proletariat settlers. The settler is the executor, the subaltern that gains many advantages of the colonial project by doing the grunt work" (Labrecque 2020). Either way, when it comes to Indigenous Peoples, the Quebec government has not shied away from being the colonizer, and the Québécois settler population has benefited, to various degrees, from both complicit and active participation in the colonial project.

Political science professor Martin Papillon comments that "the energetic needs of the province were a source of preoccupation, constant preoccupation," but that it was important for Quebec, "from a nationalist perspective, from a state-building and nation-building perspective, to occupy the land" (von Rosen 2010). Indeed, the hydroelectric megaproject was also intended to "secure Quebec's economic independence" through the creation of "a national identity ... that could unite and engage the entire population" (Martin 2008, 228). However, neither the Eeyou nor the Nunavimmiut were consulted nor even informed about the government's unilateral decision to begin construction (Richardson 1991, 20; Martin 2008, 230), even though "hunting and trapping grounds were literally being blasted to bits" already in Eeyou Istchee, and that "two rivers in Inuit lands – the Great Whale and Caniapiscau – were to be partially dammed and diverted" (Nungak 2017, 39, 52–3).

In 1973, the Eeyou and Inuit won a landmark court decision to halt the hydroelectric project (Martin 2008, 232). Quebec Superior Court Justice Albert Malouf ordered the provincial government and its agents to "cease trespassing on Cree and Inuit lands" (Nungak 2017, 65). However, the injunction was overturned a week later in the Quebec Court of Appeal on the basis of "balance of convenience" (Nungak 2017, 65), highlighting that "the rights and interests of the Aboriginal minority could not interfere with ... [those] of the general population of Quebec" (Dupuis 2008, 216). Late Waskaganish Grand Chief Billy Diamond's assessment of the loss was incisive: "We were only 5,000 Cree and Inuit, and 5,000 [Indigenous] people were not as important as 5 million Quebecers" (von Rosen 2010). Construction of the hydroelectric project resumed immediately, but the important matter of Indigenous Rights raised by Malouf's decision remained. Eeyou and Inuit opposition had forced the provincial government to negotiate; the alternative was going to the Supreme Court of Canada, with an uncertain outcome for all parties (Nungak 2017, 65–6).

Nungak was one of the Inuit negotiators and highlights "the paradox of Inuit being forced to claim what they believed had been their own lands *from the Qallunaat*," even though the "Inuit had never knowingly ceded their land to others, or lost it in war" (Nungak 2017, 90; emphasis in original). Nunavimmiut "ought to have been the acknowledged holders of all the land their ancestors had wandered for millennia" (90). At the time, Nungak affirmed that "it's up to the people who are invading it to try to disprove our ownership" (von Rosen 2010). Similarly, Eeyou negotiator Diamond pointed out,

"The land was never won in battle, the land was never given away, the land was never surrendered, so … the land was stolen. And what is stolen must be returned" (von Rosen 2010). In response to government "offers" during the negotiations, former Chisasbi Chief Roderick Pachano wondered, "How can you offer us something that's ours?" (von Rosen 2010).

Acrimonious negotiations led to the James Bay and Northern Quebec Agreement (JBNQA) being signed in 1975 "under heavy duress" (Richardson 1991, xvi). The Naskapi Nation, which was also impacted, signed the Northeastern Quebec Agreement in 1978 (Viens Commission 2019, 365n2556; Dupuis 2008, 220). The JBNQA outlined the provision of local public services for Eeyou and Inuit communities in northern Quebec, including education, health care, and social services (Nungak 2017, 79; see also Dupuis 2008, 219). The provincial and federal governments also allocated the sum of $225 million over the next two decades to twenty-two Indigenous communities in northern Quebec (Nungak 2017, 108), who nonetheless had to file multiple and repeated legal motions during the same period "to force the governments to honor their signatures" (Richardson 1991, xvii).

A second phase of the megaproject, the Great Whale Project, was ultimately defeated by the joint resistance of Eeyou and Nunavimmiut (Martin 2008, 227). Their highly publicized Odeyak expedition – a contraction of "canoe" and "kayak" in iiyiyuu ayimuun (Eeyou language) and Inuktitut – stopped throughout Quebec and the northeastern United States in the spring of 1990 to "rally opposition and challenge elected officials to boycott electricity from Hydro-Québec," the provincial utility (Martin 2008, 234). As sociology professor Thibault Martin explains, "The symbolic victory of the Crees and Inuit peoples, evidenced by the suspension of the project and their capacity to bear upon the execution of projects in exploiting international opinion, is certainly the origin of the Paix des Braves, a veritable alliance between Quebec and First Peoples" (Martin 2008, 243). Officially known as the Agreement Concerning a New Relationship Between the Gouvernement du Québec and the Crees of Québec (2002), the Paix des Braves calls for "the abandonment of a series of legal proceedings intended by the Crees," and allows the provincial government to build new hydroelectric projects in Eeyou Istchee, in exchange for "Cree participation in the development of this territory and of fees of $3.5 billion dollars to be paid by the government and the utility … for the right to exploit resources [including forestry and mining] in this region" (Dupuis 2008, 222). The new agreement was regarded by many as an important step forward in nation-to-nation negotiations (Saganash 2008, 205). As lawyer Renée Dupuis explains, then-premier Bernard Landry referred to it as a shining example of "new, more harmonious relationships between the Quebec government and the Crees of Quebec" (Dupuis 2008, 222), a characterization that government officials and politicians are quick to repeat to this day, particularly because of the pervasive rhetoric around "reconciliation" with Indigenous communities in recent years. However, the Paix des Braves "would never have materialized without the resistance of the Braves" (Martin 2008, 252). Moreover, as Dupuis points out, "This new deal does not supplant the JBNQA"; in fact, any related social change "will occur in the context of the JBNQA" (Dupuis 2008, 222).

Perhaps most pertinently, not everyone shares the government's enthusiasm, particularly among those initially impacted by the James Bay project. At the time, Abraham Weapinacappo, an Eeyou hunter, shared his regret: "I am one of those who went to Quebec City to put my signature on the James Bay Agreement. I should not have gone" (Richardson 1991, 336). More recently, in the documentary *Together We Stand Firm*, former Mistissini Chief Philip Awashish affirms that "there wasn't a single Cree who wanted the hydroelectric project, but we were faced with the reality that a project of some kind was going to eventually be built, with or without our consent" (von Rosen 2010). Eeyou and Inuit leaders felt that they could either make a deal to mitigate the damage and "get some money and some breathing space to prepare for the full weight of what the industrial world was proposing to dump on them – its wealth, technology, and insatiable appetite for energy – or hold out, and be completely swallowed" (Richardson 1991, xvi).

As Nungak notes, any benefits from the JBNQA came at a significant price: "Nobody else in Quebec ever had to trade the essence of their identity to gain access to public services" (Nungak 2017, 79). Quebec's "colonialism on steroids" meant that Inuit were forced to "surrender and extinguish their rights in and to the lands" (25, 88). The Inuit Tunngavingat Nunamini, a self-organized group representing dissenting voices from the communities of Ivujivik, Puvirnituq, and part of Salluit, was opposed to such an imposition and refused to sign the JBNQA; this group's ultimate goal was an autonomous

government by and for Inuit in Nunavik, not simply Nunavimmiut participation in provincially controlled bureaucracies administering services to the
population (Koperqualuk 2014; see also Nungak 2017, 85–7). Critics derisively
called the parcels of land allocated to Inuit through the JBNQA *sikkitaapiit*
(tiny squares): "Not only were they tiny in size compared to the total expanse
of the territory; Inuit would only own the surface rights, and not the sub-
surface" (Nungak 2017, 91). This was intentional on the part of the Quebec
government, which had overseen mineral claims registered on Inuit lands
since the 1950s (72). It should, therefore, come as no surprise that "officials
from hydro, energy, and development corporations [were] at the [negoti-
ations] table" in the 1970s; these "blasters and dynamiters" were there to "protect and promote their interests" (72). The provincial government went to
"great pains to prevent any known mineral or other wealth from being
owned by Inuit" (91).

Once underway, the megaproject had health consequences for communities impacted by the dams. Hydro-Québec claims that "more than 99%"
of its power output is "clean and renewable" (Hydro-Québec 2019, 3). But
clean for whom? Within a few years of the first phase's completion, mercury
was contaminating the waters where people fished. Activist and writer
Winona LaDuke noted that over two-thirds of the population of Chisasibi
"were found to have excessive levels of methyl mercury already in their
bodies," with some Elders exhibiting symptoms of mercury toxicity, including neurological damage (LaDuke 1991, xi). The situation must have been
dire because "Hydro-Québec advised the Cree to stop eating river fish and
instead to harvest fish from James and Hudson's bays" (xi). This "fish disease," which the Eeyou called *nimass aksiwin*, caused a lot of fear. George
Lameboy, an Eeyou fisherman and trapper, said, "It's like being told that
armageddon has started, and people are scared as hell" (xi). Bill Namagoose,
of the Cree Regional Authority, referred to the situation as an example of
"environmental racism" (xii). LaDuke highlights the double standards inherent in such a project having gone forward at all: "If Hydro-Québec proposed to flood the villages, farms, homes, and gravesites of thousands of
French-speaking white people, well, it just wouldn't happen" (xii).

Ultimately, though, as LaDuke reminds us, "Perhaps most horrendous is
that this massive experiment is all about making money" (1991, xiii). Based

on its 2018 annual report, almost half of Hydro-Québec's hydroelectricity and over a third of its total electricity was generated on Eeyou, Inuit, and Naskapi Traditional Lands, covered by the JBNQA and the Northeastern Quebec Agreement (Hydro-Québec 2019, 118; see Figure 14.1). The report boasts about a public satisfaction index of 93 per cent, owing at least in part to a residential rate (between 7.13¢/kWh and 8.04¢/kWh in 2018) considered the lowest in Canada (Whitmore and Pineau 2020, 56) or even all of North America (Hydro-Québec 2019, 2). Meanwhile, only Newfoundland-Labrador has a cheaper commercial rate than the 4¢/kWh offered in Quebec (Whitmore and Pineau 2020, 56). This is undoubtedly an incentive for large companies – including from extractive (i.e., mining) and transformation (e.g., aluminum) industries – to set up shop in Quebec and may explain why the rate of industrial electricity consumption in the province on a per capita basis is the second highest in Canada, after Saskatchewan (Pierre-Olivier Pineau, chair in energy sector management at HEC Montréal, pers. comm., 2020). Hydro-Québec's annual report states its "contribution to the Québec government's revenue exceeded $4 billion, totaling $4.5 billion" in 2018 alone (Hydro-Québec 2019, 40). Since Hydro-Québec is fully nationalized, this amount included a huge $2.3 billion dividend (i.e., 75 per cent of Hydro-Québec's net income), paid to the utility's sole shareholder, the Quebec government (Hydro-Québec 2019, 39, 42). Hydro-Québec's remarkably lucrative status in 2018 resulted in performance bonuses of almost $29 million shared among its 20,000 employees and another $7 million for its 180 upper managers, including an annual bonus of $250,000 for its CEO, Éric Martel, formerly of Bombardier (Nadeau 2019; Bernier and Posca 2020, 5). While the Eeyou and Inuit were forced to "surrender and extinguish their rights in and to the lands" when they signed the JBNQA (Nungak 2017, 25, 88; Dupuis 2008, 218–19), Hydro-Québec's management, the government of Quebec, and the settler population have profited – and continue to profit – handsomely from the expropriation.* In light of this, Health Minister Gaétan Barrette invoking limited "budgetary capacities" during the #aHand2Hold

---

* In February 2020, the Eeyou Nation of Eeyou Istchee and the government of Quebec signed a memorandum of understanding for the Grande Alliance, an "economic development agreement" worth $4.7 billion over thirty years, and described as being in continuity with the JBNQA and the Paix des Braves (Bell et al. 2020).

campaign appears all the more farcical, given that the government benefits from the dispossession experienced by the very same Eeyou and Inuit communities whose children were disproportionately impacted by ÉVAQ's non-accompaniment rule.

The James Bay hydroelectric project was a massive and unprecedented initiative, necessitating the expropriation of nearly 350,000 square kilometres to build roads, airports, and construction sites, diverting rivers and flooding over 10,000 square kilometres of land, and creating the dams that "wreaked ecological havoc" on another 175,000 square kilometres of Indigenous Territory (Richardson 1991, 20–1; LaDuke 1991, x). However, the Eeyou, Naskapi, and Nunavimmiut are not the only Indigenous Peoples impacted by Hydro-Québec's dam projects (Hydro-Québec 2018, 4–5; see Figure 14.1). These projects have also been opposed by other Indigenous Nations – including the Innu, whose territory generates a third of Hydro-Québec's hydroelectricity, and the Atikamekw (Delisle L'Heureux 2018, 33–5; Baril 2018).

In fact, to some extent, virtually all Indigenous communities throughout Quebec and Canada have experienced displacement from and theft of their lands, which are often left destroyed and poisoned by the colonial governments and corporate entities who pillage and plunder them. According to Paul Dixon, director of the Cree Trappers Association, mining companies and the forestry industry in Quebec have normalized mass-scale exploitation of the land to make short-term profits without any regard for the future or for those who are impoverished as a result: "The land is left in ruins, and they call it wealth" (Nadeau 2020). Leilani Farah, the United Nations Special Rapporteur on the Right to Housing, has stated that Indigenous Peoples are disproportionately impacted by such exploitative activities; they are forced off their lands and migrate to Canadian cities where "apartheid-like" housing conditions prevail (Riopel 2019). Meanwhile, land defence initiatives against resource exploitation are repressed and criminalized, as exemplified by the long-standing struggle of the Wet'suwet'en against the construction of TC Energy's 670km-long Coastal GasLink pipeline (Dhillon and Parrish 2019) or the Innu resistance to Hydro-Québec's La Romaine dam complex (Giroux 2016, 67–8, 72). Profiting from the land has always been at the core of the colonial project, whether hundreds of years ago or today.

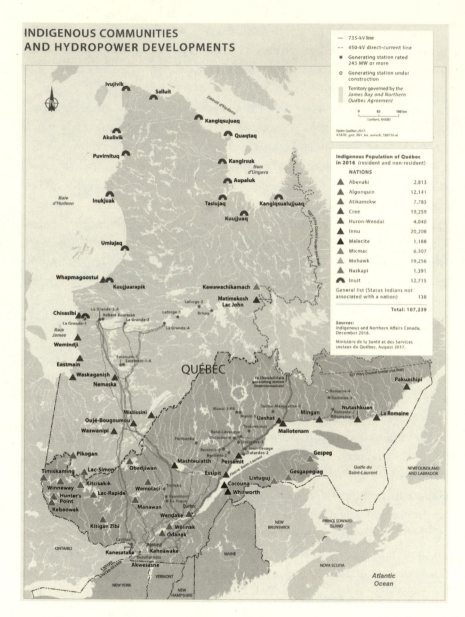

INDIGENOUS COMMUNITIES AND HYDROPOWER DEVELOPMENTS

— 735-kV line
-- 450-kV direct-current line
● Generating station rated 245 MW or more
○ Generating station under construction
Territory governed by the James Bay and Northern Québec Agreement

0   83   166 km
Lambert, NAD83

Hydro-Québec, 2017.
41870_geo_061_bv_avtech_160716.ai

Indigenous Population of Québec in 2016 (resident and non-resident)

NATIONS

Nation	Population
Abenaki	2,813
Algonquin	12,141
Atikamekw	7,783
Cree	19,259
Huron-Wendat	4,040
Innu	20,208
Malecite	1,188
Micmac	6,307
Mohawk	19,256
Naskapi	1,391
Inuit	12,715

General list (Status Indians not associated with a nation)   138

Total: 107,239

Sources:
Indigenous and Northern Affairs Canada, December 2016.

Ministère de la Santé et des Services sociaux du Québec, August 2017.

14.1 Indigenous communities and hydropower developments
The original image, with colour-coded symbols for Indigenous Nations represented on the map, is available in "Hydro-Québec and Indigenous Communities" (Hydro-Québec 2018, 2).

Land, Indigenous Self-Determination, and Sovereignty: An Antidote to Medical Colonialism

Actions and movements to reclaim and assert stewardship of Traditional Territories are critical for Indigenous Nations and communities. These include initiatives like "walking the land," harvesting practices (e.g., hunting, fishing, gathering), and cultural production activities (e.g., hide-tanning, carving) that assert Indigenous sovereignty (Coulthard 2014, 171). It is also critical to recognize that "interrelated systems of dispossession" have shaped Indigenous experiences "in *both* urban and land-based settings" (Coulthard 2014, 176; emphasis in original). Because of the relationships many Indigenous Peoples have "with their land and the ecology that has traditionally culturally defined and sustained them," the Pan American Health Organization has recommended that Indigenous Land itself should be considered a determinant of health (PAHO 2019, 74). Children's health and well-being also stand to benefit from such a recognition. For example, research published in 1998 found that a handful of "markers of cultural continuity" were protective factors against suicide for Indigenous youth in British Columbia. Land claims and land titles were one of them. History suggests that "suicide is in part a *normal human reaction to conditions of prolonged, ruthless domination*" (Chrisjohn et al. 2017, 9, emphasis in original). This may explain the researchers' finding that youth living in communities where there were "long-standing efforts to exert control over their traditional land base" had a "substantially lower" rate of suicide (Chandler and Lalonde 1998, 211). The other cultural continuity markers identified in the study were "self-government (particularly the involvement of women), control of education, security and cultural facilities, as well as control of the policies and practice of health and social programs" (Reading and Wien 2009, 21). Communities where all six markers were present had no suicides over the study period of five years (Chandler and Lalonde 1998, 215).

The study supported what Indigenous communities identified long ago as being critical to ensuring that they thrive as a people: self-determination. More recently, the 2014 Inuit Tapiriit Kanatami report on SDH concluded that a "key action for future success is the support of increasing levels of self-determination in Inuit regions" (ITK 2014, 6). The NCCAH has stated that "self-determination has been cited as the most important determinant of health among Aboriginal peoples" (Reading and Wien 2009, 24). To this end, Indigenous Peoples "*must participate equally* in political decision-making, as well as *possess control over* their lands, economies, education systems, and social and health services" (Reading and Wien 2009, 24; emphasis added). Indigenous self-determination can't happen as long as colonial governments forcefully prevent it through legislation, laws, policies, and practices that seek to maintain their domination and advantages.

This is where the disastrous handling of ÉVAQ's non-accompaniment practice comes back into the picture: to recognize people as self-determining, they have to be treated like human beings. Not like caricatures, not like cargo, not like experimental materials, not like animals. Human beings. Human beings with dignity who deserve to be treated with respect. And this is what was always missing in how this issue was handled, whether decades ago, or in response to the #aHand2Hold campaign in 2018.

Even if we ignore the many years that this practice could have been changed and rewind to the fall of 2017, when ÉVAQ decided to take well-intentioned, albeit modest, steps that could eventually have led to a change in practice, its actions were tainted by a medical colonial approach. ÉVAQ leadership reached out to medical and nursing teams – overwhelmingly made up of white health care providers – in Kuujjuaq and Puvirnituq (see Bernier et al. 2018, 129–30). The input of these teams was undoubtedly necessary, but informed sources had confirmed to me then that the perspectives and experiences of Inuit families who had experienced child-caregiver separation weren't directly solicited. In February 2018, after the health minister announced an imminent FCC policy, efforts could have been made to reach out to Eeyou and Inuit families, as well as other impacted communities, to learn how to improve medevac airlift services. Instead of inviting someone from these communities to do cultural safety training for ÉVAQ staff anticipating the change in practice, ÉVAQ invited a physician from Kuujjuaq to talk about the "context of the patients" (Bernier et al. 2018, 118). Aside from the Nunavik Regional Board of Health and Social Services, as well as (mostly non-Indigenous) medical and nursing teams from health care centres in Nunavik, no "other partners or Indigenous organizations" were consulted in the elaboration of the FCC framework (122–3). When it was released on 29 June 2018, there was no version in Inuktitut or any of the other Indigenous languages spoken in the communities served by ÉVAQ (119). Yet, decades ago, in 1964, René Lévesque, then the minister of natural resources (who would go on to become one of the most influential premiers in Quebec history), had told Inuk leader Taamusi Qumaq that Inuit should be able to speak their languages and that it should be "the whites who work in Inuit communities that should speak Inuktitut because they are here to serve the Inuit" (Qumaq 2010, 94).

Indigenous communities were not invited to participate equally in the political decision-making that established and maintained the non-accompaniment rule for all these years. In this case, as in so many others, they did not possess control over health care services that were meant for them. At the end of the day, it was ÉVAQ, along with the provincial Ministry of Health and Ministry of Transport, that was calling the shots.

The #aHand2Hold campaign's demand to end the non-accompaniment rule could have ignored the conditions that caused Indigenous children from northern and remote areas of Quebec to bear a disproportionate burden of the practice. However, this was much more than a simple human-interest story, which is why there was an explicit emphasis, as the campaign evolved, on the economic and social conditions that were produced by governing colonial powers. This could have been an opportunity for the Ministry of Health and the provincial government to partner with Indigenous communities and leaders to tangibly commit to addressing the structural determinants of health and understand why Indigenous children are more likely to require medevac airlifts in the first place. Such an exercise would have gone a long way toward improving the health care of Indigenous children.

Instead, the health minister went from invoking limited budgetary capacities that played off the anti-Indigenous "freeloader" trope in May 2018 to overtly perpetuating racist stereotypes of the "drunken Indian" barely weeks later in June. In its press release in response to Barrette's now-infamous comments, the Assembly of First Nations of Quebec and Labrador wondered what efforts had been made by high-level government officials "to ensure that their Cabinet colleagues do not send a discriminatory message in the ministries and entities under their authority" (AFNQL 2018). Chief Ghislain Picard went on to recommend seeking out "the roots of discrimination" within the government's executive (AFNQL 2018). There was no meaningful public response by the provincial government to these calls for change.

The silence speaks loudly. It echoes the structural determinants of health that allowed the non-accompaniment practice to persist all these years. Using a sdh lens to analyze the government's handling of the issue – up until and including the #aHand2Hold campaign – allows us to peel away at the various layers that reinforce the status quo to expose a rotten core: systemic racism and colonialism infect everything.

Chapter 15

Decolonizing Health Care: Reparations before Reconciliation

If you stick a knife in my back nine inches and pull it out six inches,
that's not progress.
If you pull it all the way out, that's not progress.
The progress comes from healing the wound that the blow made.
– El-Hajj Malik El-Shabazz (formerly known as Malcolm X)

I don't believe in reconciliation. I don't believe in that word.
There's too much to do for us to be able to talk about reconciliation.
– Lara Kramer, in Catherine Lalonde, "Windigo: manger le corps,
la terre et le pays," *Le Devoir*

Vos doctrines ont créé des sévices
C'est beau pardonner, mais j'ai soif de justice.
– Samian, "REZ"

Decades ago, when ÉVAQ's non-accompaniment rule was first applied, the intention may not have been to discriminate against Indigenous communities in northern Quebec. We'll never know for certain though as no paper trail tracing its origins exists since there was no written policy in the first place. However, it became a practice of medical colonialism, rooted in systemic anti-Indigenous racism, when the long-standing calls to change the practice – coming from the northern Indigenous communities themselves – were ignored by successive governments; when the Ministry of Health and Social Services chose not to implement the clear consensus in the medical literature favouring parental accompaniment as an integral part of child- and family-centred care; when caregiver accompaniment during emergency medevac airlifts became the standard of care in comparable jurisdictions across the country and ÉVAQ didn't follow suit; when the Ministry of Transport didn't prioritize finding ways for ÉVAQ planes to accommodate a caregiver at times when the fleet was being upgraded. Perhaps more tangibly, every time ÉVAQ prevented a caregiver from accompanying their child on a Challenger medevac was another missed opportunity to right a historical wrong.

The Role of Health Care Providers: Claiming a False Neutrality

The Viens Commission's final report specifically cites the ÉVAQ example as being one of many situations where government inaction in response to the "real needs expressed by Indigenous peoples" resulted in "preventing trust from being restored between Indigenous people and public services" (Viens Commission 2019, 211–12). Indeed, the ultimate responsibility goes beyond ÉVAQ and lies with the provincial government for having allowed this practice to persist for so long. However, do individual health care workers have the agency and a responsibility to disrupt unjust practices and policies? Is simply "following the rules" an acceptable justification for allowing inequities to persist? If Indigenous children living in northern communities are more likely to be sick or injured through no fault of their own based on the accident of birth (i.e., the conditions they are born into, over which they have no control), weren't the actions of health care personnel preventing caregivers and parents from accompanying them only adding insult to injury?

In some cases, the nurse or physician working at the referring centre may have had to break the news to the parent or caregiver that their child was going to be airlifted alone. Dr Geneviève Bois, a spokesperson for Médecins québécois pour le régime public when it came out in support of the #aHand2Hold campaign (MQRP 2018), recounted how onerous this task was. As a family physician working in the community of Whapmagoostui, she was particularly marked by an Eeyou child who was placed on the plane while yelling for her mother, with no one to reassure her (Gervais 2018b). Those of us who ultimately took care of these children in pediatric hospitals in Montreal (and in Quebec City) and didn't try to do something are not without blame either. The practice had been ongoing for decades, but we hadn't put an end to it. In my case, before the summer of 2017, I wasn't even aware that members of the Northern and Native Child Health Program at the MCH had tried. A pediatric emergency physician colleague had brought this issue to my attention many times in the preceding few years, but it took two particularly jarring cases for me to finally do something. There was a tangible consequence of having done nothing, of having accepted the untenable status quo, instead of intervening sooner – the suffering inflicted on the hundreds of children who were transferred by medevac alone every year.

And for this, no apology I offer to those children or their families will be sufficient. But I am sorry.

As I mentioned in the Introduction, a former pediatric resident struck right at the heart of the problem for those of us working in public health care: our complicity with a system that, at best, accepts health inequities and injustices borne by Indigenous Peoples and that, at worst, exacerbates or produces them. Some may argue that, as health care providers just doing our job in a system that ostensibly seeks to alleviate suffering, cure diseases, and keep people healthy, we can only do good. Or, at the very least, that we can't cause harm if we do our best because we consider ourselves to be "neutral." I wish this were true. It's not.

I don't doubt the genuine intentions of most people who enter the health care field. Some of us are even fuelled by a burning desire for social justice. But we are not neutral. Claiming neutrality ignores history, politics, and the privileges that come – or don't come – from one's social position. As the late radical historian of people's movements and Second World War veteran Howard Zinn was fond of saying, we simply "can't be neutral on a moving train" (Zinn 1994, 7–8). The train in question here is that of colonialism, and it has never stopped. Its cargo is violence, dispossession, exploitation, oppression, and genocide.

The medical establishment, heavily influenced by physicians, has its own rules, priorities, and values, its own ideologies and its own culture. Just like so much of the anatomy, physiology, and pharmacology that we're taught in medicine is based on the "norm" of a young white able-bodied 70-kilogram male (see Chapter 5), so is the health care system structured by those in power to cater to certain parts of the population more than others.

Unquestionably, various demographic groups (certainly Indigenous, but also Black and other racialized people, women, individuals with disabilities, 2SLGBTIQ+, those living on the street, drug users, the elderly, etc.) face various barriers preventing them from accessing dignified health care. Uninsured migrants – some of whom are Indigenous Peoples from other parts of the world – may avoid seeking care in public institutions if they are non-status out of fear of being detained and deported by government authorities. Others may delay seeking medical attention in the hopes that their symptoms abate; medical coroners have issued reports lamenting how some have even died as a result (Rioux Soucy 2007). The uninsured are simply not entitled to receive services at all without paying exorbitant fees or going into crushing debt because of the borders erected within the public health care system itself (Bettache and Shaheen-Hussain 2017). Access to health care for prisoners in Canada has been described as "deplorable" (Martin and Walia 2019, 134). Prison bars ensure that those who are incarcerated will not receive the health care services that everyone should be entitled to, penalizing them further even though they are already serving their sentence. Indigenous Peoples in particular are "disproportionately criminalized by the criminal justice system – from arrest to incarceration" (Monchalin 2016, 144). Indigenous women in Montreal are eleven times more likely to be stopped by the police than white women (Armony et al. 2019, 11); they are one of the fastest-growing prison populations in the country (PSCPCSC 2018, 63) and are often sentenced for poverty-related offences (Martin and Walia 2019, 132–3). This reality for Indigenous Peoples informs the powerful social critique made in the song "REZ" by Abitibiwinni (Algonquin) hip-hop artist Samian: "Un Indien au Canada, c'est un prisonnier politique."

These barriers don't occur randomly or by accident. If they did, the people who are impacted could understandably be considered "vulnerable." But, when a state of vulnerability is created by the very way society is structured and functions, the term "vulnerable" is a euphemism that erases the process of marginalization. Inequalities in health care follow the fault lines of societal injustices. Systems that dominate and oppress create categories of people who are subordinated, dispossessed, and exploited. This can only be characterized as structural violence.

As Cindy Blackstock has argued, "good intentions and conviction are not enough" to address this state of affairs; rather, it is "what we do in our actions that is most important" (Blackstock 2009, 36). I'm quite certain that those of us who work in the public health care system do not *want* to perpetuate or commit injustices. However, even though we inherit both the privileges and injustices we are born into, and we have no control over what happened in the past, we can't ignore them. We also can't ignore that we have the agency to act now. If social justice is a priority in this society, then we – especially those of us who benefit from various societal privileges – have a responsibility to actively confront the medical colonialism that is rooted in anti-Indigenous systemic racism. Taking up our responsibilities to work both within and outside the health care system means committing to confronting the status quo that has devastating effects on the lives of Indigenous Peoples. The alternative – doing nothing – means that we are complicit in the colonial system.

Systemic Change: Going to the Roots

So, what can we do? Gaining a historical perspective of the system within which we work is an important first step. Historically, grassroots social movements have won victories for better access or more dignified health care. Very few of these victories were top-down changes implemented by governments and institutions purely because they were the right thing to do; most came after being pushed in some form or another from below. Top-down initiatives often run counter to the spirit of movements for social justice, including in health care (Jones 2019, 304–5). When those in power do make concessions, their motivation is rarely obtaining justice, but rather self-interest (whether financial, political, or social). The development of Medicare, the public system in Canada, is an example of the importance of such grassroots mobilization (Jones 2019, 16–19; Fuller 1998, 18–19). Yet, the Canadian narrative is fixated on the mythology created around the charismatic figure of Reverend Tommy Douglas, known as "the father of medicare" (Jones 2019, 15).

Few of us know that Douglas espoused eugenicist perspectives. In his 1933 master's thesis, "The Problems of the Subnormal Family," he considers as "subnormal" any family who is "mentally defective" or "delinquent" and who may be subject to "social disease" and/or "be a public charge" (Douglas 1933, 1). His thesis focused on a town in Saskatchewan studying a dozen women whom he qualified as "immoral" (i.e., "common prostitutes") or "non-moral" (i.e., "mental defectives"); what was common to them was that they, and their children, were all "indigents who are entirely dependent upon charity for their support" (2). He divided his "suggested remedies" according to the roles played by the state, the school, and the church (19–20). Among his state-based solutions for these "subnormal families," Douglas advocated sterilization, which "would deprive them of nothing that they value very highly, and would make it impossible for them to reproduce those whose presence could contribute little to the general well-being of society" (26). He also proposed "social segregation" by placing families "on a state farm, or in a colony where decisions could be made for them;" the men would work in the fields and the women would become "better housewives and better managers of the family finance" (24–5). He reproduced many of the same themes and conclusions in an article he wrote for his socialist Cooperative Commonwealth Federation (CCF) the following year, entitled "Youth and the New Age" (Shevell 2012, 37–8). For Douglas, nothing less than the fate of society hung in the balance: "Upon the degree to which we respond to this problem will depend the permanence of our civilization" (Douglas 1933, 55). His convictions may have evolved with time, including around forced sterilization (Shevell, 2012, 38). However, it is likely that some of his ideas stayed with him through the years, including when he was in power. In 1944, when he was elected the premier of Saskatchewan as the leader of the CCF, he continued and expanded on "social planning" schemes initiated by the previous government. This included the development of Métis colonies designed as model farms where "Métis heads of families would learn skills to maintain a modern farm under the supervision of white instructors ... to integrate ... into the modern workforce" (MMIWG 2019a, 291). Many Métis found these farms to be "alienating and unworkable;" Douglas's CCF government "did not consider a Métis perspective, and [the attempted solutions] amounted to little more than a high-handed attempt to restructure Métis life according to Canadian racial and gender expectations" (MMIWG 2019a, 292).

There is no reason to think that such an approach in social policy was not adopted in health care as well. Indeed, historian Esyllt W. Jones points out that the "greatest structural inequity" of the "socialized medicine" that was implemented by Douglas around the same time in Saskatchewan was "its failure to ensure that Indigenous peoples benefited equally" (Jones 2019, 305). Grassroots movements pushing for a visionary model of health care were not immune to the pervasive anti-Indigenous racism that existed in broader colonial-settler Canadian society. This was doubly disappointing because it "was both a missed opportunity to formulate a health politics based on racial equality and a failure to join forces with Indigenous activists who were already struggling to improve health access" (Jones 2019, 140). The future would have been very different if the goal was building a socialized medical system that was based on equity and social justice. Instead, the system that developed was "generated without Indigenous input and shaped by a colonialist mentality" (Jones 2019, 140).

Several years later, when the public health care system we now know as Medicare was implemented across the country, many Canadians celebrated. However, it only made matters worse for Indigenous Peoples because "national hospital and health insurance finally provided the federal government with a golden opportunity to jettison its legal responsibilities for Aboriginal people's health" (Lux 2016, 191). Responsibility for Indigenous health care was shifted to the provinces and as a result, "jurisdictional disputes … exposed Aboriginal people to the excesses of aggrieved provincial administrations and local boards, which dismissed them as interlopers and less worthy of care" (193). Medical historian Maureen Lux notes that what was "more ominous still was the understanding that Medicare would enable the federal government to fulfil its assimilationist goal and abandon its legal and treaty obligations" (193). Ultimately, as Jones observes, "it is impossible to read a history of Canadian health care without acknowledging exclusion, segregation, and experimentation upon Indigenous bodies in the name of medicine" (Jones 2019, 20). Health care activists either didn't care, ignored, or actively excluded the issues being raised by Indigenous Peoples at the time. This is why it is not only imperative for changes to occur now, but these changes must be radical: we have go to the roots.

Representation and Disruption

Ensuring that Indigenous Peoples have equitable access to the educational opportunities that have been historically restricted to them is imperative. This requires an upstream restructuring of educational initiatives by centring the histories and knowledge systems of Indigenous Peoples and their communities. Children can be empowered from a young age to cultivate their interest in science and health care as they grow older. The innovative Eagle Spirit Science Futures Camp, a week-long summer camp for Indigenous youth from across the country, is one such example. Under the leadership of Kent Saylor, a Kanien'kehá:ka pediatrician, McGill University's Indigenous Health Professions Program team has run the camp for the last few years (an earlier iteration of the camp was initially organized by the First Peoples' House). The camp has a major focus on science taught from an Indigenous perspective (Kent Saylor, pers. comm., 2019).

More downstream, in terms of medical admissions, the Royal Commission on Aboriginal Peoples (RCAP) recommended that ten thousand Indigenous health care and social service providers be trained over ten years, including in priority areas identified by Indigenous Peoples such as community development, health administration, and public health (RCAP 1996b, 246). That was in 1996. With major underrepresentation in health care remaining almost two decades later, the TRC of Canada called on all levels of government to increase the number of Indigenous professionals working in health care (TRC 2015a, 164). In May 2019, a landmark report by a working group of the Indigenous Health Network (IHN) included ten actionable items, approved by the Association of Faculties of Medicine of Canada representing all medical schools across the country. The IHN recommended that medical schools admit "a specific minimum number of First Nations, Métis and Inuit students each year by employing distinctions based approaches and practising holistic file reviews" (IHN 2019, 11).

Certainly, increasing Indigenous representation is important for several reasons. Persons from Indigenous communities are more likely to serve Indigenous (or other underrepresented) populations, and increasing Indigenous involvement in various processes (admissions, promotions, and hiring) can lead to individuals with a greater diversity of backgrounds and experiences in medicine that can only expand what and how we learn (Razack et al. 2019, 5). Despite the significant backlash to the revamped admissions processes within McGill's Faculty of Medicine (discussed in Chapter 5), other medical schools across Canada have had a smoother transition. As a result, 10 per cent of the medical class at the University of Manitoba is Indigenous, while Indigenous students make up 12 per cent of the class at the Northern Ontario School of Medicine (Friesen 2019b). However, as Angela Robertson, a long-time health-justice advocate based in Toronto, stated during the

"Police Violence, anti-Black Racism and Health Care" session of the Liberation Health Convergence in 2019: "representation is not disruption." Greater representation by historically underrepresented and marginalized groups will not on its own fundamentally disrupt the medical establishment, nor its elitism and hierarchies. Increasing representation to achieve "diversity" checkmarks risks simply having "more brown faces in white spaces" (Gaudry and Lorenz 2018, 220).

Cultural Safety

Improving Indigenous representation in medical schools without fundamentally changing medical culture will not prevent students from experiencing racism throughout their training and will have limited impacts on the health care services provided to Indigenous Peoples and communities in the clinical setting. Based on her experience as a Cree-Anishnaabe physician and drawing on the experiences of other Indigenous physicians and trainees, Marcia Anderson, chair of the IHN, notes that "a lot of the racism that students experience is from their classmates" (Passi and McGill, 2019). In light of this and because tools with racial bias are still used in medical admissions processes, the IHN also recommended that the "assessment of knowledge of Indigenous studies, cultural safety, anti-racism" be added to the admission process for all candidates through new tools "that are developed and assessed by Indigenous people" (IHN 2019, 10–11). Drawing on previous recommendations by the RCAP (1996b, 259) and the TRC (2015a, 164), the IHN has called on medical schools to "commit to the development and implementation of a longitudinal Indigenous health curriculum with anti-racism/anti-colonialism as the core pedagogical approaches" (IHN 2019, 14). Because students need to recognize that "the tendency to attribute Aboriginal peoples' poor health to personal life choices is rooted in a neoliberal ideology of individualism that justifies decreasing commitment to the promotion of social justice," one approach could include developing a "facilitated process to confront, understand and dismantle stereotypes" (Ly and Crowshoe 2015, 620). Critically examining the practice of medical colonialism is important to understand the colonial underpinnings of the medical establishment in Canada. The longitudinal Indigenous health curriculum recommended by the IHN is meant to continue through into postgraduate medical education with the additional core focus on cultural safety, to "prepare physicians for anti-racist, culturally safe independent practice" (IHN 2019, 16).

Cultural safety can be conceptualized "as being on a continuum or part of a process-orientated approach from cultural awareness to cultural sensitivity to cultural safety" (Gerlach 2012, 153; see also Tam 2019, 46–8). The idea was elaborated in the 1980s by the late Irihapeti Ramsden, a Maori nurse and educator who identified that "the significant health disparities experienced by the Maori people of New Zealand were a direct outcome of over a century of colonialism and chronic cycles of poverty" (Gerlach 2012, 152).

Cultural safety is "an educational framework for the analysis of power relationships between health professionals and those they serve" (Ellison-Loschmann 2003, 453). At its core is the principle that "historical, economical, and social contexts influence health status and health care services," which is why the lens is shifted from the individual to the "social, economic, and political position of certain groups within society" (Gerlach 2012, 152). Fundamentally, cultural safety "aims to unveil often deeply rooted, and largely unconscious and unspoken, assumptions of power held by health educators, students, and providers, and to transfer some of this power to health care recipients ... prompting health care providers to critically reflect on and question their personal cultural heritage, colonial history, and the contemporary cultural nature of health care and the respective impact of each on health care encounters and relationships" (152–3). The responsibility falls on "the dominant health care culture to undertake a process of change and transformation" (153). More recently, the scope of cultural safety "has expanded to include a focus on institutional change" (Tam 2019, 46). This critical approach to power is a useful tool to understand "how taken-for-granted practices, policies, and research approaches can inadvertently create health inequities" (Gerlach 2012, 153). Grounded in Indigenous values and knowledge systems, cultural safety "also reflects a collective and community desire for social transformation and innovation on the part of the Indigenous peoples ... based on the cornerstone principle of social justice, and above all, is part of a clear and legitimate affirmation of identity politics and Indigenous governance" (Viens Commission 2019, 368).

Indigenous Peoples have been leading the charge promoting cultural safety for years, along with more specific approaches including experiential learning in education (Arkle et al. 2015, 8; Ly and Crowshoe 2015, 620) and trauma-informed care in the clinical setting, which shifts the paradigm of care provision from asking "what is wrong with you?" to that of exploring "what happened to you?" (Tam 2019, 49; see also Martin and Walia 2019, 184; MMIWG 2019b, 180). In November 2018, the Viens Commission heard from Minnie's Hope, a social pediatrics centre created and led almost exclusively by women in the neighbouring communities of Whapmagoostui (Eeyou) and Kuujjuaraapik (Inuit). It has been described as a "health clinic, community centre, therapy room and support group all rolled into one" (MacKinnon 2018). Johanne Morel, pediatrician and director of the Northern and Native Child Health Program at the MCH, who is involved with Minnie's Hope, considers it to be unique in the country (although similar initiatives are cropping up elsewhere) because it "offers a new model of care with respect, a non-judgmental approach, and cultural safety as core values" (Johanne Morel, pers. comm., 2019). The Viens Commission's final report has called for supporting such culturally safe initiatives by and for Indigenous Peoples (Viens Commission 2019, 370).

The IHN's call for a focus on anticolonialism, antiracism, and cultural safety training is ambitious and innovative, and highlights the important role of Indigenous leadership more broadly in medical education (i.e., not compartmentalized to "Indigenous-focused" curricula). If these programs are properly implemented in compulsory longitudinal Indigenous health curricula, future generations of trainees may be able to shift the medical culture in such a way to provide culturally safe health care to Indigenous Peoples. The rest of the population can only stand to benefit by more engaged, reflective, and respectful health care workers and the systems they would re-shape. The ripple effects can be far-reaching. As educator and historian Howard Zinn once wrote: "I'm not interested in just reproducing class after class of graduates who will get out, become successful, and take their obedient places in the slots that society has prepared for them. What we must do – whether we teach or write or make films – is educate a new generation to do this very modest thing: change the world" (Zinn 2004, 15).

Decolonizing Health Care

Informed by the health care-specific calls to action of the TRC and pushed by Indigenous physicians within their organizations, the College of Family

Physicians of Canada (via their Indigenous Health Working Group) and the Royal College of Physicians and Surgeons of Canada have taken steps to acknowledge the impacts of systemic racism and colonialism, and to begin to counter them (IHWG 2016; RCPSC 2019). Such shifts are important. Going further, a 2015 Canadian Federation of Medical Students position paper proposes "interventions to begin the process of decolonization within Canadian medical éducation" (Arkle et al. 2015, 1). For its part, the IHN has called on medical schools to develop "focused and strategic professional development activities based in anti-racism, cultural safety and decolonization" (IHN 2019, 9).

But what exactly is decolonization? As Mi'kmaq legal scholar Pamela Palmater explains, for Indigenous Peoples "decolonization is about realizing that we have power to take back what is rightfully ours and ensure a future for our future generations" (Palmater 2017, 78). It "should be a balance of both resistance and resurgence, where we withdraw from harmful government processes and relationships and reengage in those relationships that have sustained us for millennia – with the land, the water, our people and our cultures" (77). Kanien'kehá:ka lawyer and professor Beverly Jacobs has written that decolonization means living in a society based on true partnerships where everyone feels safe and people treat each other with respect (Jacobs 2017, 50–1). Decolonizing approaches aim "to resist and undo the forces of colonialism and to re-establish Indigenous Nationhood" by recognizing "the principle that Indigenous Peoples have the right to govern themselves" (MMIWG 2019b, 170–1). Indeed, decolonization necessarily occurs through self-determination (Mowbray 2007, 30).

The implications within the health care system are significant. After all, the limitations of the dominant, colonial medical paradigm for Indigenous Peoples have been described for some time (O'Neil 1993, 39). As such, exclusively reform-based strategies within the current public health care system are not a panacea. Tibetha Kemble, director of Indigenous Health in the Faculty of Medicine and Dentistry at the University of Alberta, stated in a recent interview that "the specific experience of colonization, the impacts of residential schools has left a legacy of mistrust in Indigenous patients in particular," which is why "Indigenous physicians understand the lived reality of Indigenous patients," including the importance of traditional healing methods (Ohler 2018). The RCAP highlighted the significance of "traditional medicine and healing practices, the possibilities for co-operation and collaboration, and the importance of recognizing, affirming and respecting traditional practices and practitioners" (RCAP 1996b, 268). The TRC developed this further by calling "upon those who can effect change within the Canadian health-care system to recognize the value of Aboriginal healing practices and use them in the treatment of Aboriginal patients in collaboration with Aboriginal healers and Elders where requested by Aboriginal patients" (TRC 2015a, 163).

Ultimately, a decolonization approach means that Indigenous Peoples are self-determining with respect to their health and healing systems, including to what extent they engage with the dominant medical paradigm. For example, the Inuulitsivik midwifery service and education program was established in the mid-1980s as a direct result of community organizing and activism by Inuit women in Nunavik because, as one proponent put it, the "medical model … separated our families, stole the power of the birthing experience from our women, and weakened the health, strength, and spirit of our communities" (Wagner et al. 2007, 384–5). Kanien'kehá:ka professor and educator Alex McComber has explained that the recently developed Indigenous Perspectives: Decolonizing Health Approaches course at McGill University "was designed to showcase the experience of health and wellness from Indigenous peoples prior to the contact with European settlers, from which we transition to the period of arrival that lead to colonization and oppression of Indigenous communities" (Mazerolle 2019). The eventual goal for graduate students and researchers from the Department of Family Medicine enrolled in the course is to come to "contemporary times when Indigenous peoples and scholars are collaborating with Western scholars and health professionals in more respectful ways to understand the impact of the experience, but also using traditional knowledge and practices to improve peoples' health" (Mazerolle 2019). Conversely, Indigenous Peoples and communities should also "be free to diverge – as far as their users want them to – from the bio-medical and social welfare models that predominate in non-Aboriginal society" (RCAP 1996b, 208).

Settlers to this land, whether recently arrived migrants or those whose families have been here for generations, have a critical role to play in decolonization efforts. In "Decolonizing Antiracism," Mi'kmaw professor Bonita Lawrence implies that antiracism work must "begin with, and reflect, the totality of Native peoples' lived experiences – that is, with the genocide that established and maintains all of the settler states within the Americas" (Lawrence and Dua 2005, 121). Addressing universities and other academic institutions, Nishnaabeg feminist, artist, and scholar Leanne Betasamosake Simpson points out that if revitalizing Indigenous intelligence on Indigenous terms is an actual priority, then "the academy must make a conscious decision to become a decolonizing force in the intellectual lives of Indigenous peoples by joining us in dismantling settler colonialism and actively protecting the source of our knowledge – Indigenous land" (Simpson 2014, 22). A parallel can be drawn for providers working in the health care system: if there is a true commitment to the health of Indigenous Peoples, then health care workers should join efforts to dismantle settler colonialism and safeguard the sources of Indigenous life and well-being. Toronto-based family physician and social justice activist Nanky Rai makes an important point when she writes that "tackl[ing] oppression does not simply improve the care we provide," but an anti-oppression approach can also "improve the culture of medical practice for the betterment of all those who participate within it" (Rai 2017, 26).

When Health Minister Gaétan Barrette's comments perpetuating racist stereotypes were made public on National Indigenous Peoples Day, Indigenous activists, leaders, and politicians immediately demanded his resignation. Provincial opposition parties had divergent responses. Only Québec Solidaire issued a formal statement in support of the demands (Québec Solidaire 2018), while the Parti Québécois deemed the comments to be "shameful" (Derfel 2018). The Coalition Avenir Québec (CAQ) was conspicuously silent on the issue. This was not surprising; for months future premier François Legault had staunchly opposed the Liberal government's plans to launch a commission into systemic racism because he denied its very existence (Legault 2017). Pediatric neurologist Lionel Carmant, one of Legault's star candidates who would become deputy minister of health and social services when the CAQ came into power in October 2018, repeatedly refused to acknowledge that systemic racism was a problem in Quebec in an interview only a few days prior to Barrette's comments being made public by the media (Carmant 2018). Instead of asking for his resignation or simply demoting Barrette, then premier Philippe Couillard (and head of the provincial Liberal party) stood by his health minister (Derfel 2018). What message did this stance send to the public at large? That racist comments perpetuating anti-Indigenous stereotypes could be made with impunity in provincial politics.

What was the response within the health care system itself? After all, Barrette was at the head of the system many of us work diligently in providing care for the sick and injured. On an individual level, many disagreed with what he said. However, if zero tolerance for racism and other discriminatory behaviours in the health care system exists, didn't we have a responsibility to categorically denounce Barrette's comments? Out of basic principles of solidarity, shouldn't we have been compelled to support Indigenous demands for his resignation? Wouldn't it be a strong show of support if health care unions, professional and student associations, and public health care system advocacy groups – many of which backed the #aHand2Hold campaign – had weighed in on the issue collectively and publicly? Couldn't holding a government minister accountable for his anti-Indigenous racist comments be considered a modest act in support of decolonization? While forcing Barrette's pre-election resignation would have been mostly symbolic, the message that there is a price to pay for perpetuating colonial stereotypes in public office would have been conveyed. The precedent would have been important. But none of this happened.

Barrette's comments had made headlines across the province and the country, but the news petered out after a few days. We can speculate as to why politicians, health care workers, and the general public in Quebec did not openly support Indigenous demands for Barrette's resignation. In conversation, some people explained this by the lull of summer when public engagement in politics wasn't a priority.

Yet, around the same time, when Black and Indigenous communities expressed opposition to their histories being told without them in the SLĀV and *Kanata* shows by reputed playwright Robert Lepage, the controversy made headlines for weeks throughout the summer. These communities were justifiably "attempting to reclaim some of the cultural real estate that has been taken from them surrounding their own stories" (Dunlevy 2018). However, the public debate was swiftly and disingenuously re-framed around the notions of freedom of expression and censorship (Aubin-Dubois et al. 2018). But censorship is rooted in institutionalized power. As one artist involved with the SLAV Resistance Collective noted in an opinion piece at the time: "We don't have the power to censor" (Lamour 2018). The issues that critics of the two shows were trying to highlight were not well received in many sectors of Québécois society, particularly the concept of cultural appropriation. Black artists and activists opposed to SLĀV were depicted as "violent" (Dunlevy 2018); Indigenous opposition to *Kanata* was deemed "dangerous" (Bellerose 2018). Many of those confronting systemic racism and colonialism in the art world were stigmatized by the public debate, which itself was often fuelled by racism and colonialism resulting in "egregious stereotypes for both groups" (Dunlevy 2018).

Clearly, the jarring public backlash faced by Black and Indigenous opponents to the plays proved that any summertime lull and political apathy could not be overcome if an issue was considered important enough in Québécois society. Barrette's comments barely had any consequence at all: although the Liberals lost the provincial elections in October 2018, Barrette was re-elected in his riding. Beyond systemic racism and colonialism, a "reconciliation" agenda that is actually watered-down and ignores decolonization provides an additional explanation for why Indigenous calls for Barrette's resignation were not supported.

Reparations before Reconciliation

As Dene scholar Glen Sean Coulthard argues in *Red Skin, White Masks: Rejecting the Colonial Politics of Recognition*, governments privilege "an approach to reconciliation that goes out of its way to fabricate a sharp divide between Canada's unscrupulous 'past' and the unfortunate 'legacy' this past has produced for Indigenous people and communities in the present" (Coulthard 2014, 121). Importantly, the RCAP and the TRC have had to operate within the confines of this framing (121, 127). This is, of course, intentional on the government's part: through the lens "of liberalism, the historical 'wrong' has now been 'righted' and further transformation is not needed, since the historic situation has been remedied" (Simpson 2011, 22). Instead, public officials adopt Indigenous calls for "decolonization" by "changing the names on buildings, placing ... art-work on currency, or wearing clothing with Indigenous cultural designs in Parliament," while "the crisis issues facing many Indigenous peoples that have directly resulted from historic and ongoing colonization remain unaddressed" (Palmater 2017, 75). Kanien'kehá:ka anthropology professor Audra Simpson explains that Canada's apology to Survivors of residential schools (see Chapter 7) formally inaugurated "a time of 'reconciliation', when the difficult past would be reconciled to the present even as that past itself remains structured through a geopolitical dispossession, starvation, death, and ongoing legal forms of dispossession" (Simpson 2016, 439). But who pays for the crimes that are wilfully erased through this process of forced collective amnesia?

Colonial governments consider "forgiveness" and "reconciliation" as crucial steps toward transcending a painful "legacy" to finally "move on" (Coulthard 2014, 125). For both (settler) Canadians and (colonial) governments, "there is an urgent political desire for Indigenous peoples to 'just get over it,' despite the fact that colonization continues in equally lethal ways" (Palmater 2017, 74). But, as Marie Brunelle, Anishinabeg Elder from Kitigan Zibi and Sixties Scoop Survivor, has argued, "you don't just get over what has happened to you," especially when the intergenerational effects of colonialism continue to this day (Varley 2017, 71). Ultimately, governmental reconciliation agendas are "about firmly cementing the power status quo and ensuring the [uninterrupted] economic exploitation" of Indigenous Land (Palmater 2017, 74).

The current reconciliation framework "presents a challenge for Indigenous decolonization efforts aimed at both resisting ongoing colonization and also undertaking resurgence efforts aimed at revitalizing Indigenous cultures, laws and governing systems in and on our territories" (Palmater 2017, 74). Leanne Betasamosake Simpson argues that radical transformation cannot depend on the state – decolonization efforts must be rooted in community and the land (Simpson 2014, 13). However, unlike transformative models of "robust resurgence" that infuse "reciprocal practices of reconciliation in self-determining, self-sustaining, and inter-generational ways" (Borrows and Tully 2018, 5), the colonial reconciliation model – not surprisingly – undermines decolonization. The push from reconciliation platitudes "hampers our ability to have the truth of Canada's genocidal legacy brought to the fore and advocate for reparations" (Palmater 2017, 74). Genuine reconciliation can't occur without reparations.

In "Reparations: Theory, Practice and Education," the Aboriginal Healing Foundation names "acknowledgement of and apology for actions causing harm," as well as "reconciliation, *through actions which demonstrate a sustained commitment to right relations,"* as two components of reparation measures (Erasmus 2003, 10; emphasis added). However, two other important components exist: "provision of support for healing" and "restitution/compensation" (10). Palmater has argued for the "Indigenous right to self-determination with the corresponding restitution of lands and resources" (Palmater 2014, 45). The connection between land and resources is important in capitalist liberal democracies like Canada because "liberalism (individualism, the free market, [and the] rights that point to and from both)" masks "the ways in which settler colonialism inheres to the making of states" (Simpson 2016, 440). Relatedly, "where there is a language and a commitment to 'multiculturalism' as the protection, preservation and perhaps even celebration of one's 'cultural' difference, there is a simultaneous commitment to the taking of territory" (440). In other words, "liberal multicultural policies act ... as avenues for the reinstitution of dispossession" (Cornellier and Griffiths 2016, 306). The colonial reconciliation model is still colonialism.

All of this has direct implications for health care. There can be no meaningful reconciliation in Indigenous-settler relations unless institutions that have been built on domination, exploitation, and oppression are dismantled (see Simpson 2014, 13n29). This book details how the Canadian health care system has been instrumental in the genocidal colonial project by targeting Indigenous children, and inflicting untold pain, suffering, and death – all wholly avoidable. If there is a true commitment to health justice for all in this country, we must recognize governmental practices and policies as structural determinants of health. This means rooting out racist and colonial thinking and creating a decolonized health care system that recognizes reparations and restitution as necessary prerequisites for any meaningful reconciliation.

However, there is a huge chasm that must be bridged if we care about living in a just society. Indeed, returning to the #aHand2Hold campaign, if the provincial government responded so ineptly to a quasi-unanimous call from the public to end the non-accompaniment rule that disproportionately hurt Indigenous children and their families, how will more contentious – but no less discriminatory and harmful – issues impacting Indigenous and other marginalized, exploited, and oppressed communities be redressed? Moving forward, we must choose a different path.

Conclusion

We, Inuit, know that we have to work with you, Qallunaat, for a long time still.
And we agree with that. But, if you wish for that relationship to work, to be
fruitful, you will have to listen to us.
– Late Elder Elashuk Pauyungie (as remembered by Dr Johanne Morel)

If you have come to help me, you are wasting your time.
But if you have come because your liberation is bound up with mine,
then let us work together.
– Aboriginal Activists Group (Queensland, Australia, 1970s)

catharsis is still elusive
so we'll save that
for another day

meet me at the underpass
rebellion is
on her way.
– Leanne Betasamosake Simpson, "caribou ghosts & untold stories,"
    in *This Accident of Being Lost*

Following the February 2018 announcement that the non-accompaniment
rule would be coming to an end, I had stated that the traumatic experiences of children being transferred alone all these years "is a legacy that
the provincial government needs to be held accountable for" (Banerjee 2018).
More broadly, the extensive history of genocidal violence inflicted on children through medical colonialism as detailed in this book is ultimately the

responsibility of public health care institutions and various levels of governments. All of those children, their families, and their communities are owed reparation measures. Drawing on the Australian *Bringing Them Home* report of the National Inquiry into the Separation of Aboriginal and Torres Strait Islander Children from Their Families, these reparations should include an acknowledgment and apology (Erasmus 2003, 14n22). However, apologies are necessary but not sufficient. It would be one thing if successive governments meaningfully changed their behaviour after issuing an apology so that they don't have to keep apologizing for other or ongoing transgressions. After all, as one of my high school history teachers was fond of saying: "Don't be sorry, just don't do it." Yet, colonial governments and institutions keep doing it. And, they keep apologizing. No wonder so many doubt the sincerity of such apologies. As such, for apologies to be considered genuine, measures of restitution, measures of rehabilitation, monetary compensation, and, importantly, guarantees against repetition must be ensured (Erasmus 2003, 14n22). Indeed, ongoing medical colonialism must end. As Cindy Blackstock has stated often, "reconciliation means not saying sorry twice" (Blackstock 2011). Part of these reparation measures would mean that health care providers and governments commit to ensuring that the services provided to Indigenous Peoples produce health outcomes that are at least equivalent to those of other Canadians (RCAP 1996b, 204).

This would necessarily imply an equity-based approach that would eliminate the health inequities plaguing Indigenous communities by addressing structural causes. Ending systemic racism and colonialism (as well as capitalism, patriarchy, and other systems of domination and oppression) would be prerequisites; a first step for the current provincial government is to recognize that they exist and are ongoing. The Indigenous Health Network's first recommendation could serve as inspiration: creating policies to implement such measures during a transitional decolonization period would necessarily involve "the development of meaningful relationships with the Indigenous communities that they serve," including the "development of accountability mechanisms," where "Indigenous communities are recognized as expert resources" and "are provided with the opportunity and resources" to oversee – from development to implementation – policies impacting their communities (IHN 2019, 6). Bill C-242, which sought to harmonize Canadian laws with the United Nations Declaration on the Rights of Indigenous Peoples, provides another transitional blueprint if governments are genuinely motivated by reconciliation. More promptly, they can implement all recommendations from the commissions and inquiries that they themselves created (e.g., RCAP, TRC, MMIWG, Viens). Beyond policies and legislation, health care providers must take leadership from Indigenous communities to support self-determination and resurgence movements, which are intrinsically tied to the land. This implies solidarity rooted in social justice from those of us who are not Indigenous.

In the early 2000s, as collective members of the Montreal-based Indigenous Peoples Solidarity Movement, we recognized that "if we are in support of [Indigenous] self-determination, we too need to be self-determining." Our understanding was that decolonization did not mean re-establishing the conditions of a precolonial North America, but rather abandoning the current relationship between Indigenous Peoples and settlers, defined by the capitalist nation-state and rooted in oppression. The end goal would be "to cut the [Canadian] state out of this relationship, and to replace it with a new relationship [between peoples], one which is mutually negotiated, and premised on a core respect for autonomy and freedom" (Burke 2004). That freedom isn't a licence to exploit and oppress. And it comes with a responsibility: ensuring that everyone is free from exploitation and oppression.

The #aHand2Hold campaign was marked by various expressions of solidarity (op-eds, petitions, public events, etc.) that fostered new relationships that weren't mediated by the state. Many were spontaneous initiatives by individuals who weren't currently implicated by ÉVAQ's non-accompaniment practice directly or indirectly, but nonetheless felt compelled to act. Catherine Hudon's pivotal letter about her son Mattéo's death is an example that stands out, particularly given the re-opening of old wounds it may have caused. Another is the anonymous person who approached, recorded, and made public the troubling exchange with then health minister Gaétan Barrette at a Muslim community centre in June 2018. This action was presumably motivated by a heartfelt concern for the well-being of Indigenous children living in northern communities and the indignation spurred by the fact that nothing was changing months after Barrette's initial announcement in February 2018.

The campaign, meanwhile, was intentionally centred around the most adversely impacted group of children: Indigenous children living in northern Quebec. This ran counter to the step-by-step approach that typically characterizes policy-change work, which aims for "low-lying fruit" first. Those most drastically impacted by an unjust policy continue to suffer while waiting for small gains for those less impacted in the elusive hope that this incremental strategy – that often takes years – will eventually succeed. In our case, the focus remained steadfastly on the injustice – rooted in a history of medical colonialism – inflicted on northern Indigenous communities. But we also always demanded that the practice must end for *all* children. The result is that the campaign improved the situation for all children who were impacted by the non-accompaniment rule across the province, whether Indigenous or not. In a modest way our approach drew inspiration from a notion popularized by women's liberation, Black Power, and labour activist Fannie Lou Hamer (née Townsend, 1917–1977): "Nobody's free until everybody's free" (Brooks and Houck 2011, xxi; see also 134–9). It can serve as a lesson that decolonization work should be in everyone's best interests.

Decolonization work by earlier Indigenous-led self-determination and resurgence movements played a critical role in the success of the #aHand2-Hold campaign. I have consistently tried to highlight this at public speaking events about the campaign. The 1990 siege of Kanehsatà:ke (commonly known as the "Oka crisis" because the municipality of Oka wanted to develop its golf course into the sacred pines in Kanehsatà:ke) played a major role in pushing the federal government to establish the Royal Commission on Aboriginal Peoples (RCAP 1996a, 199). Legal actions, including class-action lawsuits, filed by Survivors of residential schools eventually forced the Canadian government to establish the Truth and Reconciliation Commission (TRC 2015a, v). Indigenous women, their families, and their communities had long been organizing, demonstrating, documenting, and calling for action to put an end to the violence impacting Indigenous girls, women, and 2SLGBTQQIA people before the federal government finally gave a mandate to the National Inquiry into Missing and Murdered Indigenous Women and Girls (MMIWG 2019a, 49). The Viens Commission was created by the Government of Quebec because Indigenous women in Val d'Or exposed and condemned the physical and sexual violence of Sureté du Québec police officers (Viens Commission 2019, 11–18). Years of land defence actions, campaigns, and confrontations (to name only a few of the more commonly known sites of struggle: Barrière Lake, Burnt Church, Clayoquot Sound, Elispogtog, Goose Bay, Grassy Narrows, Gustafsen Lake, Haldimand Tract, Ipperwash, Kitchenuhmaykoosib Inninuwug, Skwelkwek'welt, Tyendinaga), as well as the Idle No More mobilizations across the province and country, had all shifted the political terrain since the first formal opposition to ÉVAQ's non-accompaniment rule in the 1990s. By exposing the injustices that stem from colonialism, these grassroots resurgence initiatives made it that much more difficult for so-called liberal democracies like Quebec and Canada to deny that Indigenous children were disproportionately impacted by a systematic practice of forced family separation. This is why the non-accompaniment rule was deemed untenable when the #aHand2Hold campaign launched; social pressure forced political action.

Yet, other injustices persist. Indigenous communities continue to resist, mostly alone, just as they have since the beginning of colonization and colonialism. But decolonization is a one-way street with two lanes. Those of us who are not the original inhabitants of this land need to get in our lane to support Indigenous resistance and resurgence movements. There are glimmers of hope that can shine a light on the path we need to take.

Arthur Manuel was born to parents of the Ktunaxa and Secwepemc nations. He was a respected leader and internationally renowned activist who influenced generations of Indigenous Peoples, as well as non-Indigenous people whom he considered his "movement family" (Klein 2017, 9). In 2017, the year he died, his "Six-Step Program to Decolonization" was published as part of *The Reconciliation Manifesto: Recovering the Land, Rebuilding the Economy*. Manuel's lucid words about hope for the future, centred on children, provide this book with a more fitting conclusion than anything I could ever write:

> Hope, for me comes from both the Indigenous youth from across the country who are ready to fight for our rights and from the non-Indigenous who I meet in university lecture halls and church basements who are not only open to re-envisioning Canada, but are willing to stand shoulder to shoulder with us in remaking it. That is our new starting point. Travelling along the path toward decolonization will take courage for Canadians. But once you begin, I think you will find the route

is not complicated and the only guide you will need is a sense of justice and decency ... We need fundamental change to fix Canada because it is Canada that is broken. Either that, or we pass on this sad legacy to our children. Mine, I know, have run out of patience. They are ready to fight it out and this is the last thing I want for them – or for your children, for that matter. So let us avoid that. Relieve your children from the international embarrassment and the moral disgrace of riding on our backs and relieve my children from the crushing burden of carrying them. If we do this right, some day they may even be able to walk freely together in friendship. (Manuel 2017, 275, 279)

Afterword

In Canadian society, the right to health care is taken somewhat for granted. The Medicare system is purported to include everyone and is considered something whereby a person expects to feel safe, cared for, and respected. That attitude has been rapidly changing with the dawn of private health care, as budget cuts by overzealous politicians slide the scales of accessibility toward those who can afford quicker access and service. While everyone has their horror stories of bad experiences within the healthcare system, for Indigenous Peoples the issue of institutionalized racism is an added factor.

Regardless of the government of Canada's insistence that this is the era of "reconciliation," Indigenous Peoples are still considered to be "wards of the state," with the quality of health care dependent upon individual decisions of health care workers and/or bureaucrats. In Kanien'ká:ha (Mohawk language), the word for "hospital" is *Tsi Iakehnheiontahiontáhkhwa*, which equates to "the place where people go to die," not an image that is welcoming or encouraging. But back in the day, the only time that Indigenous Peoples actually went to a hospital was to die.

Today, the public is unaware of the level of state/government control in every aspect of our lives, from birth to death. Through Indigenous and Northern Affairs Canada (INAC), Canada wields its power over Indigenous communities by dictating funding amounts through the release of funds from an 1874 trust fund created for Indigenous Peoples. This fund was created from resource development on unceded Indigenous Peoples' homelands, and it has never been directly accessible to Indigenous Peoples. Nor is there any transparency on how it is used. The royalties are used to fund communities' needs from health and education to roads, housing, and so on.

The framework of Indigenous health policy is created by bureaucrats and rubber-stamped by the minister of INAC, now Indigenous Services; each decision about health policy is made by bureaucrats in Ottawa, then approved by the minister of health. There is not much wiggle room for bands to change funding agreements. They must sign or risk losing funding.

Health care for many generations pre- and post-contact remained under the control of Indigenous communities through one or many medicine persons – please do not call them shamans – whose Traditional Knowledge was revered and respected. Each person was aware that the medicine person was the healer for individuals.

Sovereignty over health care meant that in the past Indigenous Peoples would pick medicines to heal ailments and maintained health through a diet including wild game and fish – all activities that meant the freedom to leave the communities. The relationship between illness and healing was understood by all. The land provided the medicines needed for healing, accompanied by our ceremonies, with songs and respect for the land and all our relations. Thus, there was retained from Traditional Knowledge the awareness that certain illnesses were rooted in an imbalance in the body, be it spiritual, physical, or mental. Once reserve systems forcibly came into being, that part of control over our own health care was stifled. The church declared our ceremonies as paganistic and devil worship; thus, parts of our mental, spiritual, and physical health were forbidden. Our whole sovereignty – how we used our lands, our environment, our bodies – changed to that of dependency upon the colonizer's will.

Today, with what we know of the impacts of colonization, of cultural shaming within the church and school systems, and of every kind of abuse committed against Indigenous children in the Indian Residential Schools, we know that oppression and trauma inflicted upon Indigenous Peoples have far more serious consequences than modern medicine can comprehend.

Through brilliant research by Maria Yellow Horse Brave Heart, a Lakota academic, it was revealed how multi-generational trauma begins with colonization and the Indian Residential School system and goes on to affect the children of those traumatized. The impacts are physical: through a chemical reaction in the body that changes one's DNA, transferred onto the baby in the womb. The impacts are spiritual: through land dispossession and denial of access and rights to our lands, affecting our spiritual and cultural life in our ceremonies and medicines and in our languages, which are land based.

The impacts are mental and emotional: consequences and repercussions are manifested through cultural self-hatred rooted in colonial education, first with the Indian Residential Schools, then with the colonial propaganda still found in schools today that erase the contributions and truths about the history of the First Peoples of Turtle Island (North America).

Today, Indigenous Peoples endure more slick and insidious forms of discrimination. Racist stereotypes of the "dirty, lazy Indian" persist in societal norms, rooted in institutionalized racism at all levels affecting Indigenous Peoples' realities. Jurisdictional arguments between provinces and the federal government on who pays for Indigenous Peoples are untenable since the provinces already control all the funding targeted for Indigenous communities. That funding remains inadequate to meet the needs of Indigenous communities. A great portion of it is absorbed into the administration costs of the province instead of helping those in need.

The state of access to health care for Indigenous Peoples continues to erode yearly, through assimilative policies. It is as if the millions of Indigenous Peoples are not oppressed, have not been colonized, and have the same experiences as the rest of society – as if a formal "Apology" for the Indian Residential School system has healed us from the genocidal impacts of colonization. We exist in an archaic, racist, bureaucratic culture that this foundation of dysfunction has been built upon, disregarding the human rights of Indigenous Peoples to health care and ignoring our economic, social, and cultural rights, along with our rights to self-determination. Colonial oppression and land dispossession impacting upon multiple generations are the root causes for many of the social ills of Indigenous Peoples, who statistically have the highest rates of poverty, suicide, murdered and missing women, and the list goes on.

Earlier generations attended Day Schools or Indian Residential Schools. Elders, especially those who could not attend post-secondary schools, worked menial labour jobs, many of which were seasonal. Community members and contract workers, such as those working in Indigenous languages, do not have the RRSPs, retirement plans, or health insurance plans that most Canadians take for granted. Hence, with no private insurance, many Indigenous Peoples are unable to keep up because of the continual cuts that the government inflicts. Without health insurance, the challenges to obtain quality health care are daunting for many Indigenous Peoples: high unemployment, lack of potable water in many First Nations communities, and a high cost of living in northern communities whose isolation is due to the fact there are no roads connecting them to the South. They pay exorbitant costs for consumer goods that must be brought in by commercial boats or airplanes.

In rural areas, there is the issue of language: French and/or English can be a challenge for those whose first language is an Indigenous language. Discriminatory practices by those who refuse to provide services in one of the colonial languages remain a source of Indigenous Peoples' frustration about the lack of quality health care. There are many workers who provide good or excellent health care, but eventually they too are often stymied by federal and provincial bureaucratic jurisdictions, eventually hitting the wall of institutionalized racism. Some health care workers are sympathetic and will go the extra mile to help, while others will not. In Quebec, it is of course a question of language and if you come from a "reserve." On leaving our communities, many Indigenous Peoples feel as if we are alien as we are forced to speak yet another colonial language. While there are many exceptions, waiting times often become longer than necessary, attitudes amongst staff change, and medical procedures are not explained in a language easily understood.

The #aHand2Hold campaign highlighted the important issue of how the federal and provincial governments deny Indigenous parents the right to be with their child when they are sick – to make the free, prior, and informed consent decision for the health plan of their sick child. No parent would tolerate it if the state made an arbitrary decision to deny them the right to make decisions to protect their child. Indigenous parents constantly experience being treated as a ward of the state as our care is rooted upon archaic, racist laws overriding a parent's right. What are considered "norms" in the rest of society do not apply for Indigenous Peoples because we remain under the tutelage of a cold bureaucracy focused on the bottom line. It remains a very frustrating situation for Indigenous Peoples and their families who get lost in the bureaucracy, causing them to reluctantly accept nightmarish conditions in institutions that are unaware of the colonial laws that leave Indigenous Peoples precariously in unfamiliar territory, often to fend for themselves.

It should be made clear at this point that any funding that Indigenous Peoples receive is from Canada's assumed fiduciary responsibility. Canada is holding hostage the funds that could make a difference in the quality of our lives: to decolonize our minds and the daily processes which affect our realities. As mentioned before, the funds that each community receives come from a nineteenth-century trust fund created from the royalties on all the resources taken from our unsurrendered homelands. Indigenous Peoples do not take from the taxpayers; in fact, it is the other way around.

The complexity of health care is one that cannot be addressed properly if the history of oppression due to colonization is not taken into consideration. It will take many generations to overcome the multigenerational trauma experienced by Indigenous Peoples at the hands of the colonizer. The hope is that those who know the health care system well, health practitioners and workers, will partner with Indigenous Peoples, Traditional Knowledge holders, and health care advocates to make the positive changes that are needed to bring quality health care to Indigenous Peoples and to respect their rights as individuals and as a collective.

This means that reconciliation, a most overused word these days, must be genuine, accompanied by reparations and restitution. In a world where climate change affects Indigenous Peoples foremost and most severely, the needs will grow greater and the need for positive change is paramount. A change whereby Indigenous Peoples can undo the chains of colonization, living lives in which their right to quality health care is respected and given without discrimination.

Skén:nen – wishing you peace
Katsi'tsakwas Ellen Gabriel
Kanien'kehá:ka (People of the Flint – Mohawk) from Kanehsatà:ke

References

AAP (American Academy of Pediatrics). 2016. "Chapter 12: Patient and Family-Centered Care." In *Guidelines for Air and Ground Transport of Neonatal and Pediatric Patients,* 4th ed., edited by Robert M. Insoft and Hamilton P. Schwartz, 239–43. Elk Grove Village, IL: American Academy of Pediatrics.

Abley, Mark. 2013. *Conversations with a Dead Man: The Legacy of Duncan Campbell Scott.* Madeira Park, BC: Douglas and McIntyre.

Adams, Howard. 1989. *Prison of Grass: Canada from a Native Point of View.* Revised edition. Calgary: Fifth House Publishers.

– 1999. *Tortured People: The Politics of Colonization.* Revised edition. Penticton, BC: Theytus Books Ltd.

AFNQL (Assembly of First Nations of Quebec and Labrador). 2018. "Discrimination from the Top," press release, 21 June 2018. https://www.newswire.ca/news-releases/discrimination-from-the-top-686160921.html (link defunct).

Alia, Valeria. 1994. *Names, Numbers, and Northern Policy: Inuit, Project Surname, and the Politics of Identity.* Halifax: Fernwood Publishing.

Allan, Billie and Janet Smylie. 2015. "First Peoples, Second Class Treatment: The Role of Racism in the Health and Well-being of Indigenous Peoples in Canada." Toronto: Wellesley Institute.

Ansell, David A. 2017. *The Death Gap: How Inequality Kills.* Chicago: University of Chicago Press.

Aodla Freeman, Mini. 2015. *Life among the Qallunaat.* Winnipeg: University of Manitoba Press.

Arkle, Madeline, Max Deschner, Ryan Giroux, Reed Morrison, Danielle Nelson, Amanda Sauvé, and Kelita Singh. 2015. "Indigenous Peoples and Health in Canadian Medical Education: Position Paper." Canadian Federation of Medical Students. https://www.cfms.org/files/position-papers/2015_indigenous_people_in_canadian_med_ed.pdf.

Armony, Victor, Mariam Hassaoui, and Massimiliano Mulone. 2019. "Les interpellations policières à la lumière des identités racisées des personnes interpellées: Analyse des données du Service de Police de la Ville de Montréal (SPVM) et élaboration d'indicateurs de suivi en matière de profilage racial." https://spvm.qc.ca/upload/Rapport_Armony-Hassaoui-Mulone.pdf.

Arnold, David. 1988. "Disease, Medicine and Empire." In *Imperial Medicine and Indigenous Societies*, edited by David Arnold. Manchester, 1–26. Manchester University Press.

Arsenault, Julien. 2017. "Airbus devient actionnaire majoritaire de la CSeries." *Journal Métro*, 16 October 2017. https://journalmetro.com/actualites/national/1212739/alerte-airbus-acquiert-une-participation-majoritaire-dans-la-cseries/.

Ashton, Nikki. 2018. House of Commons. Hansard #355 of the 42nd Parliament, 1st Session, Debates of 21 November 2018. https://openparliament.ca/debates/2018/11/21/niki-ashton-1/.

Aubin-Dubois, Kateri, Carole Charbonneau, Maya Cousineau Mollen, Yvon Dubé, André Dudemaine, Dave Jeniss, Maïtée Labrecque-Saganash, et al. 2018. "Encore une fois, l'aventure se passera sans nous, les Autochtones?" *Le Devoir*, 14 July 2018. https://www.ledevoir.com/opinion/libre-opinion/532406/encore-une-fois-l-aventure-se-passera-sans-nous-les-autochtones.

Bacon, Patrick. 2013. "Mémoire: Racisme et discrimination envers les Premières Nations. Portrait sommaire et recommandations." Wendake: First Nations of Quebec and Labrador Health and Social Services Commission.

Banerjee, Sidhartha. 2018. "In Reversal, Quebec to Allow Parent to Accompany Children on Air Ambulances." *Globe and Mail*, 16 February 2018. https://www.theglobeandmail.com/news/national/in-reversal-quebec-to-allow-parent-to-accompany-children-on-air-ambulances/article38006990/.

Banerji, Anna, Val Panzov, Michael Young, Joan Robinson, Bonita Lee, Theo Moraes, Muhammad Mamdani, et al. 2016. "Hospital Admissions for Lower Respiratory Tract Infections among Infants in the Canadian Arctic: A Cohort Study." *Canadian Medical Association Journal Open*, 4, no. 4: E615–E622. doi: 10.9778/cmajo.20150051.

Baril, Hélène. 2018. "Barrage Gouin: les Atikamekw poursuivent Hydro-Québec," *La Presse*, 13 October 2018. https://www.lapresse.ca/affaires/economie/energie-et-ressources/201810/13/01-5200123-barrage-gouin-les-atikamekw-poursuivent-hydro-quebec.php.

Barrette, Gaétan. 2018. "Déclaration du ministre Gaétan Barrette." Cabinet du ministre de la Santé et des Services sociaux, 21 June 2018. http://www.newswire.ca/fr/releases/archive/June2018/21/c5077.html.

Basile, Suzy, Carole Lévesque, Sebastien Brodeur-Girard, Wanda Gabriel, Ellen Gabriel, Viviane Michel, and Marjolaine Sioui. 2019. "Silence de Québec sur la stérilisation forcée des femmes autochtones." Radio-Canada (*Espaces Autochtones*), 18 February 2019. https://ici.radio-canada.ca/espaces-autochtones/1153624/silence-quebec-sterilisation-forcee-femmes-autochtones-lettre-ouverte.

Bean, William B. 1966. "Osler, the Legend, the Man and the Influence." *Canadian Medical Association Journal* 95 (November): 1031–7.

Beaulne, Pierre. 2018. "La politique d'austérité budgétaire au Québec à la suite de la crise financière. " Institut de recherche et d'informations socio-économiques (IRIS), 20 March 2018. https://iris-recherche.qc.ca/blogue/la-politique-d-austerite-budgetaire-au-quebec-a-la-suite-de-la-crise-financiere.

Bell, Susan, Betsy Longchap, and Christopher Herodier. 2020. "Cree Leaders Work to Calm Fears over Surprising $4.7B Infrastructure Deal." *CBC News*, 20 February 2020. https://www.cbc.ca/news/canada/north/cree-grande-alliance-lithium-infrastructure-environment-quebec-1.5469210.

Bellerose, Patrick. 2018. "Annulation de Kanata: c'est 'dangereux,' dit François Legault." *Le Journal de Montréal*, 27 July 2018. https://www.journaldemontreal.com/2018/07/27/annulation-de-kanata-cest-dangereux-dit-francois-legault.

Bernier, Nicole, and Julia Posca. 2020. "Les super-riches et l'explosion des inégalités: portrait et pistes de solutions." January 2020. Montreal: L'Institut de recherche et d'informations socioéconomiques. https://cdn.iris-recherche.qc.ca/uploads/publication/file/IRIS_noteRevenu_maximum_2020_WEB.pdf.

Bernier, Richard, Sylvie Côté, and André Lizotte. 2018. Joint testimony at the Public Inquiry Commission on Relations between Indigenous Peoples and Certain Public Services in Québec (Viens Commission). Transcription by Monique Le Clerc, Volume 154 (24 October 2018). https://www.cerp.gouv.qc.ca/fileadmin/Fichiers_clients/Transcriptions/Notes_stenographiques_-_CERP_24_octobre_2018.pdf.

Bettache, Nazila, and Samir Shaheen-Hussain. 2017. "Lorsque les politiques de santé tuent." *Le Devoir*, 7 August 2017. https://www.ledevoir.com/opinion/idees/505100/lorsque-les-politiques-de-sante-tuent.

– 2018. "Réplique: Les clichés racistes du ministre de la Santé." *La Presse*, 27 June 2018. http://mi.lapresse.ca/screens/631af78b-80bc-4f98-904c-be83621762da__7C___0.html.

Blackstock, Cindy. 2009. "The Occasional Evil of Angels: Learning from the Experiences of Aboriginal Peoples and Social Work." *First Peoples Child & Family Review* 4, no 1: 28–37.

– 2011. *Reconciliation Means Not Saying Sorry Twice: How Inequities in Federal Government Child Welfare Funding, and Benefit, on Reserves Drives First Nations Children into Foster Care.* Submission to the Standing Committee on the Status of Women, 15 February 2011. Ottawa.

– 2013. "Opening Statement of the First Nations Child and Family Caring Society of Canada: Canadian Human Rights Tribunal." *Kanata* 6 (winter 2013): 6–21.

– 2019. "Blackface and About Face: How Canada's Reconciliation Agenda Went Wrong." *Toronto Star*, 7 October 2019. https://www.thestar.com/opinion/contributors/2019/10/07/black-face-and-about-face-how-canadas-promise-of-reconciliation-went-wrong.html

Blas, Erik, and Anand Sivasankara Kurup, eds. 2010. *Equity, Social Determinants and Public Health Programmes.* Geneva: World Health Organization.

Bloomberg, Frederic Tomesco. 2018. "Quebec Plans to Balance Budget for 4th Straight Year." *Toronto Star*, 28 March 2018. https://www.thestar.com/business/2018/03/28/quebec-plans-to-balance-budget-for-4th-straight-year.html.

BMA (British Medical Association). 1992. *Medicine Betrayed: The Participation of Doctors in Human Rights Abuses.* London, UK: Zed Books.

Bocquier, Arnaud. 2018. Interview with Sue Smith, CBC Radio: *Homerun*. 31 August 2018.

Bonesteel, Sarah. 2006. "Canada's Relationship with Inuit: A History of Policy and Program Development." Minister of Public Works and Government. https://www.aadnc-aandc.gc.ca/DAM/DAM-INTER-HQ/STAGING/texte-text/inuit-book_1100100016901_eng.pdf.

Borrows, John, and James Tully. 2018. "Introduction." In *Resurgence and Reconciliation: Indigenous-Settler Relations and Earth Teachings*, edited by Michael Asch, John Borrows, and James Tully, 3–25. Toronto: University of Toronto Press.

Bouie, Jamelle. 2018. "The Enlightenment's Dark Side: How the Enlightenment Created Modern Race Thinking, and Why We Should Confront It." *Slate*, 5 June 2018. https://slate.com/news-and-politics/2018/06/taking-the-enlightenment-seriously-requires-talking-about-race.html.

Boyer, Yvonne, and Judith Bartlett. 2017. External Review: *Tubal Ligation in the Saskatoon Health Region: The Lived Experience of Aboriginal Women*. Saskatoon Health Region, 22 July 2017.

Brooks, Maegan Parker, and Davis W. Houck, eds. 2011. *The Speeches of Fannie Lou Hamer: To Tell It Like It Is*. Jackson: University Press of Mississippi.

Brown, Helen, Colleen Varcoe, and Betty Calam. 2011. "The Birthing Experiences of Rural Aboriginal Women in Context: Implications for Nursing." *Canadian Journal of Nursing Research* 43, no. 4: 100–17.

Brown, Helen J., Gladys McPherson, Ruby Peterson, Vera Newman, and Barbara Cranmer. 2012. "Our Land, Our Language: Connecting Dispossession and Health Equity in an Indigenous Context." *Canadian Journal of Nursing Research* 44, no. 2: 44–63.

Brown, Theodore M., and Anne-Emanuelle Birn. 2013. "The Making of Health Internationalists." In *Comrades in Health: U.S. Health Internationalists, Abroad and at Home*, edited by Anne-Emanuelle Birn and Theodore M. Brown, 15–42. New Brunswick, NJ: Rutgers University Press.

Bryce, Peter Henderson. 1907. *Report on the Indian Schools of Manitoba and the North-West Territories*. Ottawa: Government Printing Bureau.

– 1922. *The Story of a National Crime – Being an Appeal for Justice to the Indians of Canada*. Ottawa: James Hope and Sons, Ltd.

Burke, Nora Butler. 2004. "Building a 'Canadian' Decolonization Movement: Fighting the Occupation at 'Home.'" *Colours of Resistance*, 20 August 2004. http://www.coloursofresistance.org/360/building-a-canadian-decolonization-movement-fighting-the-occupation-at-home/.

Burke, Stanley. 1954. "Canada's Arctic Ship Dirty and Inefficient." *Vancouver Sun*, 10 September 1954: 3.

CAP (Canadian Associated Press). 1914. "Determined to do Utmost for Canada." *Montreal Gazette*, 29 May 1914.

Cardinal, Harold. 1999. *The Unjust Society*. Madeira Park, BC: Douglas and McIntyre.

Carmant, Lionel. 2018. Interview by Mike Finnerty, CBC Radio: *Daybreak Montreal*, 19 June 2018. https://www.cbc.ca/listen/live-radio/1-15-daybreak-montreal/clip/15551582-caq-candidate-lionel-carmant.

Carmichael, Stokely, and Charles V. Hamilton. 1967. *Black Power: The Politics of Liberation in America*. Toronto and New York: Random House.

Carreiro, Donna. 2017. "'Our People were Experimented On': Indigenous Sanatorium Survivors Recall Medical Tests." *CBC News*. 22 September 2017. https://www.cbc.ca/news/canada/manitoba/indigenous-sanatorium-suvivors-medical-experiments-1.4301131.

CBC. 2013. "Aboriginal Children Used in Medical Tests, Commissioner Says." *CBC News*, 31 July 2013. https://www.cbc.ca/news/politics/aboriginal-children-used-in-medical-tests-commissioner-says-1.1318150.

– 2018a. "Quebec Will Allow Parents to Accompany Children on Air Ambulances." *CBC News*, 16 February 2018. http://www.cbc.ca/news/canada/montreal/air-ambulance-parent-child-1.4538443.

– 2018b. "Read the Transcript of Gaétan Barrette's Comments on Medevac Planes." *CBC News*, 22 June 2018. https://www.cbc.ca/news/canada/montreal/read-the-transcript-of-gaetan-barrette-s-comments-on-medevac-planes-1.4718196.

CBC Radio. 2018. "The Millennium Scoop: Indigenous Youth Say Care System Repeats Horrors of the Past." *The Current*, 25 January 2018. http://www.cbc.ca/radio/thecurrent/a-special-edition-of-the-current-for-january-25-2018-1.4503172/the-millennium-scoop-indigenous-youth-say-care-system-repeats-horrors-of-the-past-1.4503179.

– 2019. "Government Subsidies for Business Are Greater Than Canada's Entire Defence Budget." *The Sunday Edition*, 24 May 2019. https://www.cbc.ca/radio/thesundayedition/the-sunday-edition-for-may-26-2019-1.5146999/government-subsidies-for-business-are-greater-than-canada-s-entire-defence-budget-1.5148266.

CHA (Children's Healthcare Australasia), Children's Healthcare Canada, European Children's Hospitals Organisation, and Children's Hospital Association. 2019. "Time to Stand Up for Child Health." 19 November 2019. Statement available for download: https://www.blog.childrenshealthcarecanada.ca/blog/2019/11/19/global-alliance-of-childrens-hospitals-calls-on-nations-to-put-children-first-and-foremost.

Chandler, Michael J., and Christopher Lalonde. 1998. "Cultural Continuity as a Hedge Against Suicide in Canada's First Nations." *Transcultural Psychiatry* 35, no.2: 191–219. doi:10.1177/136346159803500202.

Chapman, Chris, and A.J. Withers. 2019. *A Violent History of Benevolence: Interlocking Oppression in the Moral Economies of Social Working*. Toronto: University of Toronto Press.

Cherrington, Mark. 2007. "Oh, Canada!" *Cultural Survival Quarterly* 31, no. 3: 14–21.

Chomsky, Noam. 1987. *The Chomsky Reader*. Edited by James Peck. New York: Pantheon Books.

Chouinard, Marie-Andrée. 2018. "Nunavik : plates excuses." Editorial, *Le Devoir*, 26 June 2018. https://www.ledevoir.com/opinion/editoriaux/531087/mot-cles-de-l-article-plates-excuses.

Chrisjohn, Roland, and Sherri Young. 2006. *The Circle Game: Shadows and Substance in the Indian Residential School Experience in Canada* (revised edition). Penticton, BC: Theytus Books.

Chrisjohn, Roland, Andrea Bear Nicholas, Karen Stote, James Craven (Omahkohkiaayo i'poyi), Tanya Wasacase, Pierre Loiselle, and Andrea O. Smith. 2008. "An Historic Non-Apology, Completely and Utterly Not Accepted." In *Dying to Please You: Indigenous Suicide in Contemporary Canada*, by Roland D. Chrisjohn, Shaunessy M. McKay, and Andrea O. Smith, 201–20. Penticton, BC: Theytus Books, 2017.

Chrisjohn, Roland D., Shaunessy M. McKay, and Andrea O. Smith. 2017. *Dying to Please You: Indigenous Suicide in Contemporary Canada*. Penticton, BC: Theytus Books.

Churchill, Ward. 1998. *A Little Matter of Genocide: Holocaust and Denial in the Americas, 1492 to the Present*. Winnipeg: Arbeiter Ring Publishing.

– 2004. *Kill the Indian, Save the Man: The Genocidal Impact of American Indian Residential Schools*. San Francisco: City Lights Books.

Clennon, Ornette D. 2018. *Black Scholarly Activism between the Academy and Grassroots: A Bridge for Identities and Social Justice*. Cham, Switzerland: Palgrave Pivot. https://doi.org/10.1007/978-3-030-00837-6.

CMQ (Collège des médecins du Québec). 2020. "The Legal, Ethical and Organizational Aspects of Medical Practice in Quebec: ALDO-Quebec Document." February 2020, Montreal. http://www.cmq.org/publications-pdf/p-1-2019-04-18-en-aldo-quebec.pdf.

Corneau, Chloé. 2018. *For Quality Educational Services in Nunavik That Respect Inuit Culture*. Special report by the Quebec Ombudsman, 24 October. Quebec City. https://protecteurducitoyen.qc.ca/sites/default/files/pdf/rapports_speciaux/education-nunavik-summary-2018.pdf.

Cornellier, Bruno, and Michael R. Griffiths. 2016. "Globalizing Unsettlement: An Introduction." Settler Colonial Studies 6 (4): 305–16. https://doi.org/10.1080/2201473X.2015.1090522.

Couillard, Philippe. 2005. Letter to Marc-André Dowd. 28 September 2005. Document P-499 filed before the Public Inquiry Commission on Relations between Indigenous Peoples and Certain Public Services in Québec (Viens Commission).

Coulthard, Glen Sean. 2014. *Red Skin, White Masks: Rejecting the Colonial Politics of Recognition*. Minneapolis: University of Minnesota Press.

Couturier, Catherine, and Carole Lévesque. [2019?]. "La tuberculose au Nunavik." Summary sheet prepared for the Public Inquiry Commission on Relations between Indigenous Peoples and Certain Public Services in Québec (Viens Commission). https://www.cerp.gouv.qc.ca/fileadmin/Fichiers_clients/Fiches_synthese/Tuberculose_au_Nunavik.pdf.

CP (Canadian Press). 2018. "Highlights of Quebec's 2018–19 Budget." *Financial Post*,

27 March 2018. https://business.financialpost.com/pmn/business-pmn/highlights-of-quebecs-2018-19-budget.

— 2019a. "Quebec Declines Talks with Feds, Provinces, Territories on Coerced Sterilization." CBC News, 15 February 2019. https://www.cbc.ca/news/indigenous/quebec-declines-working-group-coerced-sterilization-1.5021765.

— 2019b. "Inuit Sue Federal Government over Medical Experiments That Included Skin Grafts." CBC News, 21 June 2019. https://www.cbc.ca/news/canada/north/inuit-experiments-skin-grafts-lawsuit-1.5185181.

CPS (Canadian Pediatric Society). 2018. "Paediatricians Call on Québec to Reverse Policy Blocking Family Members from Accompanying Sick Kids on Air Ambulance Flights," press release, 6 February 2018. https://www.cps.ca/en/media/paediatricians-call-on-quebec-to-reverse-policy.

Cree Nation of Chisasibi. 2020. "History and Geograpy." https://chisasibi.ca/?page_id=136.

CSDH (Commission on Social Determinants of Health). 2008. *Closing the Gap in a Generation: Health Equity through Action on the Social Determinants of Health. Final Report of the Commission on Social Determinants of Health.* Geneva: World Health Organization.

CSSS (Commission de la santé et des services sociaux). 2018. "Ministère de la Santé et des Services sociaux, volet santé et accessibilité aux soins." *Journal des débats de la Commission de la santé et des services sociaux* 44, no. 202 (1 May 2018). http://www.assnat.qc.ca/fr/travaux-parlementaires/commissions/csss-41-1/journal-debats/CSSS-180501.html.

CTV. 2018. "More Doctors Demand Quebec Change Air Ambulance Policy." *CTV Montreal News*, 6 February 2018. https://montreal.ctvnews.ca/more-doctors-demand-quebec-change-air-ambulance-policy-1.3791824.

Curtis, Christopher. 2019. "Indigenous Children Are 'Warehoused,' Face Racism from Youth Protection: Report." *Montreal Gazette*, 7 November 2019. https://montrealgazette.com/news/local-news/batshaw-report.

Czyzewski, Karina. 2011. "Colonialism as a Broader Social Determinant of Health." *The International Indigenous Policy Journal* 2, no. 1. doi: 10.18584/iipj.2011.2.1.5.

Dalton, Melinda. 2018. "Quebec Health Minister Gaétan Barrette Says Comments on 'Drugged' Medevac Passengers Were 'Misinterpreted.'" *CBC News*, 21 June 2018. https://www.cbc.ca/news/canada/montreal/barrette-indigenous-remarks-misinterpreted-1.4715907.

Daneman, Denis. 2017. "History of SickKids Is an Integral Part of History of Paediatrics." Canadian Paediatric Society. https://www.cps.ca/en/blog-blogue/history-of-sickkids-is-an-integral-part-of-history-of-paediatrics.

Daschuk, James W. 2019. *Clearing the Plains: Disease, Politics of Starvation, and the Loss of Aboriginal Life.* Regina: University of Regina Press.

Davies, J., S.M. Tibby, and I.A. Murdoch. 2005. "Should Parents Accompany Critically Ill Children during Inter-Hospital Transport?" *Archives of Disease in Childhood* 90: 1270–3.

de Leeuw, Sarah, Margo Greenwood, and Emilie Cameron. 2010. "Deviant Constructions: How Governments Preserve Colonial Narratives of Addictions and Poor Mental Health to Intervene into the Lives of Indigenous Children and Families in Canada." *International Journal of Mental Health and Addiction* 8, no. 2: 282–95. doi:10.1007/s11469-009-9225-1.

Delgamuukw v. British Columbia, 1997. CanLII 302 (SCC), 3 SCR 1010. http://canlii.ca/t/1fqz8.

Delisle L'Heureux, Catherine. 2018. *Les voix politiques des femmes innues face à l'exploitation minière*. Quebec: Presses de l'Université du Québec.

Derfel, Aaron. 2014. "Quebec Inaugurates 'Flying Intensive-Care Unit.'" *Montreal Gazette*, 19 July 2014. https://montrealgazette.com/news/local-news/quebec-inaugurates-flying-intensive-care-unit/.

– 2018. "'Barrette Has My Trust,' Premier Says after Health Minister Apologizes." *Montreal Gazette*, 21 June 2018. http://montrealgazette.com/news/local-news/inuk-leader-disappointed-by-barrettes-comments-about-parents-in-quebecs-north.

Deshaies, Thomas. 2018. "Évacuations médicales: le gouvernement interpellé il y a plus de 10 ans." *Radio-Canada*, 24 October 2018. https://ici.radio-canada.ca/nouvelle/1131731/evacuations-medicales-gouvernement-commission-viens-evaq.

Dhillon, Jaskiran, and Will Parrish. 2019. "Canada Police Prepared to Shoot Indigenous Activists, Documents Show," *Guardian*, 20 December 2019. https://www.theguardian.com/world/2019/dec/20/canada-indigenous-land-defenders-police-documents.

DiAngelo, Robin. 2018. *White Fragility: Why It's So Hard for White People to Talk about Racism*. Boston: Beacon Press.

Dirks, Yutaka. 2018. "Canada's Incredible Expanding Wealth Gap." *Rabble*, 4 October 2018. https://rabble.ca/books/reviews/2018/10/canadas-incredible-expanding-wealth-gap.

Diubaldo, Richard J. 1981. "The Absurd Little Mouse: When Eskimos Became Indians." *Journal of Canadian Studies* 16, no. 2: 34–40.

Dossetor, John B. 2005. *Beyond the Hippocratic Oath: A Memoir on the Rise of Modern Medical Ethics*. Edmonton: University of Alberta Press.

Douglas, T.C. 1933. "The Problems of the Subnormal Family." Master's thesis, McMaster University. http://hdl.handle.net/11375/7736.

Downie, Gord, and Jeff Lemire. 2016. *Secret Path*. Toronto: Simon and Schuster Canada.

DSMGP (Direction des services médicaux généraux et préhospitaliers). 2005. "Rapport du Comité sur la révision de la politique de non-accompagnement à bord de l'avion-hôpital." 20 October 2005. Document P-499-1 filed before the Public Inquiry Commission on Relations between Indigenous Peoples and Certain Public Services in Québec (Viens Commission).

DSP (Direction de santé publique). 2012. "Rapport du directeur de santé publique 2011: Les inégalités sociales de santé à Montréal, Le chemin parcouru" (2nd ed). Agence de la santé et des services sociaux de Montréal.

Duchaine, Gabrielle, and Olivier Jean. 2017. "La mystérieuse disparition des enfants Ruperthouse." *La Presse*, 3 December 2017. http://www.lapresse.ca/actualites/ enquetes/201712/03/01-5145711-la-mysterieuse-disparition-des-enfants-rupert house.php.

Duchaine, Gabrielle, and Philippe Teisceira-Lessard. 2018a. "Une pratique d'évacuation 'barbare.'" *La Presse*, 24 January 2018. http://www.lapresse.ca/actualites/ sante/201801/24/01-5151227-enfants-autochtones-une-pratique-devacuation-barbare.php.

– 2018b. "Évacuations médicales aériennes en solitaire : 'Voir un enfant partir comme ça, c'est terrifiant.'" *La Presse*, 25 January 2018. http://www.lapresse.ca/ actualites/sante/201801/25/01-5151357-evacuations-medicales-aeriennes-en-solitaire-voir-un-enfant-partir-comme-ca-cest-terrifiant.php.

– 2018c. "Une mère inuite n'a pu accompagner sa fille à bord de l'avion-hôpital." *La Presse*, 3 March 2018. http://www.lapresse.ca/actualites/201803/03/01-5155972-une-mere-inuite-na-pu-accompagner-sa-fille-a-bord-de-lavion-hopital.php.

Dunlevy, T'Cha. 2018. "Lepage, Mnouchkine Resort to Stereotypes in Defence of *Kanata* and SLĀV." *Montreal Gazette*, 24 July 2018. https://montrealgazette. com/entertainment/arts/dunlevy-lepage-mnouchkine-resort-to-stereotypes-re-kanata-slav.

Dupuis, Renée. 2008. "Should the James Bay and Northern Quebec Agreement Serve as a Model Agreement for Other First Nations?" In *Power Struggles: Hydro Development and First Nations in Manitoba and Quebec*, edited by Thibault Martin and Steven M. Hoffman, 215–25. Winnipeg: University of Manitoba Press.

Ellison-Loschmann, Lis. 2003. "Irihapeti Ramsden: Nurse Who Campaigned for the Specific Healthcare Needs of Indigenous Peoples to Be Addressed." Obituary, *British Medical Journal* 327: 453. https://www.ncbi.nlm.nih.gov/pmc/articles/PMC 188521/pdf/3270453.pdf.

Engel, George L. 1977. "The Need for a New Medical Model – A Challenge for Biomedicine." *Science* 196, no. 4286: 129–36. doi: 10.1126/science.847460.

– 1981. "The Clinical Application of the Biopsychosocial Model." *The Journal of Medicine and Philosophy* 6, no. 2: 101–23.

Equi Institute. n.d. "Our Mission." Accessed 9 August 2019. https://www.equi-institute.org/about-us.

Erasmus, George. 2003. "Reparations: Theory, Practice and Education." Paper presented at University of Windsor. The Aboriginal Healing Foundation, 13 June 2003. http://www.ahf.ca/downloads/clea-roundtable.pdf.

ÉVAQ (Évacuations aéromédicales du Québec). n.d. "Évacuations par avion-hôpital de la clientèle pédiatrique, 2012–2018." Document P-791-96.1.13 filed before the Public Inquiry Commission on relations between Indigenous Peoples and certain public services in Québec (Viens Commission).

– 2015. "Rapport d'activité, 2013–2015." Direction clientèle urgences, Centre Hospitalier Universitaire (CHU) de Québec. https://www.chudequebec.ca/getmedia/b09f dc45-fa27-41f9-beb3-af709e8818a2/Rapport_2015_EVAQ-final_1.aspx.

– 2016. "Plan stratégique, 2016–2018." February 2016. Direction clientèle urgences, Centre Hospitalier Universitaire (CHU) de Québec. https://www.chudequebec. ca/getmedia/9aa02175-97d2-48a5-bf69-b6de6bef8d86/Plan_strategique_2016-01-26.aspx.

– 2018a. "Rapport d'activités, 2015–2018." June 2018. Document P-791-96.1.14 filed before the Public Inquiry Commission on Relations between Indigenous Peoples and Certain Public Services in Québec (Viens Commission).

– 2018b. *Cadre de référence sur l'accompagnement parental.* 29 June 2018. Direction des communications du ministère de la Santé et des Services sociaux. https://publications.msss.gouv.qc.ca/msss/fichiers/2018/18-929-03W.pdf.

– 2018c. "Document de travail: Accompagnement parental lors de missions de rapatriement de la clientèle pédiatrique par le Service d'Évacuations aéromédicales du Québec." 31 July 2018. Document P-791-96.1.6 filed before the Public Inquiry Commission on Relations between Indigenous Peoples and Certain Public Services in Québec (Viens Commission).

– 2018d. "Préparation commission d'enquête." 10 October 2018. Document P-791-96.1 filed before the Public Inquiry Commission on Relations between Indigenous Peoples and Certain Public Services in Québec (Viens Commission).

Fast, Elizabeth, Nakuset, Vicky Boldo, Alana-Dawn Phillips, Marti Miller, Melanie Lefebvre, and Lance Lamore. 2019. *One Step Forward, Two Steps Back: Child Welfare Services for Indigenous Clientele Living in Montreal.* https://aptnnews.ca/wp-content/uploads/2019/11/One-step-forward-two-steps-back-_FINAL-REPORT-2019.pdf.

Fava, Giovanni A., and Nicoletta Sonino. 2017. "From the Lesson of George Engel to Current Knowledge: The Biopsychosocial Model 40 Years Later." *Psychotherapy and Psychosomatics* 86: 257–9. doi: 10.1159/000478808.

Feir, Donna, and Randall Akee. 2019. "First Peoples Lost: Determining the State of Status First Nations Mortality in Canada Using Administrative Data." *Canadian Journal of Economics* 52, no. 2: 490–525. doi:10.1111/caje.12387.

Fidelman, Charlie. 2018a. "Fix Policy of Airlifting Children to ER without Family Members: MDs." *Montreal Gazette,* 24 January 2018. http://montrealgazette. com/news/quebec/indigenous-children-airlifted-to-montreal-er-without-family-members.

– 2018b. "Airlifting Sick Kids: Quebec Has Long Ignored Pleas to Let Parents Accompany Them, Health Workers Say." *Montreal Gazette,* 25 January 2018. http://montrealgazette.com/news/local-news/airlifting-sick-kids-quebec-has-long-ignored-pleas-to-let-parents-accompany-them-health-workers-say.

– 2018c. "Airlifting Sick Kids: More Doctors Appeal to Quebec to Revise Policy." *Montreal Gazette,* 6 February 2018. http://www.montrealgazette.com/news/local-news/airlifting-sick-kids-more-doctors-appeal-to-quebec-to-revise-policy.

– 2018d. "Mother Recounts Horror of Having Critically Ill Child Flown to Hospital without Her." *Montreal Gazette,* 7 February 2018. http://www.montrealgazette.

com/news/local-news/mother-recounts-horror-of-having-critically-ill-child-flown-to-hospital-without-her.

– 2018e. "Airlifting Sick Kids: Quebec to Allow Family Member on Plane." *Montreal Gazette*, 15 February 2018. http://montrealgazette.com/news/local-news/air lifting-sick-kids-quebec-to-allow-family-member-on-plane.

– 2018f. "Airlifting Sick Kids: Nunavik Baby Flown without Mom, Despite Revised Policy." *Montreal Gazette*, 2 March 2018. http://montrealgazette.com/news/local-news/airlifting-sick-kids-nunavik-baby-flown-without-mom-despite-revised-policy.

– 2018g. "Barrette Promises Air Ambulances to Allow Parents This Month after Letter Appeals Directly to Couillard." *Montreal Gazette*, 6 June 2018. http://www.montrealgazette.com/news/local-news/sick-inuit-children-continue-to-air lifted-alone-to-montreal.

– 2018h. "Quebec Ends 'Cruel' Air Ambulance Policy of Separating Kids from Parents." *Montreal Gazette*, 5 July 2018. https://montrealgazette.com/news/quebec-ends-cruel-air-ambulance-policy-of-separating-kids-from-parents.

Finestone, Debra S. 2013. "McGill Med School's Admissions Policy Stinks." Letter to the editor, *Montreal Gazette*, 12 August 2013. http://www.montrealgazette.com/news/Letter+McGill+school+admissions+policy+stinks/8778224/story.html (link defunct).

Friesen, Joe. 2019a. "Mortality Rates for First Nations Young Women and Girls May Have Worsened: Study." *The Globe and Mail*, 26 May 2019. https://www.theglobeandmail.com/canada/article-mortality-rates-for-first-nations-young-women-and-girls-may-have.

– 2019b. "In a Push for Diversity, Medical Schools Overhaul how they Select Canada's Future Doctors." *The Globe and Mail*, 29 July 2019. https://www.theglobeandmail.com/canada/article-in-a-push-for-diversity-medical-schools-overhaul-how-they-select/.

Fuller, Colleen. 1998. *Caring for Profit: How Corporations Are Taking Over Canada's Health Care System*. Vancouver: New Star Books.

Funk, Robyn Neely, and Jessica Strohm Farber. 2009. "Partners in Care: Implementing a Policy on Family Member Passengers." *Air Medical Journal* 28, no. 1: 31–6. doi: https://doi.org/10.1016/j.amj.2008.06.001.

Gaudry, Adam, and Danielle Lorenz. 2018. "Indigenization as Inclusion, Reconciliation, and Decolonization: Navigating the Different Visions for Indigenizing the Canadian Academy." *AlterNative* 14, no. 30: 218–27.

Geddes, Gary. 2017. *Medicine Unbundled: A Journey Through the Minefields of Indigenous Health Care*. Toronto: Heritage House Publishing Company.

Gerlach, Alison J. 2012. "A Critical Reflection on the Concept of Cultural Safety." *Canadian Journal of Occupational Therapy* 79, no. 3: 151–8. doi: 10.2182/cjot.2012.79.3.4.

Gershman, John, and Alec Irwin. 2000. "Getting a Grip on the Global Economy."

In *Dying for Growth: Global Inequality and the Health of the Poor*, edited by Jim Yong Kim, Joyce V. Millen, Alec Irwin, and John Gershman, 11–43. Monroe, ME: Common Courage Press.

Gervais, Lisa-Marie. 2018a. "Avion-ambulance: de jeunes patients sont encore évacués du Nunavik sans leurs parents." *Le Devoir*, 4 May 2018. https://www.ledevoir.com/societe/526876/des-enfants-sont-encore-evacues-du-nunavik-sans-leurs-parents.

– 2018b. "Évacuations aéromédicales: des médecins relancent le débat." *Le Devoir*, 6 June 2018. https://www.ledevoir.com/societe/sante/529571/transport-non-accompagne-par-avion-des-enfants-malades.

– 2018c. "Barrette accusé de nourrir les préjugés anti-autochtones." *Le Devoir*, 21 June 2018. https://www.ledevoir.com/societe/530813/autochtones-barrette-accuse-de-nourrir-les-prejuges.

Giroux, Dalie. 2016. "La resistance innue au projet hydroélectrique de La Romaine (2009–2014): limites légales, politiques et épistémologiques à la contestation politique." In *Au nom de la sécurité! Criminalisation de la contestation et pathologisation des marges*, edited by Diane Lamoureux and Francis Dupuis-Déri, 65–80. Saint-Joseph-du-Lac, QC: M Éditeur.

Golden, Richard L., ed. 1999. *The Works of Egerton York Davis, MD. Sir William Osler's Alter Ego*. Montreal: Osler Library (McGill University).

Goodman, Jordan, Anthony McElligott, and Lara Marks. 2003. *Useful Bodies: Humans in the Service of Medical Science in the Twentieth Century*. Baltimore: Johns Hopkins University Press.

Government of Ontario. 2017. "A Better Way Forward: Ontario's 3-Year Anti-Racism Strategic Plan." https://files.ontario.ca/ar-2001_ard_report_tagged_final-s.pdf.

Government of Quebec. 2018. "Budget 2018–2019: Accessible, Quality Health Services." http://www.budget.finances.gouv.qc.ca/budget/2018-2019/en/documents/Health_1819.pdf.

Goyal, Monika K., Nathan Kuppermann, Sean D. Cleary, Stephen J. Teach, and James M. Chamberlain. 2015. "Racial Disparities in Pain Management of Children with Appendicitis in Emergency Departments." *JAMA Pediatrics* 169, no. 11: 996–1002. doi:10.1001/jamapediatrics.2015.1915.

Greenwood, Margo Lianne, and Sarah Naomi de Leeuw. 2012. "Social Determinants of Health and the Future Well-Being of Aboriginal Children in Canada." *Paediatrics and Child Health* 17 (7): 381–4. https://www.ncbi.nlm.nih.gov/pmc/articles/PMC3448539/pdf/pch17381.pdf.

Grekul, Jana, Arvey Krahn, and Dave Odynak. 2004. "Sterilizing the 'Feeble-Minded': Eugenics in Alberta, Canada, 1929–1972." *Journal of Historical Sociology* 17, no. 4: 358–84.

Grenier, A. 2019. "Conflicted and Worried: CBC Poll Takes Snapshot of Canadians Ahead of Fall Election." *CBC News*, 30 June 2019. https://www.cbc.ca/news/politics/cbc-election-poll-1.5188097.

Grygier, Pat Sandiford. 1994. *A Long Way from Home: The Tuberculosis Epidemic among the Inuit*. Montreal and Kingston: McGill-Queen's University Press.

Ha, Tu Thanh. 2016. "Leilani Muir Made History Suing Alberta Over Forced Sterilization." *The Globe and Mail*, 16 March 2016. https://www.theglobeand mail.com/news/alberta/woman-who-made-history-suing-alberta-over-forced-sterilization-dies/article29256421/.

Hafferty, Frederic W., and Ronald Franks. 1994. "The Hidden Curriculum, Ethics Teaching, and the Structure of Medical Education." *Academic Medicine* 69, no. 11: 861–71.

Hamilton, Charles, and Guy Quenneville. 2017. "Report on Coerced Sterilizations of Indigenous Women Spurs Apology, but Path Forward Unclear." *CBC News*, 29 July 2017. https://www.cbc.ca/news/canada/saskatoon/report-indigenous-women-coerced-tubal-ligations-1.4224286.

Hanes, Allison. 2018. "Shame on Quebec for Leaving Behind Parents of Airlifted Children." Opinion, *Montreal Gazette*, 29 January 2018. http://montrealgazette.com/opinion/columnists/allison-hanes-shame-on-quebec-for-leaving-behind-parents-of-airlifted-children.

Harper, Stephen. 2008. "Statement of Apology to Former Students of Indian Residential Schools." Prime Minister of Canada, 11 June 2008. http://www.aadnc-aandc.gc.ca/eng/1100100015644/1100100015649.

HC-77. 2018. Confidential testimony at the Public Inquiry Commission on Relations between Indigenous Peoples and Certain Public Services in Québec. (Viens Commission). Transcribed by Gabrielle Clément, Volume 153 (23 October 2018). https://www.cerp.gouv.qc.ca/fileadmin/Fichiers_clients/Transcriptions/Notes_stenographiques_-_CERP_23_octobre_2018_HC-77.pdf.

Healey, Jenna. 2019. "Joke on Who? Gender, Race, and Professional Identity in William Osler's 'Professional Notes.'" Vancouver: Canadian Society for the History of Medicine Annual Meeting.

Helquist, Michael. 2015. *Marie Equi: Radical Politics and Outlaw Passions*. Corvallis: Oregon State University Press.

– 2019. "National Park Service, Oregon Sec State Honor Marie Equi." *Politics & Passions* (blog), 24 June 2019. http://www.michaelhelquist.com/politics—passions-blog/national-park-service-or-sec-state-honor-marie-equi.

Hendry, Leah. 2018. "Inuk Leader Calls for Quebec Health Minister's Resignation over 'Racist' Remarks." *CBC News*, 21 June 2018. https://www.cbc.ca/news/canada/montreal/inuk-leader-calls-for-ga%C3%A9tan-barrette-s-resignation-over-racist-remarks-1.4715217.

Hick, Sarah. 2019. "The Enduring Plague: How Tuberculosis in Canadian Indigenous Communities is Emblematic of a Greater Failure in Healthcare Equality." *Journal of Epidemiology and Global Health* 9, no. 2: 89–92. https://doi.org/10.2991/jegh.k.190314.002.

Hicks, F.H. 1969. "The Eastern Arctic Medical Patrol." *Canadian Medical Association Journal* 100, no. 11: 537–8.

Hilberg, Raul. 2003. *The Destruction of the European Jews*, 3rd ed. New Haven and London: Yale University Press.

Hivon, Véronique. 2018. "Pétition: Accompagnement des enfants lors des transferts par avion-hôpital," petition deposited at Quebec National Assembly on 9 March 2018. https://www.assnat.qc.ca/fr/exprimez-votre-opinion/petition/Petition-7157/index.html.

Holleran, Renée Semonin. 2013. "Transporting the Family by Air." *Pediatric Emergency Care* 19, no. 3: 211–14.

Holmes, B. 1915. "The Relation of Medical Literature to Professional Esteem." *The Lancet - Clinic* 114: 113–15.

Hoye, Bryce. 2019. "2 Indigenous Women Allege They Were Sterilized against Their Will in Manitoba Hospitals – One of Them in 2018." CBC *News*, 9 July 2019. https://www.cbc.ca/news/canada/manitoba/forced-sterilization-lawsuit-manitoba-1.5204771.

Hudon, Catherine. 2018. "Témoignage: Mon fils est mort sans moi." *La Presse+*, 5 February 2018. http://plus.lapresse.ca/screens/74167d30-6c8a-4f96-8d94-9fd47cef8265___7C___0.html.

Hydro-Québec. 2018. "Hydro-Québec and Indigenous Communities." https://www.hydroquebec.com/data/a-propos/pdf/partnership-indigenous-communities-2017g422a.pdf.

– 2019. "Clean Energy to Power Us All: Annual Report 2018." http://www.hydroquebec.com/data/documents-donnees/pdf/annual-report-2018.pdf.

IACHR (Inter-American Commission on Human Rights). 2019. "IACHR Expresses Its Deep Concern over the Claims of Forced Sterilizations against Indigenous Women in Canada," press release, 18 January 2019. http://www.oas.org/en/iachr/media_center/PReleases/2019/010.asp.

ICRP (International Commission on Radiological Protection). 1975. *Report of the Task Group on Reference Man*. ICRP Publication 23. New York: Pergamon Press.

IHN (Indigenous Health Network). 2019. "Joint Commitment to Action on Indigenous Health." The Association of Faculties of Medicine of Canada, 23 May 2019. https://afmc.ca/sites/default/files/pdf/AFMC_Position_Paper_JCAIH_EN.pdf.

IHWG (Indigenous Health Working Group). 2016. "Health and Health Care Implications of Systemic Racism on Indigenous Peoples in Canada." The College of Family Physicians of Canada.

IPAC (Indigenous Physicians Association of Canada) and AFMC (Association of Faculties of Medicine of Canada). 2009. "First Nations, Inuit, Metis Health Core Competencies: A Curriculum Framework for Undergraduate Medical Education." https://afmc.ca/pdf/CoreCompetenciesEng.pdf.

Ipsos–La Presse. 2018. "Sondage: Perceptions des Québécois sur la discrimination." 9 September 2018. https://www.ipsos.com/fr-ca/news-polls/la-presse-discrimination-au-quebec.

Irwin, Alec, and E. Scali. 2007. "Action on the Social Determinants of Health: A

Historical Perspective." *Global Public Health* 2, no. 3: 235–56. doi: 10.1080/1744 1690601106304.

Isaac, Dan. 2018. "'I'm Only Six Years Old, I Can't Travel Alone': Cree Parents Prevented from Accompanying Son on Medevac to Montreal." *The Nation*, 28 September 2018 http://formersite.nationnewsarchives.ca/im-six-years-old-cant-travel-alone-cree-parents-prevented-accompanying-son-medevac-montreal/.

ITK (Inuit Tapiriit Kanatami). 2014. *Social Determinants of Inuit Health in Canada*. https://www.itk.ca/wp-content/uploads/2016/07/ITK_Social_Determinants_Report.pdf.

– 2018. *Inuit Statistical Profile 2018*. https://www.itk.ca/wp-content/uploads/2018/08/20191125-Inuit-Statistical-Profile-revised-1.pdf.

Jacewicz, Natalie. 2016. "Why Are Health Studies So White?" *The Atlantic*, 16 June 2016. https://www.theatlantic.com/health/archive/2016/06/why-are-health-studies-so-white/487046/.

Jacobs, Beverly. 2017. "Decolonizing the Violence against Indigenous Women." In *Whose Land Is It Anyway? A Manual for Decolonization*, edited by Peter McFarlane and Nicole Schabus, 46–51. N.p.: Federation of Post-Secondary Educators of BC.

James, Yolande, and Yves-François Blanchet. 2018. Round-table interviews with Annie Desrochers. *Radio-Canada: Le 15–18*, 21 June 2018. https://ici.radio-canada.ca/premiere/emissions/le-15-18/episodes/409986/audio-fil-du-jeudi-21-juin-2018/25.

Jones, David S. 2004. *Rationalizing Epidemics: Meanings and Uses of American Indian Mortality since 1600*. Cambridge, Massachusetts: Harvard University Press.

Jones, Esyllt W. 2019. *Radical Medicine: The International Origins of Socialized Health Care in Canada*. Winnipeg: ARP Books.

Joyce, Crystal N., Rachel Libertin, and Michael T. Bigham. 2015. "Family-Centered Care in Pediatric Critical Care Transport." *Air Medical Journal* 34, no.1: 32–6.

Juster, Fern R., Robin Camhi Baum, Chrisopher Zou, Don Risucci, Anhphan Ly, Harold Reiter, Douglas Miller, and Kelly L. Dore. August 2019. "Addressing the Diversity–Validity Dilemma Using Situational Judgment Tests." *Academic Medicine* 94, no. 8: 1197–203.

Karetak, Joe, and Frank Tester. 2017. "Introduction: Inuit Qaujimajatuqangit, Truth and Reconiciliation." In *Inuit Qaujimajatuqangit: What Inuit Have Always Known to Be True*, edited by Joe Karetak, Frank Tester, and Shirley Tagalik, 1–19. Winnipeg: Fernwood Publishing.

Kassam, Ashifa. 2017. "Canada Indigenous Women Were Coerced into Sterilizations, Lawsuit Says." *Guardian*, 27 October 2017. https://www.theguardian.com/world/2017/oct/27/canada-indigenous-women-sterilisation-lawsuit.

Kasudluak, Janice, and Jobie Kasudluak. 2018. Joint testimony at the Public Inquiry Commission on Relations between Indigenous Peoples and Certain Public

Services in Québec (Viens Commission). Transcribed by Nadia Szaniszlo and Ann Montpetit, Volume 160 (15 November 2018). https://www.cerp.gouv.qc.ca/fileadmin/Fichiers_clients/Transcriptions/Notes_stenographiques_-_CERP_15_novembre_2018_HC-79_HC-80.pdf.

Kelm, Mary-Ellen. 1998. *Colonizing Bodies: Aboriginal Health and Healing in British Columbia, 1900–50*. Vancouver: UBC Press.

– 2004. "Wilp Wa'ums: Colonial Encounter, Decolonization and Medical Care among the Nisga'a." *Social Science & Medicine* 59, no. 2: 335–49.

Kimelman, Edwin C. 1985. "No Quiet Place: Final Report to the Honourable Muriel Smith, Minister of Community Services." Review committee on Indian and Métis Adoption and Placements, Manitoba Community Services. http://digitalcollection.gov.mb.ca/awweb/pdfopener?smd=1&did=24788&md=1 and http://digitalcollection.gov.mb.ca/awweb/pdfopener?smd=1&did=24789&md=1.

Kirkup, Kristy. 2017. "National Review Needed Following Report on Tubal Ligations: Researchers." *CTV News*, 31 July 2017. https://saskatoon.ctvnews.ca/national-review-needed-following-report-on-tubal-ligations-researchers-1.3526549.

– 2018a. "AFN National Chief Urges Action on 'Gross Human Rights Violation.'" *CTV News*, 14 November 2018. https://www.ctvnews.ca/politics/afn-national-chief-urges-action-on-gross-human-rights-violation-1.4177296.

– 2018b. "'There Has to Be Accountability': Victims of Sterilization Demand Action." *CTV News*, 21 November 2018. https://www.ctvnews.ca/canada/there-has-to-be-accountability-victims-of-sterilization-demand-action-1.4186782.

– 2018c. "TRC Heard Concerns about Coerced Sterilization of Indigenous Women: Sinclair." *CTV News*, 22 November 2018. https://www.ctvnews.ca/health/trc-heard-concerns-about-coerced-sterilization-of-indigenous-women-sinclair-1.4188517.

Klein, Naomi. 2017. "Speech at the Funeral of Arthur Manuel." Preface to *The Reconciliation Manifesto: Recovering the Land, Rebuilding the Economy*, by Arthur Manuel, 9–13. Toronto: James Lorimer & Company.

Koperqualuk, Lisa. 2014. "Mouvements politiques des Inuit: Pour l'autodétermination du Nunavik." *À bâbord!* April/May 2014, No 54. https://www.ababord.org/Mouvements-politiques-des-Inuit.

Krieger, Nancy. 1983. "Queen of the Bolsheviks: The Hidden History of Dr Marie Equi." *Radical America* 17, no. 5 (September-October): 55–73.

Krieger, Nancy, and Anne-Emanuelle Birn. 1998. "A Vision of Social Justice as the Foundation of Public Health: Commemorating 150 Years of the Spirit of 1848." *American Journal of Public Health* 88, no.11: 1603–6. doi:10.2105/ajph.88.11.1603.

Kripalani, Sunil, Jada Bussey-Jones, Marra Katz, and Inginia Genao. 2006. "A Prescription for Cultural Competence in Medical Education." *Journal of General Internal Medicine* 21, no. 10: 1116–20.

Krol, Ariane. 2018. "Pour en finir avec les orphelins des airs." Editorial, *La Presse*, 8 February 2018. http://www.lapresse.ca/debats/editoriaux/ariane-krol/201802/07/01-5153051-pour-en-finir-avec-les-orphelins-des-airs.php.

Labrecque, Marie. 2020. "Le retour aux sources d'Alain Deneault." *Le Devoir*, 13 January 2020. https://www.ledevoir.com/culture/theatre/570712/theatre-le-retour-aux-sources-d-alain-deneault.

LaDuke, Winona. 1991. Foreword to *Strangers Devour the Land*, new ed. [2008?], by Boyce Richardson, ix–xiv. White River Junction: Chelsea Green Publishing Company.

Lagacé, Patrick. 2018. "Chronique: À la défense de Gaétan Barrette." *La Presse*, 22 June 2018. http://www.lapresse.ca/debats/chroniques/patrick-lagace/201806/21/01-5186807-a-la-defense-de-gaetan-barrette.php.

Lamour, Ricardo. 2018. "Comment déshumaniser la critique en criant à la censure." *La Presse+*, 26 July 2018. http://plus.lapresse.ca/screens/ab2c1309-f03e-4a03-bc84-a6c168da9464__7C___0.html.

Latimer, Margot, John R. Sylliboy, Emily MacLeod, Sharon Rudderham, Julie Francis, Daphne Hutt-MacLeod, Katherine Harman, and Gordon Allen Finley. 2018. "Creating a Safe Space for First Nations Youth to Share Their Pain." *Pain Reports* 3 (Suppl 1), e682: 1–12. https://doi.org/10.1097/PR9.0000000000000682.

Lavallé, Omer (update by Tabitha Marshall). 2008. "Canadian Pacific Railway." *The Canadian Encyclopedia*, 6 March 2008. https://www.thecanadianencyclopedia.ca/en/article/canadian-pacific-railway.

Lavoie, Martin. 2018. "Un parent pourra bientôt accompagner son enfant à bord de l'avion-hôpital, confirme Barrette." *Journal de Quebéc*, 15 February 2018. http://www.journaldequebec.com/2018/02/15/un-parent-pourra-bientot-accompagner-son-enfant-a-bord-de-lavion-hopital-confirme-barrette.

Lawrence, Bonita, and Enakshi Dua. 2005. "Decolonizing Antiracism." *Social Justice* 32, no. 4 (102): 120–43.

Lebel, Anouk. 2018. "Des enfants débarquent encore seuls à l'urgence, dénonce un médecin." Radio-Canada (*Espaces Autochtones*), 21 March 2018. https://ici.radio-canada.ca/espaces-autochtones/a-la-une/document/nouvelles/article/1090688/des-enfants-debarquent-encore-seuls-a-lurgence-denonce-un-medecin.

Lechat, Robert. 1976. "Intensive Sterilization for the Inuit." *Eskimo* no. 12 (Fall/Winter): 5–7.

Legault, François. 2017. "Point de presse de M. François Legault, chef du deuxième groupe d'opposition," press conference, 4 October 2017. http://www.assnat.qc.ca/fr/actualites-salle-presse/conferences-points-presse/ConferencePointPresse-43199.html.

Lella, Joseph W. 2000. *Willie: A Dream. A Dramatic Monologue Portraying Sir William Osler*. Montreal: Osler Library (McGill University).

Levinson-King, Robin. 2018. "Why Quebec Doctors Have Rejected a Pay Rise." BBC *News*, 8 March 2018. https://www.bbc.com/news/world-us-canada-43336410.

Lombard, Alisa R. 2019. "Mistreatment & Violence against Women during Reproductive Care, with Focus on Childbirth – RE: Forced Sterilization of Indigenous Women in Canada." Correspondence addressed to Dubravka Šimonovi , United Nations Special Rapporteur on Violence against Women, 17 May 2019. https://

www.ohchr.org/Documents/Issues/Women/SR/ReproductiveHealthCare/SEMA
GANIS%20WORME%20LOMBARD.pdf.

Loppie, Samantha, Charlotte Reading, and Sarah de Leeuw. 2014. *Indigenous Experiences with Racism and Its Impacts*. Prince George, BC: National Collaborating Centre for Aboriginal Health. https://www.nccih.ca/495/Aboriginal_Experi ences_with_Racism_and_its_Impacts.nccih?id=13.

Lortie, Marie-Claude. 2018. "Catherine Hudon – personnalité de la semaine." *La Presse*, 11 February 2018. www.lapresse.ca/actualites/personnalite-de-la-se maine/201802/11/01-5153418-catherine-hudon-personnalite-de-la-semaine.php.

Lowrie, Morgan. 2018. "Quebec Doctors Urge Province to Let Parents Accompany Kids on Medical Flights." *CTV News*, 24 January 2018. https://www.ctvnews.ca/ health/quebec-doctors-urge-province-to-let-parents-accompany-kids-on-medical-flights-1.3773749.

Lux, Maureen. 1998. "Perfect Subjects: Race, Tuberculosis, and the Qu'appelle BCG Vaccine Trial." *Canadian Bulletin of Medical History* 15, no. 2: 277–95.

– 2001. *Medicine That Walks: Disease, Medicine and Canadian Plains Native People, 1880–1940*. Toronto: University of Toronto Press.

– 2016. *Separate Beds: A History of Indian Hospitals in Canada, 1920s–1980s*. Toronto: University of Toronto Press.

– 2017. "Indian Hospitals in Canada." *The Canadian Encyclopedia*, 17 July 2017. https://www.thecanadianencyclopedia.ca/en/article/indian-hospitals-in-canada.

Ly, Anh, and Lynden Crowshoe. 2015. "'Stereotypes Are Reality': Addressing Stereotyping in Canadian Aboriginal Medical Education." *Medical Education* 49, no. 6: 612–22. doi:10.1111/medu.12725.

Macdonald, N.E., R. Stanwick, and A. Lynk. 2014. "Canada's Shameful History of Nutrition Research on Residential School Children: The Need for Strong Medical Ethics in Aboriginal Health Research." *Paediatrics & Child Health* 19, no. 2: 64. doi:10.1093/pch/19.2.64.

Mackenbach, J.P. 2009. "Politics Is Nothing but Medicine at a Larger Scale: Reflections on Public Health's Biggest Idea." *Journal of Epidemiology and Community Health* 63, no. 3: 181–4. doi:10.1136/jech.2008.077032.

MacKinnon, Catou. 2018. "Minnie's Hope, Where Culture and Medicine Go Hand in Hand." *CBC News*, 28 December 2018. https://www.cbc.ca/news/canada/ montreal/minnies-hope-nunavik-child-health-quebec-north-1.4954548.

MacLellan, Ainslie. 2018. "Indigenous Youth in Quebec Child Protection Told Not to Speak Their Own Languages, Sources Say." *CBC News*, 12 December 2018. https://www.cbc.ca/news/canada/montreal/quebec-indigenous-nakuset-batshaw-language-1.4941393.

Mahood, Sally C. 2011. "Medical Education, Beware the Hidden Curriculum." *Canadian Family Physician* 57, no. 9: 983–5.

Mann, Alexandra. 2009. "Refugees Who Arrive by Boat and Canada's Commitment to the Refugee Convention: A Discursive Analysis." *Refuge* 26, no. 2: 191–206.

Manuel, Arthur. 2017. "The Six-Step Program to Decolonization." In *The Reconcili-*

ation Manifesto: Recovering the Land, Rebuilding the Economy, 275–9. Toronto: James Lorimer & Company.

Marois, Pierre, Céline Giroux, and Marc-André Dowd. 2005. "Transport des enfants en bas âge par les avions-ambulances." Letter to Philippe Couillard, 7 July 2005. Document P-498 filed before the Public Inquiry Commission on Relations between Indigenous Peoples and Certain Public Services in Québec (Viens Commission).

Marmot, Michael, Sharon Friel, Ruth Bell, Tanja A.J. Houweling, and Sebastian Taylor. 2008. "Closing the Gap in a Generation: Health Equity through Action on the Social Determinants of Health." *Lancet* 372, no. 9650: 1661–9. doi:10.1016/S0140-6736(08)61690-6.

Martin, Carol, and Harsha Walia. 2019. *Red Women Rising: Indigenous Women Survivors in Vancouver's Downtown Eastside*. Vancouver: Downtown Eastside Women's Centre.

Martin, JD. 1981. "Health Care in Northern Canada: An Historical Perspective." In *Proceedings of the Fifth International Symposium on Circumpolar Health, Copenhagen, Nordic Council for Arctic Medicine Report Series*, edited by J.P. Hansen and B. Harvald. 33: 80–7.

Martin, Thibault. 2008. "The End of an Era in Quebec: The Great Whale Project and the Inuit of Kuujjuarapik and the Umiujaq." In *Power Struggles: Hydro Development and First Nations in Manitoba and Quebec*, edited by Thibault Martin and Steven M Hoffman, 227–53. Winnipeg: University of Manitoba Press.

Mawow Ahyamowen Partnership. 2019. *Learning from our Ancestors: Mortality Experiences of Communities Served by Maamwesying North Shore Community Health Services*. http://maamwesying.ca/wp-content/uploads/2019/07/Maam wesying-North-Shore-V32-July-08-2019-1-compressed.pdf.

Mazerolle, Frédérique. 2019. "Indigenous Perspectives: Decolonizing the Approach to Health Research in Primary Care." *Med e-News*, 5 September 2019. https:// publications.mcgill.ca/medenews/2019/09/05/indigenous-perspectives-decolo nizing-the-approach-to-health-research-in-primary-care/.

McCallum, Mary Jane. 2005. "This Last Frontier: Isolation and Aboriginal Health." *Canadian Bulletin of Medical History* 22, no. 1: 103–20. doi:10.3138/cbmh.22.1.103.

McCallum, Mary Jane Logan, and Adele Perry. 2018. *Structures of Indifference: An Indigenous Life and Death in a Canadian City*. Winnipeg: University of Manitoba Press.

McConnachie, Kathleen Janet Anne. 1987. "Science and Ideology: The Mental Hygiene and Eugenics Movements in the Inter-war Years, 1919–1939." PhD diss., University of Toronto.

McGibbon, Elizabeth A. 2012. "Introduction to Oppression and the Social Determinants of Health." In *Oppression: A Social Determinant of Health*, edited by Elizabeth A. McGibbon, 16–31. Winnipeg: Fernwood Publishing.

McKinley, Rob. 1998. "Rumors of Abuse, Cover-up at Clinics." *Windspeaker News* 16, no. 5 (September 1998): 44.

McLachlin, Beverley. 2015. "Reconciling Unity and Diversity in the Modern Era: Tolerance and Intolerance." 2015 Annual Global Center on Pluralism Lecture. Delivered 28 May 2015 in Toronto.

McLaren, Angus. 1990. *Our Own Master Race: Eugenics in Canada, 1885–1945*. Toronto: McClelland & Stewart Inc.

McNamee, Stephen J. 2018. *The Meritocracy Myth*, 4th ed. Lanham (Maryland): Rowman & Littlefield.

Meijer Drees, Laurie. 2013. *Healing Histories: Stories from Canada's Indian Hospitals*. Edmonton: University of Alberta Press.

Millard, Mark W. 2011. "Can Osler Teach Us about 21st-Century Medical Ethics?" *Baylor University Medical Center Proceedings* 24, no. 3: 227–35.

Millette, Lise. 2018. "Avions-ambulances: 'un enfant transporté d'urgence, ce n'est pas une balade de loisir.'" *Radio-Canada*, 16 February 2018. https://ici.radio-canada.ca/nouvelle/1084355/avions-ambulances-un-enfant-transporte-durgence-ce-nest-pas-une-balade-de-loisir.

Milke, Mark. 2015. "Quebec's Bombardier Bailout Is Not an Investment; It's Corporate Welfare." *The Globe and Mail*, 4 November 2015. https://www.theglobeandmail.com/report-on-business/rob-commentary/quebecs-bombardier-bailout-is-not-an-investment-its-corporate-welfare/article27081111/.

Milloy, John S. 1999. *A National Crime: The Canadian Government and the Residential School System, 1879 to 1986*. Winnipeg: University of Manitoba Press.

MMIWG (National Inquiry into Missing and Murdered Indigenous Women and Girls). 2019a. *Reclaiming Power and Place: The Final Report of the National Inquiry into Missing and Murdered Indigenous Women and Girls*, Volume 1a. https://www.mmiwg-ffada.ca/wp-content/uploads/2019/06/Final_Report_Vol_1a-1.pdf.

— 2019b. *Reclaiming Power and Place: The Final Report of the National Inquiry into Missing and Murdered Indigenous Women and Girls*, Volume 1b. https://www.mmiwg-ffada.ca/wp-content/uploads/2019/06/Final_Report_Vol_1b.pdf.

— 2019c. *Reclaiming Power and Place: A Supplementary Report of the National Inquiry into Missing and Murdered Indigenous Women and Girls: Kepek-Quebec*, Volume 2. https://www.mmiwg-ffada.ca/wp-content/uploads/2019/06/Final_Report_Vol_2_Quebec_Report-1.pdf.

— 2019d. *A Legal Analysis of Genocide: A Supplementary Report of the National Inquiry into Missing and Murdered Indigenous Women and Girls*. https://www.mmiwg-ffada.ca/wp-content/uploads/2019/06/Supplementary-Report_Genocide.pdf.

Monchalin, Lisa. 2016. *The Colonial Problem: An Indigenous Perspective on Crime and Injustice in Canada*. Toronto: University of Toronto Press.

Montreal Gazette. 2014. "Editorial: McGill Med-School Policy Fosters Diversity." 9 May 2014. https://montrealgazette.com/opinion/editorials/editorial-mcgill-med-school-policy-fosters-diversity.

Moore, Holly. 2017. APTN *Investigates*. Season 9, episode 6, "The Cure Was Worse."

Aired 27 October 2017 on Aboriginal Peoples Television Network. https://www. youtube.com/watch?v=0_Z11n9by-8.

Moore, P.E. 1941. "Tuberculosis Control in the Indian Population of Canada." *Canadian Public Health Journal* 32, no. 1: 13–17.

– 1946. "Indian Health Services." *Canadian Journal of Public Health* 37, no. 4: 140–2.

Moore, P.E., H.D. Kruse, F.F. Tisdall, and R.S.C. Corrigan. 1946. "Medical Survey of Nutrition among the Northern Manitoba Indians." *Canadian Medical Association Journal* 54: 223–33.

Moran, Padraig. 2018. "Indigenous Women Kept from Seeing Their Newborn Babies until Agreeing to Sterilization, Says Lawyer." CBC Radio: *The Current*, 13 November 2018. https://www.cbc.ca/radio/thecurrent/the-current-for-november-13-2018-1.4902679/indigenous-women-kept-from-seeing-their-newborn-babies-until-agreeing-to-sterilization-says-lawyer-1.4902693.

Moriarty, Shannon, Mazher Ali, Brian Miller, Jessica Morneault, Tim Sullivan, and Michael Young. 2012. "Born on Third Base: What the Forbes 400 Really Says about Economic Equality & Opportunity in America." *United for a Fair Economy*, 17 September 2012. http://www.faireconomy.org/bornonthirdbase2012.

Morin, Annie. 2018. "Avion-hôpital: Les enfants malades pourront être accompagnés, mais…" *La Presse+*, 16 February 2018. http://plus.lapresse.ca/screens/9edef 03f-1336-4f45-b78f-bae246dec801%7C_0.html.

Mosby, Ian. 2013. "Administering Colonial Science: Nutrition Research and Human Biomedical Experimentation in Aboriginal Communities and Residential Schools, 1942–1952." *Social History* 46:145–72.

Mowbray, Martin. 2007. *Social Determinants and Indigenous Health: The International Experience and Its Policy Implications: Report on Specially Prepared Documents, Presentations and Discussion at the International Symposium on the Social Determinants of Indigenous Health for the Commission on Social Determinants of Health.* Adelaide, Australia. https://www.who.int/social_determinants/ resources/indigenous_health_adelaide_report_07.pdf.

MQRP (Médecins québécois pour le régime public). 2018. "Medical Evacuation of Children without a Caregiver on ÉVAQ Challenger Aircraft," letter to Quebec Premier Philippe Couillard, 6 June 2018. http://mqrp.qc.ca/wp-content/uploads/ 2018/06/Lettre-au-PM_Tiens-ma-main_MQRP_6juin2018_FR-and-ENG.pdf.

MSSS (Ministère de la Santé et des Services Sociaux). 2019. "Comptes de la santé du ministère de la Santé et des Services Sociaux: 2016–2017, 2017–2018, 2018–2019." Direction des communications du ministère de la Santé et des Services sociaux. https://cdn-contenu.quebec.ca/cdn-contenu/adm/min/sante-services-sociaux/ publications-adm/rapport/RA_18-614-01FW_MSSS.pdf.

MUHC (McGill University Health Centre). 2019. "RUIS McGill." https://muhc.ca/ health-professional-information/ruis-information.

Murthy, Vivek K., and Scott M. Wright. 2019. "Osler Centenary Papers: Would Sir William Osler Be a Role Model for Medical Trainees and Physicians Today?" *Postgraduate Medical Journal.* 95: 664–8.

Nadeau, Jean-François. 2019. "Le choc électrique." *Le Devoir*, 6 May 2019. https://www.ledevoir.com/opinion/chroniques/553665/punition-le-choc-electrique.

– 2020. "Les souris des Cris." *Le Devoir*, 5 February 2020. https://www.ledevoir.com/societe/572218/les-souris-des-cris.

Nadeau, Jessica. 2017. "Femmes autochtones: qu'est-il arrivé à Laurianne?" *Le Devoir*, 28 November 2017. https://www.ledevoir.com/societe/actualites-en-societe/514080/enquete-federale-sur-les-femmes-autochtones.

Nadeau, Jessica, and Lisa-Marie Gervais. 2018. "Insatisfaits des excuses du ministre Barrette, les autochtones réclament sa démission." *Le Devoir*, 22 June 2018. https://www.ledevoir.com/politique/quebec/530836/propos-juges-racistes-barrette-doit-demissionner-reclament-les-autochtones.

Napier, David. 2000. "Ottawa Experimented on Native Kids." *Anglican Journal* 126, no 5 (May): 1, 3.

NAS (National Academy of Sciences). n.d. "The International Biological Program (IBP), 1964–1974." http://www.nasonline.org/about-nas/history/archives/collections/ibp-1964-1974-1.html.

Navarro, Vicente. 2009. "What We Mean by Social Determinants of Health." *International Journal of Health Services* 39, no. 3: 423–41. doi:10.2190/HS.39.3.a.

Neu, Dean, and Richard Therrien. 2003. *Accounting for Genocide: Canada's Bureaucratic Assault on Aboriginal People*. Winnipeg: Fernwood Publishing.

Nguyen, Minh. 2016. "Document de réflexion: Bilan de l'observatoire sur les conséquences des mesures d'austérité, 2014–2016." Institut de recherche et d'informations socio-économiques (IRIS). https://cdn.iris-recherche.qc.ca/uploads/publication/file/Bilan_observatoire_WEB.pdf.

Niosi, Laurence. 2018. "Des enfants autochtones malades continuent d'être évacués en solitaire." Radio-Canada: *Espaces Autochtones*, 30 August 2018. https://ici.radio-canada.ca/espaces-autochtones/1120760/evacuations-nord-quebec-barrette-autochtones.

Nixon, P.G. 1988. "Early Administrative Developments in Fighting Tuberculosis among Canadian Inuit: Bringing State Institutions Back In." *Northern Review* 2: 67–84.

– 1989. "Percy Elmer Moore (1899–1987)." *Arctic* 42, no. 2: 166–7. doi:10.14430/arctic1653.

NRBHSS (Nunavik Regional Board of Health and Social Services). 2018. "Emergency Medical Evacuations: Children May Now Be Accompanied by Parent or Legal Guardian," press release, 29 June 2018.

Nungak, Zebedee. 2017. *Wrestling with Colonialism on Steroids: Quebec Inuit Fight for Their Homeland*. Montreal: Véhicule Press.

Ohler, Quinn. 2018. "Access to Aboriginal Doctors a Struggle for Indigenous Population." *Global News*, 17 December 2018. https://globalnews.ca/news/4769750/access-aboriginal-doctors-struggle-indigenous-population/.

Olofsson, Ebba, Tara L. Holton, and Imaapik 'Jacob' Partridge. 2008. "Negotiating Identities: Inuit Tuberculosis Evacuees in the 1940s–1950s." *Inuit Studies* 32, no. 2: 127–49.

O'Neil, John O. 1993. "Aboriginal Health Policy for the Next Century." In *The Path to Healing: Report of the National Round Table on Aboriginal Health and Social Issues*, 27–48. Vancouver: Royal Commission on Aboriginal Peoples, Ministry of Supply and Services Canada.

Oudshoorn, Kieran. 2019. "'We Are Not Monkeys' – Inuit Speak Out about Skin Grafts Done without Consent in 1970s." *CBC News*, 13 May 2019. https://www. cbc.ca/news/canada/north/inuit-skin-grafts-nunavut-experiment-1.5128279.

Page, Julia. 2017. "'He Broke the Values We Had': Innu Women at Quebec MMIWG Hearing Recount Priest's Alleged Abuse." *CBC News*, 29 November 2017. https:// www.cbc.ca/news/canada/montreal/indigenous-mmiwg-inquiry-abuse-1.442 4087.

PAHO (Pan American Health Organization). 2019. *Just Societies: Health Equity and Dignified Lives*. Report of the Commission of the Pan American Health Organization on Equity and Health Inequalities in the Americas, Washington, DC. http://iris.paho.org/xmlui/handle/123456789/51571.

Palmater, Pamela. 2014. "Genocide, Indian Policy, and Legislated Elimination of Indians in Canada." *Aboriginal Policy Studies* 3, no. 3: 27–54.

– 2017. "Decolonization Is Taking Back Our Power." In *Whose Land Is It Anyway? A Manual for Decolonization*, edited by Peter McFarlane and Nicole Schabus, 73–8. N.p.: Federation of Post-Secondary Educators of BC.

Panasuk, Anne. 2015. "Où sont passés 8 enfants de la communauté de Pakuashipi, sur la Côte-Nord?" *Enquête (Radio-Canada)*, 12 November 2015. https://ici.radio-canada.ca/nouvelle/748777/pakuashipi-enfants-disparus-cote-nord-quebec-innus (video: https://www.youtube.com/watch?v=TR-wYQSRiYo).

– 2017. "Enfants atikamekw hospitalisés… puis portés disparus." *Enquête (Radio-Canada)*, 30 November 2017. https://ici.radio-canada.ca/nouvelle/1070045/ enfants-hospitalises-portes-disparus-atikamekw (video: https://ici.radio-canada.ca/tele/enquete/site/episodes/395415/enquete-paradise-papers-mulroney-autochtone-enfant-disparu).

– 2019. "Enfants disparus – l'impasse." *Enquête (Radio-Canada)*, 14 February 2019. https://ici.radio-canada.ca/tele/enquete/site/segments/reportage/105625/enfants-innus-disparition-atikamekws-archives-medical-hopitaux?isAutoPlay=1.

Parent-Bouchard, Émilie. 2018 "Charlie, 2 ans, transportée d'urgence de Val-d'Or à Montréal sans sa mère." *Radio-Canada*, 10 May 2018. https://ici.radio-canada. ca/nouvelle/1100398/fillette-2-ans-transport-urgence-val-dor-montreal-mere-ste-justine-avion-ambulance.

Passi, Morgan, and John McGill. 2019. "Cree-Anishinaabe Doctor 'Optimistic' about Plan to Combat Anti-Indigenous Racism." *CBC Radio: As It Happens*, 24 May 2019. https://www.cbc.ca/radio/asithappens/as-it-happens-thursday-edition-1.5146761/ cree-anishinaabe-doctor-optimistic-about-plan-to-combat-anti-indigenous-racism-1.5148775.

Paul, Alexandra. 2015. "Brandon Experiments Exposed. Residential School Kids ESP Test Subjects in '40s." *Winnipeg Free Press*, 12 January 2015. https://www. winnipegfreepress.com/local/Brandon-experiments-exposed-288248311.html.

Paul, Daniel N. 2006. *We Were Not the Savages*. Blackpoint, NS: Fernwood Publishing.

Pedicelli, Gabriella. 1998. *When Police Kill: Police Use of Force in Montreal and Toronto*. Montreal: Véhicule Press.

Pelley, Lauren. 2018. "$1.1B Class-Action Lawsuit Filed on Behalf of Former 'Indian Hospital' Patients." *CBC News*, 30 January 2018. https://www.cbc.ca/news/canada/toronto/indian-hospital-class-action-1.4508659.

People. 1977. "Lily Tomlin." *People Magazine*, 26 December 1977. https://people.com/archive/lily-tomlin-vol-8-no-26/.

Perez, Caroline Criado. 2019. *Invisible Women: Data Bias in a World Designed for Men*. New York: Abrams Press.

Picard, André. 2018. "Quebec's Air Ambulance Policy Separating Kids from Parents Reeks of Paternalism." Opinion, *The Globe and Mail*, 6 February 2018. https://www.theglobeandmail.com/opinion/quebecs-air-ambulance-policy-separating-kids-from-parents-reeks-of-paternalism/article37869514/.

Picard, Isabelle. 2018. "Ceux qui sont loin." Opinion, *La Presse+*, 6 February 2018. http://plus.lapresse.ca/screens/8541b325-3fbe-491a-aa46-88bf79eec190%7C_0.html.

Plotnick, Laurie H., Samara Zavalkoff, Stephen Liben, June Ortenberg, Joyce Pickering, Aimee Ryan, and Ingrid Chadwick. 2018. "Increasing Women in Medical Leadership: Gender-Discrepant Perceptions about Barrier and Strategies." *Canadian Journal of Physician Leadership* 5, no.1: 48–56.

Porter, Jody. 2013. "Ear Experiments Done on Kids at Kenora Residential School." *CBC News*, 8 August 2013. https://www.cbc.ca/news/canada/thunder-bay/ear-experiments-done-on-kids-at-kenora-residential-school-1.1343992.

PSCPCSC (Public Safety Canada Portfolio Corrections Statistics Committee). 2018. *Corrections and Conditional Release: Statistical Overview (2017 Annual Report)*. Ottawa: Public Works and Government Services Canada.

QIA (Qikiqtani Inuit Association). 2014 "Qikiqtani Truth Commission: Thematic Reports and Special Studies 1950–1975." Inhabit Media Inc.

QNW (Quebec Native Women Inc.). 2018. "QNW Reacts to Minister Gaetan Barrette's Remarks," press release, 29 June 2018. https://www.faq-qnw.org/en/news/qnw-reacts-to-minister-gaetan-barrettes-remarks/.

Québec Solidaire. 2018. "Le ministre Barrette doit faire face à la musique: Amir Khadir," press release, 22 June 2018. http://www.fil-information.gouv.qc.ca/Pages/Article.aspx?lang=fr&idArticle=2606221889.

Qumaq, Taamusi. 2010. *Je veux que les Inuit soient libres de nouveau: autobiographie (1914–1993)*. Montreal: Les Presses de l'Université du Québec.

Radio-Canada. 2005. "Le bébé part, mais la mère reste." 7 July 2005. http://ici.radio-canada.ca/nouvelle/258005/avion-bebe.

– 2018. "Évacuations en avion : les parents devraient pouvoir accompagner leur enfant, dit une mère endeuillée." *Gravel le matin*, 6 February 2018. https://ici.radio-canada.ca/premiere/emissions/gravel-le-matin/segments/entrevue/58068/region-eloigne-mourir-seul-avion.

Rai, Nanky. 2017. "Uprooting Medical Violence: Building an Integrated Anti-Oppression Framework for Primary Health Care." Final residency project (in preparation for publication). Department of Family and Community Medicine, University of Toronto, 1 April. https://goo.gl/XkZztY.

Raphael, Dennis. 2011. "A Discourse Analysis of the Social Determinants of Health." *Critical Public Health* 21, no. 2: 221–36. doi:10.1080/09581596.2010.485606.

– 2012. "Critical Perspectives on the Social Determinants of Health." In *Oppression: A Social Determinant of Health*, edited by Elizabeth A. McGibbon, 45–59. Winnipeg: Fernwood Publishing.

Razack, Saleem, Torsten Risør, Brian Hodges, and Yvonne Steinert. 2019. "Beyond the Cultural Myth of Medical Meritocracy." *Medical Education* 00:1–8. doi: 10.1111/medu.13871.

RCAP (Royal Commission on Aboriginal Peoples). 1996a. *Report of the Royal Commission on Aboriginal Peoples: Looking Forward, Looking Back.* Volume 1: Ottawa.

– 1996b. *Report of the Royal Commission on Aboriginal Peoples: Gathering Strength.* Volume 3: Ottawa.

RCPSC (Royal College of Physician and Surgeons of Canada). 2019. "What Does It Mean to Provide Culturally Safe Care for Indigenous Patients?" https://newsroom.royalcollege.ca/what-does-it-mean-to-provide-culturally-safe-care-for-indigenous-patients/.

Reading, Charlotte L., and Wien, Fred. 2009. *Health Inequalities and Social Determinants of Aboriginal Peoples' Health*. Prince George, BC: National Collaborating Centre for Aboriginal Health.

Reading, Charlotte. 2013. *Understanding Racism*. Prince George, BC: National Collaborating Centre for Aboriginal Health.

Reiter, Harold, and Armand Aalamian. 2013. "External Review: The Office of Admissions, Equity and Diversity Program." Office of Admissions, Faculty of Medicine, McGill University, 8 October 2013. https://www.mcgill.ca/medadmissions/about/guiding-principles/external-review.

Richardson, Boyce. 1991. *Strangers Devour the Land*. White River Junction: Chelsea Green Publishing Company. New edition [2008?].

Riopel, Alexis. 2019. "Les conditions de logement des Autochtones, une honte pour le Canada." *Le Devoir*, 25 October 2019. https://www.ledevoir.com/societe/565580/entrevue-avec-leilani-farha.

Rioux Soucy, Louise-Maude. 2007. "Les accommodements, parfois une question de vie ou de mort." *Le Devoir*, 11 December 2007. https://www.ledevoir.com/societe/sante/168015/les-accommodements-parfois-une-question-de-vie-ou-de-mort.

Robinson, Cedric J. 1983. *Black Marxism: The Making of the Black Radical Tradition*. Chapel Hill: University of North Carolina Press.

Rogers, Sarah. 2018. "Inuit Suffer from Quebec's Restrictive Air Ambulance Policy – Doctors." *Nunatsiaq News*, 26 January 2018. http://www.nunatsiaq.com/stories/article/65674inuit_suffer_from_quebecs_restrictive_air_ambulance_policy/.

Roy, Arundhati. 2004. "Peace and the New Corporate Liberation Theology." Sydney Peace Prize Lecture, 3 November 2004. Seymour Theatre Centre, University of Sydney. https://sydney.edu.au/news/84.html?newsstoryid=279.

Roy-Brunet, Béatrice. 2018. "Sondage Léger: le Québec est-il plus raciste que le reste du Canada?" *HuffPost-Quebec*, 2 February 2018. https://quebec.huffingtonpost.ca/2018/02/26/sondage-leger-le-quebec-est-il-plus-raciste-que-le-reste-du-canada_a_23370786/.

RRSSSN (Régie régionale de la santé et des services sociaux Nunavik) and l'Institut national de santé publique du Québec. 2015. "Portrait de santé du Nunavik 2014 – Les jeunes enfants et leur famille." Government of Quebec.

SAA (Saskatchewan Air Ambulance). 2018. "Section IV – General Policies. 4-408 Escort/Family Member Accompaniment."

Sabin, Janice A., and Anthony G. Greenwald. 2012. "The Influence of Implicit Bias on Treatment Recommendations for 4 Common Pediatric Conditions: Pain, Urinary Tract Infection, Attention Deficit Hyperactivity Disorder, and Asthma." *American Journal of Public Health* 102: 988–95. doi:10.2105/AJPH.2011.300621.

Saganash, Romeo. 2008. "The Paix des Braves: An Attempt to Renew Relations with the Cree." Foreword in *Power Struggles: Hydro Development and First Nations in Manitoba and Quebec*, edited by Thibault Martin and Steven M. Hoffman, 205–13. Winnipeg: University of Manitoba Press.

– 2018. "Statement by Romeo Saganash Regarding the Comments Made by Minister Barrette." Public statement, 22 June 2018. http://www.ndp.ca/news/statement-romeo-saganash-regarding-comments-made-minister-barrette.

Saimaiyuk, Sarah. 1990. "Life as a TB Patient in the South." *Inuktitut* 71: 20–4.

Salée, Daniel. 2005. "Peuples autochtones, racisme et pouvoir d'État en contextes canadien et québécois : Éléments pour une ré-analyse." *Nouvelles pratiques sociales* 17, no. 2: 54–74. https://doi.org/10.7202/011226ar.

Savard, Rémi. 1975. "Des tentes aux maisons à St–Augustin." *Recherches amérindiennes au Québec* 5, no. 2: 53–62.

SCC (Supreme Court of Canada). 1939. "In the Matter of a Reference as to Whether the Term 'Indians' in Head 24 of Section 91 of the British North America Act, 1867, Includes Eskimo Inhabitants of the Province of Quebec." SCR 104, 1939 CanLII 22 (SCC). https://www.canlii.org/en/ca/scc/doc/1939/1939canlii22/1939canlii22.pdf.

Schoepf, Brooke G., Claude Schoepf, and Joyce V. Millen. 2000. "Theoretical Therapies, Remote Remedies: SAPs and the Political Ecology of Poverty and Health in Africa." In *Dying for Growth: Global Inequality and the Health of the Poor*, edited by Jim Yong Kim, Joyce V. Millen, Alec Irwin, and John Gershman, 91–126. Monroe, ME: Common Courage Press.

Schwartz, D. 2015. "Truth and Reconciliation Commission: By the Numbers." *CBC News*. https://www.cbc.ca/news/indigenous/truth-and-reconciliation-commission-by-the-numbers-1.3096185.

SDH Frameworks Task Group (Social Determinants of Health Frameworks Task Group). 2015. "A Review of Frameworks on the Determinants of Health."

Canadian Council on Social Determinants of Health. http://ccsdh.ca/images/uploads/Frameworks_Report_English.pdf.

Seidman, Karen. 2013. "The Changing Face of McGill Medical Students." *Montreal Gazette*, 9 August 2013. http://www.montrealgazette.com/news/changing+face+McGill+medical+students/8770876/story.html (link defunct).

– 2014. "Frustration over Med School Admissions at McGill." *Montreal Gazette*, 7 May 2014. https://montrealgazette.com/news/local-news/frustration-over-med-school-admissions-at-mcgill.

Selway, Shawn. 2016. *Nobody Here Will Harm You: Mass Medical Evacuation from the Eastern Arctic, 1950–1965*. Hamilton, ON: James Street North Books.

Shaheen-Hussain, Samir, Harley Eisman, and Saleem Razack. 2017. Letter to Sylvie Côté, clinical-administrative coordinator of ÉVAQ, 19 December 2017, with erratum dated 9 January 2018. Document P-502 filed before the Public Inquiry Commission on Relations between Indigenous Peoples and Certain Public Services in Québec (Viens Commission). https://www.cerp.gouv.qc.ca/fileadmin/Fichiers_clients/Documents_deposes_a_la_Commission/P-502.pdf.

Shaheen-Hussain, Samir. 2018a. Testimony at the Public Inquiry Commission on Relations between Indigenous Peoples and Certain Public Services in Québec (Viens Commission). Transcribed by Gabrielle Clément and Ann Montpetit, Volume 75 (21 March 2018). https://www.cerp.gouv.qc.ca/fileadmin/Fichiers_clients/Transcriptions/Notes_stenographiques_-_CERP_21_mars_2018.pdf.

– 2018b. "Separating Sick Inuit Kids and Parents Is Medical Colonialism All Over Again." *Guardian*, 17 May 2018. https://www.theguardian.com/world/commentisfree/2018/may/17/separating-sick-inuit-kids-from-their-parents-is-medical-colonialism-all-over-again.

– 2018c. Testimony at the Viens Commission (Public Inquiry Commission on Relations between Indigenous Peoples and Certain Public Services in Québec). Transcribed by Monique Le Clerc, Volume 150 (18 October 2018). https://www.cerp.gouv.qc.ca/fileadmin/Fichiers_clients/Transcriptions/Notes_stenographiques_-_CERP_18_octobre_2018.pdf.

Shapiro, Martin. 1978. *Getting Doctored: Critical Reflections on Becoming a Physician*. Toronto: Between the Lines.

Shevell, Michael. 2012. "A Canadian Paradox: Tommy Douglas and Eugenics." *The Canadian Journal of Neurological Sciences* 39, no. 1: 35–9.

Shewell, Hugh. 2004. *Enough to Keep Them Alive: Indian Welfare in Canada, 1873–1965*. Toronto: University of Toronto Press.

Shield, David. 2018. "The Night the Residential School Burned to the Ground – and the Students Cheered." *CBC News*, 25 November 2018. https://www.cbc.ca/news/canada/saskatoon/fire-thunderchild-residential-school-saskatchewan-1.4914731.

Shingler, Benjamin. 2018. "Troubling 'Pattern' Emerges of Indigenous Children Treated in Quebec Hospitals, Never to Return Home." *CBC News*, 16 March 2018. https://www.cbc.ca/news/canada/montreal/montreal-mmiwg-michele-audette-1.4575552.

SickKids (The Hospital for Sick Children). 2019. "Frederick Tisdall." http://www.sickkids.ca/AboutSickKids/History-and-Milestones/Our-History/Frederick-Tisdall.html.

Simpson, Audra. 2016. "Whither Settler Colonialism?" *Settler Colonial Studies* 6 (4): 438–45. https://doi.org/10.1080/2201473X.2015.1124427.

Simpson, Leanne Betasamosake. 2011. *Dancing on Our Turtle's Back: Stories of Nishnaabeg Re-Creation, Resurgence, and a New Emergence.* Winnipeg: ARP Books.

– 2014. "Land as Pedagogy: Nishnaabeg Intelligence and Rebellious Transformation." *Decolonization: Indigeneity, Education & Society* 3, no. 3: 1–25.

Sinclair, Murray. 2017. Standing Committee on Canadian Heritage. 1st Session, 42nd Parliament. 2 October 2017. http://www.ourcommons.ca/DocumentViewer/en/42-1/CHPC/meeting-75/evidence.

Sinclair, Raven. 2017. "The Indigenous Child Removal System in Canada: An Examination of Legal Decision-making and Racial Bias." *First Peoples Child & Family Review* 11, no. 2: 8–18. http://journals.sfu.ca/fpcfr/index.php/FPCFR/article/view/310.

Sinha, Vandna, Nico Trocmé, Barbara Fallon, Bruce MacLaurin, Elizabeth Fast, Shelley Thomas Prokop, Tara Petti, et al. 2011. *Kiskisik Awasisak: Remember the Children. Understanding the Overrepresentation of First Nations Children in the Child Welfare System.* Ontario: Assembly of First Nations.

Sioui, Marie-Michèle. 2020. "Les Autochtones veulent un projet de loi distinct sur les enfants disparus." *Le Devoir*, 11 February 2020. https://www.ledevoir.com/societe/572699/enfants-disparus-les-autochtones-veulent-un-projet-de-loi-distinct.

Smart, A. 2019. "Canadians Need to Be Patient, Present and Unconditional in Reconciliation: Trudeau." *CTV News.* https://www.ctvnews.ca/politics/canadians-need-to-be-patient-present-unconditional-with-reconciliation-trudeau-1.4515227.

Solar, Orielle, and Alec Irwin. 2010. *A Conceptual Framework for Action on the Social Determinants of Health. Social Determinants of Health Discussion Paper 2 (Policy and Practice).* Geneva: World Health Organization.

Spratt, Michael. 2019. "Canada's Treatment of Indigenous Peoples Fits the Definition of 'Genocide.'" *Canadian Lawyer*, 10 June 2019. https://www.canadianlawyermag.com/author/michael-spratt/canadas-treatment-of-indigenous-peoples-fits-the-definition-of-genocide-17368/.

Starblanket, Tamara. 2018. *Suffer the Little Children: Genocide, Indigenous Nations and the Canadian State.* Atlanta: Clarity Press.

Starr, Paul. 1982. *The Social Transformation of American Medicine.* New York: Basic Books.

Statistics Canada. 2013. *Aboriginal Peoples in Canada, First Nations People, Métis and Inuit: National Household Survey, 2011.* Ottawa: Minister of Industry. http://www12.statcan.gc.ca/nhs-enm/2011/as-sa/99-011-x/99-011-x2011001-eng.pdf.

Statistics Canada. 2017. "Education in Canada: Key Results from the 2016 Census."

The Daily, 29 November 2017. https://www150.statcan.gc.ca/n1/en/daily-quoti dien/171129/dq171129a-eng.pdf.

Stote, Karen. 2015. *An Act of Genocide: Colonialism and the Sterilization of Aboriginal Women*. Winnipeg: Fernwood Publishing.

Sun, Amy. 2014. "Equality Is Not Enough: What the Classroom Has Taught Me about Justice." *Every Day Feminism*, 16 September 2014. https://everydayfeminism. com/2014/09/equality-is-not-enough/.

Sunahara, Ann (update by Mona Oikawa and Eli Yarhi). 2011. "Japanese Canadians." *The Canadian Encyclopedia*, 31 January 2011. https://www.thecanadianencyclope dia.ca/en/article/japanese-canadians.

Swanky, Tom. 2012. *The True Story of Canada's "War" of Extermination on the Pacific*. N.p.: Dragon Heart Enterprises.

– 2016. *The Smallpox War in Nuxalk Territory*. British Columbia: Dragon Heart.

Tam, Theresa. 2019. "The Chief Public Health Officer's Report on the State of Public Health in Canada 2019: Addressing Stigma – Towards a More Inclusive Health System." Ottawa: Public Health Agency of Canada. https://www.canada.ca/content/ dam/phac-aspc/documents/corporate/publications/chief-public-health-officer-reports-state-public-health-canada/addressing-stigma-what-we-heard/stigma-eng.pdf.

Tester, Frank James, Paule McNicoll, and Peter Irniq. 2001. "Writing for Our Lives: The Language of Homesickness, Self-Esteem and the Inuit TB 'Epidemic.'" *Inuit Studies* 25, no. 1–2: 121–40.

Tester, Frank. 2017. "Colonial Challenges and Recovery in the Eastern Arctic." In *Inuit Qaujimajatuqangit: What Inuit Have Always Known to Be True*, edited by Joe Karetak, Frank Tester, and Shirley Tagalik, 20–40. Winnipeg: Fernwood Publishing.

TRC (Truth and Reconciliation Commission of Canada). 2015a. *Honouring The Truth, Reconciling for the Future: Summary of the Final Report of the Truth and Reconciliation Commission of Canada*. http://nctr.ca/assets/reports/Final%20 Reports/Executive_Summary_English_Web.pdf.

– 2015b. *Canada's Residential Schools: The Final Report of the Truth and Reconciliation Commission of Canada (The History, 1939–2000: Part 2)*. Volume 1. Montreal and Kingston: McGill-Queen's University Press.

– 2015c. *Canada's Residential Schools: The Final Report of the Truth and Reconciliation Commission of Canada (The Legacy)*. Volume 5. Montreal and Kingston: McGill-Queen's University Press.

– 2015d. *The Survivors Speak: A Report of the Truth and Reconciliation Commission of Canada*. http://nctr.ca/assets/reports/Final%20Reports/Survivors_Speak_ English_Web.pdf.

Trudeau, Justin. 2018. House of Commons. Hansard #355 of the 42nd Parliament, 1st Session, Debates of 21 November 2018. https://openparliament.ca/debates/2018/ 11/21/justin-trudeau-23/.

– 2019. "Statement of Apology on Behalf of the Government of Canada to Inuit for the Management of the Tuberculosis Epidemic from the 1940s–1960s." Prime Minister of Canada, 8 March 2019. https://pm.gc.ca/eng/news/2019/03/08/statement-apology-behalf-government-canada-inuit-management-tuberculosis-epidemic.

UN (United Nations). 1951. "Convention on the Prevention and Punishment of the Crime of Genocide." Approved and proposed for signature and ratification or accession by General Assembly resolution 260 A (III) of 9 December 1948; Entry into force on 12 January 1951. https://www.un.org/en/genocideprevention/genocide-convention.shtml.

– 1990. "Convention on the Rights of the Child." Adopted and opened for signature, ratification and accession by General Assembly resolution 44/25 of 20 November 1989; entry into force on 2 September 1990. https://www.ohchr.org/Documents/ProfessionalInterest/crc.pdf.

– 2007. "United Nations Declaration on the Rights of Indigenous Peoples." Resolution adopted by the General Assembly on 13 September 2007, https://undocs.org/A/RES/61/295.

UN CAT (United Nations Committee Against Torture). 1987. "Convention against Torture and Other Cruel, Inhuman or Degrading Treatment or Punishment." Adopted and opened for signature, ratification and accession by General Assembly resolution 39/46 of 10 December 1984 entry into force 26 June 1987. https://ohchr.org/Documents/ProfessionalInterest/cat.pdf.

– 2018. *Concluding Observations on the Seventh Periodic Report of Canada*, adopted on 5 December 2018. https://tbinternet.ohchr.org/Treaties/CAT/Shared%20Documents/CAN/CAT_C_CAN_CO_7_33163_E.pdf.

Uttak et al v. Canada (A.G). 2019. "Statement of Claim." Nunavut Court of Justice, Action No: 07-19-283-CVC, 6 June 2019.

Vallières, Pierre. 1971. *White Niggers of America*. Translation by Joan Pinkham. Toronto: McClelland and Stewart Limited.

Vanast, Walter J. 1991. "Hastening the Day of Extinction: Canada, Québec, and the Medical Care of Ungava's Inuit, 1867–1967." *Inuit Studies* 15, no. 2: 55–84.

Vang, Zoua M., Robert Gagnon, Tanya Lee, Vania Jimenez, Arian Navickas, Jeannie Pelletier, and Hannah Shenker. 2018. "Interactions between Indigenous Women Awaiting Childbirth Away from Home and Their Southern, Non-Indigenous Health Care Providers." *Qualitative Health Research* 28, no. 12: 1858–70.

Van Praet, Nicolas. 2020. "Bombardier to Depart Commercial Plane Business: Quebec, Airbus to Divvy Up Company's A220 Stake." *Globe and Mail*, 14 February 2020: B1, B5.

Varley, Autumn. 2017. "'You Don't Just Get Over What Has Happened to You': Story Sharing, Reconciliation, and Grandma's Journey in the Child Welfare System." *First Peoples Child & Family Review* 11, no. 2: 69–75. http://journals.sfu.ca/fpcfr/index.php/FPCFR/article/view/306.

Venugopal, Raghu. 1996. "Reading between the Lines: A Glimpse of the Cushing Files and the Life of Sir William Osler." *Osler Library Newsletter* no. 82 (June 1996): 1–4.

Viens Commission (Public Inquiry Commission on Relations between Indigenous

Peoples and Certain Public Services in Québec). 2019. *Final Report*, Government of Quebec. https://www.cerp.gouv.qc.ca/fileadmin/Fichiers_clients/Rapport/Final_report.pdf.

Ville de Montréal. 2018. "Profil sociodémographique: Recensement 2016. Arrondissement de Côte-des-Neiges – Notre-Dame-de-Grâce." Montréal en statistiques, Service du développement économique. http://ville.montreal.qc.ca/pls/portal/docs/PAGE/MTL_STATS_FR/MEDIA/DOCUMENTS/PROFIL_SOCIOD%C9MO_CDN-NDG%202016.PDF.

Vivian, R.P., Charles McMillan, P.E. Moore, E. Chant Robinson, W.H. Sebrell, F.F. Tisdall, and W.G. McIntosh. 1948. "The Nutrition and Health of the James Bay Indian." *Canadian Medical Association Journal* 59, no. 6: 505–18.

von Rosen, Franziska, dir. 2010. *Together We Stand Firm*. Grand Council of the Crees (Eeeyou Istchee). Pinegrove Productions. https://www.pinegroveproductions.ca/portfolio/the-eeyouch-of-eeyou-istchee-ep-1/ and https://vimeo.com/37667349.

Wachowich, Nancy, Apphia Agalakti Awa, Rhoda Kaukjak Katsak, and Sandra Pikujak Katsak. 1999. *Saqiyuq: Stories from the Lives of Three Inuit Women*. Montreal and Kingston: McGill-Queen's University Press.

Wagner, Vicki, Brenda Epoo, Julie Nastapoka, and Evelyn Harney. 2007. "Reclaiming Birth, Health, and Community: Midwifery in the Inuit Villages of Nunavik, Canada." *Journal of Midwifery & Women's Health* 52, no. 4: 384–91. https://doi.org/10.1016/j.jmwh.2007.03.025.

Wahlsten, D. 2003. "Airbrushing Heritability." *Genes, Brain, and Behavior* 2, no. 6: 327–9.

Wallis, Faith. 1997. "Piety and Prejudice: In His Respect for the Jewish People, Osler Was Less a Man of His Time than a Man of His Profession." *Canadian Medical Association Journal* 156, no. 11 (June): 1549–51.

Washington, Harriet A. 2006. *Medical Apartheid: The Dark History of Medical Experimentation on Black Americans from Colonial Times to the Present*. New York: Harlem Moon (Random House).

Wesley-Esquimaux, Cynthia C., and Magdalena Smolewski. 2004. *Historic Trauma and Aboriginal Healing*. Aboriginal Healing Foundation. Kitigan-Zibi, QC: Anishinabe Printing.

Whitehead, Margaret, and Göran Dahlgren. 2006. *Concepts and Principles for Tackling Social Inequities in Health: Levelling Up Part 1*. Copenhagen: World Health Organization Regional Office for Europe.

Whitmore, Johanne, and Pierre-Olivier Pineau. 2020. "État de l'énergie au Québec 2020." Chair in Energy Sector Management, HEC Montréal. Prepared for *Transition énergétique Québec*. Montreal. https://energie.hec.ca/wp-content/uploads/2020/03/EEQ2020_WEB.pdf.

WHO (World Health Organization). n.d. *Equity*. https://www.who.int/gender-equity-rights/understanding/equity-definition/en/.

– 2006. "Constitution of the World Health Organization." Basic documents, 45th edition (Supplement), October 2006. https://www.who.int/governance/eb/who_constitution_en.pdf.

Wilkinson, Richard, and Kate Pickett. 2010. *The Spirit Level: Why Equality Is Better for Everyone*. Toronto: Penguin Books.

Williams, Robert A. 2012. *Savage Anxieties: The Invention of Western Civilization*. New York: Palgrave.

Woodward, George A., and Eric W. Fleegler. 2001. "Should Parents Accompany Pediatric Interfacility Ground Ambulance Transports? Results of a National Survey of Pediatric Transport Team Managers." *Pediatric Emergency Care* 17, no. 1: 22–7.

Wright, Erik Olin. 2003. "Class Analysis, History, and Emancipation." In *Marx and Modernity: Key Readings and Commentary*, edited by Robert J. Antonio, 371–8. Oxford, UK: Blackwell Publishers.

Young, Meredith E., Saleem Razack, Mark D. Hanson, Steve Slade, Lara Varpio, Kelly L. Dore, and David McKnight. 2012. "Calling for a Broader Conceptualization of Diversity: Surface and Deep Diversity in Four Canadian Medical Schools." *Academic Medicine* 87, no. 11 (November):1501–10. doi: 10.1097/ACM.0b013e31 826daf74.

Young, Michael. 1994. *The Rise of the Meritocracy*. New Brunswick, NJ: Transaction Publishers.

– 2001. "Down with Meritocracy: The Man Who Coined the Word Four Decades Ago Wishes Tony Blair Would Stop Using It." *Guardian*, 29 June 2001. https://www.theguardian.com/politics/2001/jun/29/comment.

Younging, Gregory. 2018. *Elements of Indigenous Style: A Guide for Writing by and about Indigenous Peoples*. N.p.: Brush Education Inc.

Zinn, Howard. 1994. *You Can't Be Neutral on a Moving Train: A Personal History of Our Times*. Boston: Beacon Press.

– 2004. "Stories Hollywood Never Tells." *The Sun*, July 2004, 12–15.

Zook, Heather G., Anupam B. Kharbanda, Andrew Flood, Brian Harmon, Susan E. Puumala, and Nathaniel R. Payne. 2016. "Racial Differences in Pediatric Emergency Department Triage Scores." *The Journal of Emergency Medicine* 50, no. 5: 720–7. http://dx.doi.org/10.1016/j.jemermed.2015.02.056.

Index